Brian De Palma's Split-Screen

BRIAN DE PALMA'S SPLIT-SCREEN
A Life in Film

Douglas Keesey

University Press of Mississippi / Jackson

www.upress.state.ms.us

The University Press of Mississippi is a member
of the Association of American University Presses.

First printing 2015
∞
Library of Congress Cataloging-in-Publication Data

Keesey, Douglas.
  Brian De Palma's split-screen : a life in film / Douglas Keesey.
    pages cm
  Includes bibliographical references and index.
   ISBN 978-1-62846-697-3 (cloth : alk. paper) — ISBN 978-1-62846-698-0
(ebook) 1. De Palma, Brian—Criticism and interpretation. I. Title.
  PN1998.3.D4K44 2015
  791.4302'33092—dc23   2014045130

British Library Cataloging-in-Publication Data available

For Helen,
the one love who'd sing my song

Contents

Brian De Palma's Split-Screen

Introduction

Brian De Palma has directed twenty-nine feature films over the last five decades. His movies have been among the biggest successes (*The Untouchables*, *Mission: Impossible*) and the most high-profile failures (*The Bonfire of the Vanities*) in Hollywood history. De Palma's films have helped launch the careers of such actors as Robert De Niro, John Travolta, and Sissy Spacek (who was nominated for an Academy Award as Best Actress in *Carrie*). Quentin Tarantino has named *Blow Out* as one of his top three favorite films,[1] praising De Palma as the best living American director.[2] *Dressed to Kill*, which was picketed by feminists protesting its depictions of violence against women, helped to create the erotic thriller and slasher horror genres, of which De Palma's own *Body Double*—with its driller-killer scene—is perhaps the most notorious example. *Scarface*, with its chainsaw sequence pushing the edge of permissible on-screen violence, embroiled De Palma in legendary battles with the MPAA over censorship. The fact that gangsta rappers have since made *Scarface* into a cult film has only added to its controversy.

Over the years, De Palma has also built up a devoted following of film aficionados and critics—most notably Pauline Kael and Armond White—who appreciate his more personal films (*Blow Out*, *Casualties of War*, *Snake Eyes*) for their emotional power and their innovative techniques.[3] The prestigious film journal *Cahiers du Cinéma* voted *Carlito's Way* the best film made during the entire decade of the 1990s. And in the twenty-first century, De Palma has continued to experiment with new filmic forms, incorporating elements from video games (*Femme Fatale*), tabloid journalism (*The Black Dahlia*), and YouTube and Skype (*Redacted*, *Passion*) into his latest works.

Of all the trademark techniques for which De Palma's films have become known (slow motion, high angles, long takes, 360-degree pans), there is one that is more closely associated with him than with any other director: the split-screen. In taking this signature style as the title for this book, I signal my intention to focus on De Palma as a man divided. Of course, all directors experience (and all films dramatize) conflict, but in De Palma's case these conflicts are often especially acute. According to his old drama teacher and mentor Wilford Leach, De Palma's filmmaking is "the work of a rational, thoughtful, intellectual person who stands outside things—and who, in fact, is the opposite of that, whose passions run deep, whose sense of outrage is limitless. He is his own opposite."[4]

One of De Palma's most striking uses of the split-screen technique occurs in *Carrie*'s prom scene where the title heroine wreaks a fiery revenge on all those who have done her wrong. (She looks at them, using her telekinetic powers, and they die in horrible ways.) Does this technique reinforce our identification with Carrie and her righteous anger, or does it distance us from her and cause us to critically examine her actions? Does the split-screen (Carrie's face on one side and the victims she sees on the other) link us to Carrie, as in a Hitchcockian point-of-view shot, or does the obtrusiveness of such a technique break our link with her, as in a Godardian alienation effect?

I use "split-screen" as a figure for the stark divisions within De Palma and his works. Four of these divisions are followed as thematic threads running throughout the book—the key contrasts to which I will keep returning. These main themes or key contrasts are:

Independence / Hollywood

De Palma began his career as an "independent" filmmaker based in New York. His early films are anarchic satires on political and social issues of the 1960s, including sexual liberalism, the draft, and theories of the Kennedy assassination. One of the main cinematic influences on these films was the French New Wave, particularly Jean-Luc Godard. "If I could be the American Godard, that would be great," De Palma said at this time in his career.[5] De Palma also felt the impact of documentary film and cinema vérité, and himself made several documentaries in the early '60s, including ones on actresses, rock stars, painters, and civil rights lawyers in the American South. Finally, it is worth noting that De Palma first came to cinema via the New York drama scene and was influenced by the street theater, happenings, and "ritualistic" dramas of the time. In fact, he filmed a live performance of the latter as *Dionysus in '69*.

When the New York "independent" De Palma went to Hollywood in 1970 to make his first studio movie (*Get to Know Your Rabbit*), he clashed with the producers and, refusing to sell out his vision, was fired from the film. Ironically, one of this film's stars was Orson Welles, living proof that a refusal to compromise with the money men could mean the end of a career. As De Palma commented, "Look at Welles. He's the greatest director in the world, and he can't get a job."[6]

Thereafter, De Palma's entire directorial career would be marked by the conflict between independence and Hollywood, between the desire for autonomy and the compulsion to conform. Indeed, some De Palma films would become allegories of this very conflict, as in *Phantom of the Paradise*: the Phantom sells his soul to a devilish record producer—ironically, in an attempt to keep his own voice. "The problem with being both a revolutionary and a film director is that you get to feeling extremely schizoid," De Palma noted. "As a director, you have to be part of the Establishment: you're dealing with great sums of money, you're wheeling and conning people, you're fighting to get an army together." But, De Palma added, you do all this "in order to make some kind of personal statement."[7] De Palma's main strategy for retaining something of his personal vision while working within the Hollywood system was to follow Hitchcock's lead and make genre films that were still distinguished by their director's unique sensibility. Yet time and again the Hitchcock gambit would prove to be something of a trap for De Palma because, even though such films usually made money and allowed him to keep working, they were often belittled as mere genre fare, and De Palma himself was relentlessly accused of being a mere imitator of Hitchcock.

Furthermore, the "independent" De Palma, remaining true to his personal vision of the world, often refused to adhere to the very formulas which made genre pictures successful at the box office. In *Blow Out*, for example, the hero and the heroine meet but do not fall for each other, and he fails to save her at the film's conclusion. Love and a happy ending would have made for a marketable film, but De Palma deliberately withheld these conventional satisfactions—and the film bombed as a result. As the director has said, "I don't believe essentially in letting people off the hook, letting good triumph or basically resolving things, because I think we live in an era in which things are unresolved and terrible events happen and you never forget them."[8] De Palma also admits that "I have a certain corrosive vision of society which seems to not be very commercial. I try to not let my vision corrode the movies to the extent that they become so dark that nobody wants to see them. I did that in *Blow Out*."[9]

Originality / Imitation

From the day De Palma's oldest brother, Bruce, was born, their parents lauded him as a genius. Brian spent the years of his childhood and adolescence in competition with Bruce for their parents' attention and acclaim, following in his footsteps at virtually every stage, reading the same science fiction magazines (though a duplicate set, for each had to have his own), and even entering the same science contests. Brian won a first prize where Bruce had garnered a third, but it made no difference—Bruce was still "the family genius."[10] Brian's other brother, Bart, who threw himself into artistic and athletic pursuits, showed that sibling rivalry was not the only way, but Brian persisted in aping and trying to best Bruce, even planning to major in physics at college, as Bruce had done.

There is thus a terrible personal irony in the fact that, for many viewers and critics, Brian De Palma continues to be known as a mere imitator of Alfred Hitchcock, as an inferior follower of the master (as he was of his brother before him). "There's a whole school of De Palma criticism that says I'm absolutely terrible, that I've never had an original idea in my life, that I'm just a poor man's Hitchcock," De Palma ruefully noted.[11] "I could make Disney pictures from now on, and they'd still be talking about the shower scene I'd stolen from *Psycho*."[12] And yet it is easy to see why critics have charged De Palma with being unoriginal. The fact is that no director has ever followed another director's themes and techniques in his own films as closely or as repeatedly as De Palma has done with Hitchcock's. De Palma even went so far as to use Hitchcock's same composer, Bernard Herrmann, and to cast the daughter (Melanie Griffith) of Tippi Hedren, one of Hitchcock's actresses (that is, when De Palma couldn't get Jamie Lee Curtis, the daughter of another Hitchcock actress, Janet Leigh).

But De Palma has claimed that his Hitchcockian films are much more than pale imitations and that he is not some slavish copier of the master's genius: "You can re-interpret good material in different ways, into your own framework. If you have a style of your own and individuality, you'll take good things from other people and make them better. Great artists have done it."[13] It is only by taking a close look at how De Palma's films relate to Hitchcock's—how they rework the master's themes and forms in personally innovative ways—that we can determine whether the younger director achieves greatness in his own right. Speaking of what he perceived as his apprenticeship to Hitchcock, De Palma said, "You learn from him; you watch his way of doing things and then you evolve beyond his work by adding your own ideas."[14]

Feminism / Misogyny

One of the most unfortunate ways in which De Palma is said to have imitated Hitchcock is in having chosen inexperienced actresses (Nancy Allen, Melanie

Griffith, Rebecca Romijn) whom he could dominate and cast as victims of voyeurism and violence in his films. A truly tremendous amount of criticism over the years has been directed at De Palma's "cruel" treatment of women, whether this be his manipulation and sexual objectification of actresses on the set or the extent to which he exposes his films' female characters to leering looks and phallic assaults (with straight razor, ice-pick, and power drill). "It always makes good copy to say I'm the guy who mutilates women," De Palma lamented.[15] Indeed, it's surprising that no one has written a viciously critical book on this director along the lines of Donald Spoto's book on Hitchcock, *The Dark Side of Genius* (Susan Dworkin's *Double De Palma* comes close), but this is not my intent. Yet neither do I plan to accept De Palma's defense of himself at face value, as when he claims that putting women in jeopardy is merely a requirement of the horror and suspense genres, that "violence is just a visual form,"[16] or that "the use of murders in movies is aesthetic stuff. Motion. Form. Shapes."[17] Given that De Palma has seemed driven to depict women as objects of voyeurism and violence in film after film, I would suggest that his motives are not purely aesthetic.

There are also personal and social factors involved. To take one account from his life, De Palma once remarked that "I think there are many sexual things you don't understand as a teenager. You look through a door and see your parents, or your brother with a girl. I spent a lot of my time watching. I would follow people around. If a girl was giving me a hard time, I'd follow her to see if she really was dating another guy. I would track her."[18] What is interesting here is how sexual curiosity and desire can turn into suspicion, jealousy, and (what borders on) stalking—how voyeurism shades into potential violence. Now, could it be that De Palma is not merely re-enacting this dangerous emotional trajectory in his films but also critically examining it? He has said that, when he first attended film screenings in college, he saw a connection between his own experiences and movies such as *Peeping Tom*, *Vertigo*, and *Psycho*. These films, like De Palma's, may put the viewer in the position of the voyeur peeping at women, but they are also highly critical of that position—both *involved* in jealous/sadistic seeing and disapprovingly *distant* from it. De Palma's first Hitchcockian thriller, *Sisters*, has us share the point of view of a man watching a blind woman undress, but this man is then revealed to be an unwitting contestant on a TV show called *Peeping Toms*. It is he who's being watched, he whose voyeurism is exposed, just as ours as viewers is exposed. And the woman's blindness was staged; she is revealed to have the power of sight, to be looking right at him—and at us.

Indeed, she turns out to have active desires, to be more forthright than he about what she wants, including, but not limited to, sex with him. In this, she reflects the times, the 1970s. "I do feel in a sense that I deal with contemporary feminist characters," De Palma has said. "Most of my women characters are very active, very strong ... they are contemporary women and are aggressively pursuing their goals."[19] But it is precisely this female strength that frightens some men, leading to a backlash, attempts to regain control through voyeurism (seeing without being seen), or violence (a physical assertion of male dominance). De Palma again: "Women are more sexually demanding now.... It was never a problem for me but I think men find women's intelligence and aggression, their ambition, threatening."[20] "It was never a problem for me"? The account De Palma gave of his teenage years—and the fact that he keeps returning to this issue in his films—would suggest that it *is* a problem for him, as it is for many men, and that he is *working on the problem* through his films.

De Palma is split between fear and understanding, between violence and compassion toward women. This is why there is often a strong link between the hero in a De Palma film and the villain, his dark double. In *Dressed to Kill*, both science geek Peter (a clear stand-in for the adolescent De Palma) and the villainous Bobbi are trackers and voyeurs of women, excited and disturbed by Liz's active sexuality. The dilemma faced by Peter/Bobbi is whether to protect or punish the woman, to love or kill Liz. This split within the De Palma hero, this uncertainty over whether his intentions regarding women are honorable or heinous, is one reason for his fatal hesitation, for why he sometimes fails to act in time to save the heroine from the villain. The hero is struggling to differentiate himself from the villain, and by the time this struggle is resolved, it may be too late.

Humility / Megalomania

When he was a senior in high school, De Palma's mother tried to commit suicide by taking an overdose of pills. She told him she had done it because his father was cheating on her. De Palma resolved to protect his mother and to help her get a divorce by obtaining proof of his father's adultery. He taped his father's phone conversations on a reel-to-reel recorder his mother had given him for Christmas. He also climbed a tree outside his father's office and surreptitiously took photos, hoping to catch him in the act with another woman. Finally, he broke into his father's office and discovered him there with a scantily clad nurse, his mistress. The revelation led to a separation between his parents and eventually to a divorce.

Years later, De Palma reworked these events from his life into one of his films, *Home Movies*. (There, the events are presented as a farcical comedy, which is perhaps De Palma's way of gaining some critical distance from them.) In the film, the teenage De Palma character, Denis, is in a tree, trying to take photos of his father with a nurse. However, Denis is also voyeuristically peering through a different window at another woman, who resembles his brother's fiancée, whom Denis desires. Thus, Denis is split between hero and villain, between selfless protector (of his mother) and lustful predator (of his brother's fiancée). Earlier, his mother had come home unexpectedly to find Denis making out with a girlfriend, a scene which seemed to greatly upset her. But it turns out that she was even more upset by the sight of his father, whom she had spied in the act of adultery. Denis is thus himself caught in the act, caught behaving more like his lustful father than like a protective son. In De Palma's movies, the hero is often a "son" struggling with a more powerful and predatory "father," and one reason for the son's impotence is the fear that he may already have too much of the father within him, that the predator he is fighting might be a part of himself.

De Palma's father, a renowned orthopedic surgeon and professor at a medical college, was seen by some as cold and aloof, closed off in his own world of work, and overbearingly commanding of the underlings—nurses, residents, medical students—who would trail after him and do his bidding at the hospital. Much the same description has been given of De Palma himself as a film director; it is said that he is like a remote patriarch on set, self-involved and obsessed with his own vision of the film, manipulating the myriad crew members who surround him as if he were their puppetmaster. That the son may become like his father, egotistical and power-mad once he has attained a position of prominence, is a danger which De Palma knows all too well: "Megalomania is a very real problem for the successful director—you think it's me, me, me."[21] "A lot of my films deal with manipulation," he has said, "because I am in a very manipulative business. And I am a very manipulative person. A director manipulates people all the time."[22]

Many De Palma films are exposés of men in patriarchal professions who, as they grow more and more isolated from human contact, increasingly abuse their power and wreak destruction on others. In *Sisters*, there is the lecherous surgeon—modeled on the worst of De Palma's father—who represents medical authority run amok and the abuse of women in the name of science. *Phantom of the Paradise* has a godlike rock promoter and drug pusher who takes advantage of 1970s-era youths who were looking for bigger and better highs. (De Palma's brother Bruce began taking psychedelic drugs and, convinced of his own genius, became more and more isolated from the scientific community, except for a coterie of devoted younger followers and fellow druggies.) And *Scarface* has a Cuban refugee (a kind of "son") who becomes a Miami gangster (a "father") driven crazy by his own excessive materialistic desires. This film was hated by the Hollywood establishment, which rightly saw it as a commentary on the coke-fueled show-business world of the 1980s.

Thus, the theme of megalomania has personal connections to De Palma's life, but it also has wide social and cultural resonance. De Palma's critiques of patriarchal power became one way for him to continue his radical "independent" filmmaking even while directing Hollywood genre pictures. As he has said, "I've always been a political filmmaker. I've never lost the spirit of the '60s. I've always been very critical of the Establishment. I've made a lot of films about corruption, greed, and power."[23]

De Palma, who studied film for two semesters at New York University and then as a graduate student at Sarah Lawrence College, is generally considered to be a member of the "film school generation," along with such fellow "movie brats" as Francis Ford Coppola, George Lucas, Martin Scorsese, and Steven Spielberg. These five men first met when they were just beginning their careers as filmmakers and have remained friends ever since. Much has been written about the connections between the lives and the films of the other directors—for example, Spielberg's childhood (*Close Encounters*, *E.T.*) and his Jewish heritage (*Schindler's List*); Lucas's adolescence (*American Graffiti*, *Star Wars*); and Coppola and Scorsese's Italian-Catholic background (the former's *The Godfather*; the latter's *Mean Streets* and *Goodfellas*). But De Palma's films have rarely been seen as rooted in his own life. Whether because they were thought of as formulaic genre films (*Carrie*, *Dressed to Kill*, *Body Double*) or as impersonal blockbusters (*The Untouchables*, *Mission: Impossible*, *Mission to Mars*), De Palma's movies are usually viewed as being devoid of biographical resonance. The director himself has sometimes encouraged this disconnect, making it seem as though he has no life, that all he is is film: "Everything I do and feel is in my movies," De Palma said in 1973. "I could leave [my] apartment tomorrow and never think about it twice—there's no personal part of me here."[24] He added, "I'm almost completely oblivious to my surroundings. I have no desire to own anything. I've never married and don't want to marry. The outside world means little or nothing to me. I'm completely obsessed with film. Everything meaningful is right here in my head, behind my eyes."[25]

But De Palma did marry—and divorce—three times, and he became a father to two daughters. He had a mother and a father and two brothers, a complex family life that marked him for good and for ill. When he was once asked, "Is it relevant for a moviegoer to know about your childhood?", De Palma replied, "Oh, I think so. I read biographies of directors."[26] De Palma also remarked that "for parents, it's always a disaster to have a son who's a director, a writer, or a poet. Because what he lived as a child always manages to turn up one day in his artistic work."[27] Indeed, De Palma has said that, even before he made any of his voyeuristic suspense thrillers, the photos he took outside his father's office window in an attempt to catch him having an affair constitute what the young director considered to be his "first film."[28]

Viewing De Palma as a mere imitator of Hitchcock has caused people to miss the fact that, through watching and then "remaking" this other director's films, De Palma found a way to *express himself*. It was just a few months after De Palma's attempt to follow and photograph his father that the young director saw Hitchcock's *Vertigo* for the first time (in VistaVision at Radio City Music Hall in 1958, when he was a freshman at Columbia University). Scottie's voyeurism and pursuit of Madeleine in that film connected with De Palma's own experience. As he has said about this and other Hitchcock films, "They seemed terrifying and wonderful to me, and suddenly I knew that I could convey my dreams on the screen. No other art form would do."[29]

What has not been sufficiently recognized is that De Palma's films are the way in which he dreams about his own life, exploring his fears and imagining possible means of overcoming them. According to him, "anyone in an artistic medium has a leg up in dealing with his obsessions, because he can express them. It's great. I don't dream much, because my dreams are all in my movies. I don't have nightmares, because I work them all out in artistic form." Speaking of his own "psychological obsessions," De Palma noted, "I sort of act them out in my movies all the time. I'm attracted to material that emanates from subconscious need through bizarre dreams."[30]

De Palma's films are thus profoundly connected to his life, but often in a metaphorical way, much as dreams are strange reworkings of moments from our waking life. If, as De Palma says, "what I *am* is up there on the screen,"[31] this does not mean that no aspects of his personal life are relevant to his films. Instead, it means that his films *are* a form of creative reflection upon his personal life. His is "a life in film." "You have to go with the emotional logic," De Palma has explained. "Your decisions [as a director] come from some private source, and they may not make sense to you at the time. It takes years, really, before you can go back and make connections—recognize the source of this or the motive of that."[32] For example, after years of making movies about heroes troubled by guilt over their failure to save others who are suffering, De Palma finally recognized one personal source of this obsessive theme. "Seeing [my brother] Bart upset over my mother being torn up [by their father's adultery] and being too small to do anything about it, that had an impact on me," the director said. "I realized that's why I always have characters who can't save people. That's me trying to save my brother. I didn't see that then, but I do now."[33]

Some viewers may question the legitimacy of reading De Palma's films in terms of his life. After all, movies are a complex creative endeavor, involving the input of multiple individuals. There are hundreds of cast and crew members who have had a significant influence on De Palma's films, making them theirs and not just his. And other directors besides Hitchcock have also had a huge impact on De Palma's works. Shouldn't a comprehensive study of these films take into account all of these varied inputs and perspectives? In fact, throughout this book I do quote from actors, actresses, screenwriters, producers, cinematographers, editors, soundmen, composers, and costume designers who have made such a major contribution to the films. And, in addition to the impact of Hitchcock (which is in itself quite varied, including not just that of *Rear Window*, *Vertigo*, and *Psycho*, but also *Sabotage*, *Rebecca*, *Saboteur*, *Notorious*, *Rope*, *To Catch a Thief*, *North by Northwest*, and *Frenzy*), I do consider the influence that numerous other directors have had on De Palma, including Michelangelo Antonioni, Jean-Luc Godard, Stanley Kubrick, David Lean, Richard Lester, Jim McBride, Frank Perry, Michael Powell, Martin Scorsese, Steven Spielberg, Orson Welles, and Billy Wilder.

But I should state upfront that this relatively short book is not intended to be comprehensive and that it does have as its central focus Brian De Palma. I hope that the reader will find that I have some interesting things to say about the way this particular director has responded in his films to significant movements and events of the last several decades, including the John F. Kennedy assassination, paranoia, and the surveillance state; feminism and the backlash against it; the violence of war (Vietnam, Iraq); and the wonder of space exploration. I also hope that the reader will be intrigued by the connections I draw between De Palma's life and his works—connections that allow the films to be seen in a new light and that help us to understand the man who made them. There may be those who object that the connections I trace are merely tenuous or highly speculative. Some might say, for example, that *Carrie* is more of a Stephen King movie than a De Palma one, or that *The Black Dahlia* is more about James Ellroy's life than De Palma's; that *Scarface* and *The Untouchables* are movies De Palma helmed as works-for-hire, lacking anything personal; or that *Mission: Impossible* and *Mission to Mars* are special-effects extravaganzas that are in no way autobiographical. I can only ask the reader to look at the evidence I provide to support the links I see between De Palma's life and these films, and to judge accordingly. I try to explain these links as carefully and completely as I can, and wherever possible, I quote De Palma and others when they have spoken about perceiving a connection. (I should note that this book was written for people who are interested in what the director, cast, and crew had to say about their intended meaning. This is not to assume that their meaning was necessarily achieved or that their meaning is the only meaning of the film.)

Some may argue that to read a director's films in terms of his life is limiting and reductive. Certainly, I have tried to vary the biographical examples that I link to the films, referring to many relevant relationships in De Palma's life, including those with his mother, his father, his brothers, his wives, his daughters, his director-friends, and leading members of his cast and crew. However, there are certain key incidents from De Palma's life to which he keeps returning in film after film: his father's adultery, his mother's near-suicide, his sense of inferiority to one brother, and his failure to save the other one from suffering. To this we should add one further event that has not yet been mentioned: De Palma as a teenager witnessing his surgeon-father perform bloody operations with a scalpel. All these early events were traumatic, and De Palma refers to them repeatedly and obsessively, and because they recur across multiple films, they will also be repeated in this book.

My hope is that, despite this unavoidable repetition, readers will still find a great deal of variety in the different forms these traumas take in individual films and the different conclusions to which they are played out. To consider some particular instances, while Dr. Breton in *Sisters* and Dr. Elliott in *Dressed to Kill* are rather clearly connected in their scalpel murders to De Palma's surgeon father, it is more surprising to see a link with the chainsaw amputation in *Scarface* and the blown-off limbs in *Casualties of War*. The competition between Denis and James in *Home Movies* and between Carter and Cain in *Raising Cain* reflects the battle for superiority between De Palma and his brother Bruce, but so does the ultimately friendly competition between Jim and Woody in *Mission to Mars*, which can be seen as an act of understanding and forgiveness on De Palma's part toward his brother. Sibling rivalry is again the theme of *Femme Fatale*, but a switch in gender seems to make it easier for the director to imagine a reconciliation between Laure and Lily, one that never actually occurred between Brian and Bruce. De Palma's failure to save his other brother, Bart, is acted out by Sue and Carrie in *Carrie*, Liz and Kate in *Dressed to Kill*, and Jack and Sally in *Blow Out*, but—for reasons which I explore—the same dilemma meets with a more positive outcome for *Body Double*'s Jake and *Femme Fatale*'s Laure, each of whom is given a second chance and ultimately succeeds in rescuing Holly and Lily, respectively.

While it is generally true that De Palma's later films are more optimistic than his early ones, this is by no means always the case. *Redacted* has as bleak an ending as any in the director's oeuvre, and the conclusions of *The Black Dahlia* and *Passion* offer at most a glimmer of hope. We have noted how De Palma's films are a form of on-screen dreaming, a visualization of traumatic material. Sometimes the films seem caught in a nightmarish loop, reliving past traumas in a compulsive repetition of the same dire events. At other times, the movies seem to allow him to master these traumas, to achieve his stated goal of "work[ing] them all out in artistic form."[34] Though one may feel an understandable desire to trace De Palma's career as a clear trajectory from pessimism to hope, I think it's important to resist imposing such a definitive structure on his body of work. The fact is that he vacillates from film to film, and often within a given film, between a compulsive repetition and a success-ful working-through of trauma. I have tried to remain true to the films them-selves in their wavering and ambiguity, while also identifying some trends and tendencies.

One consequence of seeing De Palma's films as ways of trying to master traumatic events is that I tend to take his characters seriously as people. Of course, movie characters are not people, but they can intrigue, frustrate, and move us as if they were. Similarly, film plots are not life stories, yet they can engage us in many of the same ways. Kate, the conflicted heroine of *Dressed to Kill*, becomes someone we feel for, grow concerned about, and mourn when she is murdered. My view of De Palma as a personally invested director who makes movies about realistic, complex characters is a far cry from another, quite prevalent view: that he is a distant director of often cynical satires filled with stylishly manipulated caricatures rather than with people we care about. For example, in talking about *Dressed to Kill* and *Blow Out*, James Blackford refers to their "paper-thin plausibility, cartoonish characters, virtuoso style and grandiose set pieces," and he considers these movies to be "magnificent manifestos of anti-realism that celebrate film as a syntax of illusion and arti-fice."[35] This is a perfectly legitimate view of De Palma (and one that has the advantage of being able to account for the stylistic games he plays with audi-ences, his satiric exaggeration, and his dark humor), but it is not my view.

I hope that readers will find my take on De Palma as a personal filmmaker to be powerful and persuasive, but I do not intend it as *the* definitive interpre-tation of this multifaceted director. There are many other wonderfully reveal-ing writings which emphasize aspects of his work that are different from, or more detailed extensions of, those that I focus on here. I see this book as one part of a larger critical re-evaluation of De Palma's oeuvre. As Robert E. Kap-sis and Chris Dumas have noted in their excellent overviews of the movie reviews and film scholarship devoted to this director,[36] De Palma's films of the '60s tended to be overlooked; his '70s and '80s works, despite some notable exceptions, were heavily criticized; and his movies from the '90s and beyond have been largely ignored or dismissed. But all this is changing.

Laurence F. Knapp led the way in 2003 with a superb collection of direc-torial interviews, and Laurent Bouzereau has added immeasurably to our understanding via a series of video interviews that can be found on DVDs of De Palma's films. David Taylor (2005) and Ken Tucker (2008) have each written whole books about *Scarface*, and Joseph Aisenberg (2011) and Neil Mitchell (2013) have devoted entire books to *Carrie*. Eyal Peretz (2008) has authored a treatise on De Palma's films as philosophy, which includes studying the effect of traumatic events on characters who witness them. David Greven

(2009, 2011, 2013) has mounted a sophisticated defense of De Palma's varied and complex representation of gender, and he has been among the few to argue that De Palma may be significantly revising Hitchcock and not merely repeating him. Chris Dumas (2012) not only delves into the many reasons why film studies as a profession has tended to mistreat and misunderstand De Palma, he also provides the most extensive reading of this director's films as Godardian social satires. Most recently, Cristina Alvarez López and Adrian Martin (2014) have created an audiovisual essay (with accompanying text) that studies elements of De Palma's style, including signature techniques and characteristic motifs that form meaningful patterns across his various films. In short, De Palma is being rediscovered in the twenty-first century, and I hope that my work—in combination with that of these others—will prompt viewers to take another look at this too-often denigrated and neglected director.

This book offers interpretations of De Palma's films in chronological order, drawing connections with his life wherever these seem to be most relevant and revealing. It can be read straight through as a way of tracking the changes in De Palma's work over time, or readers can skip to the sections on the particular films they find to be of most interest, for each chapter is relatively self-contained and designed to make sense if read separately. This book was written for all those who want to know more about De Palma's controversial films, and for anyone who was ever curious about what kind of man could make such films. De Palma once expressed the fear that he will be forever "remembered by everyone as a misogynist and as the man who ripped off Hitchcock."[37] He came to believe that most critics have these "preconceptions" about him "going in" to his films, which they review "against their preconceptions"; "they don't really watch"[38] the films. This book was written for those who want to watch the films.

CHAPTER 1

The Wedding Party (1964–65)

De Palma's first feature film, *The Wedding Party*, was shot in winter 1964 and summer 1965. Because no distributor could be found for the film, it was not released until 1969, after the success of *Greetings*. *The Wedding Party* was a collaborative effort: De Palma did most of the directing and editing; his drama teacher, Wilford Leach, worked with the actors; and Cynthia Munroe, a student at Sarah Lawrence College, financed the production ($100,000) and wrote the script. Originally, De Palma, Munroe, and three other friends were each going to direct separate segments of an anthology film, along the lines of *Love at Twenty*, a European movie about the state of young love in the early 1960s. (One of its five directors was François Truffaut.) But De Palma thought that Munroe's script was better than his and so the two decided to make it the basis of a full-length film.

The film was autobiographical in that its events were inspired by the wedding of Jared Martin, who had been De Palma's roommate at Columbia University, along with William Finley. De Palma and Finley served as groomsmen at these nuptials, which were held on a Long Island estate in 1963, the year before shooting began. In the film, the groom is called Charlie (played by Charles Pfluger), while his two friends are Alistair (William Finley, playing a version of himself) and Cecil (Robert De Niro, cast in the De Palma role). Martin's bride, Nancy Fales, is Josephine in the film, played by Jill Clayburgh. These were Clayburgh's and De Niro's very first movie roles. In fact, since De Niro wasn't yet of legal age, his mother had to sign his contract for him. De Niro had answered an open casting call in New York and had greatly impressed De Palma with his youthful energy and his ability to improvise, both of which would be essential to this film.

The Wedding Party begins with a sense of hopeful exuberance as Charlie, Alistair, and Cecil arrive on the island by ferry and are whisked off by car to the family estate. The madcap car ride, replete with crazy hijinks, is shot in speeded-up motion similar to a Mack Sennett silent film. All this comes to a crashing halt when Charlie reaches the house and meets his fiancée's elderly aunts on the veranda. A stinger chord sounds and a freeze-frame shows his crestfallen face, then slow motion depicts his fearful labor as he must greet each ancient lady while their voice-over carping about him fills his ears. (These criticisms—that young men don't do any work these days, that they go to college but they're not *in* college; God knows what they're doing instead— are ones that De Palma must have heard fairly often from the older generation, including his parents.) The film's title credit has a backwards *N* in *THE WEDDING PARTY*, indicating that something is terribly wrong: this wedding isn't going to be any kind of party. A card listing all the bride's relatives and guests has so many names on it that they blot out the screen, as Charlie will be stifled by all this stale WASP tradition.

And what has happened to all the men in the family? Cecil points to some gravestones, suggesting that the males have been done in by all the old biddies. To prop up Charlie's masculinity, Cecil offers him a "non-wedding present," the key to his city apartment and his little black book of girls' numbers, and Alistair offers him his Playboy Club key. Then, continuing a dialogue that seems drawn from improvisation, they jointly offer Charlie "the key to freedom": a car key so that he can drive away. Later in the film, as Charlie waits in vain for his friends to take him to his bachelor party (they have forgotten him), jump cuts emphasize Charlie's discomfort as he fails to find any position in bed that will allow him to sleep, and he finally ends up just lying there with his arms stretched out in a facetious reference to Christ on the Cross. Still later, when the minister walks Charlie and his bride-to-be through the woods, advising that "we must cleave to the path that calls us to keep our promises," Charlie literally takes another path, splitting off from them at a fork in the road and enjoying a brief encounter with some bikini-clad women who admire his he-man strength. (He lifts a large log that has impeded their car, and they thank him in an orgiastic rush of hugs and kisses.)

These scenes show neophyte director De Palma deploying a battery of experimental techniques to dramatize the conflict between youth and old age, between a bachelor's freedom and his confinement within the institution of marriage. With these techniques—fast and slow motion, freeze-frame, jump cuts, title cards, improvisational dialogue, narrative digressions, and jokey allusions—De Palma brings to America the youthful energy of French New Wave directors like François Truffaut (*Jules and Jim*) and Jean-Luc Godard (*Breathless, A Woman Is a Woman, My Life to Live*).

Stanley Kubrick's satiric films are another likely influence on De Palma here. Just as one actor (Peter Sellers) played multiple roles in *Lolita* and *Dr. Strangelove*, so Richard Kollmar, Jr., played all three of the bride's former suitors in *The Wedding Party*: Jean-Claude, I. Singh, and Klaus. Each suitor is literally foreign—much as Charlie is metaphorically so—to the conventional environment of Josephine's Eastern Establishment family. "You can't know anything about love unless you've been to Paris," says Jean-Claude (also sounding like Jean-Luc), who provides startling dinner-table conversation by adding, "After all, we're living in the twentieth century. You have your Dr. Kinsey; we have our Marquis de Sade." And I. Singh, a young Hindu, almost crashes his plane glider into Josephine and the family mansion, which is surely how her family feels about his unwanted intrusion into their lives. (An earlier shot of one plane towing another plane in the sky could be a reference to *Dr. Strangelove*.)

In his feature-film debut, De Palma also pays homage to two of the masters of cinema, Orson Welles and Alfred Hitchcock. As Charlie listens, increasingly horrified, while Josephine's father tells him what married life has in store for him—"you lose track of your friends, learn to sit at a desk, eat what's good for you instead of what you like" and you take up "chess, gardening, and taxidermy"—the nervous groom is surrounded by stuffed wild animals, neutered as Charlie is about to be. A fox has its jaws near Charlie's crotch, much as in *Psycho* where a stuffed bird had its beak near the head of Norman Bates (Anthony Perkins), henpecked by his mother. Throughout his stay in the family mansion, older women cut off Charlie's access to Josephine, constantly intervening whenever he tries to make love to her. Her mother sends her upstairs and insists that Charlie sleep downstairs with the men. He sneaks into her room, but a nanny interrupts them in bed—"I just hope this wedding isn't completely superfluous"—and contrives to get him to leave. "They came; they saw; and I'd like to get out of here before anything else happens," thinks Charlie, almost conquered by their intrusive gaze. Finally, he pulls Josephine down onto a couch in a remote tower room, but even this scene is shot from outside a rain-lashed window as if prying eyes were looking in, a voyeur's gaze watching the two of them together. The shot is similar to the one in *Citizen Kane* where Welles's camera peers in at two characters through a rainy window skylight.

Charlie's worst fear is that Josephine may have internalized this disapproving gaze; she seems to be growing older and more like her repressively conventional female elders every minute. When he requests something special for their wedding night, she says she could wear her "granny nightie." At breakfast, she peels a banana and feeds it into a juicer, making Charlie feel further emasculated. When he approaches her with animal passion, she symbolically declaws him, telling him that he is not a lion and refusing to let him make out with her. When Charlie imagines their wedding ceremony, two thought bubbles open above his head: one shows an aged Josephine who needs glasses to read her vows, and another shows Charlie throwing himself under a car to avoid having to spend a lifetime with her. It's interesting to note that De Palma dated Jill Clayburgh when they were students at Sarah Lawrence before he cast her as Josephine. The Charlie-Josephine relationship appears to represent some of De Palma's own ambivalence regarding the prospect of marriage, the loss of a bachelor's freedom and of virile passion within the female-dominated realm of matrimony and family. (Years later, in 1975, De Palma would be the best man at—and would film—the wedding of his friend William Finley [Alistair]. Finley's wife recalls that De Palma "interviewed us in the car en route to the ceremony. He asked Bill if he was 'sure he really wanted to go through with this?' . . . With me sitting between them.")[1]

As with Clayburgh, De Palma was also close to fellow student Cynthia Munroe, though the two were never a couple: "Contrary to what I've often read, Cynthia was not my girlfriend. But I liked her a lot! We were both studying with Wilford Leach at Sarah Lawrence."[2] In addition to writing and producing *The Wedding Party*, Munroe also cooked for the cast and crew, serving as a kind of mother figure. With $100,000 of her own money invested in the project, Munroe would not entrust De Palma with the direction of the film: "Judging that I still had very little experience, Cynthia asked [Leach] to supervise the direction. So I didn't have free rein."[3] Although Josephine's mother is a terrible driver, she insists on driving the car from the ferry to the house, and as a result the chauffeur ends up hanging from the car's running board while Charlie attempts to steer the car over the mother's shoulders from the backseat. At another point in the film, we find out that Josephine's mother makes the chauffeur do all the chores around the house, in fact everything except the one thing he wants to do: drive the car. Is De Palma making a sly reference to the fact that he was not granted sole directorial control of the film? We do know that he and Munroe had many disagreements over how the film's budget was to be spent.

Though in the end De Palma did most of the directing, Munroe as producer had put Leach in charge, so he "more or less had control of what actually happened. His word was the final word," recalled De Palma,[4] who had numerous arguments with his father figure and mentor. If De Palma rather than Leach had coached the lead actor, Charlie would have been played as less of a shallow wiseass. Leach, in turn, took issue with De Palma's use of fast motion, jump cuts, title cards, and movie references.

In short, the older teacher objected to much of De Palma's enthusiastic experimentation with film techniques and attempted to exert a moderating influence on the young director. There is perhaps an analogy to the advice given by the minister to Charlie in the film: "Miniature golf . . . teaches you . . . restraint of your passions. Have you ever noticed how anyone can drive, but it takes real good judgment to sink a putt?" Similarly, Josephine's father, who plays golf *inside* the house, advises Charlie to curtail his ambitions. Rather than being like a "college . . . captain of the bicycle team," he should "swim with [the rest of] the school" and "drink a bit too much, learn to mow the lawn, and wash the car on Sunday." However, it should be noted that De Palma and Leach did not break up due to their disagreements over *The Wedding Party*: "Will had been too good to me, too helpful, to let that happen. It was just that now, I thought I knew more than he did. And I thought to myself: well, now, I am going to have to do this on my own."[5]

CHAPTER 2

Murder à la Mod (1966)

If Godard had made a Hitchcock film, or if Hitchcock had made a Godard film, it might look something like *Murder à la Mod*, De Palma's second feature-length movie. Mixing self-reflexive humor about filmmaking with the horror of a murder and the suspense of its investigation, De Palma here combined the styles of the two directors who arguably had the most influence on him in his novice years. "We have three suspects," De Palma explained, and "we go back to the murder three times. Three different perspectives."[1]

The first segment is told from the (implied and sometimes literal) point of view of Karen (Margo Norton) and presented in the style of a soap opera as she chitchats with her friend Tracy (Andra Akers) and has a melodramatic scene with her boyfriend Chris (Jared Martin). In Godardian fashion, the handheld camera follows Karen with over-the-shoulder shots as she is walking down the streets of New York, while jump cuts move us quickly from moment to moment in her indoor conversations. The second segment, beginning after Karen is mysteriously murdered, transitions through Tracy's perspective on events and on to that of Wiley (Ken Burrows), a sleazy film producer. Edited for maximum suspense, this section is Hitchcockian in style and theme. Like *Psycho*'s Marion (Janet Leigh), Karen steals some money and is eyed by a suspicious policeman. She is also watched while undressing to shower and then fatally stabbed—the sudden death of a lead character early in the picture. Her dying body slides down the wall like Marion's, and the murderer's cleanup includes a shot of bloody water running down the drain similar to a shot in *Psycho*. In *Murder à la Mod*'s third segment, events are replayed from the perspective of Otto (William Finley), a crazy prankster who stabs Karen with a fake ice-pick and douses her with ketchup for blood. Otto is like Harpo of the Marx Brothers, and since he sees everything as a joke, his section of the movie is filled with the slapstick humor and the speeded-up motion of a silent-film comedy.

But whodunit—Otto, Wiley, or Chris? Did loony Otto use a real ice-pick on Karen instead of the trick one? The deaf-mute Otto's pranks are his way of attracting female attention. (In *The Wedding Party*, Alistair—who was also played by William Finley—theorized that the reason Beethoven "never had a woman in his life" was that he "was deaf.") But surprising women with a fake stabbing also empowers Otto in a voyeuristic and implicitly violent way, catching them unawares and making phallic advances upon them. While he may hope that they will love his joke, the prank also seems to punish them for the rejection of him that he assumes is coming—a rejection that, ironically, this very kind of gag is likely to bring on with its aggression. "I can't *wait* to see her face," Otto thinks before attacking Karen with the trick pick, but this only provokes her to beat him off: "She hit me! She didn't get the joke."

Could Karen's rejection have led Otto to increasingly desperate bids for attention—gags whose aggression gradually melds into a truly violent punishment of her for not loving him? Did Otto, accidentally/on purpose, mix up the real and fake picks? One of Otto's gags is to pretend that his disembodied hand is crawling toward the ice-pick as if it had a murderous mind of its own, and after Karen's murder, Otto wonders about the real pick that was used to kill her: "How did it get out of my pocket?" Perhaps he half-deliberately let his phallic aggression out—on Karen. Otto, who acts in S&M sex films, is seen going a little too far in a scene where he uses scissors to cut off a woman's dress. "He thinks ripping that girl's dress off is a great joke," comments Chris. "He'd kill her if he thought he could get a laugh out of it."

And what about Wiley, the dirty-movie producer? Did he set up a secret camera in the ceiling above a bed in order to capture unsuspecting women in the nude, to "trick" them into being filmed? Although he claims that it is Chris's camera, Wiley—with his dark shades and phallic cigar—seems awfully excited about this voyeuristic view of female flesh. "Did you see what I see?" he asks Otto. "Wow, what a tomato! I was wondering how [Chris] got those high-class broads to take it off.... I can't *wait* to see that hot scene he just shot with the secret camera!" Wiley's voyeurism has something sadistic about it, an excitement at catching women unawares and capturing their vulnerable nakedness, reducing them to objects bound by his gaze, as in his S&M film about "Joan of Arc" tied to the stake in her "Maidenform bra." Would Wiley go so far as to film a stabbing lust-murder for his viewing enjoyment? When Otto shows him a trunk, Wiley asks, "What do you got in there, a body or something?" and then pats the film canister he's holding, saying "*I'm* the one who's got the body, right in this can." Someone who can so jokingly equate a woman in a porn film to a corpse in a trunk is a potential monster. Like Otto's, Wiley's humor is pretty horrible.

Finally, there is Chris, Karen's boyfriend and the final suspect in her murder. If Wiley is a producer and Otto is an actor, Chris is a director and thus the closest metaphorically to De Palma himself. While Ken Burrows (playing Wiley) was De Palma's actual producer on the film and William Finley (Otto) was De Palma's former college roommate, Jared Martin (Chris) was not only a former roommate but also De Palma's best friend at the time. (We recall that *The Wedding Party* is based on Martin's real-life wedding, at which De Palma and Finley were groomsmen.) Chris (Martin) is De Palma's nearest alter ego in *Murder à la Mod*, in ways that suggest De Palma was using film as a medium to work through some of his own issues regarding women.

Early in the movie, we watch through a camera's viewfinder as an actress auditions for a film, and we hear the director in voice-over trying to convince her to take off her top. The actress is played by Jennifer Salt, who had briefly dated De Palma when they were students at Sarah Lawrence College, and the director is voiced by De Palma himself. The director's mumbled instructions make him sound both insecure and overly insistent as he nervously persists in getting the reluctant actress to strip. "I remember directing a scene in college," De Palma said, "and it was on a bed with a girl and for a moment, I stopped and thought to myself: This is the most beautiful girl I have ever been this close to."[2] Directing becomes an awkward young man's means to approach intimacy, while also maintaining a certain amount of distance and control.

The actress in *Murder à la Mod* establishes that she is supposed to play the girlfriend (Karen) of the director (Chris), who claims he is making this skin flick only to finance a divorce from his wife using the money he will get from the producer (Wiley): "She won't let me go until I finish this film and I'm completely degraded." Later, we find out that Chris has heard a radio play about another director beholden to his wife, Cynthia, who is herself a producer: "If I didn't do what she asked, the show would close tomorrow. Cynthia's our biggest backer." We recall that a wealthy Sarah Lawrence student named Cynthia Munroe put up most of the money for De Palma's first film, *The Wedding Party*, and that he chafed under her influence.

If Munroe was one model for Chris, the producer in *Murder à la Mod*, then the actual co-producer of that film was another. This man (whose name is no longer known) invested with the expectation that De Palma was really going to make a sexploitation film. Wiley, the sleazy producer in *Murder à la Mod*, has the same expectation of Chris, the director, as the co-producer had of De Palma. "I was reflecting the people who were making the circumstances that I was working under," De Palma later said, comparing his situation to that of Godard when he was directing *Contempt* and pressured to insert some nudity: "If the [producer] asks to see Bardot's ass, that's all you show."[3] And, when it comes to self-reflexivity, don't forget that the other producer of *Murder à la Mod*, Ken Burrows, plays Wiley, the producer in this film!

"We're making a sendup—a joke of a joke," De Palma explained about his quasi-sexploitation film about a sexploitation film, admitting that it "still is garbage . . . but garbage from a different viewpoint."[4] De Palma's smut movie is one step removed from the actual thing, a director looking at a director's way of looking at women in order to examine it from a critical perspective. Although Chris isn't a fashion photographer, his pictures of Karen in her mod '60s clothes are artistic, and his photos of her in the nude are similarly idealizing: "My studies of you are perfections of the human form. They celebrate the beauty in your innocence." If this comment suggests that he tends to take an infantilizing view of her, seeing her as an innocent young girl, another remark—that she looks "like a little Madonna"—shows that he spiritualizes her, too.

What she cannot be, in his eyes, is a sensual, adult woman. Noting that she has "stood naked before" him and that he's "never even touched" her, Karen asks Chris if that's why he's divorcing his wife—because she "went to bed with" him. When Chris had tried to get one of the auditioning actresses to disrobe— "This is an art scene. Are you afraid of your body? C'mon, *I'm* not afraid of it"—her response actually revealed the truth about *him*: "I don't care whether *you're* afraid of it, but I didn't really know that you made these type of films." He makes porn films because he's afraid of female flesh.

In part, this has to do with a disgust he feels for his own sexual desires. "This dirt degrades the human body by pandering to the basest lust," Chris says, referring to one of his sex films. He tells Karen, "When are you going to open your eyes and see what you're in love with?"—that is, his own "filthy" self. At the same time, Chris's self-disgust is linked to a fear of being rejected by women, whom he idealizes as models of purity who would—indeed, should— never let themselves be sullied by his "base" desires. Describing the kind of man like himself who goes to sex films, Chris says that he "watches girls on the screen do everything in the world he's always wanted to make them do but never dared." The actress on screen must disrobe as if unaware that she is being watched, for if she saw the viewer looking, she—as a "good woman"—would be shocked at his voyeuristic intrusion and reject him for his "base" desires. Or, if she returned his lustful gaze, she would become a "dirty slut," a woman whose desires might be more than he could handle, sexually and emotionally insecure as he is. "Sex is out of control . . . and love is out of control," De Palma has said, admitting that "I don't like to be out of control." "Taking control" is "the nature of directing," according to De Palma, although he admits that he "couldn't be a director if [he] didn't also feel the arousal, the fear."[5]

During one of Chris's photo sessions with Karen, his viewfinder's cross-hairs are right over her eye. He, with his directorial gaze, is the one to do the looking, his camera keeping her at a distance and maintaining his control, and she is to be looked at. If she returns his gaze, her eye will be viewed as a threat, as indeed the camera's crosshairs resemble those in a rifle's sight. "Once he caught me peeking into my photo-biography and he got really angry," Karen says about Chris, and in another scene she unexpectedly intrudes upon his viewing of one of his porn films, where he warns her that "I don't want you to see" such "filthy smut," to see the kind of thing "a pervert, a dirty old man, a sex maniac" views.

When she insists on watching the film and on making love with him, Chris leads Karen over to a bed, but just when she thinks he is going to kiss her, he shows her a camera hidden in the eye of a female figure painted on the ceiling. He cannot bear to have her see his lustful state, as she would if she made physical contact with him. He needs the camera in order to preserve his voyeuristic distance from her. Chris tells her that, while the two of them might make love as a "sweet, innocent young couple," a perverted actor named Otto would be watching and filming them with that hidden camera. In fact, the camera belongs to Chris. It is he who, unable to be un-self-consciously intimate with Karen, would also be imagining her looking at him—and imagining himself looking down at both of them, desiring her but feeling guilty about it, wanting her but fearful of her rejection. Thus, when Chris describes the voyeuristic Otto's reaction, he is really describing his own: "It's too much for him. He wants to join in—and in and in with his ice-pick—in and in and *in*!" The frustrated voyeur commits a lust-murder, both expressing and repressing his desire through phallic violence, punishing the woman whose look incited his lust.

Later, when Chris actually kills Karen (for it is he who is the murderer), we look from her point of view as, lying on the bed, she sees the camera in the eye of the painted woman on the ceiling, followed by the ice-pick stabbing down into her own eye. The ice-pick and the camera (which is filming the murder) forcibly re-establish Chris's distance from and control over Karen, obliterating her threatening gaze to ensure that he is the one doing the looking. As Otto realizes when he sees Chris's movie of the murder, "he killed the lady. He killed her and he put her in the picture"—that is, Chris killed her so that she would remain objectified on film, thus guaranteeing his mastery as the male voyeur.

In Michael Powell's *Peeping Tom*, a key source of inspiration for De Palma's character Chris, a would-be director named Mark (Carl Boehm) not only takes nudie photos and shoots "screen tests" of scantily clad women, he also films prostitutes and kills them with a blade attached to his camera so that he can see the look of fear on their faces as they die. Like Chris, Mark uses his camera to contain the threat of female sexuality, and his blade to defeat the female gaze. In the end, though, in order to save the woman he loves, Mark turns that camera and that blade on himself, filming his own self-destruction.

In *Murder à la Mod*, Chris has already killed Karen, but even he is assailed by guilt at the end, showing that he still has a conscience. Watching film of Karen just before her death, Chris sees her looking out at him from the screen and he seems to imagine that her eyes are accusing him, making him face his crime. (This effect is increased by the fact that the screen image of Karen seems to witness Chris's strangling of Wiley, whom he kills in an effort to keep Wiley from seeing the projected film of Karen's murder.) Chris stabs Karen's screen image with an ice-pick, trying to deflect her accusing gaze, but she keeps on looking and then seems to come at him from out of the screen, materializing in the flesh. (Actually, Otto is holding up Karen's dead body, moving it toward the guilt-stricken Chris.) Karen's eyes stare at Chris as she approaches him with an ice-pick in her hand (actually manipulated by Otto), while bright light from the film is projected onto Chris's face. Now *he* is the object of her eyes, of the camera's gaze, and of the blade's thrust (as Otto has her dead hand stab him with it). The ice-pick now comes at Chris, as seen from his point of view. In a sense, then, what the film allows this director to see is a blinding truth: his voyeuristic objectification of women is not only a kind of murder, but it also cannot fail to rebound upon himself. In denying them their humanity, he deprives himself of his own.

Shot on a shoestring budget ($25,000) over a period of a mere eleven days in 1966, *Murder à la Mod* did not see its premiere until two years later. The film played for only two weeks in one New York theater. Nevertheless, the *New York Times* praised the film's "exuberant enthusiasm,"[6] and *Variety* said that it "proves that its director could have an industry future."[7] Indeed, billed as a "horror comedy," *Murder à la Mod* stands as the first example of a genre which De Palma would make his own—that stylized combination of humor and horror to which he would return in such films as *Sisters, Carrie, Dressed to Kill, Body Double, Raising Cain,* and *Passion*.

CHAPTER 3

Greetings (1968)

But it is comedy that De Palma would emphasize in his next feature. One of the few films about the 1960s counterculture actually shot by members of that culture at the time, *Greetings* shows the continuing influence of Jean-Luc Godard on De Palma. "If I could be the American Godard," he said, "that would be great. I think there are more interesting social and political things going on here in the United States than in France."[1] Among the topical issues explored by the film are the Vietnam War draft, computer dating, the Kennedy assassination, and pornographic movies. Made for $43,000 by a non-union crew of friends, relatives, and students from New York University, *Greetings* was De Palma's "contemporary statement of what was going on in my life and the lives around me at that period."[2] Fellow "movie brats" Francis Ford Coppola and Martin Scorsese were also shooting their early films—*You're a Big Boy Now* and *Who's That Knocking at My Door?*, respectively—on the streets of New York at around this time, and in fact Scorsese edited the latter film at NYU while De Palma was in the next booth editing *Greetings*.

Greetings' three male protagonists are strikingly similar to the trio in *The Wedding Party*, only this time the catastrophe to be avoided is going to war rather than getting married. Paul (Jonathan Warden), Lloyd (Gerrit Graham), and Jon (Robert De Niro) are young men of draft age, and Paul has just been called up to serve. The film's ironically jovial title is taken directly from the actual draft notice of the time: "From the President of the United States, Greetings." In the crooningly inviting words of the Beatles-like pop song that plays during the film, "Greetings, greetings, greetings! Wouldn't you like to go away? Come and see me, don't delay. Spend a day or two with Uncle Sam." As Lloyd and Jon try to keep Paul awake for days so that he will fail when he goes for his pre-induction physical, one fast-motion sequence shows the three friends leaping and cavorting in a park to the tune of "Greetings," in an homage to Richard Lester's Beatles movies *A Hard Day's Night* and *Help!* However, less funny are other "zany" shots of the young men crawling on the ledge of a high building and standing under a giant cube sculpture precariously balanced on one of its points; the shots hint at the real threat posed by the draft which hangs over them or looms like a precipice.

As De Palma said about the actors and the male members of his crew, "*all* those guys *are* afraid of being drafted. Every time we went down to Whitehall Street [where filming was done outside the actual draft induction center] everybody was scared stiff because next week *he* was going to go down for real, or he had just come back from taking his physical the previous week."[3] De Palma, too, had felt this fear, and in thinking up advice for Lloyd and Jon to give Paul on how to flunk his army physical, the director drew upon his own experience before the draft board where he had contrived to bring on an asthma attack, declared his intention of becoming a communist, and tried to pass for homosexual. In the end, De Palma was deemed unfit for military service.

When Lloyd suggests that Paul shave his whole body with Nair and put on black silk panties so that all eyes will "scope in on that zone," Paul objects to being made into a feminized object of the gaze, which is what these men see homosexuality as being. "I'm no fag, man," he says, reasserting his masculinity. "No, we're *making* you a fag for the induction," Lloyd explains, and then proceeds to demonstrate a limp-wristed, swishily seductive walk that Paul is supposed to direct at the draft officer, saying, "The fellas call me Gerry, but you can call me geranium. All my friends think I smell like a flower." Gerry is a version of Paul's middle name (Paul Gerald Shaw), but it is also a variant of Gerrit, the first name of the actor playing Lloyd. Gerrit Graham would go on to play gay characters in two other De Palma films (*Phantom of the Paradise* and *Home Movies*), and in this scene Lloyd enacts a homosexual seduction (of Paul, who is standing in as the draft officer) in a way that suggests Lloyd could have a gay side. And so could Paul, who, now following Lloyd's example ("we're *making* you a fag" indeed!) and taking on the part himself, improvises his own line—"You want me to take my clothes off now?"—which is enthusiastically approved by Lloyd, much to Paul's pleasure.

However, this gay role-play comes to an abrupt end when Paul despairs of being able to use it to evade the draft: "It's not gonna work. I can't act like a fag, and if they believe me, they're gonna stick me in the front lines with the rest of the fags." Paul can't win either way: if he's man enough, he'll have to go to war, and if he passes as homosexual, he'll just be killed sooner, placed on the front lines to be picked off as an undesirable. As a disposable young man of draft age, Paul thus comes to feel a little something of what it's like to be a vulnerable gay man in a homophobic society.

While attempting to dodge the draft, Paul also tries computer dating, but these efforts do not do much to reaffirm his manhood. Paul lies on his computer application, claiming to be more attractive than he actually is, only to find out that two can play at this game: the "gay divorcée" he dates turns out to be a tired woman who answers the door with a baby in her arms. The computer system designed to unite persons with compatible traits becomes an occasion for deception and disappointment, further distancing people from each other. Paul's obsession with sexual conquest tends to blind him to other aspects of his female partners that could form the basis of a longer relationship. At the same time that he is filling his computer dating form with lies, his current girlfriend is in the background, being ignored and packing up to leave him.

When Paul goes to date a Bronx secretary (Ashley Oliver), she accuses him of having nothing but sex on his mind, and while he protests that this isn't so, he did arrive at her apartment with no car to take her to dinner and having already eaten by himself. She seems obsessed with the price of each item of apparel she has donned for their date, but her point is that she has gone to a lot of trouble for someone who just sits there staring at her cleavage. Does she want him to see her as a whole person, or is she as trapped in society's notion of how "a lady" should behave on a proper date as Paul is caught in the belief that it is the man's role to be sexually aggressive?

After criticizing him for leering at her, she goes into her bedroom, strips, and lies naked on the bed, leaving the door ajar, presumably so that Paul will see and join her. Has she given up on the prospect of a meaningful date with him and is just settling for sex, or is she realizing the freedom of the sexual revolution to drop all pretense of playing "hard to get" in order to enjoy the physical pleasure that she really wanted all along? Paul does gaze upon her nude body, but then he leaves her apartment. Perhaps her ready accessibility has deprived him of a sense of manly conquest, or maybe he now feels guilty about seeing her as a mere sex object.

As Paul stares at her nakedness, a book—*The Boston Strangler*—with two male eyes on its cover is also visible within the frame. (The case of the Boston Strangler, who between 1962 and 1964 sexually assaulted and strangled a series of single women after they let him into their apartments, was of such interest to De Palma that he would later give serious consideration to it as a possible subject for a movie.) Is Paul, who in a sense sweet-talked or lied his way into this single woman's apartment in order to take advantage of her, wondering whether there might not be a strange kinship between himself and the Boston Strangler, whether his own lust might not be a metaphorical kind of murder?

On a different date, the computer matches Paul with a female devotee of Eastern mysticism, whose tenets were popular among certain segments of the counterculture at that time. This woman (Mona Feit) frustrates Paul with her sublimated version of sexuality. To the sound of sitar music and viewed through a curtain of hanging beads, she tantalizes him by pressing up against his body while the two are standing in her apartment. When he hungrily kisses her, she puts him off by saying that he's "jumping to the result." When he responds to her hand near his crotch ("the source"), she argues, "We've got to raise that energy up from that swamp, away from all those murky thoughts, all that lower force." While she may be a true believer, a playful seductress, or a repressed woman who needs to think of sex as spiritual before she can enjoy it, Paul seems to experience her as an agonizing tease. By the time she has certified his readiness for "becoming one" with her, he has reached a premature climax before the manly penetration he desired can occur. "Your source! What's happened to your source?" she laments.

On his final computer date, which a title card represents as "Paul's Last Stand," he seems to achieve masculine dominance by having sex in a variety of positions with a housewife (Sara-Jo Edlin). However, it is she who pulls him inside her apartment, throws him down onto her bed, and jumps on him. Moreover, silly close-ups of his grimacing face show how much he dislikes it when she bites his chest and sticks her foot in his face during their sexual gymnastics. In a scene that gave *Greetings* an X rating and that may have influenced Kubrick's *A Clockwork Orange*, their naked lovemaking is shown in speeded-up motion, emphasizing its brute physicality. If sex is what Paul wanted, sex is what he gets, empty of any emotional or spiritual connection. Shot as if viewed through a peephole to the sound of old-fashioned piano music, the scene presents Paul—figuratively or perhaps literally—as an actor in a silent-film-style porn loop, which a title card identifies as "The Delivery Boy and the Bored Housewife." He is thus no longer the masterful voyeur but instead rendered the object of another's gaze, even as his female bed partner sexually objectifies him. At the end of their encounter, she collapses asleep on top of him (something that men are more conventionally depicted as doing), and he has to struggle to pull himself out from under the weight of her physicality. Paul's last stand proves to be more like Custer's, defeated by his "enemy."

Like Paul, Lloyd too finds that his relations with women are compromised by problems within his own male psyche. After gazing in a problematic (Boston Strangler-like?) way at the naked body of that Bronx secretary, Paul passes her on to his friend Lloyd, who doesn't have sex with her either. Instead, obsessed with the idea that there has been a conspiracy to cover up the real culprits in the Kennedy assassination, Lloyd uses a black felt-tip pen to trace bullet trajectories and to mark entry and exit points on the secretary's nude flesh. When she tries to pull him into an amorous embrace, he rejects her advances, continuing to treat her more like a dead body than a live human.

In another scene, after Lloyd studies a frame enlargement of the grassy knoll site of the Kennedy assassination, he lowers the photo and sees behind it a male photographer taking pictures of a female model. A connection is again made between gunshots and camera shoots, between dead bodies and women as targets of the sexually objectifying male gaze. The photo session is an allusion to the highly sexualized scene in Michelangelo Antonioni's *Blow-Up* where Thomas (David Hemmings) snaps pictures of the model Verushka, asserting his dominance over her. Like Lloyd, Thomas also enlarges photos of a grassy murder scene, and his investigation into that death increasingly takes precedence over any sexual interest he once had in women. In Lloyd's case, it is as though the shooting of Kennedy has unmanned him, and Lloyd will not feel empowered again until he has identified and contained the forces that objectified the president, a symbol of American manhood, behind that rifle's scope.

Like Thomas, Lloyd thinks he sees a murder weapon in the blurry image of the blown-up photo, but a woman (Tina Hirsch) at the photo lab is sensibly skeptical: "You're not going to be able to see anything but grain the size of golf balls. Look, I saw *Blow-Up*. I know how this turns out: you can't see anything." For De Palma, *Blow-Up* is a film in which you see the limits of what can be seen. The scene where Thomas follows the movements of an invisible tennis ball is like the one where Lloyd traces bullet trajectories: both are highly speculative, as much about the unknown as the known. When Thomas returns to the grassy murder site, he finds that the corpse has disappeared, much as Kennedy's body went missing from the morgue for a time, giving rise to more speculation and further theories about conspiracies to cover up the truth.

The character of Lloyd has autobiographical roots in that De Palma himself had been obsessed with the Kennedy assassination. He first learned about the assassination from a TV news report when he was passing in front of a store window while strolling through Bronxville with his date, actress Jill Clayburgh. Is this where De Palma first got the idea for a male character who turns his attention from a live woman to images of death? Like Lloyd, De Palma got increasingly caught up in conspiracy theories. "That was me in *Greetings*," he said. "I read all the books. I knew about bullet no. 399 [the 'magic bullet' that supposedly passed through two bodies and yet emerged in near-pristine condition]. I was tracing bullet paths, trying to figure out why did the bullet do this, why did it go that way?"[4] De Palma, too, studied the Zapruder film frames that had been published in *Life* magazine, believing that if he looked closely enough at them, he could eventually see the truth, only to decide in the end that no conclusive proof would be forthcoming and that to place such faith in images was naïve. "The Kennedy assassination was the most investigated murder case, probably, in the history of mankind," De Palma said. "But the more you investigate, the more murk you come up with. It's like the Zapruder film.

The more you blow it up looking for hidden details, the harder it becomes to make out the picture."[5]

Interestingly, Lloyd compares his blow-ups of the Kennedy assassination to the paintings of British pop artist Richard Hamilton, who appears in the film as himself. (Hamilton designed the album cover and poster insert for the Beatles' *White Album*.) In showing Lloyd some artwork that resembles enlargements of picture postcards, Hamilton comments that at first you can identify a boy and his mother but then, when the picture is blown up, you can no longer tell what it is. Lloyd says it's the same with his Zapruder enlargements: "You blow it up like this and you still can't see anything. You know, it's all there but it's not really there." If only Lloyd had heeded Hamilton's implicit warning about how an obsessive investigation can make him lose touch with humanity, how in following his conspiracy theories and trying to see more, he can end up missing the real life around him. Lloyd is looking so closely at the bullet trajectories on the woman's bare skin that he doesn't see *her* or the loving connection they could have.

Lloyd wants to see the truth, to restore the power that was taken when the president was made the object of a rifle's scope, but instead Lloyd finds himself unable to master the threat, to locate or contain the danger, which comes to seem as though it is everywhere and could strike at any time. Lloyd's desire to be *the one who sees* gives way to a paranoid fear that he is being spied upon; his goal of masculine re-empowerment becomes a terror of total vulnerability. "They're watching us," a crackpot conspiracy theorist tells Lloyd. "They're watching you now. You know about all those witnesses [to the Kennedy assassination]? Sixteen witnesses killed. They're watching me. I'm number seventeen. You're number eighteen."

In the end, despite hiding behind a newspaper while waiting to meet some mysterious contact who supposedly has secret information about the assassination, Lloyd appears to be shot down by a rifle bullet, holding the back of his head and staggering down a ramp similar to the one at Dealey Plaza where Kennedy was killed. It's possible that Lloyd was right about the conspiracy and that he has become its latest victim. However, we see no shooter and no blood. Could it be that Lloyd has been taken down by his own traumatized identification with Kennedy's demise, his own fear of being made the object of the gaze and the gun? Does his paranoid isolation become a self-fulfilling prophecy, causing him to die of fright? We see what appears to be an actual New York family, unaware that they were being filmed, walk past Lloyd's body. Are they oblivious to the dark forces surrounding them, or smart enough to stay connected and live their lives without crazily magnified fear?

A troubled masculinity is also what afflicts *Greetings'* third protagonist, Jon, whose obsession is peeping and pornography. Here again, there is a strong connection with De Palma himself, who has admitted that "my obsession with voyeurism was embodied in the character played by De Niro."[6] Consulting a book of psychology to understand why he would want to spy on unsuspecting women, Jon reads that voyeurs often suffer from "timidity and an overwhelming fear of rejection." In one case study that Jon peruses, a young man had had to share a bed with his married sister and, not knowing what to do with his arousal, had exposed himself to her, thereby incurring a violent rejection and a lengthy harangue about his vileness. It is possible that De Palma, too, felt guilt over incestuous desire. After his revelation of his father's adultery prompted his parents to separate, De Palma ended up living alone with his mother, a fact about which he experienced very mixed feelings: "This crisis allowed me to resolve my Oedipus complex. I had removed my father, and my mother was mine and mine alone! I then understood why he had left her! Life with my mother was a true nightmare."[7] It may also be telling that De Palma's "favorite guilty pleasure" reading is a book (*Savage Grace*) about mother-son incest, which is also the theme he highlights in one of the movies he cites as a guilty pleasure, Luchino Visconti's *The Damned*.[8]

In one scene in *Greetings*, Jon peers from behind a book display on the mezzanine level of a store while a woman (Linda, played by Rutanya Alda) on the floor below surreptitiously shoplifts. The Doberman pinscher book next to his staring eyes suggests that his is a domineering gaze, and the fact that he has caught her not only unawares but committing a crime gives him power over her. When he then approaches her outside the store and asks her to appear in an "art film" he wants to make about a woman undressing in front of a window, how can she refuse? However, though there may indeed be an implied blackmail threat to his request (as well as a con involved in the pretense of an "art film"), Jon also seems to feel some empathy with this woman. When the store manager wants her arrested for shoplifting, Jon rushes to her rescue, covering for her theft. He befriends Linda, paying her compliments. And he seems to half-believe his own lie about how his strip film could be high art, something commissioned for a museum: "You've heard of pop art. Well, this is called peep art."

When Linda is taking off her clothes in the window for Jon's camera, he wants her to pretend that "this is a private moment and no one is watching." The power of his voyeuristic eye comes from his being able to see her, to invade her privacy, to imagine taking her without himself being seen or susceptible to rejection. However, De Palma calls attention to the limits of Jon's masterful gaze by making him anxious that his camera will run out of film if Linda doesn't disrobe more quickly: "Now, let's do this a little faster." In fact, De Palma himself had exactly this anxiety about his own camera and was giving actress Rutanya Alda similar instructions, as she has reported: "Brian would say, 'I've got only three minutes of film—we've got to get the scene in three minutes.'"⁹ Furthermore, while it may be partly the wiliness of a predator, Jon is remarkably empathetic with his prey, telling her that "this is a beautiful moment" and "don't feel ashamed in front of me." Is he remembering his own shame when exposed in front of the opposite sex and wishing for her the acceptance he also wants for himself? It seems significant that, with the camera still whirring, Jon himself enters the frame at the end, climbing through the window and into Linda's bed. The scene cuts out at this point so it is unclear whether Jon's voyeuristic gaze has hardened him into a predator who now takes his prey, or whether it has gradually enabled him, from a safe distance, to overcome his fear of rejection so that he can risk embodiment and have intimate relations with a woman.

In a later scene, Jon eyes a blonde (Carol Patton) at a party while a Vietnam vet tells a tale of how two GIs shot each other over a woman. Here, desire is linked to jealousy and violence. Jon trails the woman as she leaves the party, spying on her wherever she goes. (His glasses emphasize his gaze upon her, as if he were looking through the camera's lens.) We have already noted De Palma's own admission that "I spent a lot of my time watching. I would follow people around. If a girl was giving me a hard time, I'd follow her to see if she really was dating another guy. I would track her."¹⁰

Jon follows the blonde to a museum, one of De Palma's favorite locations for picking up women. However, too timid to ask her out, Jon remains outside the museum, watching her through one of its plate-glass windows. An unsavory man (Allen Garfield) sidles up to Jon and notices his furtive longing for the blonde: "You'd like to bang her, huh? Yeah, you can't kid me. C'mon, I know. You're a regular guy. I'm a regular guy." In a conversation that seems to have been influenced by the dialogue in Kubrick's *Lolita* where the pornographer Quilty (Peter Sellers) insists that he and the pervert Humbert (James Mason) are just "normal guys," this smut peddler tries to convince Jon that he can find an outlet for his "regular" desires by buying and watching a porn loop in "beautiful taste" about a Great Dane that "screws" a woman. This man draws Jon back into the "Doberman pinscher" world of predatory voyeurism, playing on his fears that, while other men may be able to establish a relationship with her, the only way that Jon can have the woman of his desires is if he possesses her through pornography, while himself remaining unseen. "Just take a look" at the woman in the porn loop, the man says, assuring Jon that "nobody's looking" at *him*.

The disempowerment that can come from being an object of the female gaze is impressed upon Jon when a woman photographer takes his passport photo, which he has gone to get as part of an ultimately failed strategy to avoid the draft. Standing above him while he is lying on a bed, she snaps his picture, saying that she finds him "terribly photogenic." He is further "feminized" when she takes his tie off and undresses him, crooning that "I'd do just about anything for a boy in uniform." To Jon, she is a femme fatale seducing him into a war death.

It comes as no surprise then that, when Jon happens upon a young Vietcong woman (Tisa Chiang) during a search-and-destroy mission in Vietnam, he sights down his rifle scope at her, preparing to shoot, as he has orders to do. A TV news crew interviewing him takes up a position behind his shoulder, looking down the length of his rifle to shoot her with their camera. It is a moment of maximum empowerment, with Jon and the male TV correspondent safely unseen behind the phallic rifle and camera, which are trained on the unsuspecting Vietcong woman. "Private [Jon] Rubin has spotted his enemy again down the scope," reports the TV correspondent. "She's in his sights, and I think Private Rubin is now going to shoot the VC."

But he doesn't. Instead, while keeping his rifle pointed at her, Jon orders her to strip in front of the camera as if "nobody" is "watching," much as he had Linda do while filming her. (Shots of Linda disrobing are intercut with those of the Vietcong woman taking off her clothes.) While one view of Jon in this scene is that he uses war as an excuse to rape this woman with his eyes, it is worth pointing out that he disobeys the orders he was given to shoot her. Although it is extremely coercive, he attempts a form of contact—impossibly incongruous in this wartime situation—like the one that may eventually have enabled him to have a relationship with Linda. "You ever been in a movie?" Jon asks the Vietcong woman. Then, after his disembodied voice instructs her to remove her shoes, Jon reaches his hand into the TV camera's frame to show her how to take off her top: "You undo it, open it up. That's it, very good." Rather than annihilating the woman from his invisible position of maximum strength, Jon risks being seen as he reaches out to her. As a move toward connection, it isn't much, but under the circumstances, it is remarkable.

Greetings was De Palma's first critical and commercial success: it won the Silver Bear jury prize at the Berlin Film Festival, and it returned more than a million dollars on its $43,000 investment. *Variety* wrote that the three actors playing the film's "freewheeling anti-heroes . . . give their oddball characterizations the breath of life" and that the movie "has a freshness that is infectious." The trade journal predicted that the film "should do well in release with the young 'in crowd'"[11]—the same groups that were flocking to counterculture films like *A Hard Day's Night* and *Blow-Up*. The success of *Greetings* also finally enabled the release of De Palma's first film, *The Wedding Party*, which was praised by critics as being "wonderfully funny and brash"[12] and as showing "vitality and ingenuity and style."[13]

CHAPTER 4
Dionysus in '69 (1970)

Dionysus in '69, De Palma's filmic record of a Greek tragedy, may seem like a misfit, bearing little relation to the two comedies, *Greetings* and *Hi, Mom!*, he shot before and after it. But the theme of voyeurism and a self-reflexive awareness of the camera provide strong links among the three films. In June and July 1968, De Palma shot two performances, which were then melded into one film, of an avant-garde play based on Euripides's *The Bacchae*, staged by Richard Schechner's Performance Group in New York City.

An experiment in "environmental theater," the play involved breaking down barriers between intellect and instinct, as well as breaking through the fourth wall separating the audience from the actors. Schechner was strongly influenced by the theories of Jerzy Grotowski, who argued that "theatre . . . provides an opportunity for what could be called integration, the discarding of masks, the revealing of the real substance: a totality of physical and mental reactions. . . . [The] actor accomplishes this act, but he can only do so through an encounter with the spectator—intimately, visibly, not hiding behind a cameraman, wardrobe mistress, stage designer or make-up girl—in direct confrontation with him. . . . The actor's act—discarding half measures, revealing, opening up, emerging from himself as opposed to closing up—is an invitation to the spectator. This act could be compared to an act of the most deeply rooted, genuine love between two human beings."[1]

To catch the interaction between the actors and the spectators, De Palma decided that he would shoot the play's performers with one camera, while his collaborator Robert Fiore would film the theater audience with a second camera. However, when serially intercutting footage from these two cameras failed to capture the actor-audience interaction in its immediacy, De Palma

got the idea of using split-screen so that both would be projected simultaneously: "I hit on the split-screen almost by accident after deciding to cover it
with two cameras: suddenly I found I had parallel action and weaving the two
strands together became very interesting."[2] Split-screen allowed De Palma to
"show the actual audience involvement, to trace the life of the audience and
that of the play as they merge in and out of each other."[3] With its split-screen
running from beginning to end, *Dionysus in '69* marks De Palma's first and
most extensive use of this effect, which would become one of his signature
techniques. (Michael Wadleigh's *Woodstock* is often credited with having pio-
neered the use of split-screen, but it is worth noting that De Palma's film was
completed more than a year before.)

As *Dionysus in '69* begins, the image on the left side shows the actors warm-
ing up, while on the right of the split-screen we see audience members waiting
in line outside and then entering the theatrical space. The screen itself thus initially maintains the traditional division between actors and spectators. Each
entering patron is asked, "Good evening, sir. May I take you to your seat?" But
there are no seats in the conventional sense, and no stage or proscenium arch.
Audience members sit on raised platforms or on the carpeted floor, while the
performers begin to move among them, asking "Would you like to dance with
us if you dig our music . . . our women . . . our men?" A right-hand image
of a couple in the audience, looking and pointing at performers on the left-
hand side, eventually gives way to shots that show a crossing of this divide, as
performers pull spectators down from the platforms or off the carpet to join
them in their dance. Now both sides of the image are filled with actors and
audience members dancing together, and the handheld camerawork adds to
the feeling of sensual immediacy, of immersion in the dance.

And yet the split-screen itself tends to distance us from the action. Even
when both of its images show the same dancing bodies from different angles,
its two points of view remind us that we are watching, making us aware of
ourselves as spectators who are not wholly identified with the participants.
Even as performers and theater patrons strip and their dancing gets wilder
(a woman's bare breasts are visible on the left at one point, and a man's naked
genitals on the right), the fact that there are always two images side by side
keeps us aware of them *as images*, not allowing us to enter and forget the
frame as we might in the case of a single image alone.

This divided consciousness—part participant and part voyeur—is a key
element in the drama itself, which pits Dionysus, the god of wine and revelry,
against Pentheus, a king who is tempted by such joyous abandon but fearful
that its wildness represents a threat to his repressive rule over his subjects
and his own body. As De Palma describes it, "Dionysus starts dancing. Everybody in the audience, some rise, some get in, and they all start dancing. And

then the troupe start dancing even more vigorously, and they start taking off their clothes, and then so does the audience. Pentheus, the king of Thebes, looks around, and everybody is naked and groping one another and dancing. He's going, 'Oh my God.' Suddenly, the audience realizes they're naked. They're humiliated, and they run back to their seats."[4] For a time, Pentheus, too, had thrown off his clothes and joined in orgiastic dancing with a woman from the audience. This was shown up-close in an image on the right, whereas the left side presented a more distant image of the same thing, as if Pentheus were torn between taking part and holding back, between self-abandon and self-consciousness.

Eventually, he separates himself from female flesh. While the left image continues to reveal the crowd's frenzied dancing, Pentheus now stands alone on the right, holding his hands in front of his genitals, as the camera zooms in on his grimacing face, showing him as isolated from the others' commingling. Pentheus "dances with the revelers and during the dance discovers and reviles his own nakedness. Ashamed and enraged, he dresses" and then has the "house lights come up full. Everyone in the theatre is caught in the midst of their bacchanal," explains Richard Schechner.[5]

Like Pentheus, the crowd suddenly becomes self-conscious about their nakedness. Seeing themselves through Pentheus's judgmental eyes, they feel ashamed of their openness and connectedness to one other. Schechner believes that the actors' and audience members' awareness of being filmed had a similar effect: "There's no doubt that the cameras were somewhat inhibiting on the audience and the performers. The caress would have been a little bit more intimate and sexual than it was if the cameras weren't going and the lights had been dimmer."[6] The camera lens itself becomes a kind of judgmental eye, pulling revelers away from their self-abandon and making them think ashamedly of voyeuristic—prurient and disapproving—eyes upon them.

To stop what he calls "this obscene disorder," Pentheus proceeds to forcibly pull the writhing bodies apart and to cover their nakedness with his hands, ordering that the revelers be arrested. (The entire cast was in fact arrested for indecent exposure when giving a road-show performance of this play in conservative Michigan. De Palma's film of the play was slapped with an X rating.) Voyeurism triumphs: Pentheus reintroduces a separation between the viewing audience, now fully clothed and watching from the left side of the screen, and the performers who hastily cover their nakedness on the right. Another shot shows Pentheus in all his repressive glory on the left, while the right side of the screen shows nothing at all, everyone having been thrown into darkness by his benightedness.

But even Pentheus, whose mind exercised such harsh control over matter, is subject to physical desire. However, unlike Dionysus who draws women to him by virtue of his openness, Pentheus tries to prove his masculine dominance by imposing himself on a woman. As De Palma describes it, "Pentheus says, 'I'm king. I can have any girl I want.' To back his boast, Pentheus has to go into the audience, grab some girl and try to have intercourse with her onstage. Let me tell you, there was enormous tension in the audience."[7]

As the right-hand image shows Pentheus kissing a woman in the audience, lying on top of her, and attempting to lift her dress, the image on the left reveals a variety of reactions from the audience members who are watching. One spectator looks up self-consciously at the camera, perhaps embarrassed to be caught watching this near-rape. Another man looks over at his female companion for *her* reaction, as if seeking a cue to how he should respond. Pentheus's act is intrusive, as are the voyeuristic eyes of the onlookers, who to some extent share in his lust and shame.

Later, after the woman has resisted his unwanted advances, Pentheus himself becomes one of the voyeurs. He denounces the performers' sensual dancing but then tells Dionysus, "If I could move closer, I could see their shameless orgies better." As another man accompanying Pentheus says, "We were like spies. We wanted to see the action without being seen."

Dionysus tries to draw Pentheus away from voyeurism and into a pleasurable participation, bidding him to "caress me, caress my body all over—very, very slowly" and to "caress my cock. Take your mouth and suck on it." As Dionysus makes this appeal, he himself is caressing Pentheus's body all over, commingling with him as if moving him toward a reciprocated sensuality, as in the punning title *Dionysus in '69*. (Unlike the film's title, the play's title— *Dionysus in 69*—deliberately omits the apostrophe to emphasize the double entendre.) Dionysus suggests that the two of them make love where "no one has to see us" so that Pentheus can get away from the audience's shaming gaze and not have to view his sexual act through their leering and reproachful eyes.

Pentheus would no longer have to uphold his status as a king, to maintain the superior and censorious distance of a male ruler. Instead, he could mingle with the people, partaking of their common pleasures. To the boast that "I am [King] Pentheus," Dionysus replies, "Pentheus? Bullshit. You're Bill Shephard. You're in the [Performance] Group, and I know you. You're no god."

Pentheus *is* played by Bill Shephard, a member of Schechner's theatrical troupe, and Dionysus is played by Bill Finley. In this moment, one Bill tells another to drop the performance, to stop acting so superior and admit his common humanity. As Shephard explains, "Schechner gradually formulated a concept of the 'personal' actor, who used the role to reveal the conflicts of his or her own life. In addition, he felt that the actor's confession or revealment of self should be articulated into the structure of the performance, not merely through the character but also through the person of the actor."[8] In the original play by Euripides, Dionysus has Pentheus dress in women's clothing, but the actors Bill Shephard and Bill Finley were determined to face their own personal demons, "to reveal and confront a hidden aspect of our natures, a fear of homosexuality."[9]

Dionysus/Finley's attempt to seduce Pentheus/Shephard into a communal sensuality is ultimately unsuccessful. One shot of the two men kissing shows a male audience member in the background with his arm over his face, barely able to watch. Could this shaming gaze—internalized by Pentheus—have gone with him, causing guilt even after he and Dionysus went to a private place to make out? Could Pentheus, who has lorded it over women for so long, have feared that engaging in gay sex would feminize and thus emasculate him?

But another possibility is that Dionysus/Finley himself is overcome by homophobia and gynophobia. Rather than seducing the other man into a mutually pleasurable 69, Dionysus/Finley became puffed up with power at the thought of the other's "cock-sucking" submission. What if Pentheus/Shephard responded as a potential equal and it was Dionysus/Finley who lorded it over *him*? An onlooker reports that Pentheus was "totally exposed to pleasure," but "barely did he begin to feel turned on by all this" when Dionysus gave a "command" to the revelers to "kill him." "It is as if Pentheus starts out as a character and learns about the person underneath, while Dionysus starts out as one of us and elevates himself to the rigidity of godhood," explains Schechner.[10] Just when Pentheus is dropping the act to admit that he is nothing more than Bill Shephard, a common man with the same open and vulnerable body as the rest of us, Bill Finley is solidifying his own performance as an indomitably masculine Dionysus. "There is no god greater than Bill Finley," as he has his worshippers proclaim.

Now the camera is positioned at a low angle looking up at distant Dionysus, who is standing atop a platform. Dressed in a conservative suit and tie while dispensing campaign buttons from a red-white-and-blue bag, he announces through a bullhorn that "a vote for Finley in '68 brings Dionysus in '69!" The revelers' libidinal energy has been co-opted as a campaign slogan. The hippies' desire for free love is being used by one man to consolidate his repressive power. After all, instinct without intellect is blind; it can be led anywhere, as we see when the revelers become "one angry mob, one single mindless body gone mad by the politics of ecstasy," as ready now to kill as they were to caress. As De Palma has said about the 1960s as represented in *Dionysus in '69*, "There's a kind of idealistic, revolutionary, anti-establishment, almost absurdist energy. . . . The establishment has just sucked it all up and made a product out of it, and that kind of destroyed it."[11]

Rather than commingling with the crowd, Dionysus/Finley is held high upon the shoulders of actors as they carry him out of the theater and into the street, followed by other actors, audience members, and us (the camera). He makes V signs using both hands with upraised arms, in imitation of President Richard Nixon. In 1968, Nixon ended up victorious in his bid for election, having promised a "peace with honor" in Vietnam that would instead lead to several more years of war. Dionysus/Finley then raises one arm in the fascist salute, like Hitler who mobilized the energies of his people toward extremely destructive ends. "Dionysus . . . becomes another Pentheus," says Schechner. The liberator becomes the dictator. "Most of us have a pretty cheap fantasy of self-liberation. And if Dionysus, or someone else, could lead us into the Promised Land, then Dionysus, or someone else, could lead us right out again."[12]

CHAPTER 5

Hi, Mom! (1970)

De Palma got the idea for *Hi, Mom!* when he saw filmgoers lined up outside a theater to attend his movie *Greetings*. Across the street from the theater was a high-rise building, and he imagined that inside each one of its apartment windows there was a story to be told. In his mind, each window became a kind of movie screen. *Greetings'* voyeuristic character of Jon (Robert De Niro) returns in *Hi, Mom!*, which is self-consciously a sequel to the earlier film. (In its initial stages, *Hi, Mom!* carried the title *Son of Greetings* and everyone hoped it would be at least as successful as that first film.) Back from Vietnam, Jon rents a rundown apartment whose sole positive feature is its view of the windows in a nicer housing complex across the way. The film's opening credits run during Jon's view of activities going on in each apartment facing him, much as the movie screen shows us the opening credits of Hitchcock's *Rear Window* over the view seen by Jeff (James Stewart) of the apartment windows across from him.

Planning to film his neighbors using a telescopic camera, Jon goes to a photo store to buy the equipment, only to find that one of these neighbors, a housewife named Jeannie (Lara Parker), is also there buying a camera of her own. She tests it by pointing it at Jon, who has his camera trained on her. This scene of each one filming the other, like the similarity in their names, suggests that Jon and Jeannie are in some way doubles, characters with a strange likeness.

The idea for Jeannie, who plans to make a home-movie record of her own life, came to De Palma when he saw Jim McBride's *faux* documentary *David Holzman's Diary*, a film that had a strong effect on De Palma himself: "When I first got my 8mm sound camera, I'd carry it around like David Holzman and try to film everything I did and look at it. My friends and I had cameras all the time and we were all film directors. I filmed a whole section of my life—people I was going out with, my friends. I just shot everything. I directed the scenes, too."[1] When David (L. M. Kit Carson) constantly films Penny (Eileen Deetz), the woman he's going out with, including shooting her when she is sleeping in the nude, she leaves him. Bereft, he masturbates in his loneliness and then resorts to surreptitious filming of her from outside her window, which gets him clubbed by a cop for being a Peeping Tom. While perhaps wanting his movie to bring him closer to Penny, David seems to end up loving his Eclair camera—which he addresses as if it were female—more than his girlfriend.

The camera appears to create a similar distance in Jeannie's relationships, despite her attempts to use it for further closeness. Her filming strives to show how her building is so much nicer than the one across the way and how her sons have to be the most talented musicians, thus stressing social-climbing ambition over neighborliness or familial love. (There is a special poignancy in the fact that the actors playing Jeannie's sons are the actress's real-life sons. De Palma himself was similarly pushed by his parents to accomplish greater and greater achievements as a boy.) The camera records Jeannie's acquisition of a fur coat, that is, her materialistic self-satisfaction. "She starts out with home movies," De Palma explained. "It gets more and more excessive. She's very concerned with *things*. She has a scene where she talks about her body the way she talks about chairs and objects. Everything becomes an object for her."[2] The scene to which De Palma refers was apparently cut when the Jeannie portion of the film was reduced in the editing room, but we do see Jeannie zoom in on the naked breasts of a woman in a poster, suggesting the camera's sexual objectification. It's also significant that the man at the photo store teaches Jeannie how to use her camera in a way that sounds like masturbation: "You can just take pictures of yourself. That's right, you just push this button. Now, are you familiar with the exposure? Well, you see this little ring around this center here? You just turn that slowly and slowly." Despite her desire to connect (she uses the camera's zoom at the photo store to bring her "closer and closer and closer" to Jon), filming traps Jeannie in a narcissistic self-enclosure.

Like Jeannie, Jon tries and fails to connect via his camera. He seeks funding for his voyeuristic movie from a porn producer—Joe Banner (Allen Garfield), the smut peddler from *Greetings*—but Jon tries hard to distinguish the film he plans to make from the kind of sleazy stag reels or dirty photos you would find at an adult bookstore: "It's what I call peep art. You get all these private moments; you get all these people [in their windows] and they don't know they're being watched. It's not like in those photographs in that bookstore. These are *real* activities."

Yet even pornography can be viewed as an attempt to make an emotional connection by means of the physical. Joe, who is homophobic ("If you come into one of these theaters, don't go into the men's room—you got that *straight*?"), nevertheless excuses a man who puts his hand on Jon's leg while they are all three watching an X-rated movie: "That's all right. He means well." This stranger is trying to move beyond filmed flesh—superficial and unsatisfying—to actual contact as something potentially more meaningful. Joe even switches places with Jon and puts the stranger's hand on Joe's own groin. This is ostensibly Joe's way of indicating that he could produce a movie that would satisfy this man's desires so that he wouldn't grope people in theaters, but the act suggests Joe's own desire for human contact beyond pornography. Even Joe the porn producer, a cynical wiseacre wary of being touched, harbors a hidden desire for deeper connection, as when he finally agrees, after refusing for some time, to shake Jon's hand. (Joe is another one of Jon's doubles like Jeannie, secretly longing for greater intimacy.)

Funded by Joe, Jon begins filming the windows across the way with his telescopic camera and gradually focuses in on Judy (Jennifer Salt), a secretary who is constantly left behind to dream about a date as her female roommates go out on real ones. Although Jon spies on Judy with lustful eyes, he also seems to sympathize with her lonely dreaming, a fact which does tend to differentiate his "peep art" film from the mere porn that Joe Banner thinks he is bankrolling. "You see that cleavage?" Joe had bragged about one of his stag reels. "You don't get that in a Fellini film. You can get that in a Banner film." Jon's potentially empathetic movie is closer to a Fellini film, such as *Juliet of the Spirits*, which follows the reveries of a lonesome woman (Giulietta Masina). Halfway between filming Judy and nodding off in front of his camera, Jon seems to share her dream of a man, played by Jon himself, who brings a bouquet of flowers to her in her apartment and sweeps her into his embrace. In this imagined scene, Jon moves from being a lonely voyeur to taking action within the frame, making actual contact with the lonely woman he longs for, his double, Judy. But when he comes out of the reverie, Jon is still the man behind the camera, separated from Judy across the way. In the words of the song we hear, "I wake up lonely and that's how I pay for looking at you from far away."

In an attempt to bridge the gap, Jon does go to Judy's apartment, pretending that a computer dating service sent him there by mistake. (This scene is reminiscent of Paul's desire to connect via computer dates in *Greetings*.) The two go out to a movie, *David and Lisa*, and Judy is moved by the character of Lisa, in whom she sees herself. "That child-woman, at times she's a little girl, terrified by the brutality and ugliness of reality, and she has to talk in rhyme to preserve her fantasy world," Judy says. "And then at times the woman— this sexual, driven, passionate woman—bursts forth like a ripe fruit, so much wanting, and then that frightens her and she has to go back into that little girl again and talk in rhyme." In fact, Judy recounts a past experience in which she gave her virginity to a boy (Roger) with whom she thought she had a special bond, only to find him laughing at her belief in love, causing her to regress into a little girl's rhyming speech. The actresses Jennifer Salt (Judy) and Janet Margolin (Lisa) were best friends, so Salt as Judy could do an excellent imitation of Margolin as Lisa. Is Judy's story about having talked in rhyme true, or did she make it up, in imitation of the movie, as a way to express her genuine longing for Jon?

In *David and Lisa*, David (Keir Dullea) gets close to Lisa by speaking to her in rhyme. Jon gets close to Judy by making up a story that "rhymes" with hers: supposedly, the very same Roger who laughed at her is the one Jon discovered having sex in the shower with the girl he loved. Roger is a lot like the playboy Jon observes in one of the apartments who pretends to share the interests of whatever girl he is with—painting a female art student, adopting the lotus position with a blonde mystic, and zooming like an airplane around the room with a stewardess—just so that she will have sex with him. Jon also uses pretense to get near Judy, but when she begins kissing him, he puts her off. He desires intimacy with her, but the "sexual, driven, passionate woman" is too much for him, so he retreats into his filmic fantasy world. In this, he resembles Jeff in *Rear Window*, who empathizes with one woman (Miss Lonelyhearts) and leers at another (Miss Torso), both of whom he watches through windows using his telescopic camera, but balks at having actual intimate contact with Lisa (Grace Kelly), the lonely, lustful girlfriend who is with him in his own apartment.

Jon cannot be with Judy without the mediation of the camera, and while this apparatus may be designed to allow him a gradual approach to her, "zooming" him from a safely voyeuristic distance to a position of increasing intimacy, Jon's filmmaking remains more of a barrier than a bridge between them, suggesting that he is not brave enough to take the risk of being rejected. While on the one hand he is taking an interest in Judy and the things in her apartment, on the other hand he is surreptitiously using a light meter to check the illumination in the room. Jon plans to film himself having sex with her, and so he plots his seduction of Judy to the second so that the camera he has rigged to a clock timer back in his apartment will capture the action in Judy's window at the right time. Thus, though Judy proves eager to make love to him, Jon keeps putting her off, sneaking glances at his watch. (The character of David in *David and Lisa* was also obsessed with clocks and couldn't stand to be touched.) As a stalling tactic, Jon tells the tale of a former girlfriend who, after they made love, got "burnt to a crisp" in a car accident. (Does the story encode Jon's fear of getting "burned" if he opens himself up to Judy's love?) Jon then starts to cry—a weeping that we saw him rehearse earlier, so it does not appear to be genuine. Nevertheless, it does draw Judy closer to him to commiserate, bringing him the contact that is his deepest desire but also his greatest fear, which is why he puts her off again.

Finally, when the timer sets off the red light in the window of his apartment to show that filming has begun, Jon hurriedly jumps her. Like the coupling in pornographic movies, their sex is awkward since Jon has to keep maneuvering her body so that it shows to best camera advantage in the window. De Palma presents their fornication in fast motion, as he did the porn-loop sex between Paul and the housewife in *Greetings*, to emphasize its sheer physicality. Rather than forming the lasting emotional connection with Judy that is surely his heart's desire, Jon has turned them both into performers in a porn film. Ironically, Jon's pusillanimous attempt at "peep art" even fails as pornography, for when he watches this film of his seduction of Judy later with Joe Banner, Jon finds that the camera in his apartment somehow drooped on its tripod, thus failing to capture his climactic moment with her. Even the distancing apparatus that was to prove his manly dominance has let him down.

What the camera tilts down to show instead is a university student, Gerrit (Gerrit Graham), in the apartment below Judy's. This middle-class white student is in the process of becoming a radical revolutionary, having grown a beard and now painting his naked body entirely black, including his penis. (This last was one revolutionary gesture too much for the ratings board, which insisted that the penis-painting be cut in order to avoid an X rating.) Jon, whose peep art has proved impotent, is inspired by this sight of phallic empowerment and decides to join this student's radical theater troupe, which is part of the Black Power movement. What Jon fails to see is the extent to which Gerrit has merely put on a show of power, an image of radical chic. His beard is modeled on that of Che Guevera, who appears in a poster on the wall behind him next to another poster of Malcolm X, whose Black Power salute Gerrit imitates while having a camera take a picture of himself. It is no accident that Jon's camera has pointed the way to a further camera image of masculine force, as Jon now grabs onto a new role in his desperate attempt to act the part of the dominant male he so wants to be. Exchanging his green army jacket for policeman's blues, Jon rehearses his theater role as a violent, racist cop addressing hippie "perverts" and student radicals, while actually talking to himself: "What did you say? Huh? What did you say?!"

The scene anticipates De Niro's later role as Travis Bickle in *Taxi Driver*, where he will practice his "You talkin' to me?!" speech in front of a mirror. In fact, it is De Palma who will be the first to formally introduce De Niro to Martin Scorsese (at a Christmas party in 1972). Paul Schrader, a friend of De Palma's who will script *Obsession* for him, will also write the screenplay for *Taxi Driver*, which seems to have been directly influenced by *Hi, Mom!* On his first date with Betsy (Cybill Shepherd), Travis takes her to a porn film, much as Jon tries to use "peep art" to connect with Judy. Both Travis and Jon are Vietnam vets whose failure to make it with women turns them toward increasingly violent alternative means of self-empowerment. At one point, disliking what he sees on television, Travis kicks over the TV set while holding a gun, much as Jon tips over a TV and then shoots it. Finally, as we will see, Jon ends up committing an act of explosive violence and then appearing in news coverage—an ending with strong similarities to Travis's in *Taxi Driver*.

Jon tried to move from voyeur to participant, using his "peep art" as a means to make a physical and emotional connection with Judy. The black theater troupe, which Jon joins, attempts to use its play, *Be Black, Baby*, to get white audiences to participate in the black experience. De Palma had earlier showed audiences and actors commingling in *Dionysus in '69*. With *Be Black, Baby*, he takes that concept and links it to the politics of race in America. As one African-American actor explains of the "environmental theater" in which white playgoers will take part: "Intellectual experiences don't have nothing to do with physical experiences. . . . You can't intellectualize it, you understand. You have to *live* it."

Having come to a rundown tenement building for what they think will be an off-off-Broadway show, white theater patrons are induced to touch the Afro-textured hair of black actors, to dance to funky drum music, and to eat black-eyed peas, pigs' feet, and collard greens. When some playgoers protest against their increasing involvement in the performance ("*You're* the actors; *we're* the audience"), they are told by the radical troupe that they must continue: "You've tasted black; you've danced black; and you've felt black, and now you've got to *be* black in order to truly know what it is to have the black experience." The whites' faces get painted black by the black actors, who have daubed their own faces white. So that they can feel the force of discrimination in America, the whites (in blackface) are then robbed, asked for their identification by a white cop (played by Jon), and not believed; instead, they are treated as the criminals. A white woman (in blackface) is sexually objectified—"We know all you niggers know how to screw, right?"—by two black actors (playing whites) who begin to rape her with a broom handle, and when a white man (in blackface) tries to stop them, he is beaten and forced to watch.

Be Black, Baby is clearly influenced by De Palma's time as a drama student at Columbia and Sarah Lawrence as well as by the unconventional performances he attended in such New York City venues as Judson Memorial Church and La MaMa Experimental Theatre Club. The play is a parodically extreme version of Antonin Artaud's Theater of Cruelty, which was designed to shock bourgeois audiences out of their complacency and to immerse them in their own monstrousness. "We abolish the stage and the auditorium and replace them with a single site, without partition or barrier of any kind," Artaud argued. "A direct communication will be re-established . . . between the actor and the spectator, from the fact that the spectator, placed in the middle of the action, is engulfed and physically affected by it."[3] Artaud went on to write that "without an element of cruelty at the root of every spectacle, the theater is not possible. In our present state of degeneration it is through the skin that metaphysics must be made to re-enter our minds. . . . One does not separate the mind from the body nor the senses from the intelligence, especially in a domain where the endlessly renewed fatigue of the organs requires intense and sudden shocks to revive our understanding."[4]

Another important source for *Be Black, Baby* lies in the films of Godard, who was still a significant influence on De Palma at this time. Godard's *La Chinoise* shows students debating the relation between theater and politics, while his *Weekend* has hippie revolutionaries who beat drums, paint their naked bodies, and rape their bourgeois captives.

In *Hi, Mom!*, the *Be Black, Baby* theater performance is being filmed as part of a documentary for educational television. Just as the theater patrons become so involved that they begin to believe the play's events are really happening, viewers of the TV program are drawn in by the documentary's "reality effect" to the point where reel images come to seem real. This effect is fostered by the grainy black-and-white used for the film, which resembles true-life news footage, and by the improvisational feel of the performance, which is shot in what appears to be one take, as if events were unfolding unpredictably in real time. De Palma compounded this "reality effect" by casting actual Black Power activists in key roles: "I try to use very real people. Like in [*Hi, Mom!*], we have a black militant. Not an actor. But a young kid who's radical and who's not play-acting."[5] When a gun is pointed at the male theater patron who tries to intervene in the woman's rape, it is also pointed at the cameraman and by extension the TV viewer, who are equally made to believe that they must now experience what it is like to be helpless witnesses to a physical assault on one of their own.

But the black troupe's Theater of Cruelty and the harrowing TV documentary both fail to shock audiences out of their complacency as distant spectators and into some greater empathy with black experience, which might have truly altered understanding and changed society. Once they have arrived safely outside the "environmental theater" in which they had been robbed and raped, the white playgoers quickly reduce their harrowing experience to just another show. "[*New York Times* theater critic] Clive Barnes was really right," they rave. "It was a great show, great theater!" "I'm tickled I came," says one audience member, diminishing and dismissing the impact of the violent event, while another proceeds to intellectualize the whole thing away: "It really makes you stop and think." When the TV documentary of *Be Black, Baby* concludes to the tune of soothing classical music ("music to write checks by," in the words of the announcer), it is implied that TV viewers ultimately have the same dismissive reaction to what they witnessed as the theatergoers from suburbia did to their inner-city black "show." As De Palma said: "I was really trying to show how you lie with documentaries, those ridiculous documentaries you see on educational TV all the time about the oppressed blacks, made by white middle-class film makers. They're being oppressed by the economics of that class, yet these people are running around saying, 'Don't worry, it's all going to be okay. Here are your food stamps.'"[6]

When playacting violence makes no lasting impression, Jon suggests to the black activist troupe that they move to the real thing: use guns to storm a middle-class apartment building and kill everyone, literally "blow their minds." The failure of theatrically and filmically represented violence results in a desperate attempt to exert it in an unmediated form. Then, when the black revolutionaries are gunned down by white apartment owners with superior weaponry, Jon plots to infiltrate the middle class by posing as a happy bourgeois.

What is interesting about the scenes of Jon "undercover" is that for three years he actually seems quite content in this conventional role, which appears to allow him ample ways to prove his masculinity. Seated on the couch in his apartment, he smokes a pipe and has pens in his shirt pocket. He's become a successful insurance salesman expected to rise in his company. He has married Judy and impregnated her.

But life as a husband is not figured as having the potency of life as a seducer. It is as though Jon has jumped from his anticipated seduction of Judy directly to the aftermath of marriage and pregnancy, without getting to experience the consummation he so desired, the moment of greatest virility *combined with* an emotional connection to her. Whereas before he sighted Judy through his telescopic camera in hopes of being with her, now he is the object of her nagging about wanting to buy a new dishwasher and not wanting to do all the housework. Feeling increasingly domesticated and emasculated, Jon says he will do the laundry but then retaliates by placing some phallic sticks of dynamite in the basement washing machine and blowing up the entire bourgeois apartment building.

Interviewed in the rubble after the blast by a TV news reporter who doesn't know who did it, Jon praises the expertise of the bomber, thus secretly bragging about his prowess with explosives. Wearing his Vietnam vet's jacket, Jon gets increasingly angry as he speaks about the violence he saw in the war, referring to "arms shot off," "faces blown up," and "***** taken off"—the word is bleeped, but Jon gestures down toward his crotch, which is below frame. If such emasculating violence could be heard and seen on TV, would it shock viewers out of their complacency? If Jon could express his anger and his desire through plays or films *in a way that would reach an audience*, would he not have blown up that building? Asked if he has anything more to add, Jon gives the camera a twisted grin and says hello to his mother. The film's title credit appears, which is De Palma's sardonic way of predicting that his own film, *Hi, Mom!*, will be viewed as just another show, failing to make any truly meaningful connection with its audience.

Several days before *Hi, Mom!* was released, some members of the Weathermen, a radical underground group, accidentally detonated a bomb they were constructing and blew up a New York City building. The film was frighteningly accurate in its depiction of the times, which may be why it did not draw big audiences. Most moviegoers seemed to want even their counterculture comedies to have a lighter tone—something more along the lines of *The Graduate* or De Palma's earlier *Greetings*. *Hi, Mom!* was just too blackly comic.

CHAPTER 6

Get to Know Your Rabbit (1972)

Hollywood was eager to cash in on the new youth market that had made movies like *The Graduate* and *Easy Rider* so profitable, particularly after the failure of more conventional, big-budget productions (*Cleopatra, Paint Your Wagon, Hello, Dolly!*). Given the recent success of his counterculture comedy *Greetings*, a fresh talent like De Palma seemed to be a good bet, so Warner Bros. brought him out from New York to LA to make *Get to Know Your Rabbit*. "Warners were making a lot of young pictures with young directors," said De Palma, "and they wanted some crazy, lunatic New York director to make this crazy, lunatic comedy."[1] De Palma's first big-studio film gave him the chance to work with movie stars and a Hollywood film crew and to experiment with different kinds of shots, including his first extensive use of the crane shots that would become a staple of his cinema.

One such shot, filmed from directly overhead, follows the film's business executive protagonist, Donald Beeman (Tom Smothers), as he walks through the rooms of his palatial, all-white apartment, king of a cold, empty universe. Another tracking shot, this one filmed at eye level, shows Donald walking through the maze of corridors in his office building, a bee-man in the corporate hive, an executive who is really nothing more than a corporate drone. Wanting more than a life of anonymous drudgery, Donald decides to make a break from the business world, as dramatized by a split-screen effect showing him "splitting off" from his boss Turnbull (John Astin) and walking away in the opposite direction. Turnbull tries to force Donald back to work by locking him in an armoire with his disappointed parents, saying, "I'm sure you're not the sort of man to go against the wishes of those near and dear to you." Behind the absurdist comedy of this scene, there is perhaps also the terror that De

Palma felt when he was trapped behind a refrigerator as a boy, combined with the sometimes suffocating pressure brought to bear on him by his parents to be competitive and successful.

Undeterred, Donald proceeds to drop out of the rat race and become a tap-dancing magician. Here begins an extended comic metaphor linking rabbits (pulling them from a hat, feeding them carrots) and male libido. When master magician and trainer Delasandro (Orson Welles) tells Donald, "Look at your hands—you're holding your rabbit all wrong," the masturbation joke is also serious in that Donald must learn how to express his individual desires after so many years of corporate conformity. Similarly, when his girlfriend Paula (Suzanne Zenor) cuts off the end of a carrot with an electric knife and then breaks a carrot in half with her hands while denying him sex until he returns to work ("I made a rule: you're not to come near me until you give up this crazy scheme of yours"), she exerts a castrating violence in the name of the Establishment.

In his first attempts to try out his newly developed libido, Donald lets himself be guided by Vic (Allen Garfield, who played the pornographer in *Greetings* and *Hi, Mom!*). But the "wild," "all-night" party they attend turns out to be filled with cigar-chomping men and heavily mascara'd women so tightly packed together in one small room that no one can even move, let alone "get it on." In this black-comedy version of the crowded cabin scene from the Marx Brothers' *A Day at the Races*, Donald finds himself shut in with sexually frustrated middle-aged types whose "wild partying" is but a conformist cliché. When Donald does meet one young woman at the party, Susan (Samantha Jones), Vic's leering attitude toward her is both prudish and prurient. Warning Donald that he "can't count on a cheap broad with no brassiere," Vic also touts her as "the type of cheap broad who knows exactly what to do in the back of a car." Vic is as excited as he is disapproving—attracted *and* repelled. Driving a car with the two of them in the back, Vic assures them that he has removed the rearview mirror so they can have sex unseen, which only emphasizes the extent to which Vic is a frustrated voyeur.

Eager to get Susan a bra (to make her respectable?), Vic takes her to a lingerie store where he leers at her bare breasts, while Donald holds up a piece of clothing to shield her from his own eyes, which gaze only upon her face. "The show's over here," Vic tells him, placing Donald's hand on her breast. Donald is still too conventionally romantic, not libidinous enough, whereas Vic is too lustful and spiteful, lacking in respect. When Susan turns out to prefer Donald, Vic jealously rejects her as a whore: "A cheap broad like this, she's always up for grabs, right?" At the same time, it seems that Vic, too—as evidenced in Allen Garfield's comic, sleazy, and ultimately touching performance—just wants to find some happy medium between prurience and propriety, a place where individual desire can fit with social convention: "I just wish that some time, some place I can find a girl who appreciates a good, medium-priced brassiere."

When Donald goes on the road to perform as a tap-dancing magician, he is also required to double as an emcee for strippers. Donald's properly respectful introduction fails to excite the crowd ("In just one moment, a lady's gonna come out here and take off almost all her clothes!"), so the manager instructs him to instead say that "every curve is loaded with dynamite!" Donald's reply that he doesn't know what this means indicates that he is libidinally challenged but also that he is refreshingly innocent, not yet associating desire with danger. "If you go into it too deep, it ruins it," says the manager, as if warning him not to overthink it but just to act on libidinal instinct. Does there have to be something impersonal or conventional about desire for it to function? Or is it just a certain kind of prudish-prurient "striptease" desire that works this way—a kind we would be better off without?

During one of his magic acts, Donald has a nameless woman (Katharine Ross) from the audience join him on stage inside "the incredible escape sack." Despite several puffs of smoke, the two do not disappear but instead end up falling to the floor of the stage, struggling within the sack. We hear her laughter and then see what appears to be Donald thrusting on top of her inside the sack. (The scene is a happier version of the one in *Dionysus in '69* where Pentheus draws a woman from the audience onto the stage to have intercourse with him.) It would seem that Donald did indeed "get to know his rabbit," that his sexual-revolutionary performance has put him in touch with libidinal energies, allowing him to connect with a woman. When her jealous boyfriend rushes the stage, there is another puff of smoke and this time Donald and she do disappear from the sack, while her boyfriend ends up caught inside it, unable to break up the couple, who stand kissing on stage before running off together.

Both material and ethereal, physical and romantic, the relationship between Donald and the woman would seem to be love, as contrasted with the jealous voyeurism of her boyfriend, which is similar to Vic's. And, unlike Paula, this woman appreciates Donald's unconventional libido, his desire to be an individual: "Those are the hands that take the rabbit out of the hat," she says. "Oh, they just make me shiver." While sexual, their relationship is also emotional, as shown in a romantic montage of the two talking and getting to know each other.

But, as foreshadowed by this clichéd romantic montage, capitalism threatens to co-opt the personal energy of this couple's love and turn it into something marketable, an image of "true love," an icon of unconventional romance. As with the famous 1968 nude photo of John Lennon and Yoko Ono, this commodification begins when a photographer snaps a picture of Donald and the woman in bed—an image that will then become part of a lucrative self-help program marketed by Turnbull to other executives like Donald who want to drop out and pursue their own unconventional desires. "Tired of the rat race?" runs the ad campaign. "Live life at the gut level. Try our 17-day drop-out plan. TDM Tap Dancing Magician, Inc." (This ad for TDM runs in the same newspaper with the headline, "LBJ Bids Viet Peace"—another false promise.)

Turnbull got the idea for TDM from a beach postcard of Donald with his head through the hole of a life-size cutout figure of a man whose hand is on a woman's breast. It is the *image* of libidinal desire that Turnbull appropriates, thereby depriving it of meaningful personal contact. Similarly, as hundreds of executives are sold their "own" rabbits so that they can also become tap-dancing magicians, it is the *image* of a personally fulfilling life that is proffered, while the reality remains as uniformly conventional as ever, as filled with te-di-um. "It's like Playboy in Disneyland," De Palma has said. "Generally the idea in *Get to Know Your Rabbit* is that anytime there's a revolutionary potential in America they find a way to merchandise it so that it's castrated and no longer threatens the system; it becomes part of the system."[2]

Turnbull tempts Donald to sell out and rejoin the system by making a *personal* appeal. After Donald's initial departure, Turnbull found that he could not run the company without him. It would seem that Donald provided the individual energy needed to fuel that faceless bureaucracy. Having lost his business and living down-and-out like Donald, Turnbull was presented with too much freedom; unable to tap his own desires, he drifted aimlessly, lost without conventional structure. Because of the personal connection they once had, Donald befriends him, supporting him as the two men cross a busy street in a scene similar to that between Joe Buck (Jon Voight) and Ratso (Dustin Hoffman) in *Midnight Cowboy*. Donald hires Turnbull as his manager, a job Turnbull builds into a corporation so big he cannot run it by himself, hiding in a small office away from the pressure (like that facing a first-time Hollywood director?) of all the people who are depending on him. Insidiously, it is the emotional plea for help which Turnbull makes to Donald as his friend that leads him back to work for an impersonal corporation.

There are two endings to *Get to Know Your Rabbit*: the one we have and the one that De Palma originally intended. In the one we have, Donald magically disappears from the escape sack while standing on his office desk in front of his window, leaving behind the life of corporate conformity symbolized by all the other office windows facing his, each looking exactly alike. Reconnecting with his individual desires, Donald goes on the road again with his magic act, pulling a rabbit out of a hat to entertain passengers on a bus, at the back of which sits the woman he first made love to on stage, smiling and holding their baby. (Katharine Ross, who plays the woman, also departed in the back of a bus with another anti-conformist hero, played by Dustin Hoffman, at the end of *The Graduate*.)

Though it has its appeal, this fairy tale ending is lightweight and sentimental, a wish-fulfillment fantasy. (How can he just disappear?) De Palma felt that "there's no dramatic conflict there."[3] True, he had wanted to make a "whimsical comedy" but said that "it's probably going to be more like [Dr.] *Strangelove* when I get through with it,"[4] referring to Stanley Kubrick's dark political satire. In what De Palma originally intended, "the humor isn't warm, it has a cruel twist that's part of me."[5]

The director's preferred ending has Donald appear as a guest on TV's *Johnny Carson Show*, where an Abbie Hoffman-esque radical confronts him with the fact that TDM (Tap Dancing Magician, Inc.) is just another example of the counterculture having been co-opted by capitalism. De Palma got the idea for this ending from his own experience promoting his counterculture comedy *Greetings* on television: "When I made *Greetings*, I found myself on talk shows, talking about the revolution, and I realized I had become just another piece of software that they could sell, like aspirin or deodorant. It didn't make any difference what I said. I was talking about the downfall of America. Who cares?"[6] In an attempt to *make a difference*, to get someone to *care*, Donald proceeds to perform a magic trick that is a spectacular, gruesome failure. "On coast-to-coast TV, it looks like he has just sawed his rabbit in half and failed. The rabbit is a bloody, horrible mess. . . . Well, the whole TDM collapses because he's done the worst thing in America that you can do, he's maimed a warm furry animal on TV,"[7] explains De Palma. Like the bloody photos of the dead and dying which, when first shown on TV, alerted American viewers to the true horrors of the Vietnam War, such as the youth sacrificed to the Establishment, the bloody rabbit is Donald's way of physically showing the public that "revolutionary potential" is being "castrated" when capitalism co-opts it to "merchandise"[8] its own nefarious products. Donald is able to "disappear" from TDM because he has thrown the bloody rabbit like a wrench into the corporate machine to destroy its functioning.

Afterward, De Palma's ending has Donald pull out the unharmed rabbit in front of the woman he loves, revealing that it was all a successful trick, a *representation* of bloody death with enough force to change reality. The revolution was not completely castrated, for Donald is now free to pursue his desires with his beloved. This is still a wish-fulfillment fantasy but certainly a more radical one than just having Donald vanish from his office, leaving the corporation to go about its bad business as usual.

The reason we do not have the director's preferred ending is that the studio fired De Palma from his first Hollywood film and brought in someone else to shoot an additional sequence, insert some discarded footage, and rearrange some scenes while chopping others. De Palma's more defiantly anti-Establishment ending was cut, in a kind of corporate castration of his individuality: "It was very difficult to create any kind of reality for a political comedy on a solid, Hollywood soundstage";[9] "I was young and I hadn't yet understood how the studios function. I believed their lies; I let myself be manipulated; and I lost control of the film. So I learned an enormous amount from that experience and I've never again let anyone else re-edit one of my films."[10]

Ironically, the film's lead actor, Tom Smothers, who shared De Palma's leftist sensibilities, played a key role in having him removed from the film. Smothers, a big TV star known for his sly satire on *The Smothers Brothers Comedy Hour*, was trying to launch a movie career with *Get to Know Your Rabbit*. Both Smothers and De Palma were concerned that Jordan Crittenden's script made the character of Donald appear too passive, merely reacting to the events around him. Growing increasingly nervous about how he was being presented in his film debut, Smothers ended up identifying De Palma with the studio and believing that neither cared about his own individual interests. "I had an unhappy star," De Palma said, "who looked at Warner Brothers as the enemy. And pretty soon, I was the enemy too."[11] This, despite the fact that De Palma's preferred ending would have presented Donald in very active defiance of the Establishment. Smothers's unhappiness contributed to De Palma's being fired and the studio's eventual shelving of the film for two years, since by the end Smothers didn't even want it released at all.

In a curious twist of movie history, the film's other star was Orson Welles, the maverick director whose career of conflict with the Hollywood studios was the stuff of legend. De Palma greatly admired the films of Welles, and the neophyte paid homage to the master's *Touch of Evil* with a long-take tracking shot and a ticking bomb that leads to an explosion near the beginning of *Get to Know Your Rabbit*. (However, the unassuming Welles, who considered himself more of a master showman than a Great Director, would carry a book around so that he could pretend to be reading and thus avoid being asked about his film's famous long take.) Welles originally took a rather lazy approach to his role as mere work-for-hire, demanding cue cards so that he would not have to memorize his dialogue. But, impressed with the young De Palma's commitment to his craft and his willingness to stand up to the studio executives, Welles eventually became a close collaborator and ally, learning his lines by heart and supporting De Palma when he was fired by Warner Bros.

The relation between master magician Delasandro and student-of-the-art Donald in the film can be seen as an allegory of the relation between Welles and De Palma. At times, Delasandro seems like an old hack only in it for the money, having to look down at his notes to remember Donald's name at the magicians' graduation ceremony and presenting him with a cheap card and T-shirt as graduation presents. "Kid, I don't care what you do," he tells Donald and then conjures up a glass of liquor to drink. At this point in his career, Welles, too, was considered by some to be a broken-down has-been, taking on dubious film roles and eventually doing wine commercials because he needed the money. "Would you like me to look upon you as the son I never had?" Delasandro asks Donald, and we wonder if his reply—"No, I don't think so"—might also be De Palma's to Welles. Just beginning his own film career, De Palma may have seen Welles as an object lesson in what to avoid. Delasandro has Donald climb into "the incredible escape sack" with him, saying that "once you've mastered this, there's nothing more I can teach you." But the disappearing act fails, with both men trapped inside the sack and falling to the floor. Welles was unable to find a successful directorial career away from Hollywood; his attempt to escape the big studios and pursue his own filmic interests foundered.

The lesson De Palma takes from Welles is *not* to split from Hollywood but to try to preserve his individuality while working within the studio system: "I've always found it very sad that a great director like Orson Welles never succeeded in working for the system and instead had to go seek financing from the most unlikely places in Europe, finding himself limited by budgets and delays. . . . Managing to deal with the system is part of a director's job, and the majority of great directors have succeeded in doing it. Look at Ford, Hitchcock, they managed to work within the system while also imposing their own vision of the world. . . . Hollywood is an industry run by greedy men, and a part of your job consists in making them work for you." Noting that Welles's *The Magnificent Ambersons* was recut by the studio much as *Get to Know Your Rabbit* was, De Palma says that Welles "did not do all that he could to keep control of his films. You have to go into the producers' office; you have to talk to people; you have to convince them, to find any means possible to save your scenes so that the studio doesn't shoot other ones behind your back."[12]

But it would be several years before De Palma would get another chance to prove that he could be more effective in dealing with the studio system, for having directed an "unreleasable picture,"[13] he was for a time *persona non grata* in Hollywood. When the film was finally released two years later, it did not receive much attention. De Palma was forced to leave Los Angeles and return to independent filmmaking in New York.

CHAPTER 7

Sisters (1973)

With *Sisters*, De Palma moved from Godard to Hitchcock, changing genres from political satire to the psychological suspense thriller. Having worked in *Greetings*, *Hi, Mom!*, and *Get to Know Your Rabbit* with episodic, freewheeling narratives, handheld tracking shots, and semi-improvisational dialogue, he decided to try his hand at a tighter script, a more structured plot (one that was carefully storyboarded), and experiments in editing. His low-budget comedies had been shot in long takes for efficiency's sake, which De Palma believed made them come across as "long and talky. It bothers me. I like films that use cuts to build suspense."[1] Cuts—related to both montage and murder—would certainly be central to *Sisters*.

The plot has Phillip (Lisle Wilson) and Danielle (Margot Kidder) meet on a TV game show, go out to dinner, and then return to her Staten Island apartment. There they sleep together, but the next morning, when Phillip brings a cake to celebrate the birthdays of Danielle and her identical twin sister, Dominique, the latter stabs him to death with the carving knife. The murder is witnessed by Grace Collier (Jennifer Salt) from the window of her apartment across the way, but by the time she is able to bring two detectives to the scene to investigate, Danielle and her husband, Emil Breton (William Finley), have hidden Phillip's body in a foldaway couch and cleaned up the blood. Grace hires a private investigator, Joseph Larch (Charles Durning), who steals a file on the twins from the apartment and then follows the couch as it is taken away by movers in a truck.

The file leads Grace to the Time-Life building in New York City where she speaks with Arthur McClennen (Barnard Hughes), a reporter who wrote a story on the Blanchion twins. She finds out from him that Danielle and

Dominique had been Siamese twins, conjoined at the hip, until the surgery that separated them led to Dominique's death. After tracking Emil and Danielle to a mental clinic, Grace is discovered and drugged by Emil, who proceeds to tell her the whole story of the Blanchion twins. Grace hallucinates scenes from this story, with herself seeing events from Dominique's point of view. Jealous of the attention that Danielle was receiving from Emil, who was Danielle's doctor and her lover, Dominique stabbed the pregnant Danielle in the belly. The operation that followed saved Danielle but left Dominique dead. Since then, the now-schizophrenic Danielle has suffered from fits in which, thinking that she is Dominique, she jealously kills any man who might make love to her sister.

Back in the present, Emil holds the bloody knife up to Danielle to make her realize that *she* killed Phillip with it, and he also makes sexual advances toward her, but Danielle (as "Dominique") grabs a scalpel and uses it to kill Emil. In the end, Danielle claims to be innocent, and Grace—who was hypnotized by Emil while under sedation—can merely repeat the words he told her to say: "There was no body because there was no murder."

In the film's opening scene, Phillip is pulling up his trousers in a locker room when Danielle, as a blind woman, enters and begins to take off her blouse right in front of his eyes, unaware of his presence. He has the voyeuristic advantage, seeing her without being seen, peeping from a position of phallic dominance. However, as we zoom in on Phillip's face and a keyhole shape frames it, we realize that this is a scene from a TV game show called *Peeping Toms* (based on *Candid Camera*) and that the watcher is himself being watched, caught in the act of peeping. Phillip is the object of our gaze (that of the TV viewing audience), and Danielle is a model and an actress merely posing as his object and acting sightless while actually having the advantage over him, setting *him* up for scrutiny.

We as viewers are split, identifying with Phillip's leering gaze but also disapproving of it, feeling guilty about having shared it and wanting the camera to be turned on him (and us) as punishment. Interestingly, Phillip does not keep on looking at what he thinks is a blind woman; instead, he gallantly turns aside and leaves the locker room. We feel proud of him and also a little sorry for him that he was set up with this voyeur's trap.

On the game show, Phillip's reward for his chivalry is two tickets to the African Room. Even though he didn't act "like a primitive" toward a white woman by leering at Danielle in the nude, the African-American Phillip is still treated like one by white society and sent to a restaurant with a jungle décor and a prominent black gorilla. If Phillip receives a racist gift, Danielle gets a sexist prize, a set of cutlery for her to use as a happy homemaker. We feel for the two of them as they are both victims of stereotyping.

Back at her apartment after their dinner date, Phillip does watch as an inebriated Danielle walks off toward her bedroom, peeling off her clothes as she goes and revealing bare breasts as she turns at the end of the hallway. Is he taking advantage to leer at her in her drunken state, proving himself to be in fact an unchivalrous voyeur, or is she aware of his gaze and performing a seductive striptease for him? As Phillip takes off his coat, we view him from outside one of the apartment's windows, and as he then pulls down a shade, he sees Grace in a nightgown, standing in a window across the way. Has Phillip become the voyeur viewed, caught looking and lusting after Danielle (and Grace), or is he merely preserving privacy before having consensual sex with Danielle?

Seated on the couch, Danielle opens her nightgown to show him her bare breasts and then pulls him down to make love, but an extreme high-angle shot of him on top of her conveys the feeling of their being watched and, as Philip runs his hand up her leg, we see (though he does not) the scar of her separation from Dominique revealed. To Dominique, men's looks and love are unwanted and intrusive, and a part of Danielle has internalized this disapproving view, which hovers over her like a sense of guilt. Whether Phillip is seen as a rapist with a predatory gaze or as a loving gentleman depends partly on whose eyes we are looking through, Danielle's accepting and hopeful eyes or Dominique's fearful and rejecting ones.

The next morning, when Phillip brings a cake ("Happy Birthday to Dominique and Danielle") along with a knife, the "Dominique" inside Danielle uses it to attack him, stabbing directly at the camera's eye, at his crotch, and at his mouth. She metaphorically blinds, castrates, and rapes him, in revenge for his having had sex with Danielle, just as Emil had had sex with her before using his surgeon's knife to separate the sisters. Through Phillip, "Dominique" strikes back at Emil for having rejected her in favor of Danielle, whose birth as a separate person became Dominique's "death day."

Birthdays were also occasions of rejection for De Palma, who said that "I don't remember their having celebrated my birthday a single time when I was a child. . . . I recall having phoned my mother once and asking her, 'Do you know what day it is today?' She told me, 'No.' How could she forget her own son's birthday?"[2] There is thus a part of De Palma that identifies with "Dominique," lashing out against rejection, even as another part of him takes Phillip's point of view as he is knifed, being punished for having peered at and penetrated Danielle. It is a punishment that, though he may feel some guilt over his actions, does seem to exceed the crime.

A split-screen shot then begins as Phillip crawls toward a window to write "Help" on it in his own blood: the camera on the right side of the screen takes up a position behind Phillip, while the left side gives us an over-the-shoulder shot of Grace looking through her window to witness his desperate plea.

With these side-by-side images, De Palma forges an empathetic link between the two characters, as Philip reaches out to Grace and she sees feelingly and determines to try to rescue him, or at least to bring his murderer to justice. As Phillip dies, our identification is transferred across the image-seam to Grace, who is still alive and able to carry on the narrative. A similar transfer occurs in *Psycho* when Hitchcock shifts our identification from Marion (Janet Leigh), a main character also shockingly stabbed early on in the picture, to her sister, Lila (Vera Miles), who will investigate the murder. To ensure that we would identify with his lead characters, De Palma wished that he could have cast Sidney Poitier as Phillip and Marlo Thomas as Grace, but the modest budget did not allow for such big stars.

At another point, the screen splits between Grace on the left—struggling to convince two detectives to go investigate the murder scene—and Emil and Danielle on the right, hurriedly endeavoring to cover up the crime. These two hide Phillip's body in the foldaway couch and then, while Emil tries to clean blood from the apartment's white carpet, Danielle touches up her face in the bathroom, as he has told her to do: "Put on some make-up. It must look as though nothing has happened." Emil would have Danielle repress the "Dominique" inside her, as he covers up all traces of her gory crime. Yet, as Danielle looks into the bathroom mirror, a seam splits her face in two, suggesting the division within her between repression and confession, between wanting to cover up her crime as if she were Dominique, and wanting to be caught and admit her wrongdoing as prompted by her Danielle side. Our identification is similarly divided; like Danielle and like the screen itself, we are split between wanting to get away with murder (Emil and "Dominique") and wanting to catch the evildoers and bring them to justice (Grace and the detectives).

When these investigators arrive at the apartment, the left side of the split-screen gives us the perspective of Grace and the detectives as they look through the open door at Danielle/"Dominique," while the right side shows us *her* point of view from inside the doorway as she faces her interrogators. We are both the investigators and the investigated, seeking and evading but partly wanting to be caught. At one point, the camera tilts down to reveal a blood spot on the back of the white couch, and we simultaneously do and do not want the detectives to see this evidence of the crime, to see that the body they justifiably seek is right under their noses.

This scene is reminiscent of the one in Hitchcock's *Rope* where the body of a murdered man has been placed in a chest right under the noses of the people at a dinner party. In fact, De Palma originally planned to keep returning to that couch, as Hitchcock had to the chest, in order to increase the audience's fear/desire that the crime will be discovered, but the camera's movement in relation to the bigger and bigger blood spot could not be worked out. For those familiar with *Rope*, that film has even further resonance for *Sisters*. Emil, a domineering doctor, can be seen as similar to Brandon (John Dall), the intellectually "superior" murderer in *Rope*, who browbeats his weaker lover, Phillip (Farley Granger), as Emil does Danielle, into covering up the crime. Emil's similarity to Brandon tends to work against our identification with Emil and to move us toward adopting Grace's perspective.

However, Grace's own similarity to another Hitchcock character, Jeff (James Stewart) in *Rear Window*, tends to problematize our identification with her. Like Jeff, Grace thinks that a murder occurred in sight of her rear window and has trouble convincing detectives to believe her. But, as Danielle's question to Grace suggests ("Miss Collier, do you spend a lot of time watching my apartment?"), Grace, as a would-be investigative journalist who smells a big story in Phillip's murder, is also motivated by self-interest when it comes to her prying, a fact which tends to alienate us from her and move us back toward identification with Emil and "Dominique." De Palma has noted that he wanted to "reverse the spectator's identification process" so that we "identify with the criminal and not with the voyeur." If he made Grace "an aggressive careerist, a snoop, a 'woman's-libber,' the public would find it less easy to identify with her," he said, arguing that to "obtain a scoop, she's ready to do anything. She gets mixed up in people's private life. She doesn't care about the tragedies she uncovers."[3]

After Grace has spied on Emil and Danielle and followed them to a mental clinic, she is discovered by Emil, who confronts her about her voyeurism: "You came to watch us, to spy on us, to feed on our sorrows, at no cost. You want to know all our secrets? All right, we will share them with you. Watch!" As Danielle's patient's gown is pulled aside to reveal the scar of her separation from Dominique, we cut to a shot of Grace's blinking eye, scared and scarred by what she is seeing. "*Sisters* is very much the story of a voyeur getting it," De Palma said. "Grace Collier watches and spies, wants to know what's really going on; and when she finally finds out, she's totally altered by it. It's like the ice-pick in the voyeur's eye."[4] We recall the knife stabbing directly at the camera's eye, which represented the point of view of Phillip, in the scene where he got punished for his voyeurism. Now Grace, too, will be forced to see her own involvement in and vulnerability to the events she witnesses.

Having been drugged, Grace hallucinates scenes from the Blanchion twins' past as she hears Emil recount them. Presented as black-and-white documentary footage which gradually becomes an expressionistic nightmare of odd angles and fish-eye distortions, these scenes show the twins' fear of being treated like freaks during the early years that they spent in another clinic. Photographers take flash photos of the conjoined twins, and visitors gawk and laugh at them alongside other medical oddities such as Eddie the Giant,

64 *Sisters* (1973)

Sealo the Flipper Man, and Cathy the Lobster Child. There is also a set of tap-dancing triplets, boys who could be a reference to the De Palma brothers—Bruce, Bart, and Brian. As always, De Palma the voyeur is also imagining what it must be like to be the object of such unsympathetic attention, which could make anyone feel like a freak.

By recounting these scenes, Emil is reminding Danielle of her past with Dominique in an attempt to help her understand the reasons why they were separated. Danielle remembers a scene in which Emil was trying to make love to her as they were being watched resentfully by the conjoined Dominique. "You're supposed to be sleeping!" Danielle tells her, then asks Emil, "Why can't you make her go away?" As heartless as it is to disregard a dependent sister, one part of us can identify with the lovers' desire for privacy. De Palma himself once dated a woman with a "twin sister who was her spitting image, except that she was mentally retarded. The two sisters were never apart and when I'd go out with my girlfriend, I had to drag along her retarded sister, who went with us everywhere. Can you imagine the scene?"⁵ *Sisters* does imagine this scene.

But *Sisters* also imagines what it is like to be the excluded one, rejected and resentful. At the same time that Emil is trying to remind Danielle of the reasons for the sisters' separation, Grace is viewing these memories *through the eyes of Dominique*, the sister who does not want to be cut off. Grace also sees herself *occupying Dominique's position*, attached to Danielle. From Dominique's point of view, Emil with his slicked-back hair and pencil-thin mustache is a villain, seducing Danielle so that he can take her—and take her away from her sister. Emil injects Dominique with a hypodermic needle to put her to sleep so that he can rape Danielle—or at least this is how Dominique sees it. Grace, viewing events through Dominique's eyes, sees it this way, too. After all, she was also drugged with a needle on Emil's orders, and earlier she saw him inject Danielle to calm her down. Grace is now "conjoined" with Dominique and Danielle, feeling menaced by Emil. (Shots of Emil leaning over her, subjecting her to needle-rape, are reminiscent of ones from *Rosemary's Baby* where a wife [Mia Farrow] experiences the husband [John Cassavetes] on top of her as a rape by the devil.) Being injected by Emil, Grace (as "Dominique") cries out for "help!" and reaches toward a clinic window, much as Phillip once did toward her. No longer a distant voyeur, Grace has become a vulnerable participant, feeling the scares and scars that she sees.

Drugged, Grace now watches through Dominique's eyes as Emil ("I am a surgeon") uses a scalpel, which is fearfully imagined as a meat cleaver, to cut her—the unwanted sister—off from the one he desires, Danielle. Of course, given that the scene is shot from Grace's point of view, De Palma's camera shares her perspective, as do we. As the director said, "The audience becomes this girl [Grace], peering through a psychological hole. Since, in a way, I am the girl, the people out there can be her, too."[6]

De Palma's statement—"I am the girl"—prompts us to consider the autobiographical elements in this scene, the ways in which Grace/Dominique's relation to Danielle and Emil might resonate with De Palma's own family relationships. Both Emil and De Palma's brother Bruce have large birthmarks on their foreheads, and indeed the director has admitted that Emil, a kind of mad scientist (one of "those megalomaniacal and malefic types who take themselves for gods"),[7] was partly inspired by Bruce, the crazed-genius physicist. Sibling rivalry was one reason De Palma resented his oldest brother, with whom he competed for his parents' attention, which always seemed to favor Bruce over Brian, much as Danielle is preferred to Dominique. "I had Bruce and Bruce was *mine*," Vivienne De Palma has said (and we note that a birthmark can be viewed as the visible sign of a former attachment to the mother), but "Brian," she admitted, "was a mistake,"[8] the result of an unplanned pregnancy.

Surely, though, the most direct inspiration for Emil was De Palma's orthopedic surgeon father, Anthony, whose adulterous liaison with a nurse constituted an improper crossing of the boundary between the professional and the sexual, as did Emil's relations with his patient, Danielle. (Given that Emil can be seen as killing Dominique so that he can rape Danielle, it's interesting to note that in 1989 Anthony wrote an unpublished novel about a doctor who kills to satisfy his sexual urges.) When De Palma went spying to catch his father with the nurse, De Palma was acting on his mother's behalf, in a sense looking through her jealous eyes, feeling excluded along with her, much as Grace and Dominique are excluded by Emil and Danielle. Anthony's relations with the nurse effectively cut off his own wife and son. In his late teens, De Palma had witnessed his father perform bloody operations. During one of these, De Palma recalled, "I was standing right next to him in front of the operating room table. He cut off a patient's leg and then gave it to me!"[9] A voyeur who suddenly finds himself involved, De Palma may have imagined his own body, like that of the patient, as being vulnerable to the father's knife. Could his own body be cut into or off, like a leg?

The actual Siamese twins Masha and Dasha, the subjects of a *Life* magazine story that inspired *Sisters*, had a "third vestigial leg," but "when doctors planned an operation to remove" it, Dasha "became so upset that the doctors dropped the idea."[10] It would seem that Dasha did not want to be separated from her third leg any more than she did from her sister Masha. After Emil has gotten Danielle to remember why he separated her from Dominique, who died as a result of the operation, Danielle does not understand or accept the loss. Instead, she gets upset: the vengeful "Dominique" inside her uses a scalpel to fatally stab Emil. He then clings to Danielle's back as the two of them fall on top of Grace, who is lying in a clinic bed. Grace is here positioned as the "third leg," "conjoined" as Dominique was to Danielle when she was with Emil. Only now, "Dominique" has cut off Emil, who has died, in order to preserve her connection with Danielle/Grace.

Actresses Jennifer Salt (Grace) and Margot Kidder (Danielle/Dominique) were best friends who, in the early 1970s, shared a house in Malibu, California. When De Palma arrived in LA to film *Get to Know Your Rabbit*, Salt—who had briefly dated De Palma in the early '60s when they were students at Sarah Lawrence—invited him to stay with her and Kidder at their beach house, where De Palma began a sexual relationship with Kidder. Could Salt, Kidder, and De Palma in the beach house form part of the real-life background to Grace, Dominique/Danielle, and Emil in the clinic in *Sisters*? (Writer-director John Milius was a frequent visitor to the beach house, and De Palma named the head of the clinic "Dr. Milius.")

It seems possible that De Palma could have imagined Kidder as feeling divided between her best friend, Salt, and her boyfriend, De Palma. It's worth noting that Kidder suffered from bipolar manic depression, so there may have been a Method-acting component to her portrayal of the cheerfully outgoing Danielle and the withdrawn, disturbed Dominique. Also, De Palma might have thought of Salt as feeling somewhat excluded and resentful regarding his relationship with Kidder, her best friend.

It's interesting that, just as Phillip brings a surprise birthday cake to both Dominique and Danielle, so De Palma gave a surprise Christmas present to both Salt and Kidder in 1971: each actress received a copy of the script for *Sisters*, which had parts in it for the two of them. "I had the idea of bringing together Jennifer and Margot in the same film," De Palma said.[11] He did indeed "bring them together." When Grace (Jennifer Salt) goes to the clinic, Emil calls her "Margaret," as in Margot Kidder (whose nickname was "Margie"), and Grace then imagines herself literally attached as Dominique to Danielle—Salt and Kidder joined together.

Emil's recounting of the past fails to make Danielle accept the reasons he separated her from Dominique and caused her sister's death. Rather than gaining conscious mastery over past trauma, Danielle unconsciously re-enacts it when the vengeful "Dominique" inside her uses the scalpel that cut off her life to fatally stab Emil, thus cutting *him* off from Danielle. Questioned by detectives, Danielle claims total innocence ("I have never hurt anyone in my life. My sister died last spring"), having once again repressed all memory of "Dominique" and covered up the crime, the way she did when she was interrogated earlier by the same detectives about Phillip's murder.

But repression is not integration; Danielle's personality is still split, and the next time a man like Emil or Phillip makes sexual advances to her, "Dominique" will come out. "The unconscious is always there, waiting to manifest itself," said De Palma about the ending of *Sisters*, "even when we believe that logic has resolved everything."[12] At the end of Hitchcock's *Psycho*, even though a doctor has attempted a full recounting of past events, madness will out: Norman (Anthony Perkins) is still schizophrenically inhabited by his "mother," who, like Danielle, can hardly be believed when she claims that she "wouldn't even harm a fly."

Earlier in *Psycho*, Norman had said that his mother "isn't quite herself today." At the end of *Sisters*, Grace is described as being "just not quite herself." Like Danielle, Grace has repressed the past ("There was no body because there was no murder"), partly due to Emil's brainwashing but also because the trauma of witnessing such terrible events has caused her mind to cover them up as a form of self-protection. She has received the ice-pick (or knife or scalpel) in the eye, having gone from the voyeuristic mastery of a prying, self-interested journalist to the vulnerable victimhood of someone who feels all too deeply the suffering of Danielle/"Dominique." Psychologically blinded by what they have seen, Grace's wide-open eyes are glazed and sightless at the end, unknowing as those of a child, and she has in fact regressed to a childhood state, retreating to her parents' house and the bed she had as a young girl to be cared for by her mother (who is played by Salt's real-life mother, Mary Davenport). Yet, as the camera arcs slowly around to reveal a large Raggedy Ann doll seated next to Grace on the bed,[13] we realize that she cannot simply forget what she has seen or deny her connection to her "sister." Traumatized by what she has witnessed, Grace has become a split personality like Danielle, outwardly innocent and trusting as a child while inwardly fearful and disturbed.

The scene changes from Grace and the Raggedy Ann to a cow standing next to the sheet-covered couch containing Phillip's body. Grace is like that glassy-eyed cow, oblivious to the corpse. Her memory has whitewashed it, covered it up: "There was no body because there was no murder." But "there *is* a body," as De Palma has said about this ending.[14] Grace may try to deny it, but that only means that, when the scarred and scared side of her comes out, she—like Danielle—will be unable to deal with it.

With the independently financed *Sisters*, De Palma was in complete control and did not suffer from studio interference: "I'm much happier with *Sisters*. That is mine from beginning to end."[15] The film did very well on the summer drive-in circuit, and critics began to take notice of the fact that De Palma could do suspense as well as comedy. John McCarty in *Cinefantastique* wrote that "*Sisters* is the freshest, most gripping suspense thriller to hit movie screens since *Night of the Living Dead*," adding that it is "also the most insightful and deeply felt homage to the art of Alfred Hitchcock that a devoted admirer has yet produced."[16] And Paul Schrader—who a few years later would pen the screenplay for De Palma's *Obsession*—wrote, "Brian De Palma, a young American filmmaker who seemed condemned to the syndrome of successful low-budget 16mm films (*Greetings, Hi, Mom!*) but unsuccessful large-budget, mass-audience 35mm films (*Get to Know Your Rabbit*), has broken free with a brilliant, wry and scary film called *Sisters.* . . . By injecting his wry humor into Guignol De Palma makes it grand again."[17] With his next film, *Phantom of the Paradise*, De Palma would add even more humor to the horror, plus an entirely new element—songs—to create a horror rock musical comedy.

CHAPTER 8

Phantom of the Paradise (1974)

Winslow Leach (William Finley) is an aspiring singer/songwriter whose music is stolen by Swan (Paul Williams), a media mogul who wants to use it to open his new rock palace, the Paradise. After all of Winslow's attempts to reclaim his music meet with rejection and his face is mangled in a record press, he dons a mask and cape, becoming the Phantom who haunts the Paradise. Using an on-stage car bomb, Winslow sabotages a surfer band to prevent them from playing his music.

To stop further destruction, Swan signs him to a contract whereby Winslow sells his soul in order to have his music performed by Phoenix (Jessica Harper), the singer he prefers and who will now be "his voice." When Swan reneges on the contract by having another singer named Beef (Gerrit Graham) open the Paradise with Winslow's music, Winslow (as the Phantom) electrocutes the performer, thus clearing the way for Phoenix to be the star. But when Winslow sees his beloved Phoenix in bed with Swan, Winslow tries to kill himself. However, his contract stipulates that he cannot die until Swan does, and Swan, who is himself under contract, cannot die until the videotape of his pact with the devil is destroyed.

Swan plans to marry Phoenix but also to have her assassinated during the wedding ceremony as a live television event. Discovering this plot, Winslow saves Phoenix from the assassin. He also burns Swan's videotaped contract, causing the simultaneous on-stage deaths of Swan and himself—both of whom are cheered in their dying by a crowd overcome with bloodlust, excited to a frenzy by wild music and violent death.

With *Phantom of the Paradise*, De Palma put his own experience as a maker *of* movies *into* the movie, for his relationship with the big Hollywood producers can be seen as parallel to Winslow's relationship with media mogul Swan. De Palma has described this film as having been "motivated by my own experiences, going into big buildings, bringing in your own material that nobody pays any attention to or rips off in one way or another."[1] We recall that when De Palma first went to Hollywood as a naïve young director to make *Get to Know Your Rabbit*, he felt lied to and manipulated, eventually having that film "stolen" from him and "mangled" by the studios, who recut it in a way they thought would be more commercial. "I plain got outmaneuvered," said De Palma. "They fired me and went and did what they wanted with the film";[2] "You get fooled into believing you have relationships with people. . . . I've finally come to realize that your head is always available to go on the block if it makes some kind of business sense. You can always be sold out if the price is right."[3] Indeed, De Palma has even gone so far as to compare working with Hollywood producers to dealing with the devil: "For me, the devil is very concrete . . . you find him in Hollywood, for example, with all those producers who are only interested in money and who seek to buy your soul."[4]

For their part, some producers have considered the headstrong, maverick artist De Palma to be a Phantom-like threat to their own control over their moneymaking operation. "De Palma was a monster," said John Calley, Warner Bros. head of production, commenting on the director's willful efforts to retain creative control of *Get to Know Your Rabbit*.[5] Moreover, De Palma's anti-Establishment film was also accompanied by anti-Establishment behavior, as when he openly—though good-naturedly—mocked some Warner Bros. executives, including studio head Ted Ashley, at a party, which the director believes contributed to his firing. In De Palma's account, "Ashley smiled, and he left the room. But I can assure you that the following week I was fired; I no longer existed. These guys never forget anything; you can't make fun of them. . . . That's what happened to me and it cost me a good four or five years of pain."[6] Like Winslow who has his music stolen and then can't even get in to see Swan, De Palma had his film taken away from him and then couldn't get any work with Hollywood producers for several years. As a result, he ended up having to buy back his unproduced scripts for *Sisters* and *Phantom of the Paradise* and to make these as independent pictures outside of Hollywood.

Winslow and De Palma are both artists fighting to retain their distinctive voice in a media industry that would homogenize it into another assembly-line product. De Palma has said that he "got the idea" for *Phantom of the Paradise* "in an elevator, listening to the Muzak version of a Beatles song. Money corrupts art."[7] Swan takes Winslow's song, a rock cantata about the Faust legend, and reworks it according to whatever musical formula is popular at the time, gutting the strength of its music and reducing its meaningful lyrics to pap. This homogenization is emphasized by having the same three performers sing

Winslow's song in different variations, simply changing their musical style each time to fit the fashion and thus presenting a travesty of Winslow's work. A group that can perform '50s bebop (as the Juicy Fruits), then surf rock (as the Beach Bums), and finally heavy metal (as the Undeads) has no personal or heartfelt connection to the music. De Palma, who had filmed the Who and the Rolling Stones in concert for his documentary *Mod* (1964), thought of using one of these groups for *Phantom*'s band, but not only were they too famous for the fee he could afford to pay them, they also had a distinctive sound, which was the opposite of what he wanted for the film's permutating performers.

Swan, the rock impresario, imposes his own voice on everyone, dictating what his performers will sing, even as this voice is in a sense no voice at all, merely the sound of whatever is fashionable. Swan is thus associated with ego and emptiness; he is simultaneously everywhere and nowhere, dictatorial and destructive. After mangling Winslow's voice, Swan uses a complex technology of audio filters to alter that voice until it sounds "perfect"—that is, until it sounds exactly like Swan's! Swan literally imposes his voice on Winslow's, just as Swan metaphorically does when his chosen performers dub over Winslow's music. When Swan wants to render Winslow speechless, he literally pulls the plug on his voice, controlling it by means of technology. After Swan hears Phoenix sing Winslow's music in her own voice, he pronounces it "perfect" but adds, "I abhor perfection in anyone but myself." He then determines to eradicate that distinctive voice, first by replacing her (with Beef), then by having her assassinated, and finally, when these attempts fail, by strangling her himself, which he tries to do in the film's finale.

As the all-controlling money man, the producer on whom everyone depends, Swan is omnipresent and oppressive. His dead songbird logo, the emblem of his media empire Death Records, is plastered everywhere—on buildings, walls, door signs, podiums, and video monitors. Swan's logo is even burned into the side of Winslow's face when he gets his head caught in the record press, a symbol for how crushing this producer's influence has been. (Originally, the words "Swan Song" were equally ubiquitous, meaning that Swan's actual name extended virtually everywhere, but Led Zeppelin's manager Peter Grant, who had recently created a real-life company called Swan Song Records, threatened to sue, so these words were edited out or matted over in the finished film. The film itself was originally titled *Phantom of the Fillmore*, but this was changed when rock impresario Bill Graham refused to grant the rights to the name of his famous music venue.)

According to De Palma, he based the character of Swan on "incredibly wealthy and powerful" people who try to "create environments that are extensions of [themselves]. You see this a lot in rich people in their homes. You go into their palaces, and they've got their things there that represent them, and you're in their space . . . and they don't want to go to your space. They want you to go, they summon you, to their space";[8] "When you have a tremendous amount of money, you can let your eccentricities be constructed into anything you like and get the most bizarre extensions of your madness."[9] Swan sits at the center of a large circular desk that looks like one of his gold records (stamped with his dead songbird logo, of course). The corridors of Swan's office building curve in spirals like the grooves of a record as Winslow runs along them, trying—and failing—to "get a meeting" with the mogul at its center. When Swan has sex with Phoenix, it is on a round bed with a black satin bedspread over which a crane hovers like the arm of a phonograph about to play a record, much as he is "playing" or manipulating her.

In *Phantom*'s original script, Swan is called Spectre, and De Palma has said that "I'd always sort of modeled Swan on [record producer] Phil Spector, this kind of very short, Napoleonesque [figure], obsessed with power [and] the way he looks."[10] Swan's megalomania is thus traced back to feelings of inferiority, at least partly owing to his small stature. (Napoleon was five feet, six inches; Spector, five feet, five inches; and Paul Williams, who plays Swan, five feet, two inches.) Similarly, Swan's narcissism can be seen as overcompensation for his lack of conventionally handsome looks. (Some reviewers likened him to a homunculus.) Swan has surrounded himself with mirrors, which not only magnify his influence but assist him in his self-admiration. Having bought into the cult of youth (the rock-'n'-roll ideal that you "die young and leave a beautiful corpse"), Swan makes a pact with the devil so that his face remains eternally youthful while his videotaped image ages in its place. (An early version of the script used the name Dorian for Swan, a reference to Oscar Wilde's *The Picture of Dorian Gray*, in which a young man's painted face grows old in place of his real one.)

De Palma also based the character of Swan and his lavishly decadent home, Swanage, on Hugh Hefner and his Playboy mansion. Just as Hefner was reputed to hold orgies in which he slept with numerous "Playmates" who wanted to appear in his magazine centerfolds, Swan has his assistant, Philbin, run a casting couch, serially bedding hopeful starlets, and Swan himself watches a group of women perform sexually for him on a waterbed before joining them as the center of their attention, like a sultan with his harem girls.

Another model for Swan was business magnate Howard Hughes, whose wealth led to increasing isolation and insanity, the kind that grows from being cut off from contact with ordinary people. De Palma described Hughes as one of those who "wind up in hotel rooms with the drapes drawn, staring at movie screens or TV sets,"[11] and Swan is similarly reclusive, refusing to be photographed and controlling his environment by means of the cameras he has placed everywhere and the video from them that he constantly watches in his private viewing room. Using his video technology, Swan claims the power of the omniscient and omnipotent eye.

But Winslow (as the Phantom) challenges this panoramic power. In one scene, as Swan sits up in his balcony box seat watching the Beach Bums rehearse their insipid version of Winslow's song, the screen suddenly splits. In the left image, we see the Phantom planting a time bomb in the trunk of a stage car; this now threatens to blow up the handpicked performers in their stage show designed by Swan, which is visible on the right. Thus, Swan's visual control is riven down the middle, as dramatized by the split-screen. In another shot, the right-hand side of the screen shows the Phantom now high up in a balcony, looking down like Swan, while the left-hand image zooms in on the trunk of the car where the bomb is ticking. The right-hand image then gives us a swish pan from the Phantom to Swan, who sees the car explode on the left-hand side, replete with fire, smoke, and performers screaming. A fade to black ends the split-screen effect. No longer the master of what he surveys, Swan has been made the object of the Phantom's eyes and been forced to witness the destruction of his own spectacle—a splitting, an explosion, and a blackout of his own gaze.

With this scene, De Palma pays homage, as he did earlier in *Get to Know Your Rabbit*, to the ticking bomb sequence that opens Orson Welles's *Touch of Evil*. In that movie, the car explosion, which ends a famously long take, is a young man's attempt to strike back at a wealthy businessman who considered the young man unworthy of marriage to his daughter. In De Palma's film, the explosion ends a long take and the split-screen, and it represents the poor Phantom's challenge to the dominance of wealthy Swan, who will soon move to block the Phantom's access to his beloved Phoenix. Also, we already noted that Hollywood producers took Welles's *Touch of Evil* away from him and recut it against his will, as happened to De Palma with *Get to Know Your Rabbit*. The car bomb sequence becomes De Palma's way of siding with the Phantom against the record producer Swan and of siding with Welles and all directors of artistic integrity against manipulative and domineering movie producers: "The film industry is a very tough profession and you're surrounded by . . . a lot of manipulators like Swan . . . as you are in the rock industry. . . . You have to struggle through these forces, as Winslow does as best he can."[12]

Winslow's explosive triumph is short-lived. Swan manipulates Phoenix into his bed with promises of fame and shows the spectacle of their lovemaking to Winslow, who tearfully watches their intertwined bodies through a rainy window skylight on the roof (an allusion to Welles's *Citizen Kane*). What should be a position of power—a view looking down from above—is turned against the voyeur as Winslow is forced to witness his exclusion from the fame and the female he desires. Moreover, since Swan has a bedside TV monitor fed by a camera on the roof behind Winslow, Swan is able to watch Winslow watching him, able to view the excluded voyeur in all his jealous sorrow and rage. Swan has re-established visual dominance. There are split-screen shots of Winslow (on the left) looking painfully down at Swan and Phoenix in bed, and Swan (on the right) looking gleefully at the TV monitor's image of Winslow's suffering. Now it is Winslow who is "split," wanting to be the one in bed with Phoenix but instead seeing himself replaced by Swan. These split-screens then become whole-screen shots of Swan's grinning face, dominating the entire scene and pushing Winslow out of frame.

The parallels between Winslow and De Palma may be personal as well as directorial. Earlier we noted how De Palma used himself as an example in a discussion of voyeurism: "You look through a door and see your parents, or your brother with a girl."[13] Winslow's jealousy of Swan and Phoenix seems to play out a certain Oedipal rivalry between De Palma and his father over his mother, who, like Phoenix, also aspired to be a singer. We also know that De Palma sought to catch his father having sex with a nurse—an act of adultery which involved a mortifying betrayal and replacement of De Palma's mother, much as Swan vows to wed but then plots to assassinate Phoenix, replacing her with another star. It is interesting that Phoenix's and Winslow's replacement is Beef, portrayed by Gerrit Graham, the same actor who will play the character who is essentially De Palma's brother Bruce in *Home Movies*. De Palma always felt that he failed in his rivalry with Bruce, who seemed to attract all the attention and was his father's favored one, much as Swan prefers Beef, who gets to go on stage instead of Winslow.

Although Winslow is victimized by Swan's villainy, it's important to see the extent to which Winslow himself becomes increasingly villainous as the movie goes on. De Palma named the character of Winslow Leach after Wilford Leach, the professor who taught drama to De Palma and William Finley (who plays Winslow) when they were at Sarah Lawrence College in the early 1960s. For the most part, Leach was the kind of mentor that Swan should have been, nurturing De Palma's budding talent even after his father had cut off all support. As De Palma said about Leach, "I became like his fair-haired boy.... He understood the aesthetic potential that I had and helped me realize it."[14] However, we also know that De Palma ended up struggling with Leach for creative control of *The Wedding Party*, De Palma's first feature film, for Leach had been given supervisory authority by that film's producer. In that role, where Leach sometimes clashed with De Palma over his directorial decisions and limited his artistic freedom, Leach was more like Swan than like Winslow.

Finley described Leach as "very timid, but he had this other side of him where, if you noodged him the wrong way, he'd get very antsy and start to get angry and then go very quiet. I just thought it was great to have a character based on that kind of introvert, who was a genius but had no idea how to get it out there."[15] The frustrated genius artist Winslow Leach gets very angry indeed, threatening a stage manager with violence when he finds out that others are set to perform his rock cantata: "*I'm* the only one that can sing *Faust!*" Is this a righteous effort to retain his distinctive voice, or is it evidence of a narcissism not so very different from Swan's? "I only sing it solo," Winslow first tells Phoenix about his music, and even after he has fallen in love with her and indicated that "she could be my voice now," we wonder how much it is *himself in her* that he loves rather than her for herself. (Caught between Swan and Winslow, each overbearing in his own way, Phoenix often resembles the female dancer in *The Red Shoes*, who is torn between a composer who values her only for her talent as a performer, and a husband who wants her with a jealously possessive love.)

Winslow (as the Phantom) strangles a stagehand so that he himself can man the spotlight that shines on Phoenix for her big performance, staring intently down at her as she sings his song. Phoenix's—and by extension Winslow's—voice is thus bought at the price of another man's permanent silence. To warn Beef against singing his music, Winslow (as the Phantom) stalks Beef when he is naked in the shower, slicing through the shower curtain with a knife and then sticking a toilet plunger over the helpless singer's mouth. The scene is humorous in *not* presenting the horror of seeing him stabbed in the way that Marion Crane is stabbed in Hitchcock's *Psycho*. But, in his violent silencing of Beef's voice, how different is Winslow from Swan when he pulled the plug on Winslow's voice? (Winslow's voyeuristic stalking of the naked Beef, shot with the camera taking Winslow's point of view, is also disturbingly similar to Swan's constant surveillance: he, too, has a camera trained on the exposed Beef.) And it is Winslow (as the Phantom) who sends a neon lightning bolt down from on high to electrocute Beef, as if Winslow had arrogated to himself the power of God—or of the devil.

Speaking about a director's obligation to involve himself with producers, with filmmaking as a profit-driven enterprise, if he wants to get his movie made, De Palma has said, "The problem is that even by dealing with the devil, you become devilish to a certain extent. You need the machine. And once you use it, you are a tainted human being . . . the very fact that you are in that world at all makes you a compromised individual."[16] A director cannot realize his artistic vision without the producers' money, but they force him to compromise that vision for commercial considerations. Winslow's distinctive voice cannot be heard unless Swan funds a performance, but Swan forces compromises to Winslow's artistic integrity, mangling that voice. Winslow is literally dependent on Swan's "machine": on the electronic voice box fitted to Winslow's chest, allowing him to speak but with a strangulated voice, and on the theater-and-recording industry which performs his music but deforms it in the process into a mutilated state.

In his attempts to fight Swan, Winslow becomes more and more like him: isolated and narcissistic, headstrong and violent, willing to manipulate and destroy others in order to get his own way. Winslow becomes the Phantom; the man is transformed into a monster. Finley has said about his Phantom mask that "I wanted it to be somewhere between a sort of bird of prey and a little bit of an alien, the notion of a human being transforming into something totally different."[17] Putting on his mask and cape, striking from on high, Winslow is increasingly dangerous and predatory, even frightening his beloved Phoenix, who now finds him practically unrecognizable.

While the masked Winslow becomes less identifiably human and more the monstrous Phantom, Swan is undergoing a change in the opposite direction, becoming less of a powerful performer and more of a vulnerable person. (We recall a similar role reversal in *Dionysus in '69* where Pentheus, the king who claimed to be a god, is revealed to be merely human, while the oppressed and rebellious Dionysus becomes a godlike oppressor. Both Dionysus and Winslow are played by William Finley.) Swan is virtually invisible in the first part of the film, seeing without being seen. Secluded in his mansion or high up in his balcony box seat, he appears only as a pair of white-gloved hands cueing audience members when to applaud the acts he approves. Swan's eyes, augmented by the gaze of his surveillance cameras, are everywhere, while he is nowhere to be found.

But once Swan's spectacle is disrupted by the car bomb explosion, we begin to see less of "Swan" and more of the man, such as his wan face as he witnesses the blow-up. The big-shot producer, playing it up with a cigar in his mouth, is revealed as vulnerable when the Phantom holds a knife to his throat. It turns out that Swan is not the devil but instead under contract to that evil entity, just as Winslow is. Swan is thus beholden to a more powerful "producer" for his own fame and fortune; he is himself trapped by the infernal machine of capitalism. Having heretofore evaded photographers and wielded the power of his own cameras, Swan has his technology turned against him, becoming vulnerable to the gaze when the Phantom discovers Swan's videotaped contract and burns it, thereby destroying him.

The difference between Swan (Paul *Williams*) and the Phantom (*William* Finley) begins to blur, much like the difference between Pentheus (*William* Shephard) and Dionysus (*William* Finley) in *Dionysus in '69*. It is, of course, Paul Williams who actually wrote the Phantom's music, and De Palma originally asked Williams to play the part of the Phantom, realizing that Williams could identify with a "composer who has had his music destroyed by bubble gum groups, the sensitive artist who has had his music commercialized to the point of its being unrecognizable to him."[18] Swan and the Phantom are both beholden to the profit-making machine, both captives of audiovisual technology, both under videotaped contract with the devil. Increasingly, both Swan and the Phantom appear in mirrors, reflected images of each other's expansive egos redoubled into emptiness, since they have sold their integrity, their substance, their souls. Midway through the film, the Phantom joins Swan in his balcony box seat, the two of them appearing only as glowing eyes gazing down upon the auditioning singers, who will perform what their godlike surveyors want them to perform.

Interestingly, behind-the-scenes photos show De Palma himself in that balcony box, a perch from which to exercise directorial control. In discussing megalomaniacs like Swan, De Palma has said that "I can identify. Making movies is a lot like that";[19] "I'm conscious that my characters create a reality to which others must conform. It's a little bit like what I myself do when I direct a film."[20] De Palma adds that characters such as Swan "live surrounded by a court which venerates them and which reflects back to them the deformed image of the world in which they imagine they are living."[21]

It's possible to see De Palma's self-critical awareness of his own Swan-like power in some of the film's audition scenes. In one of these, a would-be starlet asks, "Do I look like a kidder?" Margot Kidder had been De Palma's girlfriend and the star of his previous film, *Sisters*. If this young woman looks like Kidder, will Swan/De Palma bed her and cast her? We recall that Swan has his assistant, Philbin, use the casting couch to "try out" girls, and indeed this young woman—played by Janit Baldwin—is selected for a further "audition," along with several other "lucky" hopefuls, on Swan's waterbed. First the women are expected to perform sexually with other each while Swan watches, but, as one of them says, "I'm saving it for Swan." Her voice is dubbed by actress Betty Buckley, who herself tried out for a role in *Phantom* but didn't get one. However, after the film wrapped, she did briefly date De Palma and was cast—as Miss Collins—in his next film, *Carrie*. Interestingly, Betty Buckley also dubs the voice of Swan's former girlfriend, Betty Lou ("We went steady in high school"), who now can't even get him to acknowledge her existence. These self-reflexive scenes show a self-consciousness on De Palma's part about how male producers and directors can exploit women by making them conform to the men's wishes.

In the end, Swan dies on stage, a victim of the very bloodlust he has incited as a rock promoter. He had planned to have Phoenix killed during a televised rock concert/wedding ceremony: "An assassination live on television coast to coast—that's entertainment!" With this idea of Swan's, De Palma alludes (as in *Greetings*) to the Zapruder film of the Kennedy assassination, repeated viewings of which revealed not an end to the mystery but an increasingly unhealthy public obsession with violent death. As De Palma notes, this trend has since gotten even worse: "Today, with the tabloid cable television, they'd be showing the Zapruder film a hundred thousand times a day."[22] But the Phantom foils the assassination attempt and stabs Swan, while the crowd, whipped into a frenzy by heavy metal music and the spectacle of violence, joins in, rushing the stage where one audience member himself stabs Swan and they all lift him up, carrying him about in celebration of his death. Having unleashed the throng's worst tendencies, Swan should not be surprised when the out-of-control crowd turns these against him.

Earlier, Swan's horror/rock creation, Beef, was assembled like a Frankenstein's monster from the severed limbs of various audience members. As his lyrics say, "Do you realize that all of you donated something horrible you hated that was part of you? Well, I'm your nightmares coming true." As Beef struts about the stage, violently thrusting his pelvis at the audience, he sings, "I'm the evil that you created, gettin' horny and damn frustrated, bored stiff and I want me a woman now." "Bored stiff" connects lust with boredom and death, as if Beef's desire, tending toward rape, is nothing but a search for stronger sensations to relieve life's ennui.

De Palma has described certain rock fans as "looking for bigger and better highs. . . . It is whatever moves them, and the intensity of what moves them is being escalated all the time. It is a very de-sensitized, de-emotionalized culture. They have turned themselves off with drugs and detachment, and they're looking for things to make them feel alive."[23] Performers like Beef and promoters like Swan become false idols, "leading" the crowd only toward the mindless pursuit of instinctive gratification. In the words of the song, "If we had fun, he would not restrain us. If we got caught, he would just explain us."

Swan's audience—cheering, dancing, and enthusiastically participating in his bloody demise—is reminiscent of the orgiastic revelers in *Dionysus in '69,* whose kisses and caresses turn to bites and tearings of Pentheus's flesh, as mere sensation-seeking leads to violence and death. In fact, William Shephard, who played Pentheus in that film, choreographed Swan's "orgiastic" death scene in *Phantom of the Paradise* and played the part of the audience member who stabs him. The televised stabbing of Swan also has a real-life referent in the notorious knifing that occurred at the Rolling Stones' 1969 Altamont concert, which was captured on film for the documentary *Gimme Shelter.* Robert Elfstrom was a cameraman on that film, and De Palma hired him for *Phantom of the Paradise* to help give Swan's death scene a cinema-vérité look.

In stabbing Swan and burning his videotaped contract with the devil, the Phantom kills himself, too. Figuratively, this suggests that the Phantom has become too Swan-like to live, too egotistical and too violent to merit salvation. While the Phantom may have overcome his ego to the extent of allowing his beloved Phoenix to sing his songs, the violence he committed to ensure her stardom and to save her from Swan ended up tainting the Phantom and fatally compromising his integrity, his soul. In dealing with Swan's devilry, the Phantom himself became too devilish. His bird-of-prey mask ultimately links the Phantom to Swan's dead songbird logo; they are birds of a feather who kill and die together. Although each of them was once a powerful performer, they both die as bleeding, screaming persons. Swan's "golden boy" mask—the godlike one he wears in public to avoid being photographed—is torn off, revealing the vulnerable human face beneath, just as Winslow's Phantom mask is also removed to show his dying.

But isn't Winslow a hero in having killed the evil Swan? Won't this act make a difference? We recall that, before producers fired him from the film, De Palma had wanted to end *Get to Know Your Rabbit* by having Donald (very effectively pretend to) kill a rabbit on live television. Its bloody body would cause such a scandal that the oppressive corporation Donald works for would be ruined: "He's such a nebbish all through the movie—I wanted him to suddenly realize he's being co-opted by all of these forces and suddenly rebel against them. . . . I wanted him to humiliate the [boss], destroy his corporation."[24]

But the nebbishy Winslow's killing of Swan does not register with this crowd as a moral victory of good over evil—or even as a warning about the ultimately self-destructive nature of violence whether used for good or ill. Instead, the crowd doesn't differentiate between Winslow and Swan, viewing both their violent deaths as the occasion for an orgy of bloodlust, the latest sensation in entertainment. Said De Palma: "A world of people killing themselves, consuming themselves, in front of you, and you're sitting there applauding, 'Jesus, do it better, do it bigger!'"[25]

In a sense, with the bloody slaughter that climaxes *Phantom of the Paradise*, De Palma finally has the *Rabbit* ending he desired, but he no longer seems to believe that it would make any difference. Swan may be dead but the corporation lives on, having found a way to profit from Winslow's (and De Palma's) bloody rebellion by selling it as a sensational event. The crowd in the theater—and presumably the TV-viewing audience—just want more extreme violence and even bloodier death. And what about the audience for De Palma's movie? What do we want?

One thing audiences didn't seem to want was to see *Phantom of the Paradise*, perhaps because the film held a mirror up to their own obsession with violent death, or maybe because audiences became confused about what kind of film this musical/horror hybrid was supposed to be. "I've always thought rock and horror were very close stylistically," De Palma said. "I felt I had a solution in combining two separate audiences. Obviously, I didn't." De Palma believed that the movie's marketers erred in selling it as a rock or concert film, and he noted that it did much better on rerelease when advertised as a "fantastic horror film."[26] Though never to the same extent as *The Rocky Horror Picture Show*, *Phantom of the Paradise* has since gone on to develop quite a cult following, including "Phantompalooza" events in Winnipeg, Canada.

As if to avoid any further confusion, De Palma's next film would not have any comic or musical distractions. *Obsession* would be a serious suspense thriller, in the classic Hitchcock mode.

CHAPTER 9

Obsession (1976)

In 1959 New Orleans, Michael and Elizabeth Courtland (Cliff Robertson and Genevieve Bujold) celebrate their tenth wedding anniversary by dancing with each other and then with their nine-year-old daughter Amy (Wanda Blackman). But that night, Elizabeth and Amy are both kidnapped and a ransom note is left in their place. Michael is persuaded by police to leave dummy money at the drop site, rigged with a radio transmitter allowing police to track the kidnappers to their lair. A chase ensues, resulting in the deaths of Elizabeth and Amy when the kidnappers' getaway car collides with an oil truck, explodes, and plummets into a river. Michael builds a funeral monument to his wife and daughter in the shape of the Florentine church where he and Elizabeth first met. Sixteen years later, in 1975, Michael revisits that same church in Florence, Italy, where he discovers a young woman, Sandra, who looks like the reincarnation of his dead wife (and who is also played by Genevieve Bujold). Michael's courtship of Sandra involves making her over into the very image of his former wife.

The two of them return to New Orleans, but, on the eve of their wedding, history seems to repeat itself: Sandra is kidnapped and a ransom note is left in her place, just as happened before with Elizabeth and Amy. This time, however, Michael is determined to bring real money, but the briefcases are switched behind Michael's back by his business partner, Bob (John Lithgow), and so once again the ransom attempt fails. Michael confronts Bob and eventually kills him in an altercation after his partner has admitted to swindling Michael out of the money—in cahoots with Sandra. Michael decides to shoot Sandra for the part she played in betraying him.

We, however, are privy through Sandra's flashbacks to information Michael doesn't have: Sandra is in fact the grown-up Amy, who actually survived the first kidnapping, which was masterminded by Bob. For years, Sandra has blamed her father for the death of her mother, and in order to take revenge on him, Sandra joined in Bob's plan to have Michael fall for her and then to stage a second kidnapping. Deep down, though, Sandra hopes that her father will prove his love for her by bringing the real money this time. When Michael fails at this second chance (since Bob switched the briefcases), Sandra attempts suicide in despair. She survives and, just as Michael is about to shoot her, sees him running toward her with the real money in his possession and falls into his arms, crying "Daddy." "Amy," he says, recognizing Sandra as his daughter, and the two of them embrace.

Let us return to the middle of the film, to when Michael is wooing Sandra in Florence. Instead of the classic "I love you just the way you are," the *Mad* magazine parody of *Obsession* has Michael say to Sandra, "I love you just the way she was!"[1]—that is, the way *Elizabeth* was. In the film, Sandra tells the story of how Dante would go to a church to watch his beloved Beatrice, while in between them sat the Lady of the Screen, whom he would gaze upon and pretend to love for propriety's sake. In Sandra's account, she is the Lady of the Screen on whom Michael is projecting his love for the woman "behind" her, his Elizabeth from the past: "You still love Elizabeth, don't you? That's why you want me." In describing Elizabeth, Michael says that she "never wore rouge" and that she had "a very Bryn Mawr walk," and he has Sandra imitate this walk, telling her not to "sashay so much . . . like a model," but "just glide, natural." Michael's instructions desexualize Sandra, turning her into an idealized woman like Dante's highly spiritual Beatrice. Towering behind Sandra during this conversation is a large white statue of a woman, like the angelic Beatrice he wants her to become. Michael is reminiscent of the sculptor (William Finley) in De Palma's short film *Woton's Wake*, who prefers the female statue he created to the live woman it turns into. There is also Winslow (William Finley) in *Phantom of the Paradise*, who sometimes seems to love the rock star Phoenix more as his creation, an extension of his own voice, than as herself.

When Michael first sees Sandra in a church, she is standing high up on a scaffold, preparing to restore a painting of the Madonna by Bernardo Daddi. It is her daddy's Madonna—Michael's Elizabeth—that Sandra restores in his mind. In gazing upon Sandra, he doesn't really *see her* but instead projects the idealized image of her mother upon her. Michael's first sight of Sandra is rendered in step-printed slow motion, as if her movements were being slowed down to become still photos or a painting. He sees her as an idealized image of static perfection, not as the living woman she actually is. After catching sight of Sandra in the church, Michael gazes upon a wallet photo of Elizabeth, marveling at the resemblance and maybe superimposing the two images in his mind. Later, Michael uses a camera to take still photos of Sandra on the church steps, just as he had taken pictures of Elizabeth there many years ago. The church background, the angelic female choir on the soundtrack, and Michael's position below each woman (as if he were worshipping them with his camera) signify that he views them as Madonna figures.

We know that Michael doesn't really see Sandra as herself, but did he ever actually see Elizabeth either—or only some projected ideal femininity of his own imagining? At the beginning of the film, for the guests attending the couple's tenth anniversary celebration in 1959 New Orleans, Michael gives a slide show of the photos he took when he and Elizabeth first met in 1948 Florence. The first photo is of Michael looking and the second is of Elizabeth as the object of his gaze. It would appear that, from the very start, his view of her has been mediated by an idealizing camera, one that fixes or captures her as what *he* wants to see. Michael's slide show ends with a title card stating "and they lived happily ever after," as if theirs was a picture-perfect romance, supernally and eternally flawless. Paul Schrader's screenplay for *Obsession* describes Elizabeth as "like the Madonna . . . pure, detached, almost too good for this world. She really isn't these things, of course, but men find in her a symbol, an icon, of the Beauty they aspire to."[2]

After journeying from Florence to New Orleans to marry Michael, Elizabeth herself wrote in her diary that "New Orleans is a nice town, and Mike is very good to me, but it is all so different now. He is busy at work all day, and sometimes I wonder if Mike loves me as much as his business." If Florence was the location of love, New Orleans is the place for profit, where Michael Courtland, a real estate developer, *courts land* rather than attending to his wife. (In this sense, he is similar to his acquisitive partner Bob *La Salle*, who is more interested in houses and *rooms* than in people.) Michael had hoped to "retain for the New South," with its "energy" and "ambition," "some of the graceful values of the Old South," but it would seem that capitalism increasingly drives him away from courtesy and caring.

Thus, the hidden reason he allows himself to be convinced by the police to use phony bills during the first kidnapping is that Michael values money over love, just as he values his own idealization of Elizabeth over the real woman. In his own selfish dream world, Michael *thinks* he worships Elizabeth while in fact discounting and neglecting his actual wife. When Michael then builds a massive funeral monument to his wife on land that he could have profited from by developing, this stands as an ostentatious attempt to show others—and to prove to himself—that he does value love over money.

While this memorial for Elizabeth may seem like a step in the right direction, indicating that Michael could feel the loss of his actual wife, it is instead problematic in several respects. The memorial is modeled after the church in which he first "worshipped" her as his "Madonna," which suggests that Michael is still idealizing her rather than recognizing her reality, including the harsh fact that she is dead and that he must mourn her and move on. De Palma uses one seemingly continuous 360-degree arc shot to take us from Michael in 1959, overseeing the construction of Elizabeth's memorial, to Michael in 1975, gazing upon the completed monument. It is as though he hasn't moved for sixteen years, instead remaining morbidly fixated upon his wife's death.

Then in Florence, as Michael walks toward the church where he will see Sandra as the "reincarnation" of his dead wife, a simultaneous zoom-in and track-out on him shows that, while he may seem to be moving forward in space, he is mentally moving backward in time, returning obsessively to Elizabeth, viewing Sandra not as who she is in the present but as who Elizabeth was in the past. The zoom-in/track-out may also indicate that, though one part of Michael wants to approach the church and "his Elizabeth" again, another part of him recoils from doing so, sensing that his is a morbid obsession that could prove fatal for himself and the woman he makes over into the mirror image of his dead wife.

As Michael is entering the church, he passes two priests on their way out; they are not only identically garbed in black robes but also identical twins. If Michael marries Sandra because she looks like the deceased wife he loved, the wedding will be more like a funeral. Indeed, a psychiatrist warns him that "you shouldn't marry . . . out of some morbid preoccupation with Elizabeth," and on the eve of Michael and Sandra's wedding in New Orleans, he dreams that the two of them cut a wedding cake that is topped by a model replica of the church/funeral monument associated with Elizabeth. Because Michael's love for Sandra is shadowed by his love for a dead woman, because Michael *loves death through Sandra*, the church becomes a tomb.

Michael's fixation on Elizabeth is thus a form of necrophilia, and if he could *see Sandra* as more than just a screen for the idealized image of his deceased wife, he might be able to realize that the most rational explanation for Sandra's remarkable resemblance to his wife is that she is Elizabeth's daughter, who has now grown up to be the same age his wife was when she died. (After the car exploded and sank into the river, Sandra was presumed dead, but her body was never found.)

And if Michael could *see Sandra* as his and Elizabeth's daughter, then he would realize that marrying her would be incest. At a dinner in Florence with fellow rich businessmen, all of whom seem to have younger female companions, Michael wonders, "How do these old guys get such young wives?" When one man shows a photo of his actual wife, a matronly woman, Michael realizes that the men are in fact surrounded by their mistresses, "girls" who make the aging men feel more youthful. But what Michael doesn't realize is that he is doing much the same thing with Sandra, trying to recapture his youthful past through her, to relive the young love he had with Elizabeth. Michael's behavior is as selfish and exploitative as theirs—indeed, more so, because in Michael's case, the "incestuous" attraction to the young woman would be more than metaphorical. (At one point in Schrader's development of the script, there were going to be allusions to Kubrick's *Lolita* in the form of a Quilty-like character, which would have made it even clearer that Michael is like Humbert in that film, a man whose incestuous desire for his stepdaughter is driven by a longing to recapture an ideal love he had years ago.)

Does Michael actually commit incest? In the original version of *Obsession*, he really does marry and bed Sandra (who is his own daughter, Amy), but the film struggled to find a distributor and so De Palma came up with a compromise that would allow the film to be released: "Originally, [Michael] does sleep with his daughter; that does in fact happen, and it's scary and dangerous and you go, 'Oh, my God!' But when we were trying to get a distributor, that scared them away, so we figured out a way to make it sort of like he *thought* he slept with her. So we put in this dream sequence where he marries her and takes her to bed in his head, and when he wakes up in the middle of the night, it's sort of left ambiguous: did he actually marry her, or didn't he actually marry her? But I always felt that he should marry her; he should have taken her to bed."[3]

By using wavy effects to make Michael's consummation with Sandra appear as though it could be a dream, the film participates in his romantic blindness to the fact that, rather than being (re)united in holy matrimony with his Elizabeth, he would be committing incest with his daughter. De Palma's preferred version with its actual incest would have been much blunter about the physical impact and, by implication, the psychological consequences of Michael's romantically deluded desecration of his daughter. But making this scene ambiguous does preserve the possibility that Sandra was not bedded by her father and that, if he does finally come to his senses, the two of them will not have to live with the fact that he may have done her irreparable damage. The dream version we have now thus holds out more hope than De Palma's original version.

In the "wedding night" dream, Michael hears Sandra say, "Now I am your wife. I am Elizabeth." But whose dream is this, his or hers? If the deluded Michael sees Sandra as Elizabeth, it's important to note that, increasingly, she sees herself the same way. If Michael wants to *have* Elizabeth again and not just someone like her, Sandra wants to *be* Elizabeth, not just to grow up to be like her. The script describes Michael as "a man possessed,"[4] so driven is he to find in Sandra the reincarnation of his dead wife, while Sandra herself is "as if compelled by forces beyond her control"[5] when she approaches and communes with the funeral monument he built to her mother. "Now Sandra is obsessed with the idea of Elizabeth," a psychiatrist tells Michael. "She's caught up in your fantasy." The psychiatrist in the script calls it "the most unique case of *folie à deux* I have ever seen" and warns that "the two of you are going crazy together."[6]

In the film's first scene (the 1959 anniversary celebration), Michael dances with Elizabeth; he and his wife then include nine-year-old Amy/Sandra in their dance; and finally Sandra is alone with her father, sharing a dance exclusively with him. The daughter has replaced her mother in her father's arms. That night, just as Elizabeth is about to go to bed with Michael, she is called away by Sandra's cries of "Mommy!" which turn out to be the first signs of the kidnapping. Once again, it is as though the daughter has intervened between her parents, removing her mother from her father to have him for herself. When the kidnapping and subsequent death of her mother make this removal permanent, it is as if the daughter's unconscious wish has come terribly true: her mother, the rival for her father's affections, has been eliminated. Thus, one reason Sandra may be so obsessed with restoring Elizabeth to life is that the daughter feels haunted by guilt over her mother's death, believing herself to be somehow responsible for it and desperately needing to make amends.

Whether or not she is overcompensating for rivalrous feelings, Sandra identifies very strongly with her mother. De Palma emphasizes this by having the adult Sandra (Genevieve Bujold) play her nine-year-old self when she remembers the time that she and her mother (also Genevieve Bujold) sat side by side, having been tied up by the kidnappers. Sandra so identifies with her mother that she imagines herself as her mother's twin, as if biologically still tied to her. (In our first viewing of the kidnap scene, we see that Elizabeth's mouth is gagged while Sandra records the plea on the ransom tape for Michael to bring the money. Thus, the daughter speaks for—and as—the mother, as if she were her mother's voice, the two of them still one body.)

When the kidnappers cut the ties that bind mother and daughter and then take Elizabeth away to what proves to be her death, the scene is reminiscent of the one in *Sisters* where Emil cuts Dominique off from her Siamese twin Danielle, a riddance partly desired by Danielle but a loss that will haunt her forever, causing her to over-identify with her dead sister. Similarly, the mother-daughter bond is severed for Sandra before she has had the time to develop into an independent person, and she, too, will maintain an overly close link to her deceased mother. (It is interesting that, when Michael finds the ransom note in Sandra's bedroom, there is a Raggedy Ann doll on her bed. Like the Raggedy Ann in *Sisters*, this doll represents innocence compromised and wholeness cut in half, for the doll has lost its "mother," Sandra, just as she has lost her mother, Elizabeth.)

In the Florentine church, Sandra tells Michael that when she first saw the Daddi painting that had suffered water damage, "I said, 'Sandra, the Madonna needs you,'" which is why she was doing the prep work for it to be restored by a specialist. We recall that Elizabeth died when the kidnappers' car exploded and fell into the water, and now Sandra is devoted to helping her daddy "restore" her mother, the woman they both idolize. Sandra asks him to tell her about Elizabeth and to show her Elizabeth's picture. When Michael takes photos of Sandra in front of the church, she knows that he took similar pictures of Elizabeth before her, pictures that were screened during the anniversary slide show in 1959.

In Hitchcock's *Rebecca*, the unnamed heroine (often called "Fontaine" by critics since she is played by Joan Fontaine) appears in home movies of her honeymoon filmed and then screened by her husband, Maxim (Laurence Olivier), who has married her after the death of his first wife, Rebecca. Fontaine believes that Maxim idolized Rebecca and that she herself is inferior and must struggle to live up to the standard of the perfect wife set by her predecessor. Like Fontaine when she goes to live in the mansion shared by Rebecca and Maxim, Sandra is seen in front of large doors that make her look like a small child when she returns to New Orleans with Michael. The thought of Rebecca's/Elizabeth's perfection seems to loom over Fontaine/Sandra as an impossible ideal, a sainted memory that outrivals any living woman. Maxim and Michael have preserved their former wives' rooms as shrines which Fontaine and Sandra long—and fear—to enter. In the hope of embodying what Maxim desires, Fontaine dresses up in a gown that she sees in a painting and that was once worn by Rebecca. Sandra gazes up at a portrait of Elizabeth and dons her mother's pearl necklace while looking at herself in the mirror, as if she could thereby *see herself as* Elizabeth and imagine herself loved by Michael.

But when Sandra discovers Elizabeth's diary with its revelation that Michael may have loved money more than he did her, it is at once a wish-fulfillment fantasy and a nightmare. The fantasy is that, if her mother was not loved as the ideal, then the daughter has a chance of replacing her in the father's affections and need no longer feel so inferior. The nightmare is the thought that, if the father didn't love the mother, he might not love the daughter, either. Would he sacrifice them both for money? Didn't he keep the cash instead of paying to ransom them?

As Sandra reads Elizabeth's diary aloud, she seems to become her mother's voice, expressing her anxiety about Michael's true feelings and character. Like Sandra, Fontaine undergoes an analogous change in attitude: she shifts from viewing Rebecca as a rival for Maxim's idolatrous affection to seeing her as a potential victim, like herself, of Maxim's hatred. What Sandra and Fontaine fear is that Michael's and Maxim's worship of women is a cover for their murderous disregard, that the shrine to their former wives is like Blue-beard's chamber filled with the wives he killed. In speaking about *Rebecca*, De Palma said that he is "a great admirer of that genre [the Gothic]" and that, with *Obsession*, he "wanted to do something in that 'woman in a dark house' area, played against an obsessed, driven character."[7] Sandra is the woman who feels threatened in Michael's dark New Orleans house, menaced by his drive to see her *as* his sainted former wife, an idolatrous obsession that could be as lethal to Sandra as it may have been for Elizabeth.

We have seen how Sandra's gazing at Elizabeth's portrait and how her trying on what Elizabeth wore, while growing increasingly anxious about Michael's true character, are similar to scenes in *Rebecca*—but they are also remarkably similar to ones in Hitchcock's *Vertigo*, which may be an even more important film source for the understanding of *Obsession*. In *Vertigo*, Madeleine (Kim Novak) stares at the portrait of her great-grandmother Carlotta and wears a matching necklace, feeling "possessed" by her lookalike predecessor, as if drawn toward a similar death. In a later scene occurring after Madeleine dies, Judy (also played by Kim Novak) looks at herself in the mirror while wearing that same necklace and thinking about how Scottie (James Stewart) has been trying to make her over into the mirror image of Madeleine, his former love.

In both films, a man's obsession with imposing his vision of a deceased love upon a living woman threatens to have fatal consequences for her. Like Michael, Scottie is associated with a simultaneous zoom-in and track-out (pio-neered by Hitchcock as the "vertigo" shot), as if to warn him that he should not approach but avoid; his attempt to recapture his past love can only result in the loss of life in the present. Both Scottie's pursuit of Judy and Michael's pursuit of Sandra are set to tragically romantic scores composed by Ber-nard Herrmann, with compulsive repetitions and dark tonalities which sug-gest that their obsessions are likely to come to a bad end. Nevertheless, both men persist in following and wooing—that is, stalking and seducing—young women, refashioning their live flesh to fit the image of the dead women the males still desire. For example, Scottie makes bra-less Judy into someone less crudely sexual, much as Michael replaces Sandra's "sashay" with that "Bryn Mawr walk."

It is interesting that Michael's egocentric imposition on Sandra appears to have had a corollary in Cliff Robertson's rather selfish behavior toward Genevieve Bujold during the making of the film, according to John Lithgow's account of what happened behind the scenes. Lithgow implies that Robert-son would often upstage Bujold, including several takes when he "lifted his shoulder, covering half her face"[8] during an over-the-shoulder shot of him embracing her. Michael similarly blankets and obscures Sandra with his own vision of her as Elizabeth. Robertson apparently saw his role as a last chance to recapture some of his past glory and made rather elaborate attempts to disguise and deny his true age. Something of the same could be said about Michael, who tries desperately to recapture his youth through Sandra. In the end, Lithgow's description of Robertson's "self-aggrandizement" as "sad, self-deluding, and almost poignant"[9] could apply equally well to Michael.

Michael may be deluded, failing to realize the extent to which his adoration of women masks a culpable neglect for their actual beings, but he is not guilty of deliberate cruelty. Yet Michael's partner, Bob, for his own selfish reasons, has lied to Sandra, leading her to believe the worst about her father: "I was raised believing you killed mother. I hated you. I lived for the day when I could revenge her."

Like Sandra, the young De Palma tended to idealize his mother and to demonize his father. If Michael, according to Elizabeth's diary, was "busy at work all day," so was De Palma's father. Elizabeth's feelings of abandonment ("sometimes I wonder if Mike loves me as much as his business") were then dealt a killing blow by the ultimate desertion—his failure to pay the ransom money, which led to her death. Young Sandra felt equally deserted, sharing her mother's pain. We recall that it was Sandra's voice on the tape recording, pleading for her father to save them. As a result of his neglect, she vowed to get revenge and undertook a secret plot against Michael. As we know, De Palma's father compounded his workaholic "desertion" by sleeping with a nurse at the office, which led to a suicide attempt on the part of De Palma's mother. (She was saved by De Palma himself, who took her to the hospital.) De Palma then used the tape recorder his mother had given him for Christmas to try to avenge her, secretly capturing his father's phone conversations—and later surreptitiously filming him—to gather evidence of adultery so that his mother could divorce him. "I identify with the avenging child," De Palma once said in a direct comparison of himself to Sandra.[10]

But the comparison doesn't stop there. Just as Sandra eventually realized how much her demonization of her father was due to Bob's manipulation of her to believe what *he* wanted her to believe—the very worst about Michael's motives ("[He] just can't come up with the money, not for Elizabeth and not for you"), so De Palma came to see that "my mother had manipulated me": "My brothers and I had only had my mother's point of view, and she spoke of daddy as an outsider, leagued against us. She told us, 'He's the bad one; you, you're with me; blame him.'"[11] In the children's eyes (Sandra's, De Palma's, and his brothers'), the father was as guilty and despised as the mother was innocent and idealized. (It is interesting to note that De Palma's brother Bart painted the portrait of Elizabeth that Sandra idolized.) However, both Sandra and De Palma later gained a more mature understanding to challenge their one-sided, childish perceptions of their fathers: "I gradually came to appreciate my father's point of view"; "in truth—but I understood this only much later—he was just a man who threw himself into his work so that he could forget his marriage troubles."[12] Similarly, in *Rebecca*, Fontaine grows to understand that her husband/father figure Maxim isn't as demonic as she feared and her predecessor/mother figure Rebecca isn't as worthy of idolatry.

The loss of childish perceptions can be traumatic, and there is always the risk that the self will succumb to disillusionment rather than pulling through to maturity. When Sandra discovers that she has been manipulated by Bob and that her father is not the pure evil she thought he was, she is overwhelmed by guilt over the vengeful plot she perpetrated against him. Her mind threatens to swing to the opposite extreme, idealizing him again and demonizing herself: "Father," she addresses him in a letter, as if he were a godlike confessor, "I do not ask forgiveness. I know there can be none." Feeling so terribly unworthy in his exalted eyes, she attempts suicide. For his part, Michael, who once idolized Sandra as the "reincarnation" of his sainted wife and who has now been told by Bob that she is a "lying little bitch," plans to commit vengeful homicide against the woman for her betrayal. The shock of disillusionment threatens to lead him from idolatry of her to total denigration.

Thus, the ending we *might have had* is one where the opposite extremes of idealization and demonization come together in a *Liebestod* or love/death. As Michael and Sandra run toward each other in slow motion, the two are like long-lost lovers about to be reunited, and when the camera circles around them as they embrace, it is as though he has regained his Elizabeth and is dancing with her again as he did at the film's beginning. (In *Vertigo*, the camera makes a similar circling motion when Scottie imagines, as he is holding Judy, that he has Madeleine in his arms again.) However, Michael not only knows that Sandra is not the woman of his dreams, he also believes that she is an evil betrayer, and he intends to kill her with the gun in his hand. Because Michael has been traumatized by the terrible discrepancy between the romantic ideal he held and the wicked reality he actually has in his arms, this love scene is likely to become a death scene instead. Much the same could be said for Sandra, whose wish to *be* Elizabeth so that she could *believe* again in Michael's love has now turned into an abject desire that she suffer a fatal punishment for her guilty plot against her father.

Yet, in the end, the film presents two characters mature enough to overcome the trauma of disillusionment and to negotiate between the childish extremes of idealization and demonization. Sandra recognizes that she is neither her sainted mother (Elizabeth) nor an unforgivable "little bitch" and that Michael, though he may have failed as the ideal father in not bringing the money the first time, has proven himself "good enough" by bringing it when given another chance. (This time, he has a briefcase of real bills with him.)

Michael realizes that Sandra is neither a saint nor a whorish betrayer, neither worthy of worship nor deserving of death, just as he is not a perfect husband or a man so evilly culpable that he can never be forgiven for his wife's death. He recognizes that Sandra is not Elizabeth but is instead, as he says, "Amy," his daughter, and that he must give up hope of ever finding his deceased wife again. The real way for him to prove his love for his wife is not by trying to recapture the past, but by embracing his daughter—as herself—in the present.

Obsession's slow pace and implied incest made it hard for the film to find a distributor, delaying its release, but it proved to be a moderate success with the public and the critics, and it was selected to be screened in competition at the Cannes Film Festival. Bernard Herrmann—who, as we noted, had scored Hitchcock's *Vertigo* as well as De Palma's *Sisters*—received an Oscar nomination for *Obsession*'s music, which he declared his favorite out of all the movie music he had written. "My *Obsession* score has two distinct elements: romance and tension," Herrmann said. "They usually go hand-in-hand."[13]

Despite the modest profits and praise garnered by *Obsession*, De Palma was not satisfied. As he has said, "You can make strange, idiosyncratic movies, and I made a lot of them—*Greetings*, *Phantom of the Paradise*, and so on—but if you do a lot of movies that don't make much money, it gets more and more difficult to raise the finance. So every once in a while, you have to move into the mainstream . . . and the first one where I did that and it was really successful was *Carrie*."[14] By this time, De Palma's friends in the business had all had significant success with mainstream Hollywood films—Francis Ford Coppola with *The Godfather*, George Lucas with *American Graffiti*, and Steven Spielberg with *Jaws*. De Palma had been fired from his first Hollywood picture, but he was ready to try again: "My first studio film, *Get to Know Your Rabbit*, had been a catastrophe at Warner Bros. I saw *Carrie* as my way of getting back into the system while still doing what I wanted to do cinematically."[15] Yet, because of this initial debacle, followed by a succession of independent films that didn't earn much, De Palma "had to beg for the job" of helming a Hollywood film: "They wouldn't hire me for *Carrie*. . . . I pleaded, *pleaded* to be allowed to direct it."[16] The result, according to De Palma's longtime editor and friend Paul Hirsch, "was a real breakthrough for Brian." *Carrie*, Hirsch said, was "the first of his pictures that really had a great commercial success; this was the first time that he really connected with an audience, and I think it gave him entrée to projects in Hollywood that he might not have had a chance with before this."[17]

CHAPTER 10

Carrie (1976)

Kept ignorant of the body by her religiously repressed mother, Carrie (Sissy Spacek) fears that she is bleeding to death when she has her first period in the high school gym shower. The other girls don't help by pelting her with tampons. Gym teacher Miss Collins (Betty Buckley) enforces the school's punishment for their bad behavior, but one of the girls, Chris (Nancy Allen), refuses to do the required physical exercises and so she is denied her tickets to the upcoming senior prom. Another girl, Sue (Amy Irving), feels bad about her role in the tampon "stoning" of Carrie and convinces her boyfriend, Tommy (William Katt), to take Carrie to the prom in her place. Miss Collins persuades Carrie to feel good enough about herself to accept Tommy's invitation, despite the opposition of Carrie's mother, Margaret (Piper Laurie), who associates boys with sex and sin, and who warns Carrie that "they're all going to laugh at you."

At first, the prom is a dream come true for Carrie: Tommy is romantically attentive to her, and the two of them are elected prom king and queen. However, Chris has connived to have her boyfriend, Billy (John Travolta), rig a bucket of pig's blood above the stage where Carrie is to be crowned prom queen. Sue discovers the plot and attempts to avert it, but she is dragged away by Miss Collins, who mistakenly believes that Sue herself is trying to ruin Carrie's crowning achievement rather than save her. The blood is dropped on Carrie. In the extremity of her shame and humiliation, she mistakenly sees everyone as laughing at her and she uses her telekinetic powers to lash out in rage, deploying water and fire to destroy all the students and teachers at the prom. A traumatized Carrie returns home to be embraced by her mother, but Margaret considers Carrie's powers to be satanic and stabs her in the back with a knife. Carrie retaliates by telekinetically crucifying her mother with knives and other kitchen implements. Carrie then embraces her mother as their house falls inward upon them, killing them both and sinking into the ground.

Near the film's beginning, De Palma's camera eye roves through the girls' high school locker room and showers, revealing the young women in varying states of undress, including full-frontal nudity. According to editor Paul Hirsch, "George Lucas once told me he thought that locker-room scene was the key to *Carrie*'s success. He said, 'Most directors, if they're going to show frontal nudity, will save it for reel nine. By putting it [early] in the film, Brian puts the audience in a place where they feel like this is a director who might do anything.'"[1]

But what, exactly, has De Palma done with this audacious opening? With one half of the population barred from women's locker rooms, the camera's entrance here—especially when combined with the nudity—is bound to feel like a voyeuristic invasion of privacy, a sight of something forbidden to the male eye. De Palma, who once planted a hidden microphone in the girls' sex education class at his Quaker high school so that he could secretly record what went on there, has described the shower scene in *Carrie* as "just the illustration of a very male fantasy: all boys have dreamed of knowing what happens in the girls' locker room. I decided to go in there with the camera."[2] As the camera snakes through the inner sanctum of these young women, who cavort naked and oblivious to its intrusive gaze, we get a naughty thrill as secret witnesses of what we shouldn't be seeing. The "hidden" camera ends its stalking movement by creeping up behind Carrie in the shower, eyeing her as she rubs soap on her breasts and between her legs. "Don't forget," De Palma has said, "that we shot *Carrie* in the first half of the 1970s, a time when all the films had naked girls."[3] With this comment, De Palma positions his film alongside others of the time that used female nudity to attract a voyeuristic audience.

But De Palma has also denied that his is a "voyeuristic" or "Peeping Tom"[4] camera in this opening scene from *Carrie*. Instead, he has argued that this scene "adopted Carrie's point of view"[5] and that he shot it in slow motion because "I wanted to get involved in this lyrical eroticism before the blood comes, and it's all wonderful, beautiful . . . the steam, Carrie's touching herself."[6] Creating an effect that is "sensuous and languorous," the "slow motion makes it slightly erotic as it moves through all these sort of half-dressed and sometimes naked girls to Carrie, a kind of erotic atmosphere before it's broken," De Palma explained.[7] The viewer may choose to *identify with* the girls cavorting in their innocent nakedness, to *get involved in* Carrie's sensual self-discovery of her body in the shower, which is as yet guilt-free because it is not even recognized as adult sexuality.

It is only when the blood flows from her first period (and the film speed drops into regular motion) that Carrie is forced to confront the "fallen nature" of adult sexuality, which is often associated with guilt and shame. When Carrie reaches out a hand to Sue for help, leaving a bloody imprint on her blouse, Sue is repulsed because Carrie's period raises in Sue a sense of shame over her own female body. The girls "stone" Carrie with tampons as a way of scapegoating her for the "sins of the flesh," projecting onto her their own fear and loathing regarding the female sex—a guilt and shame induced in them by patriarchal society. The girls have gone from innocent naked-ness to guilty exposure; they now see themselves through judgmental eyes and turn that shaming gaze on Carrie. Carrie, too, has transitioned from a guilt-free sensuality in the shower to a shame-filled sense of her own body, a self-loathing that will be further intensified when her mother blames Car-rie's period on lustful thoughts and associates her bleeding with the "sins of woman," as defined by patriarchal religion.

It is interesting to note that the actresses playing the girls had to struggle to appear "innocent" in their naked cavorting during the slow-motion portion of the scene; the thought that they would be seen in the nude by a voyeuris-tic movie audience kept making them feel self-conscious and "dirty." "They had all kinds of anxieties about doing it," according to De Palma, "and a few of the actresses finally balked and said, I can't do this" and "were crying";[8] "Certain actresses started to panic; others vomited right before the take; still others tried to negotiate with me."[9] Sissy Spacek herself (Carrie) also found the nudity to be challenging: "That shower scene—of course I worried about that and wanted it to work, wanted it to be authentic, wanted to be able to lose myself in it and not think about being naked in front of the world."[10]

The actresses themselves thus experienced a version of the split within their characters between an un-self-conscious, Edenic nakedness and a post-lapsarian sense of exposure before a shaming gaze. "Brian told us it would be a beautiful dream, so we're thinking it's ethereal and very smoky," Nancy Allen (Chris) said. "So when we saw the dailies, it was a surprise. It was beautiful. And you saw pretty much everything."[11] In the end, it was Spacek's coura-geous self-display in the slow-motion shower scene, which included close-ups of intimate parts of her body, that helped her fellow actresses to feel less ashamed. "I didn't know if I should laugh or crawl under my chair," Spacek said, commenting on her first viewing of herself in the dailies. "I decided to laugh. 'Thanks a lot, Brian!' I said, as sarcastically as I could, as I left the screening room. After that, Brian later told me, the female cast members stopped complaining about their topless locker room scene."[12] "They thought, if Sissy can do this, we can do this," De Palma commented.[13] Unfortunately, unlike the actresses playing them, the female characters in the film adopt patriarchy's shaming gaze toward themselves and Carrie, abjecting her "sinful" woman's body.

Just as Sue pushes Carrie's bloody, beseeching hand away and joins the other girls in pelting her with tampons (indeed, Sue is the first to open the dispenser), Miss Collins is initially repulsed by Carrie's bleeding female body. Carrie's hand marks Sue's blouse and Miss Collins's gym shorts with blood, providing an unwelcome reminder to each woman of her own "unclean" and "sinful" female nature (again, as seen through patriarchal eyes). As with Sue, Miss Collins's first reaction is to refuse this mark of "sin" by abjecting and scapegoating Carrie for it. Miss Collins slaps Carrie across the face and shakes her body, ostensibly to help her overcome her hysterical reaction to the bleeding, but underneath there is a sense of punishing her for the bleeding body that Miss Collins and the girls know—but want to deny—that they, too, have. As Miss Collins later tells the school principal (a man who is looking in disgust at the bloody mark on her shorts), "The thing is, Morty, I knew how they felt [when they attacked Carrie]. The whole thing just made me want to take her and shake her, too." When Carrie returns home, her mother slaps her across the face with a Bible tract and preaches to her from the tract about the "sins of woman," asserting that "the Lord visited Eve with a curse, and the curse was the curse of blood.... If she had remained sinless, the curse of blood would never have come on her.... She may have committed the sin of lustful thoughts." When Carrie denies this, her mother says, "I can see the sin as surely as God can." Carrie's mother views her through the eyes of patriarchal religion, condemning Carrie for her bleeding, sinful body.

Both Miss Collins and Carrie's mother slap Carrie, but Miss Collins will then spend the rest of the movie trying to differentiate herself from Carrie's mother. Miss Collins will attempt to see Carrie—and herself—through female-affirming eyes rather than those of a judgmental patriarchy. Someone has scrawled "Carrie White Eats Shit" on the gym walls, but Miss Collins tries to convince the girls that they "did a really shitty thing" when they abjected Carrie in the locker room. The punishing physical exercises that Miss Collins orders the girls to do can be seen as a way to force them to recognize their own vulnerable bodies, their corporeal connection to Carrie. De Palma presents these exercises as a montage of shots in which the girls sink lower and lower to the ground, feeling the weight of their bodies. When Chris refuses to accept this punishment, wanting to quit detention early, Miss Collins tells her that "the period's not up," again linking their bodily suffering to Carrie's bleeding, insisting on a somatic sympathy.

When Chris then insults Miss Collins, the teacher slaps her. While Chris might seem to deserve this reprimand, the violence of it is disturbing, as is the way it repeats the slap Miss Collins gave to Carrie. As Betty Buckley

(Miss Collins) has said about this slap, "The woman was very judgmental and angry at these girls. She knows she shouldn't act like that as a teacher, but she's kind of compelled to."[14] Too eager to prove her own acceptance of Carrie as opposed to Chris's denial, too ready to be right this time rather than wrong (slapping Chris instead of Carrie), Miss Collins fails to realize that she is now abjecting *Chris*, acting like an angry and judgmental God toward her rather than reaching out in compassion.

It is interesting to note that, while Buckley "wanted to do a stage hit" on Nancy Allen (Chris), De Palma "really wanted that whack." According to Allen, "My face didn't feel good! My ear was bruised also. It was completely hideous. We kept doing it again and again. Brian would say, '*Hit her harder!*'"[15] Apparently, De Palma "wanted a particular reaction and for some reason didn't trust that he could just tell me that," Allen said.[16] Whether or not De Palma's violent approach to Allen was as ill-considered as Miss Collins's to Chris, the effect is one of excessive force. The impact on Chris will be to make her feel victimized and to set her on a course of revenge against Miss Collins and Carrie. For scenes where Miss Collins wanted Sue to feel bad about her mistreatment of Carrie, De Palma also had Buckley use personal information she had about actress Amy Irving (Sue) to make her cry. Again, the goal may be laudable, but the means used to achieve it seem excessive.

Miss Collins's attempt to differentiate herself from Carrie's mother by helping Carrie see herself in a more positive light is evident in the scene where the two of them stand reflected in a mirror, and the teacher has Carrie imagine how pretty she would look with her hair out of her face and the application of some mascara and lipstick. Miss Collins's admiring gaze reflects back to Carrie a validating view of herself. Later, Carrie will carry this female-affirming view with her when she tries out lipsticks in a drugstore mirror, despite disapproving looks from a shop assistant, and when she puts on lipstick in her bedroom mirror before the prom, in direct defiance of her mother's judgmental gaze. Earlier, when her mother had made her see herself as sinful, Carrie's bedroom mirror had warped and cracked into pieces as if she was too ashamed to look at her own image. (Given the lack of compassion shown by Carrie's mother, it's not surprising that a reflected image of Jesus also cracks when the mirror fragments and that the mirror's shards fall near a Madonna and Child lamp.) However, after Miss Collins shores up Carrie's image of herself—and after Carrie uses her telekinetic powers to reform the fragments of the mirror—she is able to use its positive reflection of her to apply make-up before the prom.

Resisting the urge to condemn herself through her mother's eyes ("I can see your dirty pillows," Margaret tells her, "everyone will"), Carrie insists on her own positive image of the female form: "Breasts, momma, they're called breasts, and every woman has them." Carrie also maintains that her prom dress is pink and not the sinful blood-red her mother sees it as (since it is not an impossibly pure white). As Piper Laurie commented about her character (Carrie's mother), "In her head, it's red."[17] At the prom, Carrie's desire for affirmation is ratified by Miss Collins, who tells her that "you look beautiful," and when Carrie is about to be crowned prom queen, she mouths "thank you" from the stage in response to Miss Collins's applause and approving gaze. It would seem that Miss Collins has indeed become the "good mother" she has strived to be ever since the moment when, after slapping Carrie in the shower, she took the naked girl in her arms as if enclosing her in a womblike comfort.

Why, then, does De Palma have Miss Collins be the one to stop Sue's attempt to rescue Carrie, dragging Sue away before she can prevent the pig's blood from being dropped? Why is Miss Collins so quick to assume that Sue is in on some plot against Carrie, that Sue is "jealous about her boyfriend [Tommy] kissing Carrie"?[18] Miss Collins's precipitate action against Sue is reminiscent of her rash slapping of Chris earlier, and both suggest a distrust of others that is rooted in a doubt about herself. Overcompensating for her fear that she is not a "good mother," Miss Collins takes excessive and hasty action, ironically setting in motion (through her abjection of Chris) and finally completing (through her removal of Sue) the plot against Carrie, the "daughter" she had tried to save.

The difference between "bad mother" Margaret and "good mother" Miss Collins is a split within Miss Collins herself, whose own doubt leads her to fail at the successful maternal role she tried to embody. One sign of this internal split can be found in that scene where Miss Collins was shown in the mirror while standing next to Carrie. At first, Miss Collins's face beams with approval, reflecting back the image of herself as a "good mother," but as the scene ends, a look of doubt troubles her visage, disturbing the image that she wishes to project. It is immediately after this scene that Miss Collins interrogates Sue about her intentions in having her boyfriend, Tommy, take Carrie to the prom—a suspicion about the other that is really an uncertainty about herself and that will ultimately lead Miss Collins to the precipitate action of a "bad mother" who drags Sue away and prevents the saving of Carrie at the prom.

When Carrie imagines that Miss Collins's approving gaze turns to mocking laughter after the pig's blood drops, Carrie is literally wrong (Miss Collins is not laughing at her), but there is some metaphorical truth to what Carrie envisions since, despite Miss Collins's good intentions, she has in fact acted like a "bad mother," contributing to Carrie's demise. Thus, when Carrie uses her powers to send a basketball backboard crashing down on the teacher ("It was meant to appear that it cut Miss Collins in half," De Palma said),[19] Miss Collins's death—though, of course, literally unjustified—does contain a certain poetic justice: it is as though her unresolved internal split, her inability to differentiate herself from the "bad mother," kills her.

Curiously, Betty Buckley (Miss Collins) would herself go on to play the "bad mother," Margaret, in the first Broadway musical version of *Carrie*.[20] It is also interesting that Buckley dubbed the voice of the boy (played by De Palma's nephew Cameron) whose taunts—"Creepy Carrie! Creepy Carrie!"—lead Carrie to use her powers to crash his bicycle. As with the slapping of Carrie, it is as though one part of Miss Collins/Buckley (and of De Palma) sides with patriarchy in condemning Carrie, while another part feels empathy for and tries to save her.

Like Miss Collins with Margaret, Sue struggles to separate herself from her opposite character in the film, Chris. While Sue is initially leagued with Chris and the other girls in their tampon "stoning" of Carrie, joining the conformist crowd in their scapegoating of "the other" as vulnerable and bleeding, Sue will spend the rest of the film ostensibly trying to help Carrie. According to screenwriter Lawrence D. Cohen, "The key was that Sue is *us*. She's the surrogate for the audience. She, like us, could be standing there tormenting Carrie, only to realize what she's done and have a moment of conscience that forever changes her life and everybody else's."[21]

Sue accepts the calisthenic punishment meted out by Miss Collins, whereas Chris rejects it. Sue self-sacrificially has Tommy take Carrie to the prom in her place, while Chris takes revenge for her exclusion from the prom by getting Billy to rig the bucket of pig's blood. Sue goes to the prom to share in Carrie's triumph of enjoying a special night with Tommy and of being crowned prom queen. (Indeed, the romantic songs played during Tommy and Carrie's dance are sung by Katie Irving, the sister of Amy Irving [Sue], so it is as though Sue is present as a guiding spirit watching over Carrie.) Chris goes to the prom to pull the rope and cover Carrie in blood, thus re-enacting and reinforcing the same abjection of her that Chris had committed in the girls' locker room.

Yet, for all these differences between "good girl" Sue and "bad girl" Chris, the movie keeps uncannily hinting at likenesses between them. Parallel editing shows Sue acting standoffish toward Tommy until he agrees to take Carrie to the prom, and Chris withholding sex from Billy until he consents to her plot against Carrie. Though Sue does it more subtly, she still maneuvers her boyfriend, much as Chris does hers. "Chris manipulates Billy using sex," said De Palma. "She teases him to get him to do what she wants. Sue Snell manipulates Tommy in the same way."[22] Similarly, it is Sue who authored the poem, supposedly written by Tommy, which convinces Carrie to go with him to the prom, much as it is Chris who has the ballot boxes stuffed so that Carrie is "elected" prom queen. Carrie's crowning is the result of manipulation and subterfuge on the part of both Sue and Chris. Then, most uncannily of all, Sue discovers the nefarious plot when she feels the rope twitch under her hand as she leans against the side of the prom stage—the rope that runs up to the bucket of pig's blood and down to Chris, who is nervously waiting to pull it. Thus, it is as though Sue, too, is holding that rope in her hand, strangely complicit in the crime against Carrie.

What sense does this make? Certainly, Sue played a key role in getting Carrie to the prom, and Sue fails to save Carrie when Miss Collins drags Sue away from the stage before she can blow the whistle on Chris. So Sue is an unwitting contributor to—and an unsuccessful preventer of—Carrie's demise. Yet there is more to the matter than this. As noted above with regard to Sue's manipulation and subterfuge, there is more of Chris in Sue, more of the "bad girl" in the "good," than Sue seems prepared to admit. And this is a problem because a character who doesn't know herself well enough, a character with too much self-doubt, is one who, since she suspects her own motives, may hesitate to act quickly enough in favor of the good when the time comes to take action. The excruciatingly drawn-out slow motion in which Sue discovers her own hand on the rope connected to the pig's blood, and in which Sue struggles to realize that it is Chris's hand—not Sue's own—that is maliciously holding that rope, suggests that Sue takes too long to differentiate herself from Chris, too long to confirm the "good girl" in herself and to take action accordingly.

Sue's moral failure is compounded by Miss Collins, who prevents Sue from acting when she does try to save Carrie because Miss Collins suspects Sue's motives, believing that one part of Sue may wish Carrie harm. An earlier dialogue exchange between Miss Collins and Sue is revealing of the teacher's suspicions but also of Sue's potential doubt regarding her own motives. After Sue claims that she had Tommy ask Carrie to the prom because Sue "thought it would be a good thing for Carrie," Miss Collins counters by saying, "Come on, Sue. We're not that stupid. Neither is Carrie." "Maybe not," Sue says; "I don't know." Sue's rebuttal is weak, suggesting uncertainties about herself and even the possibility that others are right to mistrust her motives. Sue's subsequently strong assertion of her good intentions toward Carrie—"We're not trying to hurt her, Miss Collins; we're trying to help her!"—comes across as more than a little desperate, as if Sue were trying to convince herself.

It's no accident that so many of this film's viewers have come away with the sense that Sue was somehow complicit in the plot against Carrie. As we have seen from the examples above, the film itself works to give this impression. It is interesting to compare Sue's discovery of the rope leading to the bucket of pig's blood with the scene where Colonel Nicholson (Alec Guinness) discovers the wire that leads to the bomb in *The Bridge on the River Kwai*, a favorite film of De Palma's and a key inspiration for this particular scene in *Carrie*. One part of Nicholson is proud of the bridge that he and his fellow prisoners of war built, and so he wants to prevent it from being blown up. But another part of him is a British officer who realizes that the bridge must be destroyed or it will further the enemy's war effort. Riven by mixed motives, overcome by self-doubt, Nicholson hesitates at the crucial moment, uncertain how to act. Like Nicholson with the wire leading to the bomb, Sue hesitates when it comes to the rope and the bucket of pig's blood, not sure enough about herself to decisively distance herself from Chris, whose hand is also on the rope. It could be argued that, if Sue had been able to more quickly resolve the "good girl"/"bad girl" split within herself in favor of the good, she might have acted in time to save Carrie.

Sue's motives have been hard for viewers—and for Sue herself—to discern. Is it possible that she shows up at the prom not only to see Carrie triumph, but also because one part of Sue *is* jealous, as Miss Collins suspects? After all, Carrie gets to go to the prom in Sue's place, to dance with Tommy, and to be crowned prom queen. Interestingly, Amy Irving (Sue) actually dated William Katt (Tommy) in high school the year before working on this film. (The photo of the two of them together displayed by Sue's mother in her home is an actual photo from that time, and Sue's mother is played by Irving's actual mother.) We think of "bad girl" Chris as the envious one, but could jealousy reside as well within "good girl" Sue? Irving has said that, during the shoot, "there was a lot of competition" between herself and Nancy Allen (Chris) over "who's going to get one of these two guys in the sack first? They ruled out William Katt because I had already dated him. So John [Travolta] was my hook. And man, I gave it a good shot."[23] Irving (Sue) thus tried to bed Travolta, who plays Chris's boyfriend, Billy, in the film. Irving also tried to date De Palma, who set her up with Steven Spielberg instead, which eventually led to their marriage (1985–89). It was Allen who began a relationship with De Palma. On their first date, he was editing the film's oral sex scene between Chris (Allen) and Billy (Travolta). Was De Palma jealous? He and Allen would go on to marry in 1979. "Basically, there was a lot of casting going on: casting of films and of life," as Irving put it.[24]

If "good girl" Sue and "good mother" Miss Collins both have some bad inhabiting them, their evil counterparts—Chris and Carrie's mother—can be seen as having at least some good in them, an element which De Palma emphasizes through casting. Before this film, Allen had only played "girl next door" roles like that of Sue, "the sweet, helpful girl." According to Allen, De Palma deliberately cast her against type: "I think a lot of it was the fact that I looked so sweet, and those nasty words coming out of my mouth help keep the audience off balance."[25] An "off balance" audience is one that is unsure what to think of a character, who has the potential for good or evil and who may sometimes even get the two mixed up.

When De Palma stresses that Chris "thinks Carrie White is a cretin and a fool who deserves everything she gets" and that Chris "thinks that she was irrationally punished by [Miss Collins] and looks at it as harassment,"[26] he does so as a way of pointing out that "the whole good and evil thing is very relative."[27] This is not to say that there is no distinction between good and evil. Rather, it is to insist on understanding and empathy for the other person's point of view. From Chris's perspective, *she* is now in Carrie's former position, having been abjected by Miss Collins's violent slap and excluded from the prom, ostracized from society as Carrie had been and forced into the position of envying the more popular girl.

As with Chris, De Palma calls attention to a similar character complexity in Carrie's mother by means of unconventional casting. Although he had originally planned to present the "bad mother" Margaret as dour and matronly—a "dark" and "hard Gothic" type like Mrs. Danvers in Hitchcock's *Rebecca*—De Palma instead chose to cast Piper Laurie, whose luxuriant hair and husky voice make her seem "very young" and "sensual."[28] In this way, De Palma makes it clear that Margaret is herself a victim, a woman whose loving instinct has been perverted by patriarchal religion's view of sex as a sin. Though she goes about it in the wrong way, keeping Carrie ignorant of her body and trying to prevent her from having any contact with boys such as Tommy at the prom, De Palma wants us to understand that Margaret—from *her* point of view—does have "positive motivations" and the "best intentions,"[29] wanting to protect Carrie from lust ("After the blood, come the boys") and scorn ("They're all going to laugh at you").

Of course, the character who manifests the most significant split self is Carrie, the "good girl" gone "bad," the victim turned avenger. It is fitting that Sissy Spacek tried out for "all the parts—she played Sue Snell [the "good girl"], Chris Hargenson [the "bad girl"], Carrie. She played everybody—and played them all really well," according to De Palma,[30] who described Spacek as having "a wider range than any actress I know," adding that "she's a phantom, with a mysterious way of slipping into a role."[31] Prior to De Palma's film, Spacek had appeared in *Prime Cut* as a naked woman confined to a pig pen to be auctioned off like meat to the highest male bidder—a part that strangely resonates with her role as a victim of pig's blood in *Carrie*. (And note that, in *Carrie*'s pig-slaughtering scene, one character comments that he "went out with a girl. . . . She was a real pig!") By contrast, in *Badlands*, Spacek played a young woman who joins up with a serial murderer on a killing spree—as if in anticipation of Carrie's mass murder at the prom.

Spacek, who had worked with her husband Jack Fisk on the art direction for *Phantom of the Paradise*, had lost out for the lead role of Phoenix in that film, and for a time it seemed as though De Palma was going to pass her over again. "It infuriated me," Spacek remembered, "and I thought, 'Screw him, I'm going to get this part.' Suddenly I felt like the underdog, which was very Carrie-esque."[32] For the day of her screen test, Spacek put on "a pale blue sailor dress that my mother had someone make for me when I was in seventh grade"[33] and proved that she could play the victim—in order to be victorious at winning the starring role! (It should be noted that Spacek had been homecoming queen of her high school senior class, so she was no stranger to being voted most popular.)

At first the queen of the prom and then the group's scapegoat (or pig), Carrie's self-image goes from being the apex of admiration to suffering the nadir of scorn. Right after she succeeds at seeing herself as beautiful in Miss Collins's eyes, the trauma of the pig's blood causes Carrie to revert to her mother's view of her as an ugly sinner. With her mother's voice ("They're all going to laugh at you") ringing in her head, Carrie imagines that she sees everyone at the prom, including Miss Collins, scorning her with laughter.

The trauma of abjection provokes a psychic splitting in Carrie whereby the victim of shame becomes an enraged avenger. The screen literally splits down the middle as Carrie, formerly the object of others' shaming gaze, turns their scornful look back on them. At various moments during the prom massacre, Carrie's stare from one side of the screen cues violent cuts to the suffering of characters on the screen's other side. Carrie, standing to the right of the split-screen, shoots a glance leftward where the gym doors slam shut, trapping the people inside. Then Carrie, sliding to the left side of the image, telekinetically pops the prom's blue lights at image right, flooding all her classmates with red light, much as she was covered in blood. After deploying her gaze so that a fire hose slams students backward with its explosive spray, Carrie looks from screen left over to the right side of the image, where water from the fire hose short-circuits the sound equipment, electrocuting two men on stage who jerk spasmodically in pain, much as Carrie herself was spectacularly "pranked." (De Palma kept telling Spacek to "open your eyes wider,"[34] in order to emphasize the vengeful force of Carrie's gaze as she stares out from a face covered in blood.)

Carrie, the victim turned victor, is sometimes at screen left and sometimes at screen right in relation to her victor-turned-victim classmates, and there are moments when Carrie occupies both sides of the split-screen, as if the avenger were gazing upon herself as victim, or vice versa. If only Carrie could have *seen herself* and recognized that she was being driven by extreme emotion, by a rage born of shame, she might have gained conscious mastery over her actions and been able to stop. But, as De Palma has noted about Carrie's telekinesis, "I wanted to use it as an extension of her emotions—her feelings that were completely translated into actions, that only erupted when she got terribly excited, terribly anxious and terribly sad . . . almost like *Forbidden Planet* where the Id monster is an intellectual man murdering people because he subconsciously wants to";[35] "It's out of her control. . . . It's very unconscious and it's very emotional."[36] With her psyche split between victimization and vengeance, between receiving looks that wound and giving wounding looks, Carrie is not able to stand outside her emotional predicament and take a conscious look at herself.

But we as viewers can, because the split-screen not only allows us to *look with* Carrie as she turns her vengeful gaze upon her oppressors, it also enables us to *look at* Carrie from the outside, to gain some critical distance from her wrath, to understand her divided self. Curiously, De Palma has come to regret his use of split-screen for the prom sequence, arguing that this technique "doesn't have enough visceral energy for action sequences" since "it removes you too much";[37] "The audience wanted to go with her destruction. They want a basic Sam Peckinpah sort of sock, hit. But suddenly, you're distracting them. . . . My mistake in *Carrie* was that you can't hit the heavy emotional things in split-screen."[38] Yet De Palma was right not simply to pander to the audience's base desire for vengeance. Rather than merely suturing us to Carrie's gaze so that we enjoy her retributive violence in conventional filmic fashion, De Palma employs the split-screen as a distancing effect. At his best, De Palma realizes that the viewer's instinctive identification with Carrie must be countered by a morally conscious repudiation of her destructive rage, which only continues the cycle of violence and revenge.

If it is too easy to glory in Carrie's revenge, it is also too easy to dismiss her thereafter as a mere monster. In Sue's dream at the film's end, when Carrie reaches out from the grave to grab Sue's arm with a bloody hand, Sue repels her as she would a monster from hell. In this, Sue repeats her earlier pushing away of Carrie when the girl had bloodily beseeched her in the high school locker room. Sue abjects the other in a desperate attempt to deny her own weakness and vulnerability. She wakes screaming from her nightmare to be held in her mother's embrace, but her mother's arms do not seem to comfort her.

Carrie, too, had reached out to *her* mother for solace, but Margaret stabbed her with a knife. The religiously repressed Margaret associated Carrie with the sin of lust. Rather than accept her own desires ("He took me, and I liked it; I liked it," a horrified Margaret shudders), she scapegoated Carrie for them, taking a knife to her as if she could thereby cut them out of her own body.

Now Sue has demonized and repelled Carrie, much as Carrie's mother did. Will Sue's mother do the same to her? Carrie's bloodily beseeching hand haunts because it is a reminder that, until we learn to respond with compassion to others' weaknesses, we must fear that they will react with aversion to our own. As De Palma has said about that hand, "it's the idea of guilt, the guilt will always be with her" as Sue keeps "remembering Carrie coming back to torment her for the rest of her life for her complicity in her tragedy."[39]

It is interesting that the main theme music from *Sisters* plays as Carrie's bloody hand reaches out for Sue. At the end of *Sisters*, Grace's mother had tried to comfort her after her nightmarish ordeal, but the Raggedy Ann doll nearby was a reminder that Grace would never be able to sever ties with her "sister" Danielle, any more than Danielle could from Dominique. Similarly, there is a Raggedy Ann doll in the room with Sue, who will be forever bound to Carrie, as Carrie was to her mother. The bleeding hand will haunt until we recognize it as our own.

There are some significant connections between key aspects of *Carrie* and De Palma's own life. Sue's sight of the bleeding Carrie can be compared to the young De Palma's traumatic witnessing of the bloody bodies on his surgeon father's operating table. In this defining moment, De Palma, like Sue, has an awareness of his body's own vulnerability forced upon him, particularly when his father "cut off a patient's leg and then gave it to me!"[40] (Later in his life, De Palma himself would be shot in the leg by a policeman.)

If Carrie's mother tells her that "I should have given you to God when you were born," De Palma's own mother has said that "Brian was a mistake," the result of an unplanned pregnancy that came when she "didn't really want to have another child."[41] Like Carrie, De Palma felt manipulated by his mother into taking an extremely negative view of his father for having left her for another woman, only later coming to see how much "my mother twisted everything" in order to get De Palma to side with her against his father, who was represented as "the bad one" and solely to "blame."[42] Carrie's mother tries to convince her that "Satan . . . carried [her father] off," but Carrie retorts that he merely "ran away with a woman, momma. Everybody knows that." Like Carrie, the young De Palma was shut up in the house alone with his mother, who gradually succumbed to a kind of self-destructive madness. As De Palma has said, with his father gone, "life with my mother was a true nightmare."[43]

Ultimately, De Palma was able to save his mother from suicide and to gain some critical distance from her distorted views, but it's possible to envision a different outcome. It seems significant that De Palma often refers to books and films about the perils of incestuous closeness, such as Luchino Visconti's *The Damned*, where the lead character "sleeps with his mother—she completely destroys him, and he completely destroys her. Totally perverse people. A totally corrosive family."[44] After her fanatical mother stabs her, Carrie has her crucified with kitchen implements, the two of them sinking together into madness and mutual destruction. The end of *Carrie* is the nightmare scenario of how De Palma's own relationship with his mother might have ended.

Carrie, De Palma's tenth feature film, was his first Hollywood hit. Made for a mere $1.8 million, the film ended up grossing more than $33 million at the U.S. box office alone. Nevertheless, De Palma felt that the movie could have been much more profitable if the studio had not been "embarrassed by it":[45] "I was very unhappy with the way the studio sold *Carrie*. They dumped it in Halloween and treated it like a B picture—just grab the [fast] money and that's it. I'd wave my reviews at them, saying 'This is an important movie.' And it fell on deaf ears."[46] De Palma was proud of the film, believing that he had "put everything into *Carrie*: I had the romantic story between Tommy Ross and Carrie White; I had all the visual suspense elements, and the terror elements; and I was using everything I knew, including comedy and improvisation, from all the other pictures I had made."[47] One sign of the film's critical acclaim was that both Sissy Spacek and Piper Laurie were nominated for Academy Awards—something practically unheard of for actresses in a horror film.

De Palma's film *was* profitable, but it did not gross nearly as much as Steven Spielberg's *Jaws* or George Lucas's *Star Wars*. "It's frustrating," De Palma said, "to have a success and not a blockbuster. I'm surrounded by associates who have monster hits."[48] Particularly galling was the fact that De Palma and Lucas had held joint auditions when they were casting for *Carrie* and *Star Wars*. (Amy Irving [Sue] had even been considered for the role of Princess Leia, and William Katt [Tommy] for the part of Luke Skywalker.) With his next film, *The Fury*, a kind of sequel to *Carrie* about two telekinetic teens, De Palma was hoping to rival or even surpass the achievements of Lucas and Spielberg.

CHAPTER 11

The Fury (1978)

Peter (Kirk Douglas), a secret agent for the U.S. government who is on the verge of retirement, is vacationing with his teenage son, Robin (Andrew Stevens), at a Middle Eastern beach resort. Suddenly, a band of ghutra-clad Arabs launches a guerilla attack, and Robin looks on helplessly as they fire machine guns at his father and then blow him up when he attempts to escape in a boat. However, unbeknownst to Robin, the attack was actually ordered by Peter's colleague, Childress (John Cassavetes), who wants the boy's father out of the way so that Robin's psychic abilities can be developed as a weapon in the Cold War against China and the Soviet Union.

But Peter survives and, with the help of Hester (Carrie Snodgress), a nurse at Chicago's Paragon Institute for paranormal research, makes contact with another gifted teenager, Gillian (Amy Irving), who has empathetic visions connecting her with her "psychic twin" Robin. First, Gillian "sees" Robin run up a staircase and fall out a window while trying to escape from the Paragon Institute, and then she imagines his pain and terror as experiments are conducted on him to increase his telekinetic abilities and his aggression. Gillian escapes from Paragon with Hester's aid, but when Peter shoots the driver of a car pursuing Gillian, it swerves and hits Hester, who dies by crashing through its windshield.

Using her psychic link, Gillian leads Peter to where Robin is being held, but the boy attacks his father, causing both of them to fall through an upstairs window. As Robin dangles off the edge of a roof, held only by his father's hand, Peter attempts to pull him to safety, but when Robin claws at his face, Peter lets go and the boy falls to his death. Peter then commits suicide, throwing himself off the roof to join his son on the ground below. With Robin gone, Childress moves on to Gillian in an effort to exploit her paranormal powers, but, not fooled by his "good father" act, she uses her telekinetic force to literally blow him up in an explosion of blood and body parts.

Like *Carrie*, *The Fury* revolves around several scenes of traumatic witness-ing.[1] After seeing Peter shot and bleeding and then (apparently) blown up, Robin responds by denying his father's and his own vulnerability and by trying to become an invincible avenger. Childress feeds Robin's fury by making him watch films of the attack, thus manipulating the boy's paranoid and aggressive response. Unlike with Alex (Malcolm McDowell) in *A Clockwork Orange*, who is induced to become pacific, Robin's film-conditioning is designed to whip him into a frenzy of retributive violence. As one result, Robin pursues ven-geance at an indoor amusement park by telekinetically causing a Ferris wheel ride to careen out of control, crashing a car full of Arabs through a restaurant window (in an homage to the runaway carousel scene in Hitchcock's *Strangers on a Train*).

But Robin's father was not attacked by Arabs, by some "enemy other"; rather, it was Childress, Peter's colleague and friend inside his own government agency, who staged the attack so that Arabs would be blamed. Though mistaken as originating from outside, the attack came from within. In this way, the film sends an anti-racist message, as it also does by mentioning the United Nations in an early scene. Childress, by having staged and filmed the attack in order to fool and manipulate Robin toward greater aggression, is a kind of evil director (played by real-life director Cassavetes). He is the opposite of De Palma, who exposes this use of film as manipulation and whose own movie works against racist scapegoating of the "other." (De Palma himself even donned one of the Arab robes during filming, as a protection against the unexpected cold.)

Striving for invincibility because he is so vulnerable, Robin develops a God complex that is fueled by his feelings of inferiority. As Childress has the boy "treated like a prince" or "royalty," catering to his every whim to puff up his pride in his psychic powers, Robin is induced into a state of paranoid compet-itiveness, compelled to lord it over everyone and everything. The competitive spirit (swimming, soccer) first encouraged in him by Peter has been pushed by Childress to a point of unfocused, total aggression. Having wanted to develop in Robin "the power of an atomic reactor," Childress has instead "pushed him too far" and made the boy "quite unstable," like "an atomic bomb" that could go off at any time, as one character warns. Indeed, while pole-vaulting, Robin flies into a rage at his own inability to perform superhuman feats, to will him-self into omnipotence. He gets violently jealous when other men show any attention to Susan (Fiona Lewis), the woman he is sleeping with, and he is envious of his "psychic twin," Gillian, fearing that she might have superior powers that would make *her* the favored one and his replacement.

Robin's paranoid aggression is so extreme that, when Peter does come to rescue him, the boy no longer recognizes him as a loving father. Instead, having used his powers to levitate himself, Robin looks down at Peter from on high—a position of apparent omnipotence that is really a cover for fears of impotence—and then attacks him as he would an enemy, causing both of them to crash through a window. Even when his father reaches down to save him as he is dangling off the roof, Robin still claws at Peter's face, leading his father to drop him to his death on the ground below. If Robin could levitate himself before, how can he die from a fall now? The fall is a metaphor, indicating that he is not all-powerful, that he is still dependent on others for survival. Robin dies as a result of his godlike hubris and his paranoid competitiveness.

De Palma's interest in the perils of pride and over-competitiveness can be traced back to his childhood relationship with Bruce and Bart. "My brothers and I grew up in a competitive environment: it was about who would be the best, 24/7!" said De Palma, adding that "when I think back on it, this competition existed only because my parents were there to stir it up."[2]

Like Robin, De Palma's brother Bruce was gifted—with an extraordinary mind for science, and he, too, was deified, resulting in an isolation from society and a kind of hubristic madness: "All his life, Bruce was considered to be a genius by my parents. . . . They literally treated him like a god, which had tragic consequences for his life. Once he was on his own, he was never able to fit in anywhere; he could never manage to connect with anyone because he didn't have anything human left anymore. He had such a high opinion of himself that he ended up losing his reason and went off to an island in New Zealand where he lived cut off from the world."[3] A brilliant physicist with a degree from MIT, Bruce invented an "N-machine" which he claimed could "release the 'free energy' latent in the space all around us" and thus "help end the world's dangerous dependence on supplies of oil, gas, and other polluting fuels."[4] However, as the scientific establishment refused to credit his research, Bruce became increasingly embattled and aggrieved as well as isolated and paranoid: "I have had my inventions confiscated by other groups. . . . Later on other groups tried to manipulate me and control me. . . . Yes, I have been threatened for my life."[5] One wonders if De Palma had Bruce in mind when a character in *The Fury* says that Robin, with his special gifts, could have been welcomed by people as "their magician, their prophet, their great healer," but "what a culture can't assimilate, it destroys."

It is interesting to compare Bruce's claim that a rotating gyroscope can display antigravity characteristics with Robin's ability to levitate himself and to lift and spin other persons and objects. It is also curious that the vein that bulges when Robin exercises his mental powers is located on his forehead, the same place where Bruce had a prominent birthmark. (Given his propensity to think beyond the bounds of normal science, it's perhaps not surprising that Bruce was also known to have experimented with mind-altering drugs.)

We have seen that Robin attacks Peter in the end rather than allowing himself to be rescued. Since this may strike some viewers as implausible, it may be worth exploring some additional reasons for this turn of events. It could be that Robin experienced Peter's (apparent) death as a form of abandonment and that, despite his father's tearful protestation that "I never gave up, I kept looking for you," Robin is still filled with an irrational rage toward him. It is also possible that Robin has lost faith in fatherhood itself. During the guerilla attack in which Robin thinks he sees Peter killed, it is Childress who shields Robin's body with his own, seeming to protect the boy from the force of the onslaught. From this moment on, Childress becomes a substitute father to Robin, at first seeming to provide for his every need. But, increasingly, Childress's kindness is revealed to be a cover for cruel self-interest as Robin is subjected to film-conditioning and other psycho-medical experiments to heighten his aggressive powers. A "bad father" has thus been surreptitiously substituted for a good one, as if what Robin gradually discovers in Childress are the flaws that he couldn't see in his idealized father Peter, so it is perhaps no wonder that, when Peter finally appears again at the end, Robin has trouble telling the good and the bad fathers apart.

When an agonized Peter asks, "What have they done to you?" he calls attention to how much Robin has been made over in the image of the "bad father," Childress, whose pernicious influence the boy has had to suffer while Peter could not get to him. De Palma has spoken of the John Ford western *Two Rode Together*, in which a sheriff (James Stewart) and a cavalry officer (Richard Widmark) "go out and find these kids grabbed by the Indians. Their families want them back, but they're like savages. . . . One guy's kid tries to kill him because he's a total savage."[6] Again, in *The Fury*, De Palma brings this critique of savagery *home*, for the corrupting force is not some racial "other," like "Indians" or Arabs, but an agent inside the U.S. government itself, a man masquerading as a good father—Childress. (Childress in effect kidnaps Robin from Peter, much as Bob kidnapped Amy/Sandra from Michael in *Obsession*, but she is able to recover from the negative influence of a "bad father" substitute and reunite with her real father, overcoming her rage at him, whereas Robin is not.)

Finally, in terms of bringing the critique home, we should consider whether some part of the fault may reside within Robin himself. *The Fury* begins with a "friendly" contest between father and son over who is the best swimmer, followed by some "good-natured" arguing over who actually won, so an undercurrent of Oedipal rivalry is present in the film right from the start. Could it be that, when Robin then witnesses the (apparent) death of his father, the trauma of this sight lies not just in its nightmarish undesirability, but in its hidden wish fulfillment? The "death" of his father reveals a split within Robin in being what he consciously least—and secretly most—desires. It is as though one part of Robin has willed (telekinetically?) his father's "death," while another part of the boy looks on in agony, unable to prevent it.

Having eliminated his father from the competition, Robin then goes on to have a relationship with a mother figure, Dr. Susan Charles, a beautiful older woman who not only provides him with medical care but also crosses the line to give him sexual attention as well. We recall that the young De Palma, having gathered evidence of his father's adultery and precipitated his parents' separation, then had his mother all to himself: "This crisis allowed me to resolve my Oedipus complex. I had removed my father, and my mother was mine and mine alone!"[7] However, De Palma came to regret his over-promixity to his mother, who, he believed, distorted the truth and used his love for her to manipulate him, much as Robin feels lied to and manipulated by Susan. Eventually, Robin kills Susan in a horrifyingly sadistic manner (he lifts, spins, and exsanguinates her), and this is at least partly due to jealousy—the fear that she might replace him with another man, the way he "replaced" his own father. So, when Robin attacks Peter in the end, it could be because the boy's viciously competitive side, once mostly latent and overruled by love and conscience, has now become the dominant part of him, leading him to enact the murderous attack on his father that had only been a repressed fantasy at the film's beginning.

As Robin was forced to view his father's "death" at the start of the film, Peter himself is subjected to a traumatic witnessing when he sees his beloved Hester hit by a car and crash through its windshield. Not only must he watch helplessly, unable to prevent the collision, but Peter must also confront his own partial responsibility for his lover's death. It was he who first put Hester's life in danger by asking her to help Gillian escape from the Paragon Institute, and it is Peter who shoots the man (one of Childress's henchmen) behind the wheel of the car pursuing Gillian, causing it to swerve into Hester. Viewers who would absolve Peter of any fault for Hester's death, seeing it merely as an ironic quirk of fate that in no way impugns Peter's excellent character, would do well to consider what De Palma presents directly after the collision: Peter fires his pistol again and again and again into another one of Childress's henchmen and then stands in a daze with his gun pointed at Gillian. Peter's overkill represents a desperate attempt to scapegoat the other man for Hester's death so that he will not have to blame himself, despite the fact that *he* exposed her to danger, as he then does to Gillian.

From the film's beginning, De Palma has presented Peter as a morally problematic hero, a man of mixed motives: Is he out to save his son Robin or to seek vengeance on Childress for having betrayed him? Is Peter driven by love or revenge? After being shot in the arm by Childress's "Arab" guerillas, Peter himself picks up a machine gun and fires at his former partner, later commenting, "If you see Childress, ask him if it was worth his arm. . . . I killed it." From that moment on, Childress—whose dead arm continues to "hurt"—and Peter seem locked in a mirror-like combat, each trying to kill the other in an attempt to overcome a sense of wounded masculinity. Childress took Peter's son, and Peter took Childress's arm. Peter sometimes seems to think of his son as an extension of himself (like an arm), with the quest for Robin being more about restoring Peter's own pride than about saving another person. Kirk Douglas was cast in the role of Peter because De Palma wanted "the kind of driven, obsessive character he plays so well. At one point I said to [producer] Frank Yablans, 'We need a Kirk Douglas type.' And he said, 'Why don't we get Kirk Douglas?'"[8]

It is creepily telling that Peter pretends to be a heavy-breathing obscene phone caller ("I want your body, baby") to avoid a phone tap and set up a secret assignation with Hester, because there is a part of him that is indeed using her: for sex and for her ability to get Gillian to lead him to Robin—and Childress. Intent on his mission, Peter pays little heed to the extent to which he is placing Hester in harm's way. When he sights down the barrel of his gun at Childress's henchman driving that car, Peter *fails to see* the effect of his plan on others. He *fails to consider* the tragic consequences that his "driven, obsessive" quest may have for Hester, and for this he is morally culpable.

To his credit, Peter does acknowledge his guilt for Hester's death ("I killed her; I knew I would the first time I said hello and conned her into helping me") and, once he has gotten Robin's location via Gillian's psychic link, Peter does try to dissuade her from coming with him, though she insists. However, after he and Gillian are captured at the house where Robin is being held, Peter leaps upon Childress, trying to strangle his archenemy, despite the fact that this act of rage could get himself killed and thus prevent him from saving his son.

More altruistically, Peter does risk his own life when he tries to pull Robin up from dangling off the roof, dropping him only when the boy claws at his face. But the very fact that De Palma has Peter drop his son is revealing. In *Saboteur*, which is one of the Hitchcock films with "dangling" scenes that inspired *The Fury*, Barry (Robert Cummings) reaches down a hand to try to save Fry (Norman Lloyd), who is hanging off the side of the Statue of Liberty. Even though Fry is a heinous villain (a Nazi spy and a saboteur, a traitor who has turned against his own country), Barry does not drop him; instead, Fry falls to his death when his sleeve, which Barry is holding, comes unstitched. By contrast, Peter actually drops Robin, who has turned against him but is still his own son. If Peter's act cannot be condemned as roundly as the self-serving Childress does ("Peter could have saved Robin; instead, he let him go—he deliberately killed his own son"), it still points to a fault in the father who had only minutes before told his boy that "I never gave up [on you]."

After Robin falls to his death, Peter commits suicide by heaving himself off the roof, apparently having given up on both Robin and himself. This resignation is rendered even more tragic by the fact that, by killing himself, Peter now leaves Gillian entirely unprotected against Childress's nefarious designs on her. It is interesting that, prior to this, De Palma had shown Peter dropping *Gillian* after reaching down a hand to try to lift her over a wall to safety. Despite Peter's former reassurance to her ("We're all [Robin, Gillian, and Peter] going to be okay—that's a promise"), Peter fails them both in the end, along with himself.

The third traumatized witness in the film, besides Robin and Peter, is Gillian. In fact, she is a kind of meta-witness who, at various moments, sees what they see, much as we do as viewers of the film. One character compares the "alpha" state in which Gillian has her psychic visions to one where you "visualize sitting in an empty theater in front of a blank screen and let that screen fill your mind."

In one scene, when Gillian almost trips on the staircase of the Paragon Institute and Dr. Jim McKeever (Charles Durning) reaches out a hand to keep her from falling, the contact with him prompts Gillian to have a vision of an event from his recent past. As the camera arcs around her, a moving image like something projected onto a blank screen takes the place of her present surroundings to reveal a time when Robin ran up that same staircase, with McKeever in pursuit. When the boy reached the top of the stairs, he fell backwards through a window, even as McKeever was reaching out toward him. McKeever cut his hand on the broken window glass, and now Gillian's hold on McKeever's hand causes the scar from that cut to open and bleed again.

While McKeever was in some ways a "good father" to Robin, trying to help the boy, the doctor also—following Childress's orders—had Robin drugged, experimented on, and virtually imprisoned within the institute. The doctor's "healing hand" actually did considerable harm. Gillian's vision reveals that, rather than reaching out to save his patient, McKeever's hand actually drove the boy to his fall. The cut that reopens, pouring out blood, is the truth that McKeever cannot deny about his complicity in Robin's fall (much as Childress's dead and still "hurting" arm is the truth about his role in the attack on Peter). Through her vision, Gillian "sees" that the kindly doctor whose hand reaches out to prevent her from falling on the staircase may in fact cause her harm, just as he did to Robin.

In another scene, when McKeever's colleague Dr. Ellen Lindstrom (Carol Rossen) is asking Gillian questions about her "psychic twin" Robin, ostensibly out of a desire to help but really to advance her own research interests, Gillian

grabs Ellen's hand and makes it bleed while having visions of the pain and terror caused to Robin by the experiments that Dr. Susan Charles is conducting
on him. In this way, Ellen is not allowed to pretend that she is just an objective
witness or a concerned doctor but is instead made to feel the pain she is causing her research subjects such as Gillian. Like Grace, the journalist investigating the Siamese twins Danielle and Dominique in *Sisters*, Ellen is forced to
realize her own involvement in the suffering she witnesses.

Gillian inadvertently causes Ellen's hand, ears, and eyes to bleed. Later, to
make his own doctor feel the pain that she has caused him, Robin deliberately
lifts, spins, and exsanguinates Susan, which Gillian "sees" happen as part of her
psychic link, crying out, "You're killing her! Stop it!" At this point in the film,
Gillian remains an empathetic witness. Having sensed Robin's suffering as a
result of Ellen's experiments, Gillian understands why he strikes back at his
cruel doctor, but she also commiserates with Ellen's pain, crying out for Robin
to stop.

The traumatic sights that Gillian sees are registered as a call for compassion, not revenge. One of Gillian's earliest visions had been of an unknown
woman's sightless, bleeding eyes—a vision that turns out to be a precognition
of the dead, upturned face of Susan after Robin has murdered her, but it could
have been Gillian's own face. Seeing with sympathy means recognizing your
own bodily connection with others in terms of a shared vulnerability and
mortality. As with Lydia (Jessica Tandy), who discovers the pecked-out eyes
of a dead farmer in *The Birds*, what Gillian sees is her own potential sightless-
ness, the "voyeur" face to face with her own vulnerability.

Yet Gillian does ultimately wreak revenge. When the "bad father" Childress
attempts to seduce her in order to use her powers for his own ends (much as
the "bad mother" Ellen seduced Robin), Gillian kisses Childress's eyes, causing
them to bleed and go blind. Then, as the camera cuts in quickly to tighter and
tighter shots of her own eyes, she telekinetically kills him with her look, blowing up his body in a spectacular explosion of bloody bits. Rather than gazing
with even a modicum of sympathy or understanding, Gillian turns her eyes
into a weapon, obliterating the other's vision and form. She blows up Childress
at the end, just as he blew up Peter (or so it seemed) in the boat explosion at
the start of the film. She thus becomes a mirror image of her own enemy.

Earlier, as Robin lay dying on the ground after his fall, he gazed into Gillian's eyes, which took on the same icy blue look that his had had, as if Robin
were transferring his vengeful wrath to her. It is interesting that Peter throws
himself off the roof *after* this moment. Could it be that seeing Gillian tainted
by his son's vengefulness is what confirmed Peter in his despair, leading him
to believe that there was really nothing left to live for? The transference of
Robin's icy blue look is a metaphor for the terrible effect that witnessing has

finally had on Gillian. As with Robin, the fearful impact of all she has seen has finally turned her from compassion to defensive loathing, from empathy to the most violent revenge.

It is interesting to compare *The Fury* to Alfred Bester's 1953 science fiction novel *The Demolished Man*, which De Palma had wanted to film ever since he first read it as a boy. (In fact, De Palma had co-authored a screenplay for *The Demolished Man* with John Farris, his co-scenarist on *The Fury*, and De Palma considered *The Fury* to be a way to "start practicing" the "interweaving storylines"⁹ and expensive special effects that would be necessary for the Bester film, which he hoped the studio would fund as his next project.)

De Palma has described *The Demolished Man* as "a psychic thriller—an Oedipal murder in a telepathic society,"¹⁰ and, though the hero of the novel does not commit incest, in the film version "he is going to be sleeping with his mother."¹¹ We have seen how Robin may unconsciously desire his father Peter's death and how the boy then goes on to sleep with his "mother" Susan. In *The Demolished Man*, a character named Reich is trying to gain a monopoly on power by using telepaths to further his own interests, much as Childress attempts to do with psychics in *The Fury*. Reich shares a special connection with his telepathic sister Barbara, imagining the two of them "linked side to side like Siamese twins," much as Robin is linked with his "psychic twin" Gillian. When Reich kills his father, D'Courtney, Barbara is the traumatized witness of it, and others attempt to use her psychic link to get to Reich, in the same way that Peter has Gillian guide him to Robin after she, linked with the boy, has "seen" the death of his father. *The Demolished Man* ends when multiple telepaths link minds and use their combined power to bring about the "demolition" of Reich for his murderous grab at total power, which is similar to Gillian's deployment of Robin's and her own telekinetic wrath to explode Childress.

However, there is one crucial difference: the enlightened telepaths of the future—the novel is set in the year 2100—do not kill Reich. They "demolish" his mind, but only to build it back up again; they show understanding of his mental illness and treat him with psychotherapy: "Three or four hundred years ago, cops used to catch people like Reich just to kill him. Capital punishment, they called it. . . . But it doesn't make sense. If a man's got the talent and guts to buck society, he's obviously above average. You want to hold on to him. You straighten him out and turn him into a plus value. Why throw him away?"¹² Bester's novel ends with the utopian vision that one day people will be able to use their mental powers to see sympathetically, to recognize their shared bond beyond the fear of difference: "*We [telepaths] see the truth you cannot see . . . That there is nothing in man but love and faith, courage and kindness, generosity and sacrifice. All else is only the barrier of your blindness. One day we'll all be mind to mind and heart to heart.*"¹³

The Fury ends with Gillian using her higher powers for the lowest form of revenge, psychically exploding Childress as though she were a mythological fury or goddess of vengeance tearing him apart. *The Fury* ends with the violent impact of her pitiless gaze, her look of utter condemnation aimed at the "monstrous other." It is the least enlightened form of seeing imaginable.

Shot for $5.5 million, *The Fury* had the largest cast and the biggest budget of any De Palma film to date. Though it pulled in modest profits, grossing $11 million, the film was far from being the blockbuster hit De Palma had wanted it to be. The reason for its less-than-stellar performance remains something of a mystery. It could be that, as with the horror musical comedy *Phantom of the Paradise*, audiences were confused by *The Fury*'s mixture of teen horror and espionage thriller. Certainly, when De Palma would later confine himself to the latter genre—in *Mission: Impossible*—he would have the biggest hit of his career. It's also possible that *The Fury*, with its spy-thriller elements, was just too different from the sequel to *Carrie* that many viewers had been expecting, and the film's box office suffered as a result.

CHAPTER 12

Home Movies (1980)

When the horror/espionage thriller *The Fury* proved less successful than had been hoped, the studio withdrew its financial backing for *The Demolished Man*, the film De Palma had intended to make next. In response, the director returned to his roots and shot a loosely structured comedy called *Home Movies*, which was similar to *The Wedding Party*, *Greetings*, and *Hi, Mom!*, all made in the '60s: "I hadn't done just a straight-out comedy in a long time, just letting an ensemble do really good character acting, having them carry the movie as in my earlier pictures."[1] As Keith Gordon (star of *Home Movies*) said about De Palma, "I think, coming off the unfair critical and commercial hits he took on *The Fury*, it might have done him good to get back to making a movie for the fun and passion of it."[2]

Another sense in which the new film marked a "coming home" for De Palma was that he returned to Sarah Lawrence, the college where as a student he had gained his first filmmaking experience under mentor Wilford Leach. Now De Palma would be the mentor, giving later students some hands-on filmmaking experience, since *Home Movies* would be made by them as part of a class that De Palma was teaching on how to make a low-budget film. De Palma recalled that his speaking tours at college campuses in the late '60s had had at least one positive outcome: "I'll never forget Terry Malick saying that my touring with *Greetings* had inspired him to become a director."[3] (Malick's films include *Badlands* and *Days of Heaven*.) De Palma himself had been inspired by the great Orson Welles during the making of *Get to Know Your Rabbit*: "Welles had a lot of impact on me. I would like to have one on the next generation of directors."[4]

And, of course, it was Leach at Sarah Lawrence who had had the most direct personal and professional impact on De Palma when he was a fledgling filmmaker: "He understood me. He understood the aesthetic potential that I had and helped me realize it. From him, I learned about acting, about directing, about writing, about design, about everything."[5] So De Palma called up Leach, offering to teach Sarah Lawrence students all these various aspects of filmmaking, much as Leach had once taught him. According to De Palma, "I was, in a way, going back to my roots, working the way I used to work when I was their age—and at the same time escaping from all those industry types who can turn you inside out."[6]

A further way in which *Home Movies* marked a return to De Palma's roots was its overtly autobiographical content. Indeed, it is the most nakedly revealing film about De Palma's youthful past that we have. Asked about his childhood, De Palma once remarked, "See *Home Movies*; it's all there,"[7] adding that "it's about me, that's my family."[8] *Home Movies* is in fact a kind of home movie about the De Palmas, as is hinted during the animated opening credits when a family home transforms into a giant projector shining an image onto a screen that says, "A Brian De Palma Film." According to Nancy Allen, who was De Palma's girlfriend at the time and soon to be his wife, "the story was actually based on Brian's own life. I don't think anyone knew that at the time."[9]

Prominently depicted in the film is what we have seen as a central event in De Palma's young life, his attempt to capture on film his father's adulterous affair with a nurse in order to help his mother gain evidence for a divorce. Interviews with the cast members many years later reveal that "during the shoot, [Keith] Gordon at one point confided to [Nancy] Allen that while he liked the movie, he wondered if the spying and filming of the father was plausible. Would he really record his own father cheating? Allen thought, You have no idea, but kept that to herself."[10] Curiously, De Palma has remarked that, to this day, he doesn't know if his parents ever saw *Home Movies* because "they never said a thing to me about it."[11]

De Palma has taken the members of his own family—his adulterous father, Anthony; his depressed mother, Vivienne; his egocentric older brother, Bruce; and his feckless young self—and exaggerated each of their characteristics, in the process turning family tragedy into farce. The director has noted that giving his life story "the comic treatment is ironic since at the time that I lived these events, I frankly wasn't in a very humorous mood."[12] The comic hyperbole grants him a certain critical distance from his family members and some clarification regarding them, for the exaggeration of certain traits brings them into sharp focus and makes them stand out from what was at the time a turmoil of emotion.

Early on in the film, Denis (Keith Gordon, playing the high school-age De Palma) is discovered making out with a girl on the family couch when his mother (Mary Davenport) comes home unexpectedly. She seems to disapprove of his actions, but then his father (Vincent Gardenia) enters through a door behind him and it turns out that she had previously witnessed his father, a doctor, having sex with a woman in his hospital office. Denis's mother thus *sees him as his father*, lumping him in with other lecherous males who are "all . . . the same—hurting me, hurting your mother, ruining her life! . . . Oh, you men and your women! You, Denis, you chip off the old block!" From this moment on, Denis will be driven by a need to differentiate himself from his lascivious father so that his mother will view him as a loving son and ally.

In real life, De Palma's mother fell into a depression over the adultery and attempted suicide by taking an overdose of sleeping pills, but he himself found her in time and brought her to the hospital, where her stomach was pumped and she survived. Afterward, his father vowed never to cheat on his mother again. In the film, it seems that Denis's mother only pretends to have swallowed the pills; her hysterical overreaction to the father's cheating is emphasized, for by the time of *Home Movies* De Palma seems to have gained some critical distance from his mother, viewing her less as a tragic sufferer and more as a histrionic manipulator.

In the film, Denis calls his father home to help his mother; the son is presented as weak and dependent rather than heroically saving his mother by himself taking her to the hospital. The father insists that Denis assist him in pumping the mother's stomach, even though she tries to protest that she hasn't in fact taken an overdose of pills and to warn Denis that "your father is trying to kill me." Denis wants to help his mother, but his subservience to his father could further endanger her. De Palma's stance here is difficult to determine: while he seems to emphasize the father's cruelty (or obliviousness to her protests) in giving the mother an unneeded stomach pump, there is also a sense that she deserves it for having histrionically feigned an overdose. Of course, the film's comedy also takes the edge off the danger: just as the mother didn't really attempt suicide, so the father's pumping of her stomach won't really kill her.

Denis is made to feel even more inadequate by the fact that his mother dotes on his older brother, James (Gerrit Graham), constantly crying out for *him* rather than Denis to save her. It would seem that, owing to the father's adulterous absence ("He was never home; he was always either teaching anatomy at Now College or 'practicing' it at the office"), the mother has unhealthily diverted all her affections to James. The situation in De Palma's actual family was similar, as he has noted: "My father's life was elsewhere [he practiced and taught at Jefferson Medical College in Philadelphia]; he was rarely home," while "my mother was absorbed with my oldest brother [Bruce]. He was her genius."[13] Three years after *Home Movies*, in 1983, De Palma said, "Even today, I could get my picture on the cover of *Time* and I don't think my mother would notice."[14]

Significantly, Denis's mother has photos of James all over the house—photos which seem to compete with Denis for her attention, even when he is there and James is not. Since the mother seems proud of James's independence and leadership ability (he is teaching a course in self-reliant manliness at Now College), Denis contemplates going to "live in the woods by myself" or obtaining some position "where I have to be a leader of men." The young De Palma likewise considered becoming a genius physicist like his brother Bruce and going off to MIT. Much as Bruce became the charismatic leader of a "free energy" movement, attracting cult followers who would obey his every word no matter how outlandish, so James leads his student disciples—who have names like Matthew, Mark, and Luke—to enact his extremist theories of masculine asceticism. In the character of James, we have another one of those "megalomaniacal and maleficent types"—"inspired by my brother Bruce"—who "take themselves for gods"[15] and who "live surrounded by a court that venerates them and reflects back to them the deformed image of the world they imagine they are living in"[16]—types like Swan in *Phantom of the Paradise* or Childress in *The Fury*.

Through James, De Palma seems to diagnose his brother Bruce's egocentrism as springing from his mother's worship of his "genius." In addition, James's much-vaunted masculinity is presented as a desperate attempt to separate himself from his doting and dependent mother. When James ends class early, telling his male students that "I need silence and solitude," it is actually to hide the fact that his weeping mother has come to him for solace, which he must now provide as a dutiful son.

As a mama's boy, James feels inferior to his father, with whom he is constantly sparring in an effort to assert his own independent manhood. When James attempts to confront his father about the adultery, standing up to him while wearing a knife in his belt, his dad kicks him in the groin and whacks him in the jaw with a phone. Later, the "castrated" James ruefully explains why he drinks carrot juice instead of taking the stalk more manfully in hand: "Ordinarily, I'd masticate these vegetables, but I had a little accident with my jaw." His doctor-father offers James some "nuts" and attempts to fix his jaw, but the wrenching realignments of his mandible only further "unman" the son.

While the lecherous father keeps ogling and pawing James's fiancée, Kristina (Nancy Allen), James is determinedly asexual with her. Despite his macho bragging, the son seems to have been rendered impotent by his dominant father, or perhaps James avoids sexual contact with Kristina because she reminds him of his mother, whose uncomfortable closeness threatens his masculinity. James's class, he keeps insisting to his fiancée and his mother, is "for men only." Holding a slab of roast beef on a knife near his crotch, which is in Kristina's face, James wants her to resist eating it. "First beef, now me," he says, commenting adversely on her appetite for meat and men. What is ostensibly for her own good—Kristina has been promiscuous in the past—is really a desperate attempt on James's part to avoid female contact and to preserve his insecure masculinity. (It is amusing to recall that Gerrit Graham [James] also played the hunky and narcissistic Beef in *Phantom of the Paradise*.)

Earlier, James's father had carved some roast beef and offered a piece to Kristina as a coded come-on, but James's disapproving look had caused her to choke on it. Kristina is caught between the father's lust and the son's repression. To "save" her, the father calls for a sharp knife to perform a tracheotomy (recalling the invasive stomach pump he used to "save" the mother), but Denis is slow to produce the knife (making him feel unmanly and unheroic). During the search for it, James manages to lock lips with Kristina and suck out the piece of meat, leading her to exclaim, "You saved my life!" However, James's "kiss of life" was clinical rather than an expression of loving desire, and it was he who endangered her in the first place when his withering glance of sexual repression provoked her to choke.

In terms of male role models, Denis, too, is split between his father, the lech, and his brother, the mama's boy. At first caught making out with a girl (acting like his father), Denis then attempts to draw close to his mother (acting like his brother). In a scene where Denis tries to comfort her while she is applying a mud mask in front of a mirror, some of the mud rubs off on his face as if to indicate his almost physical sympathy with her and her besmirched reputation, her indignity at the father's adultery. In this moment of alliance with her, Denis's mud-covered image gives him the idea to disguise himself in blackface and to hide in a tree outside his father's office in an attempt to snap photos of him cheating with a nurse—photos that could serve as evidence to support his mother's suit for a divorce. As we know, the young De Palma himself took a camera up into a tree and tried to capture photographic evidence of his father *in flagrante delicto* with a nurse.

Denis's situation in that tree is fascinatingly ambiguous. On the one hand, his photographic spying is on his mother's behalf, so he looks with a disapproving eye upon his father's philandering. On the other hand, Denis is in the classic position of the voyeur or Peeping Tom, gazing upon a sexual scene, including the nurse's nubile body, which provokes desire similar to his father's lust. Does Denis (like his mother) want to stop his father's lechery, or does Denis (like his father) want to enact it with the nurse? This dilemma is further exacerbated when, in a nearby window, Denis spies another woman undressing and finds himself distracted from disapproval of his father's lust by the sight of a female who provokes Denis's own illicit desire.

At this point, a famous director called the Maestro joins Denis up in the tree and chides him for his voyeurism, revealing that the woman in the window watched by Denis "isn't real flesh" but instead "a film of a girl undressing, a film used to trap Peeping Toms" like him. Since the Maestro's conversation with Denis is itself being filmed, Denis becomes a peeper caught peeping, much as Phillip in *Sisters* was (almost) caught watching a blind woman undress on what turned out to be a *Candid Camera*-style TV show called *Peeping Toms*. The Maestro, played by star Kirk Douglas, exhorts Denis to become the star of his own life and not just a bit player or extra. According to De Palma, "Voyeurs are not participating in their lives. They're basically extras, not leading characters." By contrast, stars are "people who have a strong sense of themselves, who want to be *in* the room, not watching from outside."[17] The Maestro offers to mentor Denis by giving him Star Therapy. As a first step toward activating the boy's star potential, the Maestro removes Denis from his voyeuristic perch by literally pushing him out of the tree.

If Denis is the young De Palma, then the Maestro is Wilford Leach, "the most influential teacher I ever had,"[18] or Orson Welles, who had "a lot of impact on me."[19] At the same time, the Maestro is also De Palma himself who, older and accomplished, is now mentoring youngsters like Keith Gordon (Denis). In fact, Gordon would go on to have a distinguished career as an actor and director, in part because De Palma took him under his wing during the filming of *Home Movies* and *Dressed to Kill*, teaching him about all aspects of the business. "Working with Brian twice was an amazing education," Gordon has said, "and what I learned could literally fill a book";[20] "In a sense, Brian was the world's best film school!"[21]

The Maestro advises Denis to turn the camera around and film himself as the one in the spotlight: "You! You're the star. Shoot a day with you living your life. Tomorrow we'll watch it, see who you are." In keeping a filmed diary of everyday moments from his own life, Denis does what De Palma himself has done for decades, beginning in the late '60s. As noted in the chapter on *Hi, Mom!*, De Palma used to carry a camera around with him all the time, shooting everything that he and his friends did. Decades later, thinking back on all that footage, he mused that "what I should ultimately do, when I retire to the Will Rogers Old Age Home, is get [the films and videos] all together" and "maybe I'll come up with some shattering insights into my life."[22]

When the Maestro and Denis watch the first scenes from his filmed diary, the insight they gain is that Denis's life lacks "action!" It is soporifically and almost terminally "boring." The camera lens and the Maestro's critical eye provoke Denis to examine his own existence, and they exert a galvanizing pressure on him to live up to higher expectations: "As usual, the Maestro was right: my movie stunk. So did my life. I never did anything heroic or exciting, except for spying on my father. Wait a minute! That's it: I'll shoot my father 'in the act' for the Maestro and get mom's divorce evidence at the same time!" Exposing the adultery on film will not only separate Denis from his lecherous father and save his mother, it will also please the Maestro, who here acts as a kind of adoptive father, inspiring the boy to assert his independence and to become a filmmaker. In a similar fashion, mentor Leach took De Palma on as "his fair-haired boy," providing him with understanding and encouragement to become a director at a time when De Palma's own father cut him off: "My father and I got into a big argument about what I should be doing with my life. He thought I should be spending my time getting out of college instead of running around making movies, and I ultimately told him I was going to make movies whether he liked it or not and he stopped supporting me after that."[23]

Denis does take action to catch his father in the act of infidelity, just as the teenage De Palma did. But De Palma's real-life raid on his father's office was more individual and direct. Although both Denis and De Palma don all-black clothing for their "commando" raid, De Palma actually pounded on some double-paned glass doors until he broke through, causing his hand to bleed. In his other hand, he held a long knife, making for a very forceful confrontation with his father. (De Palma had originally planned to bring a .22-caliber rifle but decided it was too heavy to carry.)[24] Instead of a knife, Denis brings an 8mm camera, and rather than conduct the raid on his own, he enlists the aid of a cop who holds a gun on the adulterous father. Denis is not so much the star of this action movie as he is its director, who films the cop applying force.

If this makes Denis seem less heroic than the bloody, knife-wielding De Palma, it also makes him seem less crazed and more aesthetically distanced. Denis accomplishes his attack indirectly by means of a camera; his is an artistic assault. It is also in a sense "authorized" by the cop, a kind of surrogate father figure who helps Denis "catch" the bad father. (Quinn—the fat, racist cop—is reminiscent of Quinlan, the role Orson Welles played in *Touch of Evil*, so it is as if Denis/De Palma has enlisted the aid of director-mentor Welles in exposing his own father's inadequacy.)

The fact that Denis wears blackface and an Afro wig in addition to the all-black clothing also makes his attack more of an artistic performance and less a matter of uncontrolled rage. Once again, the blackface links Denis to his denigrated, betrayed mother on whose behalf he launches the attack, but it also connects him with African-Americans as an oppressed minority. Many viewers are likely to find this connection offensive, since the injustices are hardly of equal magnitude, but Denis—feeling oppressed by his family—does appear to link his own suffering with that of racial minorities, as if he were somehow "black." In addition, Denis feels that he will be denigrated as an out-law if he fights back against oppression. "Hey, colored boy! Hey, nigger!" the cop calls him when he sees Denis around his father's office building, and the boy responds, "You talkin' to me?" Denis is white, but he feels "black." He is a member of the Establishment, but he turns against his doctor-father.

In *Taxi Driver*, the "you talkin' to me?" speech of Travis Bickle (Robert De Niro) showed his split between white and black, between a racist atti-tude toward African-Americans and an identification with them as outcast and oppressed. In *Hi, Mom!* (which, as we saw, was a likely influence on *Taxi Driver*), Jon (De Niro) gives a similar speech; he is dressed up as a white racist cop but only to give a performance in a play put on by black revolutionar-ies, with whom Jon partly identifies. And this play, we recall, involves whites wearing blackface in order to feel what it's like to suffer the indignities of Afri-can-Americans in a racist society. In *Home Movies*, the blackface Denis, by appealing to the cop's desire to be on camera, is able to get him to switch from racism to civil rights advocacy and to help Denis with his filmic exposé of his father as a white oppressor. (Denis feigns being an undercover TV reporter and tells the cop that the nurse—whom the father "dominates" during sex—is an oppressed minority.)

Thus, the law is on Denis's side in *Home Movies*, whereas in real life the teenage De Palma's confrontation with his father seemed to be more the act of a crazed outlaw. "You're crazy," his father told De Palma when the boy, bloody and holding a knife, accused him of adultery even though there was no woman present in the room.[25] De Palma did then discover the evidence of his father's infidelity, but only after a floor-by-floor search of his father's office building revealed a nurse "cowering in her slip"[26] behind one of the doors. By contrast, Denis—wielding a camera instead of a knife—catches his father on top of the nurse, thus coolly capturing him on film, "shooting" him *in flagrante delicto* but with the calm control of a director's disapproving eye. If the cop is in one sense the star of the scene, barging in on the unfaithful father and holding a gun on him, Denis may actually have more power, for the camera enables him to sublimate his rage, to fight back against his father without sinking to the same bestial level, to exert control without crazed violence.

If the action he takes toward his father and the nurse is complex, so are Denis's actions regarding his brother, James, and James's fiancée, Kristina. Once again, despite the Maestro's urgings, Denis finds it hard to move from voyeur to participant, from extra to action-hero star. In one scene set to lyri-cal violin music, Denis imagines Kristina walking toward him in slow motion, her hair billowing in the wind, while he uses a masher to pound potatoes in a bowl. Here, Denis is the masturbatory voyeur, unable to bridge the gap between his physical desire and the idealized image he has of a woman.

Later, Denis will peep through a keyhole as Kristina dons black stockings and a miniskirt, while she listens to a taped message from James, who is testing whether she can dress sexily but resist the temptation to sleep with men and thus prove that she is not a "whore." This less-idealized image of Kristina seems to excite Denis even more, but he is caught between his desire for her, which makes him like his lecherous father, and his sense that such desire is wrong, which makes him like his repressed brother who seems incapable of a physical relationship because every woman reminds him of his mother. Denis, in his blackface disguise, follows Kristina to a biker hangout and, watching the upstairs window from a position outside the house, sees one of the men rip her clothes off and jump her. It is as though Denis is again perched in that tree outside his father's office, watching his father with the nurse and paralyzed by the unresolved conflict between desire and repression.

Denis's dilemma is complicated by the fact that it has elements of Oedipal rivalry and the primal scene. Even if his urge to save the woman from sexual degradation weren't undermined by his fear that he just wants her for himself, there is also the sense that these women "belong" to the older men—the nurse (and his mother) to his father, and Kristina to his brother or the biker—and that Denis is just an inexperienced boy with no claim to an adult woman. It is interesting to note that, since Nancy Allen (Kristina) was De Palma's girlfriend at the time, he himself occupied Denis's rivalrous position in relation to that biker. As De Palma commented, "There was a scene of [the biker] raping Nancy, the female lead. It started to go on and on, and I finally said cut, cut. I told him not to be quite so real."[27] Moreover, Keith Gordon (Denis) was in a similar position in relation to De Palma. Gordon has admitted to "the crush I had on Nancy Allen," but "I knew she was Brian's girlfriend, and making out with his paramour in front of him was a bit unnerving."[28]

Seeing Kristina jumped by the biker, Denis takes action, barging into the house and up the stairs, punching the biker, and taking Kristina away. In so doing, Denis moves from being an extra to being the star, following the advice and the example of his mentor, the Maestro. (Earlier, during a Star Therapy course, the Maestro had punched a male student when the boy was coming on to a female classmate.) Denis's action with regard to the biker and Kristina is even more conventionally heroic—more individual and direct—than were Denis's actions toward his father and the nurse, where it was the cop who forced his way in and held a gun while Denis was behind the camera. Here, it is Denis alone who rushes in and commits violence against the biker, then takes Kristina away with him.

One of James's male students—assigned by him to see if Kristina will resist having sex with the biker—is perched in a tree, filming the scene. This student is a voyeur the way Denis was when he sat in a tree outside his father's office, snapping photos of him with the nurse. Denis has now become an active participant, someone who barges into the room and not just watches from outside. (The Maestro shows up next to the male student in the tree as he once did next to Denis, turning the spotlight on this new boy and trying to get *him* to take "action!" and be a star in *his* own life.)

But for Denis, the problem with conventional heroism is that its violence links him to the same brutish males that he wants to save Kristina from. When Denis punches and kicks that biker and then steals Kristina away, his actions are too close to those of the brawling members of the motorcycle gang who fight over who gets to jump her. Denis's violence is also reminiscent of the kick to the groin and the whack across the face that his father gave to his brother, James, when the two of them were fighting for alpha-male dominance and the former was trying to take possession of the latter's fiancée, Kristina.

When Denis does take Kristina to bed after saving her from the biker-rapist, Denis's approach may be compassionate, but in the back of his mind he fears that he is also acting out of selfish lust and thus hurting her. This fear is signified by the crassly libidinous Bunny, a hand puppet which Kristina holds near Denis's back and which urges him to hump away on top of her. (Bunny is a split-off side of Kristina, who also fears that the sex she is having with Denis is merely lust and that she is slipping back into a life of promiscuity.) Did Denis save Kristina from the biker (and from his brother and his father) just so that Denis could use her himself? His fear that his lust has caused her injury seems confirmed when, the next morning, he discovers that she swallowed an overdose of his mother's sleeping pills.

Now family history begins to repeat itself. As he did when his mother had (apparently) taken an overdose, Denis seeks his doctor-father's help, this time going to his office. There, the father demands privacy in order to pump Kristina's stomach, but Denis, suspecting that his dad might make a move on her, climbs the tree outside the office in order to watch them through the window. Meanwhile, his mother and his brother, James, have arrived by car in the street below, accidentally bumping into a cop, whom James tries to stop from frisking his mother. Denis is once again the voyeur, unable to take action due to unresolved conflict. Wanting to save Kristina from his lecherous father, Denis fears that he is too much like him in lusting after her himself. At the same time, Denis also suffers from the opposite fear—that he is too much like James, a feckless mama's boy. Split between two "screens" (the scene of his father with Kristina and the scene of his brother with his mother), torn between equally unacceptable role models (hypermasculine and female-dependent), Denis struggles to define himself and is paralyzed with self-doubt. He knows he must act but is unsure how.

He falls out of his voyeur's perch in the tree but ends up lying dazed on the ground, remaining a mere witness to the events that ensue. As Kristina and the lecherous father are leaving the building, she eludes him, only to have jealous James point a gun at her and pull the trigger. The gun doesn't fire, but in her attempt to escape, Kristina is hit by an arriving ambulance. (Shades of De Palma's previous film, *The Fury*, in which Hester is hit by a car as a result of gun-wielding Peter's rivalry with Childress.) As Kristina is apparently killed by the father's and the brother's alpha-male competition over her, Denis just lies there, unable to act because uncertain of what kind of man to be.

Despite the Maestro's attempt to push Denis out of that tree and into meaningful action, the boy has remained an onlooker in his own life, a traumatized witness to death rather than a lifesaver. As the Maestro laments about Denis, "He was on the brink of stardom and then he plunged into the depth of anonymity—forever an extra, never a star." This is a tragic ending, and it says something about the darkness of De Palma's vision that, comedic as *Home Movies* is, this is actually the way his original script for the film ended. As revealed in a 1981 interview with the director, "In De Palma's original version the girl was killed and the autobiographical [Denis] character was left alone and desolate. However, De Palma was persuaded to have a 'happy ending' because the original was 'too grim' in the context of the rest of the film."[29]

In the ending we now have, Kristina miraculously survives ("Luckily, I was hit by an ambulance and they rushed me to the hospital"), coincidentally runs into Denis ("I feel great about everything, especially about us"), and the two of them go off happily together. It is tempting to read the blatant artificiality of this ending as De Palma's wink to the audience, a telltale sign that he knows we know that endings in real life don't conform so easily to such comedic conventions.

But this ending is significant for another reason: Denis "gets the girl" *even though* he failed to become a conventional hero and save her. Or perhaps we should put this another way: does Kristina choose him in the end *because* his self-doubt kept him from becoming like the other lustful males and entering into a violent rivalry over her? The unlikely comedic ending to *Home Movies* opens a space for Denis to be rewarded for being a new kind of hero.

To add to the personal funds De Palma invested in *Home Movies*, his director friends George Lucas and Steven Spielberg chipped in their own money. De Palma approached the film with great confidence ("I think we made a fabulously funny movie"), and for the sake of the students whose class project this was, he very much hoped that it would be profitable: "I think it might start a new generation of low-budget filmmakers";[30] "It's so important to make this film a success. Otherwise this kind of film will never be done again."[31] Unfortunately, the movie bombed at the box office, perhaps because the distributor put very little money into marketing it (De Palma had to pay for some of his own ads), or maybe because audiences now associated De Palma with thrillers like *Carrie* and *The Fury* and were unwilling to take a chance on a comedy from this director. "When I did something totally out of the ordinary from what a suspense-horror director does, I got no feedback, no support, not one break,"[32] De Palma complained, adding that "if I had been Truffaut . . . and had made *Home Movies*, it would have been infinitely more successful, because the critics are used to Truffaut making this sort of movie—about his youth, a kind of sweet, personal, sentimental, quirky, ironic, funny film. But they're not used to me doing it."[33]

Thus, when De Palma returned to the suspense-horror genre for his next film, *Dressed to Kill*, it was in part because he felt typecast. But De Palma also stated that, as a director, "you've got to know what you do well and not be embarrassed by it."[34] This genre would give him another opportunity to develop the *visual* storytelling at which he excels ("Personally I think the horror genre is a very filmic form. Certainly it's the closest thing we have today to pure cinema"),[35] but it would also allow him to further explore elements from his own life, albeit in a somewhat less direct way than he did in *Home Movies*. "I'm dealing with things close to me more than I've done before," De Palma said, linking *Home Movies* to *Dressed to Kill*. "I'm getting to the point where I'm able to express what I'm feeling . . . no matter what perverse street it takes me down."[36]

CHAPTER 13

Dressed to Kill (1980)

Dressed to Kill notoriously begins with a fantasy scene of wealthy housewife Kate (Angie Dickinson) masturbating in the shower while watching her husband shave in front of the bathroom mirror. Languorous violin music plays, accompanied by breathy female vocals, as Kate runs soapy hands over her breasts and between her legs. But these moments of soft sensuality, along with the music and heavy breathing, are suddenly cut short when a strange man comes up behind her in the shower, clapping one hand over her mouth to stifle her screams and grabbing her with the other hand between her legs while forcibly taking her from behind. Kate's husband looks over in her direction, but either the shower steam prevents his view of the sexual assault on his wife or he is indifferent to it, for he then turns back to his shaving. The fantasy scene ends when Kate is finally able to cry out, and we cut to reality where the husband is having pounding intercourse on top of Kate. She moans histrionically in feigned pleasure while a radio weather report about frost in cold regions indicates her true lack of fulfillment.

Kate's shower fantasy can be compared to Carrie's sensual self-communion in the high-school gym shower, which also ended abruptly when blood from her first period took her by surprise. This blood was associated with punishment for the "sin" of female sexuality, as though Carrie's Edenic enjoyment of her body were suddenly invaded by prurient/prudish eyes, by a postlapsarian sense of shame. In Kate's case, the innocent purity of her self-pleasuring—we note that the hands with which she touches herself have fingernails that are painted white—gives way to a sense of shame that she is enjoying *herself*, that she is experiencing pleasure *apart from her husband*. (Her wedding ring is also quite prominent during her masturbation.)

Thus, one interpretation of the stranger who attacks Kate in the shower is that he is a figment of her guilty conscience, conjured up to punish her for her transgression against marriage and her proper "wifely" role. In this view, her husband doesn't save her because she doesn't deserve saving; indeed, he would want to see her punished. In a way, he might be said to have sent this man— who actually looks very much like her husband—to punish her. In a different but related interpretation, the stranger *is* the husband, as Kate's dreamy fantasy of what sex with her husband ought to be like (she gazes longingly at him while touching herself) is forced to yield to the cold and painful reality of what it actually is: a brutish, loveless encounter which she later describes as "one of his wham-bang specials." (It is worth noting that her husband has his head down, not even looking Kate in the face while he has sex with her.)

A third interpretation is that the shower scene is Kate's "rape fantasy," that being taken by a stranger excites her. When she cries out in the end after being forcibly and repeatedly penetrated, is her cry one of pain or of pleasure? De Palma's script has Kate thinking that "it doesn't matter anymore [if] she's being fucked in the shower by a madman right in front of her husband because it feels so unbelievably good. Her excitement is wild, out of control, as she finally manages to pull his hand away from her mouth and scream out in a spasm of pleasure."[1]

When Women Against Violence Against Women organized groups to protest the film, demonstrators passed out leaflets saying, "*Dressed to Kill* asserts that women crave physical abuse, that humiliation, pain, and brutality are essential to our sexuality."[2] According to WAVAW spokesperson Stephanie Rones, the film "entices, eroticizes and perpetuates violence"; scenes such as the one with "Angie Dickinson fantasizing rape" are dangerous because they promote the "myth" that "women subconsciously want to be raped. With rising rape statistics, there are still these kinds of movies."[3] Whether directors should refrain from depicting rape fantasies on film because they might lead some disturbed individuals to act them out is a question for each filmmaker's conscience, but such a prohibition would certainly limit the range of cinema's exploratory power.

Some women do fantasize about rape, as is evident from Nancy Friday's collection of female sexual fantasies—probably *My Secret Garden* or *Forbidden Flowers*—that actress Nancy Allen read to prepare for her role in *Dressed to Kill*. Allen noted that it's "always a stranger in those fantasies" and that the women are "always being forced. For whatever reason at the time, women's fantasies were like that."[4] Nancy Friday speculates as to the reason: "Not one woman I have ever met actually wanted to be raped in reality; what she wanted from a fantasy of being forced was release from responsibility. 'I'm a good girl, but he made me do it. It's not my fault.'"[5]

Perhaps, then, Kate's fantasy of being forced by a stranger is the only way that she can imagine enjoying sex—or enjoying it with a man other than her husband—without bearing the responsibility and the guilt for the self-pleasuring or the extramarital liaison. If the pleasure she gets is against her will, then how can she be blamed for it? If the illicit orgasm is wrenched from her, then she is not guilty even if her husband's eyes are watching her have it.

Interestingly, when De Palma first approached Angie Dickinson about acting in this intimate scene, she balked at the self-exposure. Like Kate, Dickinson found it hard to convey un-self-conscious sensuality while at the same time feeling all those eyes upon her. "It was hell!" she said with nervous laughter. "Being naked on a soundstage is very difficult, then also, in the shower, worrying about your hair and your make-up and all that stuff, it makes it very trying. So, as much as you are aware of all the crew and the camera and the lights and the microphone, we also then have to forget it all, and that's what acting is about."[6]

De Palma asked Dickinson if doing the shower scene would be easier for her if he used a body double and she agreed it would, so *Penthouse* model Victoria Lynn Johnson was hired for the close-ups of "Kate" caressing her naked breasts and pubes. In a sense, then, Kate is literally split between the respectable housewife and her sexual double, between the reputable actress (Dickinson, the beloved star of TV's *Police Woman* whose face had been on the cover of *Ms.* magazine) and the sexy model (Johnson, a *Penthouse* Pet and nude centerfold). This split between face and body mirrors the attempt by Kate's mind to disown her flesh, to disclaim responsibility for its illicit enjoyment. The respectable woman does not want to be seen by penetrating/punitive eyes. It is rumored that, to bring more viewers to the film, the producers tried to get Dickinson to claim that the shower nudity was hers. *Mad* magazine quipped, "The audience is now on the edge of its seats, wondering . . . is it really happening? Or is it really a dream? But mainly, is it really Angie Dickinson's naked body we're seeing in the shower?"[7]

Kate's subsequent encounter with an actual stranger in a museum, with a man whom she both approaches and avoids, provides further evidence of this same split within her. On the one hand, she wants to be desired by him. In De Palma's script, Kate muses to herself, "What's so interesting about that painting? Is it that much more interesting than me?"[8] On the other hand, when the man shows an interest in her, Kate demurs, thinking, "He's got a lot of nerve trying to pick up such a respectably dressed married woman in the middle of the morning—for God sakes!"[9] In certain shots, Kate the virtuous matron—blonde and wearing all white—is visible on one side of the frame, while on the other side can be seen the naked pubes of a dark-haired nude woman in a painting. Kate's divided nature is perfectly captured in the moment when she removes a glove, and her wedding ring becomes visible—a sight which causes the man to leave her. Does she deliberately show him the ring to get him to go away, as the script would indicate, or, as some viewers think, does she take off the glove absentmindedly or even seductively, not realizing that the sight of the ring would send him away and then regretting that it had this effect?

When she later allows the stranger to make love to her in the back of a taxi, Kate is hyper-aware of the cab driver stealing desirous and disapproving glances at them in his rearview mirror. (Shades of voyeuristic Vic from *Get to Know Your Rabbit*, who was tempted to leer in his rearview mirror at "the type of cheap broad who knows exactly what to do in the back of a car.") Like Kate, Dickinson, too, felt the eyes upon her and the disjunction between respectability (in her former role as an established TV star) and illicit desire (in this taxi sex scene). Referring to the scene as both "wondrous and horrendous," Dickinson explained that "the camera was hidden. Every tall bus and truck came down while we were shooting and all they saw through the window was me getting laid in the backseat. I've never been so embarrassed in my life. Some kids got out of a bus and yelled, 'Hey, Police Woman, right on!' They were so thrilled, it was hysterical."[10]

Given her sense of shame, it is no wonder that Kate tries to stifle her moans of pleasure until she can no longer do so. Her orgasmic cry, which sounds like the scream she emitted at the end of the shower fantasy, seems to be one of pain as much as pleasure, and De Palma cuts to an extreme long shot where her cry seems to echo through the city streets, as if she were ashamedly afraid that everyone could hear it. Interestingly, Kate's cry was actually dubbed by actress Rutanya Alda, who played the woman who stripped in the window for Jon's "peep art" in *Greetings*. Thus, Kate has a voice double for her orgasmic cry, much as she had a body double for her sex in the shower. Both visually and aurally, Kate's matronly mind seems separated from her desiring body, fearing the shaming gaze and the disapproving ear.

After sleeping with the stranger in his apartment and achieving at least a brief sense of sexual fulfillment, Kate's guilt begins to get the better of her. The wedding ring that she removed before having sex sits on top of a digital clock with an LED display like the one on the computers her son builds. It is as though her husband and her son are now present in the adulterous apartment with her, their accusatory eyes judging her for her failure as a wife and a mother. When she tries to phone home, she imagines her son and her husband at the other end of the line and, mortified by her behavior, she cannot bear to speak to them. The discovery of a health notice indicating that the stranger has VD, which she must now fear having contracted, acts as a nightmarish punishment for the illicit pleasure she just had. Like the sexual assault in her shower fantasy-turned-nightmare, the shock of VD seems almost to have been conjured up by her guilty conscience.

A series of split-screens presents Kate's face on one side, while on the other she remembers: having dropped a glove, which the stranger picked up and used to lure her into the cab; having left behind her underwear, which the stranger stripped off her in the cab; and having forgotten her wedding ring, which she leaves beside the stranger's bed when exiting his apartment. In each case, the matronly Kate recalls and regrets her "bad girl" actions, split between propriety and prurience. Kate must wonder: if she had remained respectably dressed, if she had kept the cover of those gloves, that underwear, and the ring, would she have been protected? When, as she is riding the elevator back up to the stranger's apartment to retrieve her wedding ring, a maniac uses a straight razor to slash her hand (the one with the missing ring), her face, and her body, it is as though the rift in Kate between the matron and the "bad girl" has torn her asunder. Kate's guilt has split her open, as if her mind were punishing her body for its wayward desire.

Given that De Palma has often been accused of callousness toward women and even of downright misogyny, it is worth noting the extent of the director's identification with Kate throughout the first part of this movie. "I've always had a feminine point of view in many ways,"[11] De Palma has said. As with Grace (in *Sisters*), Carrie, and Sue (in *The Fury*), Kate is the character whose viewpoint we share, whose desire and guilt we are made to feel, as De Palma has attempted to imagine bridging the gap between his lived experience and hers. Kate goes to a museum to pick up a guy because De Palma used to go to museums to pick up girls: "In my student days, I was in the habit of going to museums to approach girls. You'd walk from one gallery to another; you'd look at the same painting as the girl would; and you'd end up engaging her in conversation."[12] (An exterior shot of the museum Kate visits shows it to be New York's Metropolitan Museum of Art, but because permission could not be obtained to film there, the interior is actually that of the Philadelphia Museum of Art. De Palma grew up in Philadelphia and was a frequent visitor to New York museums when he was a student at Columbia University.)

In the script, De Palma has Kate go to the gallery with Monet's "Water Lilies" because the room "reminds her of Quaker meetings she had to attend in prep school. Once a week for one hour the whole school would meet in the gym and sit in silence. At first she couldn't stand it but over the years she got used to it and finally even looked forward to it . . . she missed those weekly silences until she discovered the Waterlily room."[13] It was De Palma himself who went to a Quaker school. Since this connection between the Waterlily room and Quaker peacefulness seems never to have been intended to make it into the finished film, it is a pure example of De Palma's blending of his own experience with Kate's.

Similarly, Kate's unpleasant discovery that the man she slept with may have given her VD is based on an event from De Palma's own life: "I ran into an old girlfriend in [Greenwich] Village. I went down to her loft and, as we were reminiscing about our college days, there was a guy who knocked on the door. . . . She talked to him for a second and she came back with this form, and apparently she had gotten VD, and you have to fill out a form to show them all of your partners you had slept with";[14] "A true nightmare!"[15] De Palma's empathy for his former girlfriend receiving this shocking news may have been facilitated by his sense that, as one of her previous partners, he, too, could have been infected, had their relationship not been more than five years in the past.

Like the venereal disease, the razor attack is empathetically imagined by De Palma as being a nightmare, and in particular a *woman's* nightmare: "I read somewhere that the most terrifying thing for a woman is disfigurement, that disfigurement is worse than death—that a woman would rather be stabbed than have her face cut up."[16] Even if the razor attack in the elevator strains credulity (how likely is such a scene?), De Palma defends its lack of realism by describing it as Kate's "worst nightmare": "Granted you may have to stretch the logic a bit in order to achieve the effect, but you can get away with it because you're dealing with Angie's [Kate's] point of view, so you're operating on a very visceral level."[17] While De Palma has been criticized for subjecting Kate to a razor attack after she commits adultery ("people say it's *me* punishing her"),[18] it's important to realize the extent to which he *is* Kate. The guilt and the nightmarish fear of punishment that she feels are what he would feel under the same circumstances: "Angie plays a woman who cheats on her husband. If I respect and love my wife and I have a sexual encounter, I am going to feel guilty and punish myself. Angie feels this way."[19]

The male maniac who slashes Kate with a razor is disguised as a blonde woman who resembles her, furthering the impression that Kate is punishing herself out of guilt, having conjured up a nightmarish double to make her suffer for her sexual transgression. As Kate is dying from the attack, she stares into the eyes of a witness, Liz (Nancy Allen), a woman who is standing there when the elevator door opens and who turns out to be another kind of double for Kate. If Kate is a respectable matron who fears that she has behaved like a "bad girl" or prostitute, Liz is a prostitute who yearns for respectability. (Right before witnessing Kate's dying supplication, Liz has been talking with a Wall Street john in an effort to further her stock investments. Later in the film, she will befriend Peter, Kate's son, acting like a mother to him.)

As Kate reaches out a bloody hand toward Liz for help, Liz extends her own hand in kind but then stops when she sees, in the elevator's convex mirror, that the killer is bringing his razor down toward the point where the two women's hands are about to meet. In this way, the killer severs the connection between them, preventing the wife and mother (Kate) from uniting with the "bad girl" (Liz), cutting them apart—much as he used his razor to cut up Kate, to insist on a separation within her between the mother and the "whore," to punish her for expressing unmatronly desires. We recall Dr. Emil Breton in *Sisters*, who uses his knife to surgically separate the Siamese twins Danielle and Dominique, cutting off the woman he wants as his "good wife" from the more strongly sexual "bad girl" who was a part of her, much as the killer cuts up Kate. And Liz can be compared to Grace in *Sisters*, who witnesses the male blade's enforcement of the mother/whore split, as Dominique, like Kate, has to die for her sexual "misbehavior" unbefitting a matron.

In the moment that Liz, cut off from saving Kate, helplessly watches her die, Liz is also struck by two other sights: the face of the killer "blonde" reflected in the elevator's convex mirror, and a blinding glint of light reflected off the blade of the killer's razor. These sights indicate the traumatic impact of Liz's witnessing, a psychic wound that becomes apparent at the end of the film when Liz dreams Kate's nightmares, finding herself bedeviled by the same fears. Having accompanied Peter to his home in her capacity as a kind of surrogate mother to him, Liz falls asleep in Kate's bed and has a dream which combines both Kate's shower fantasy-turned-nightmare and the razor attack upon her in the elevator. Liz imagines she is in Kate's shower, running the water spray from a handheld shower head over her breasts and between her legs, but this sensual scene is filmed rather more realistically than was Kate's erotic fantasy, perhaps because Liz—as a sexually independent young woman—is more accepting of her own desires. However, as Liz dreams of a voyeuristic stalker approaching the house, breaking a window, and turning the bathroom doorknob, and as she covers her naked body with her arms, it is clear that even she is susceptible to shame, open to fear that the expression of her female sexuality is somehow deserving of punishment.

Liz leaves the shower, walks determinedly toward the medicine cabinet, and tries to reach the straight razor inside it before the killer can get to her. She attempts to fight back against the fear induced in her, to grab hold of the power to accept herself as sexual *and* maternal, to cut the man who would cut her off from any vital part of herself. But the razor blade in the cabinet throws off a reflected glint of light and, as Liz is reaching for it, the killer "blonde"—reflected alongside Liz in the cabinet mirror—comes up behind her and slashes her throat with another straight razor. The fact that blonde Liz is murdered by a killer "blonde" in a mirror suggests that Liz's own fears get the better of her, that in effect she slits her own throat with that razor. (In De Palma's script, this nightmarish self-defeat is even more apparent because "a disembodied arm wielding a straight razor"[20] emerges from inside the medicine cabinet itself, coming from the very place where Liz's own reflection would be in the cabinet mirror.) After her nightmare, Liz wakes up screaming in Kate's bed—an appropriate place given that Liz has caught the contagion of Kate's fear, that the blinding sight or traumatic witnessing of blood pouring from Kate's throat has led Liz to imagine a split opening up in her own.

Nancy Allen has commented on her own fear of self-exposure, her own sense of lustful/lacerating eyes upon her while she was playing Liz in the film's concluding shower scene: "So there you are on that set. You're naked. You're vulnerable. There are people around. I just think that to do that piece of it you have to feel that certain vulnerability."[21] Interestingly, she also noted that some of this fear may have been instilled in her by having watched the shower murder scene in Hitchcock's *Psycho* at an impressionable age: "It [filming the *Dressed to Kill* shower scene] had a certain creepiness to it. I think that probably having seen *Psycho* as a kid did it to me."[22] Hitchcock had died three months prior to the release of *Dressed to Kill*, and the film's distributors were keen to market De Palma as the new "master of the macabre" on movie posters and in newspaper ads.

Certainly, De Palma's film is a deliberate reworking of *Psycho*: both films have major stars (Angie Dickinson and Janet Leigh) shockingly killed early on in the narrative by blade-wielding, schizophrenic transvestites (Michael Caine and Anthony Perkins). The close connections between the two films led to a certain amount of ridicule. In the *Mad* magazine parody *Undressed to Kill*, Liz witnesses the murder of Kate and thinks, "Gasp! Do YOU see what I see?! I don't believe it! It CAN'T BE HAPPENING!! . . . I mean a major character getting knocked off this early in the film! It hasn't happened since Janet Leigh in *Psycho*!"[23] When the transvestite killer is unmasked at the end of this De Palma parody, he is revealed to be Anthony Perkins, who went on a killing rampage "because you were stealing the classic horror movie of all time . . . MY movie . . . and you were RUINING IT!!"[24]

More seriously, respected critics like Andrew Sarris did accuse *Dressed to Kill* of being "a shamefully straight steal from *Psycho*," arguing that "there is no depth of feeling in De Palma's Hitchcockian flourishes."[25] In George Morris's view, "De Palma lacks the searing vision that would assimilate Hitchcock's techniques into a coherent work of personal expression,"[26] and Richard Combs maintained that "in *Dressed to Kill* there is no illusion that the movie connections [to *Psycho*] connect with anything but the director's yen for free-floating visceral excitement."[27] Even more damningly, John Simon wrote of the elevator murder scene: "This is to treat murder (quite unlike Hitchcock, for all his serving as model to De Palma) as fashion-magazine chic à la Helmut Newton—perhaps the ugliest form of titillation. . . . It is moral aphasia, and something uglier still: the drawing out of murder into languorous, lascivious excitation."[28]

My discussion above of *Dressed to Kill*'s elevator murder scene and its two shower scenes has, I hope, demonstrated that they are searing, coherent, and *personal* explorations by De Palma of women's sexual fantasies and fears, and not simply there for visceral excitement or necrophiliac titillation. Here, I would like to note that the connections with *Psycho* are not just incidental flourishes, but deep and significant.

In *Psycho*, Marion (Janet Leigh) has sex with a married man in a city hotel, and the camera peers in on them through a window, emphasizing Marion's fear of being watched by desiring/disapproving eyes as she engages in illicit intercourse. To help fund her lover's divorce, she then steals money from her boss and holes up in a seedy motel, where Norman (Anthony Perkins), the motel clerk, voyeuristically spies on her through a peephole in the wall as she undresses. After deciding that she will do the right thing and return the money, Marion takes a shower. This scene of Marion under the water's spray is shot in a way that emphasizes her attempt to cleanse her conscience and to take unashamed pleasure in her own body. However, the different angles from which her naked body is viewed convey a creepy sense of her being watched, as if Marion—despite her attempt to feel good about herself—is still struggling with a fear of being caught out in an illicit act, of being punished for her sexual transgression. It is at this point that the killer, as the virtual embodiment of Marion's own fear, comes up behind her with a knife and stabs her to death in the shower.

In *Dressed to Kill*, Kate has a fantasy of enjoying her own body under the shower, but the idea that she is taking pleasure in herself apart from her husband brings on a nightmare of punishment in which a strange man comes up behind her and forcibly penetrates her with his phallus. Kate has adulterous sex with another stranger in a taxi and in the man's city apartment, while anxious that she might be observed or found out by others (the cab driver, her son, her husband). Deciding that she will do the right thing and take the elevator back up to retrieve her wedding ring, Kate tries to clear her conscience and feel better about herself, but a killer—who is "blonde," like Kate—attacks her with the blade of a straight razor, first slashing her hand (the one with the missing ring). As with Marion, it is as though Kate, unable to overcome her guilt, has conjured up a disapproving double to punish herself. Then Liz, the "whore" who becomes a surrogate mother to Kate's son, attempts to find a "clean" enjoyment and an un-self-conscious pleasure in her body under the shower, but succumbs to her own fantasized fear of judgmental eyes, imagining a split-off part of herself—a "blonde" with a blade—who kills her in condemnation.

The connections by which Kate and Liz are linked with Marion are thus extensive and deep, as are the parallels between the elevator/shower scenes in *Dressed to Kill* and *Psycho*'s shower scene. De Palma is as invested in his female characters' fears and desires as is Hitchcock, belying critic Richard Combs's claim that "De Palma's suspense mechanisms are so free of emotional content, they become enjoyable simply as absurd conceits, more dada than Hitchcock."[29] And when George Morris argues that De Palma is *unlike* Hitchcock because the "violence and terror in [Hitchcock's] films are rooted in the psychological truths of character and erupt within a potentially responsible but morally precarious universe,"[30] the critic seems to be missing both the psychological depth of De Palma's characters and the moral complexity of his movie world.

There are also significant links between both films' schizophrenic transvestites. In *Psycho*, Norman peeps lustfully at Marion while she is disrobing, but the "mother" side of Norman disapproves of his desire and, shifting the blame onto Marion for being a seductive "bad girl," knifes her in the shower. Norman's split personality thus contains both a lustful male side and a lacerating female side that cuts in condemnation of sex as sinful. By knifing Marion, Norman simultaneously expresses his phallic desire by means of a violent penetration, and represses that desire by punishing the woman who gave rise to it.

In *Dressed to Kill*, Kate's psychiatrist, Dr. Elliott, is also a male/female split personality torn between prurience and prohibition. When Elliott finds himself getting aroused by women patients in his office—first by Kate and later by Liz—he imagines his female side, Bobbi, staring back at him from a mirror, fixing him with a forbidding gaze. The disapproving Bobbi takes a razor to Kate (in the elevator) and to Liz (in Elliott's office), scapegoating them as "seductresses" for having excited Elliott's lust. As another psychiatrist explains, "Elliott's penis became erect and Bobbi took control, trying to kill anyone that made Elliott masculinely sexual." But the phallic razor blade is also Elliott's way of asserting his masculine desire. It is a violent stab at proving his male dominance over Bobbi and other women; it is a desperate attempt to show that he has the phallus and they do not, as when, in the elevator murder of Kate, he "plunges the razor deep between her legs."[31] In the script, it is revealed that Elliott/Bobbi "once tried to hack off" his own male "genitals."[32] So he/she wavers between phallic dominance over women and an urge to castrate himself out of guilt over his own lust.

Bobbi, the disapproving *double* who stares back at him from the mirror, is thus a sign that Elliott is in fact *split*, with the male and female sides of himself at war with each other—"opposite sexes inhabiting the same body," according to his psychiatrist. In one split-screen shot suggestive of the man/woman divide within him, Elliott is in his office at screen left while on the right can be seen a blonde, who resembles Elliott when he is cross-dressed as the killer, using binoculars to peer in through Liz's window while she is changing clothes. On the one side, there is the male psychiatrist, while on the other, there appears to be the female Bobbi gazing disapprovingly at Liz's body for having aroused the male's desire. (In fact, the figure on the right is police-woman Betty Luce, assigned to keep a watchful eye on Liz in order to help rather than to hurt her. But the actress who portrays Luce, Susanna Clemm, also plays Bobbi in all but one of the scenes where Elliott cross-dresses as her. The role of Elliott/Bobbi is thus itself split between Michael Caine as the masculine side and Susanna Clemm as the feminine side.)

On the left half of the screen, Elliott is listening to an answering-machine message from Bobbi, a message that was, of course, left by him/herself. Bobbi's female voice was actually dubbed by male actor William Finley, who as Lloyd in *Greetings* had pretended to be an effeminate man, and who as Winslow in *Phantom of the Paradise* had cross-dressed as a woman. Finley's characteristic gender indeterminacy adds to the "war between the sexes" inside Elliott. This war was very uncomfortable for Michael Caine, whose nervousness about having to cross-dress in his one scene as Bobbi betrays a fear of his feminine side that seems a lot like Elliott's anxiety: "I had never worn female clothing before, I swear, and my first worry was—supposing I became a transvestite! I was truly so anxious about this that I refused to wear the panties (because nobody was ever going to see them) and kept my own underpants on as a sort of safety shield against a lapse of masculinity."[33]

In another split-screen shot, Elliott—whose face is partly doubled in a mirror—watches a TV show about a male-to-female transsexual on the left, while on the right, Liz, while watching the same transsexual on TV, applies make-up to her face using a vanity mirror before going out on a "date" as a prostitute. Watching that TV program is like looking into a mirror for Elliott because he is himself a transvestite and would-be transsexual. The gender divide within Elliott is revealed by the doubling between his male self and the female transsexual on TV. The mirroring of Liz's face also reveals a split within her, which is between a "respectable" woman and the "bad girl" she is making herself up to be. (Right before this, Liz just had two phone conversations that displayed this same division, one as a reputable businesswoman speaking with her stockbroker, and the other as a prostitute speaking with her madam, Norma, to whom Liz lied in saying that she was talking to her mother on the other line. The idea of having *Norma* on one line and *mother* on the other is a reference to *Psycho* and the Anthony Perkins character, who is schizophrenically split between being *Norman* and being *mother*.)

The fact that the TV image of the transsexual, which obviously reminds us of Bobbi, hovers over both the Elliott and the Liz halves of the screen suggests that *they, too*, are being watched, that Bobbi is looking for signs of the "bad girl" in Liz and for signs of the lust that she might provoke in Elliott. If Liz is getting provocatively attired and made-up as a prostitute—metaphorically, "dressed to kill"—then Elliott as Bobbi will get cross-dressed to kill *her*.

The murderous transvestite in *Dressed to Kill* may seem like a unique character, but there are a number of creepy connections between him and the other males in the film. In the movie's opening fantasy, while he is looking into the bathroom mirror, Kate's husband shaves with a straight razor like the one that the killer will use on Kate after Elliott looks into the mirror and sees "Bobbi" telling him to punish Kate for her sexuality. (In fact, the killer even uses the razor from Elliott's shaving drawer.) The razor links the husband and the killer in terms of phallic violence. As we saw, the husband sometimes seems to be watching while Kate is raped by the strange man—the husband's double—in the shower, as if the husband were punishing her for her self-pleasuring under the water's spray. And, in reality, the husband is having impersonal, pounding intercourse with her, hurting her in bed.

The stranger in the museum also watches Kate and then sexually harms her in bed. Wearing dark glasses, the stranger spies on Kate at the museum, just as the killer—also wearing dark glasses—voyeuristically eyes her throughout the film, including as she leaves the museum with the stranger. At his apartment, the stranger beds Kate, quite possibly infecting her with VD (as revenge because some other woman infected him?), while right after that, in the elevator, the killer invades her with his phallic razor blade, including between her legs.

And yet there are other ways that the stranger and the husband are linked to the transvestite killer which are not examples of phallic aggression or punitive violence. Kate drops her gloves at the museum. The killer, who himself wears women's gloves, picks up one of Kate's, while the stranger picks up the other one and *puts it on*. If, as seems to be the case, he merely intends to return it to her, why does he don it himself? Is there a sense in which the stranger identifies with Kate as a woman? Does his partial cross-dressing indicate a potential for empathy that is the other side of this predatory male? As for the husband, it is worth noting that in the original script, his shaving was to continue beyond his face to include the hair on his chest, legs, and pubes; in the end, he would take the razor to his own penis, just as Elliott/Bobbi tried to do. Does the husband's guilt over his own phallic violence toward Kate lead him to punish himself? Is he trying to imagine what it might feel like to be a woman? It is possible that, like the transvestite and would-be transsexual killer, the husband and the stranger are also split between aggression and guilt, between predatory male desire and empathy for the female victim. (Interestingly, just as E*ll*io*tt* contains a double-*l* and a double-*t*, so the husband's name—Mike *Miller*—and the stranger's name—Wa*rr*en Lockman—contain similar doublings.)

In thinking about transvestites, De Palma himself imagined cross-dressing: "I was at a dinner party, and I asked, quite innocently, 'Wouldn't it be terrific to dress up in women's clothes and go out and see how people related to you?' And everyone looked at me like I was a lunatic."[34] Notice that "lunatic" is others' reaction, not De Palma's; rather, he seems to take the idea seriously as a way of exploring how people view gender and possibly as a way of feeling what it is like to be looked at as a woman.

De Palma has also imagined wanting to rid himself of his own masculinity: "Once in college when I was shaving, I started to shave my face and then I started to shave my neck and then I started to shave—I said, 'What happens if I shave off my chest hair? What happens if I shave off my pubic hair?'" Going on to talk about his original plan for the film's opening in which the husband takes a razor to himself, De Palma says (and we note that he begins to use "I" as if speaking as a transsexual), "It's done in very big close-ups, and then he gets to this penis, which is this big problem with transsexuals—'When am I going to get my penectomy? When am I going to get this thing taken off and have a woman's organ created for me?'—and so suddenly he hacks off his penis."[35] Here, male sexuality is experienced as such a problem that the offending organ must be removed. There is an absolute man/woman split: the alternative to male phallic aggression toward females is emasculation—to become a woman.

This split is also apparent in Peter, the character who serves as De Palma's avatar in the film. At one point, Cameron De Palma—the director's nephew, who played the boy on the bike in *Carrie*—was considered for the role, but instead Keith Gordon, who played Denis or the young De Palma in the autobiographical *Home Movies*, was chosen. As we know, De Palma's mother was suicidally despondent over his doctor-father's affair with a nurse. In order to help his mother obtain evidence for a divorce, the young De Palma recorded his father's phone calls and shot film of him from outside his office. Similarly, Peter bugs the police station where Dr. Elliott is being questioned in connection with the murder of Peter's mother (Kate), and he rigs a time-lapse camera to take photos outside Elliott's office. As De Palma has said about Peter, "He is obsessed with technology like me; he has all this photo equipment like me; and he uses it for spying, as I did when I tracked my father."[36] With the murder of Kate, which turns out to have been committed by Elliott's phallic razor in the elevator, it is as though De Palma has imagined that his father's lust did cause his mother's death, prompting the son to track him down for it. In addition, when Liz becomes a mother-surrogate to Peter and when Elliott threatens *her* with the razor, it is as if Peter is given a second chance to save his "mother" from the consequences of male sexual aggression.

Peter is halfway between (mama's) boy and (phallic) man. The computer that the boy is constructing—an exact replica of the one that young De Palma built for a science fair—is a kind of transitional object on the way to manhood. Dubbed "a Peter," the computer becomes part of a masturbation joke his mother tells about "working on your Peter." Originally, the boy's role was written for a preteen, but when De Palma could not find a child actor experienced enough to carry the part, he cast teenage Keith Gordon in the role. As Gordon explains, there used to be "a much more 'golly gee' edge to the dialogue. Sometimes we'd take it out, and sometimes we'd let it stay, but with a more double-edged/double-entendre feel. For example, in the script, Peter clearly wasn't in on the joke when his mom talked about 'working on your Peter.' At first Brian thought of dropping the joke, but then we realized it showed something nice (if a bit Oedipal) about the relationship if they could share a slightly sexual joke."[37] Thus, Peter is part innocent boy and part Oedipal young man.

Peter's awareness of adult desire seems to grow further around Liz, the mother-substitute who is also a young prostitute. When Liz tells him that "I'm going to miss having you on my tail," their relationship begins to take on erotic overtones. Is he a boy following his "mother" to protect her, or is he stalking her out of desire? According to Gordon, "Some of the stuff with [Liz] took on little bit of sexual tension that wouldn't have been there if [Peter] had been a little kid, and by not changing the [double entendre] dialogue, it actually added some layers of meaning."[38]

When Peter is in the police station listening to the bug he planted, he hears his mother being described by a detective as "some hot-pants broad cruising around for some action. . . . There's all kinds of ways to get killed in this city if you're looking for it." The detective makes Kate sound like a "bad girl" who got what she deserved. Elliott, Kate's psychiatrist, reacts indignantly and protectively against this characterization of his patient, but as we know, another side of Elliott has a different reaction; it is Elliott who actually killed her with the razor for having excited him with her "seductiveness." Is there another side to Peter, too? As he listens to this description of his mother as a "whore," is Peter the indignantly protective son, identifying with his mother and out to catch her murderer, or is he a kind of "audio voyeur," pruriently and punitively excited by what he hears about her? As Gordon explained about this scene, "I liked the idea that there might be a moment or two where even Peter would seem suspicious."[39]

Believing that the killer is somehow connected with Elliott, perhaps as one of his patients, Liz goes to his office to investigate, with Peter stationed outside to watch over her through a window. To distract Elliott so that she can get a look at his appointment book, Liz strips down to a black bra, garter belt, and stockings, calling herself a "very bad" girl and telling him a "dirty" rape fantasy in which she is sexually assaulted with a razor. While Elliott appears to main-tain the professional demeanor of a psychiatrist caring for a female patient, the other side of him is aroused and angry, getting ready to lustfully lacerate the "bad girl."

Peter, standing outside in the rain and using binoculars to try to peer in through the window, is also psychologically split in terms of his attitude toward Liz. (The pouring rain and his inability to get a good look represent his confusion.) On the one hand, he identifies with Liz and is there to protect her from phallic aggression, like a boy given a second chance to save his "mother." On the other hand, he is a voyeur with binoculars watching a woman strip and beginning to feel his own lustful desires. As the novelization of the film has it, "Now, across the street from Elliott's office, [Peter] saw Liz take her clothes off. He couldn't figure it for a moment, thinking only that she had a real terrific body, like the kind he sometimes sneaked a look at in *Playboy* or *Gallery*. But what the hell was she doing? He wiped the smears of rain from the lenses of the binoculars."[40] Interestingly, actress Nancy Allen (Liz) felt a similar growth of potentially threatening lust on the part of the male crew while shooting this scene: "When you put the black lingerie on, that's when you get into trouble. I don't know what it is, but men behave very badly. It brings out the eighth grader in them, looking at *Playboy* magazine or something."[41]

De Palma himself has been criticized for subjecting Allen, who was his wife at the time, to such scenes where she is prey to dangerous desires: "De Palma put his wife in lingerie, sent a razor-wielding transvestite schizophrenic after her, and then filmed the scene, knowing it would be shown to thousands, pos-sibly millions of people. This was troublesome to many. How could you perpe-trate such violence on your wife? Why display your wife nearly naked, and so consistently? Why your wife, why not some other actress? *Why?*"[42] On the one hand, De Palma would sometimes show a husbandly protectiveness on set. According to Allen, "At one point, he said, 'What am I doing with my wife run-ning around naked in front of all these people?!' He was really flipping out!"[43] On the other hand, given the obsessiveness with which he keeps returning to scenes where sexually assertive women are preyed upon, De Palma himself would seem to be struggling with the tendency to punish sex as sin. Years later, reflecting on the "controversy" over *Dressed to Kill* and whether or not it showed "Brian being a misogynist and not being kind to women," Allen acknowledged that "there was a lot of violence against women" in his films: "What's that all about? I don't know. You'll have to talk to his psychiatrist, I suppose. I don't know what it all means. It does seem that there's a lot of con-flict there, somewhere internally, a lot of conflict about saving someone but ripping them apart at the same time."[44]

De Palma has said about Liz's scene in Elliott's office that viewers don't want her to be saved from the killer, that "the audience wants Nancy [as Liz] to get the s--- slashed out of her then and there."[45] But the only audience that wants this is one with a prurient and punitive attitude toward a strongly sexual woman like Liz. Is De Palma a member of *this* audience? "I've always felt that sex and guilt worked very well," he has said. "It's a device that people respond to. If the characters do something sexually bad, then the audience is willing to have the characters pay for it on some level or other. Now, *that may be because I believe that or because I think that it works*. I don't consider myself a puritan who says, if you have illicit sex you're going to die. But I use that device a lot in my movies because I think *audiences* believe it and because I think it works."[46] This strikingly honest statement reveals a split in De Palma: he may believe in the puritan view that "illicit sex" or "bad girls" should be punished, but he may not. It seems to me that, while one part of De Palma may view females through prurient, prudish, and punitive eyes, another part of him is struggling to move away from that view and to see women differently.

Watching Liz strip in front of Elliott, Peter struggles not to see her the way Elliott does, to view her empathetically as her savior and not voyeuristically as a potential ripper. In this, Peter is like Denis (also played by Keith Gordon) at the end of *Home Movies*, who looks through the window of his father's office to see Kristina (also played by Nancy Allen) with his doctor-father. Denis is also torn, wanting to save Kristina, a former stripper, from his father's predatory lust, but also fearing his own latent desire to take sexual advantage of her—a domineering lust that seems little different from his father's.

Similarly, in Hitchcock's *Rear Window*, Jeff (James Stewart) gazes from across the way through a window at Lisa (Grace Kelly) when she is menaced by Thorwald (Raymond Burr) in that man's apartment. (Sometimes Jeff uses binoculars to watch Thorwald's window, as Peter has used them to watch Elliott's.) Ostensibly, Jeff feels Lisa's terror as she is exposed to Thorwald's manhandling and to possible murder as his next victim, since he has already killed his wife and she is investigating that death. However, another side of Jeff has been troubled by Lisa's sexual assertiveness, and this dark side of him may be enjoying Thorwald's male dominance over her and his violent punishment of her female effrontery. The confusion in Jeff's mind over whether he is an empathetic protector or a murderous punisher seems to result in a psychological paralysis (symbolized by the cast on his leg), impeding his ability to come to Lisa's aid. She is saved by the police, not by him.

Plagued by the same confusion with regard to Liz, Peter also hesitates, trying to see what is going on inside that window of Elliott's office and inside himself: is he a savior or a ripper? To dramatize this split within Peter, we are shown his image doubled as a reflection in the window glass where, standing outside, he seems to be looking at himself standing inside. Another split double occurs when the killer blonde standing inside seems to come up behind Peter from outside and attack him. In fact, the blonde who grabs Peter from behind is the policewoman assigned to help them, whereas the "blonde" inside is the cross-dressed Elliott who wants to hurt them. Thus, these two blondes can also be seen as representing the split within Peter between a desire to attack Liz and an urge to rescue her. This unresolved division within Peter makes it hard for him to act decisively to save Liz, and though he does try to warn her about Elliott's impending attack, the warning is late and ineffectual. Liz is saved by the policewoman, not by Peter.

The remainder of the film sees this split within Peter become further exacerbated instead of resolved. One side of him has felt true empathy for the vulnerability of women. When he was grabbed from behind, Peter thought he was being attacked in the way that his mother and Liz were. Positioned like them on the receiving end of violence, he comes to feel what they felt. This identification with women may be one reason why, when Liz later tells him about the surgery transsexuals undergo, Peter says that "it's giving me some wonderful ideas for a science project. I mean, instead of building a computer, I could build a woman—out of myself." Rather than "working on [his] Peter" (the computer that is his phallic masculinity), Peter imagines forgoing manhood and remaining a boy connected to his mother, so identified with her that he *becomes* her. Ostensibly, Peter's relationship to Liz seems very much that of a protective son to his "mother," and he even invites her home to take his mother's place so that, as they put it, he can have the "company" and she can feel "safe." (It is interesting that, throughout this restaurant conversation between Peter and his surrogate mother, Liz, the elderly woman seated at a table behind him is played by Mary Davenport, the actress who played Denis's mother in *Home Movies*.)

Yet there is another side to Peter that is not empathetic but defensively masculine. We get a glimpse of this side when, after hearing further details of the transsexual surgery, Peter decides that he will stay on the path to conventional manhood: "I think I'm going to stick to my computer." In the script and the novelization, Peter is much more overtly phobic about feminization, about men who become (too much like) women: "They're fags." "Nut case[s]."[47] "Sounds sick."[48] To Liz's retort—"What's the matter with being a girl? It's not so bad"—Peter's reply is that he "sure wouldn't want to be one."[49] As was the case with Elliott, Peter's masculine defensiveness then goes on the offensive, assaulting women to prove his power as a man. While the "son" side of Peter takes mother-surrogate Liz home to protect her, the violently lustful side of him attacks, which is shown in fantasy as Elliott's assault on the nurse (in the mental hospital) and on Liz (in the shower). The real Elliott has been caught by police and locked up. The fantasy "Elliott," who attacks in the end, is a figment of Liz's fear—and of Peter's murderous desire. It is as though, while the protective Peter is asleep (in the script) or working on his computer (in the film), his nightmare id—the prurient/punitive Peter—is out committing lust-murder.

The nurse, who looks after patients, is a kind of mother figure. The nurse wears all white, as Peter's mother, Kate, did. Kate was a mother who—as some men saw it—acted like a whore, letting her clothes be stripped off and sleeping with a stranger. She was murdered by a man who blamed her as a seductress for arousing his lust. That same man tried to kill the prostitute Liz, who was stripping in front of him. The nurse, too, is murdered and stripped by her killer to reveal that she is wearing a bra, garter belt, and stockings, just as Liz was. The white-clad nurse has seductive undergarments; the mother (Kate) is revealed to be a whore (Liz) in the eyes of the killer, provoking a lust-murder. As we have seen, Peter's sense of his mother's "goodness" was altered when he overheard the detective say "dirty" things about her, and Peter's view of "good girl" Liz was changed when he watched through the window as she stripped in front of Elliott. At the end of this film, the side of Peter that is like Elliott has a nightmare in which he punishes the sexy nurse, the way Elliott punished Kate and Liz. (It may be worth recalling that, after the teenage De Palma broke through some glass doors and—knife in hand—confronted his philandering father, De Palma also went in search of the nurse his father had slept with, finding her "cowering in her slip"[50] behind a door—clearly afraid of what might be done to her.)

Peter's nightmare as "Elliott" continues as he imagines first watching from outside the house as Liz strips off her clothes and then breaking through window glass to get at her. After "Elliott" reaches out and cuts her throat with the phallic blade of the straight razor, Liz wakes up screaming in bed to find Peter reaching out to her. Significantly, she fights him off, taking him to be her nightmare aggressor, and in a sense she is right. Despite his attempts at calming reassurance—"It's me! It's Peter! It's all right!"—it was the dark side of him that attacked her; her nightmare was his. Peter is conflicted between love and lust, between empathetic protection and violent penetration.

The implied connection linking Peter to Elliott might have been even more striking if De Palma had chosen to go with one of the two alternate endings he had originally considered. According to a psychologist who interviewed the director shortly after the film's release, "there was to be a 'double twist' ending in which Liz wakes, goes to the door, and lets Peter into the bedroom. She is again slashed by [Elliott] and then awakens for 'real.'"[51] Letting Peter in to help her leads only to Liz getting slashed again by Elliott. In this ending, there is a kind of flicker between Elliott and Peter as well as between nightmare and waking, a fluctuation between them that blurs the two. Peter has a dark side just as Elliott did—a side that could actually emerge as real phallic aggression against women, like the kind committed by Elliott when under the influence of *his* alter ego. (The other ending considered by De Palma, which appears to be the one published in his script, has Liz "wake up in bed with a john"[52] after her nightmare, rather than have Peter come to her bed. As a character, the john suggests the guilty lust that could be growing in Peter and that might turn him into Elliott.)

Dressed to Kill proved to be a commercial success for De Palma. Financed by Samuel Z. Arkoff, the same independent producer who had bankrolled *Sisters*, *Dressed to Kill* returned a $31 million domestic gross on its $7.5 million investment. Consequently, Arkoff was more than happy to green-light De Palma's next project. But the director did not want to make *Dressed to Kill II*. Instead, De Palma was eager to leave the horror genre behind and to try his hand at something more serious and reputable. The result would be *Blow Out*.

Brian De Palma in a photo taken around the time of his first Hollywood film, *Get to Know Your Rabbit* (1972). Photofest.

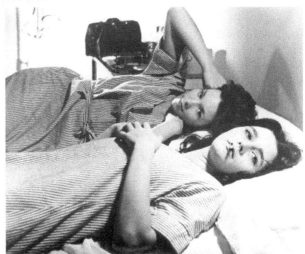

Jennifer Salt grows strangely attached to Margot Kidder in the Siamese-twins thriller *Sisters* (1973). Author's collection.

William Finley, who appears in eight De Palma films, here has the starring role in *Phantom of the Paradise* (1974). Author's collection.

Piper Laurie shows the wrong kind of maternal devotion to Sissy Spacek in *Carrie* (1976). Both actresses were nominated for Academy Awards. Author's collection.

Kirk Douglas and Keith Gordon as older and younger versions of De Palma in the autobiographical *Home Movies* (1980). United Artists Classics/Photofest.

Angie Dickinson conjures up a blonde double to punish herself for committing adultery in *Dressed to Kill* (1980). Author's collection.

De Palma directs actress and first wife Nancy Allen in *Dressed to Kill* (1980). They were married from 1979 to 1984. Author's collection.

John Travolta tries to solve a murder by repeatedly playing an audiotape of it in *Blow Out* (1981), a film influenced by investigations of John F. Kennedy's assassination. Filmways/Photofest.

Al Pacino in his over-the-top performance as gangster Tony Montana in *Scarface* (1983), a film vilified for its violence but revered by its fans. Universal Pictures/Photofest.

Craig Wasson with Melanie Griffith in *Body Double* (1984), trying to turn a porn shoot into a romantic interlude. Columbia Pictures/Photofest.

Brian De Palma and Robert De Niro in matching poses on the set of *The Untouchables* (1987). Years earlier, the director gave the star his first movie role in *The Wedding Party* (1964–65). Author's collection.

Michael J. Fox attempts to protect Thuy Thu Le from Sean Penn in *Casualties of War* (1989). Columbia Pictures/Photofest.

Wall Street broker Tom Hanks learns what it's like to live as one of the less fortunate in *The Bonfire of the Vanities* (1990). Warner Bros./Photofest.

Gale Anne Hurd, producer and De Palma's second wife (photo circa 1992). They were married from 1991 to 1993. Photofest.

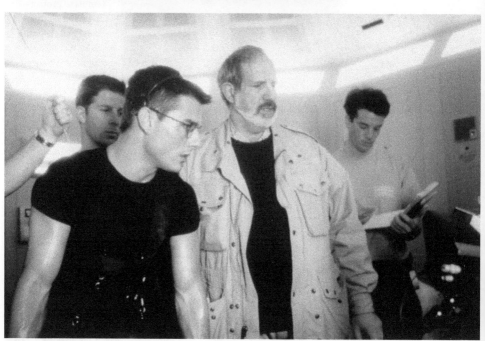

De Palma advises Tom Cruise on how to infiltrate and rob CIA headquarters in *Mission: Impossible* (1996), the director's most financially successful film. Author's collection.

De Palma instructs Nicolas Cage to pay attention or he will get lost in the dizzying complexities of the conspiracy thriller *Snake Eyes* (1998), one of the director's trickiest films. Buena Vista Pictures/Photofest.

Married astronauts Kim Delaney and Gary Sinise stay connected in *Mission to Mars* (2000), a film about family ties and spiritual vision that many were surprised to see coming from De Palma. Buena Vista/Photofest.

De Palma's director-friends—Francis Ford Coppola, George Lucas, Martin Scorsese, and Steven Spielberg—at the Academy Awards in 2007. They have all won Oscars, while De Palma has not. AMPAS/Photofest.

De Palma, still fiercely independent, directing his anti-war film, *Redacted* (2007). Magnolia/Photofest.

Workplace competition gets out of hand between frenemies Noomi Rapace and Rachel McAdams in *Passion* (2012). Entertainment One/Photofest.

CHAPTER 14

Blow Out (1981)

Starting with a blade-wielding killer who attacks a woman in the shower, *Blow Out* begins where *Dressed to Kill* ended, but only so that De Palma can distance himself from the kind of stalk-and-slash film that he has been pigeonholed as making. "I'm typed as . . . the specialist in B-movie horror," he has said,[1] and so *Blow Out* begins with a scene that is gradually revealed to be from a film-within-the-film, a low-budget horror movie called *Coed Frenzy*. Made as a kind of parody of *Halloween* (according to Steadicam operator Garrett Brown),[2] the scene is deliberately bad, with the camera adopting the perspective of the heavy-breathing killer as he leers at scantily clad coeds before plunging his knife into one. The parody announces De Palma's new distance from this type of subject matter, as does the Brechtian moment of the showering woman's feebly unconvincing scream, which throws us out of the B-grade horror movie and into the more serious film that De Palma really wants to make—one where he is "dealing with a kind of material that I'd never dealt with before and trying not to pander to the bloodlust of the audience, which is what I've been accused of doing many times."[3]

Jack (John Travolta), a soundman on cheap horror movies, is recording some nocturnal noises in a park when his microphone picks up the pop of a tire blow out, which causes a car to careen into a river. The car's male driver drowns, but Jack is able to dive in and save the female passenger, Sally (Nancy Allen). The driver was Governor McRyan, possibly the next U.S. president, and Jack hears what he thinks may be a gunshot just prior to the tire blow out on his recording of the incident, making him suspect that it might have been an assassination rather than an accident. It turns out that a photographer, Manny (Dennis Franz), was also present on the scene, and Sally reveals that he was there to take compromising pictures of the governor's adulterous dalliance with her. By syncing up Manny's still photos with his own audio recording, Jack is able to confirm both the sound and the bright explosion of a gunshot preceding the blow out. Thus, it is revealed that there was yet another man at the scene, Burke (John Lithgow), an operative for the opposing campaign, who exceeded his orders—which were to compromise, not to kill—and shot out the governor's tire, leading to his death. Now, to cover up all evidence of the crime, Burke impersonates a TV news reporter and meets with Sally, who brings him the synced-up film. Jack has planted a bug on Sally, enabling him to locate her by following her screams and to kill Burke just before the man is about to plunge an ice-pick into her. But it is too late: Burke has already strangled her to death with a wire. With Burke having destroyed the film, there is no longer any convincing evidence of the politically motivated crime that Jack was trying to prove. In a gesture of cynical despair, Jack dubs Sally's screams into the low-budget horror movie *Coed Frenzy*. They are very convincing.

In some ways, *Blow Out* marks a return to De Palma's earlier film, *Greetings*, where Lloyd (Gerrit Graham) is obsessed with proving that there was a conspiracy behind the John F. Kennedy assassination. Like Jack, Lloyd tries to solve the mystery by studying photos of the incident (blown-up frames from the Zapruder film). Lloyd's obsession with his investigative work also takes precedence over any relationship he might have with a woman, as when he traces bullet trajectories on the nude body of his would-be girlfriend. The danger to her that is merely implied is made manifest in Jack's case, when he persuades Sally to go alone to meet with the man who ends up being her killer. True, Jack thinks this man is a TV news reporter, not Burke; Jack has wired Sally so that he can listen in; and Jack believes that the only way both of them will be safe is if the truth about the assassination is made public, in which case there would no longer be any point in killing them to shut them up. But Jack is also hell-bent on proving that his theory about the conspiracy is correct, and in this he puts his own ego above Sally's safety. As De Palma says, "[Jack] manipulated [Sally] to prove that he is right. He didn't think that his experiment was maybe going to cost the life of the girl he loves; no, for him, the truth must be divulged, whatever the price."[4] In Jack, De Palma recognizes a surrogate for himself, for he, too, is prone to such an obsessive involvement in his own work that his relationship with those he loves can be imperiled: "When I'm making a film, nothing else matters to me. The outside world no longer exists. I have only one obsession: to realize the project that is in my head. I no longer pay any attention to my wife or my children and sometimes I've lost everything because of it."[5]

Besides the John F. Kennedy assassination, another historical influence on *Blow Out* is the 1969 Chappaquiddick affair, in which lingering questions about Ted Kennedy's involvement in an incident where his car drove off a bridge and into the water, leaving his female companion dead, ended the possibility of his becoming president. Not only has De Palma reversed the outcome, as if to punish the man for his philandering (the politician dies while the woman survives), but with Manny there to take photographs of the man *in flagrante delicto*, De Palma seems to make another obsessive reference to that incident from his own past when he attempted to film his father committing adultery in order to obtain evidence for his mother's divorce. (Sally claims that the photos Manny took of her in bed with adulterers would be used by their wives in divorce cases.) We also know that the young De Palma tried to capture his father's adulterous conversations on tape and that he considered taking a .22-caliber rifle with him to the confrontation with his father and the mistress, so it would seem that there are additional connections between De Palma and Jack, who tapes McRyan in the car with Sally, and between De Palma and Burke, who shoots McRyan as De Palma had thought of shooting his philandering father.

It is as though De Palma had split and scattered himself across three characters—Jack, Manny, and Burke—each of whom is gradually revealed to have been present at the scene of adulterous McRyan's death: Jack listening (with his shotgun mike taping the incident), Manny viewing (with his camera shooting photos), and Burke shooting (with his rifle). Throughout *Blow Out*, Jack can be read as someone who tries to confirm his identity as a good man by differentiating himself from his dark doubles, Manny and Burke.

At first, the difference between Jack and Manny may seem clear-cut. Manny put Sally in the car with McRyan, using her to take compromising photos, and he may even have known about Burke's plan to shoot out the tire, in which case Manny would have placed Sally in danger of death. Manny flees the scene whereas Jack dives in to save her. However, there are strange similarities between the two men. The office where Manny works on his sleazy photos is located above an X-rated movie theater, and Jack is the soundman on cheap slasher films containing elements of softcore porn. Manny's photos of Sally in bed with other men make him a kind of voyeur, while Jack's phallic microphone intrudes upon two lovers in the park at night, prompting the woman to wonder, "What is he, a Peeping Tom or something?" After rescuing Sally from the river, Jack takes her to a motel where he chastely puts her to bed, but later, when he discovers Manny's photos of Sally in bed with other men *at the same motel*, Jack's attitude toward her changes from chivalrous to contemptuous, speaking to her as he would to the "tits and ass" models who feature in his softcore porn slashers: "You got nice tits. Who was payin' you to flash them for McRyan?"

Although Sally protests that she "didn't really . . . screw" her clients, Jack's view of her is now clouded, with the "good girl" shadowed by hints of the whore. Similarly, in Hitchcock's *Vertigo*, after Scottie (James Stewart) saves Madeleine/Judy (Kim Novak) from drowning and puts her chastely to bed, he is disturbed to find out that she was involved with another man and part of a nefarious plot against Scottie. From the moment of that revelation, Scottie loses trust in her, suspecting her of further duplicity (like Sally, she is a shop-girl and actress associated with make-up or a possible "false front"), and his energies turn from loving her toward making sure that he is not the victim of any further plot, even if that means endangering her.

Likewise, Jack—though at one level still very much concerned for Sally—is also prey to subterranean doubts about the kind of woman she is. In one shot, Jack is backgrounded by a store window displaying a row of female manne-quins whose attire alternates between bridal white and sensual red: is Sally a "good girl" he could marry or a prostitute? Red-haired Sally is dressed entirely in red in the scene where, after his flash of anger at her for her pecuniary par-ticipation in Manny's compromising photos, Jack tries to convince her not to trust Manny. Is Jack also trying to convince himself that she is not a whore but a "Raggedy Ann doll" or innocent victim of Manny's scheme? (Nancy Allen has said that she "saw 'Sally' as being some sort of rag-doll. Brian wanted me to change the color of my hair for it. So I took it deep red.")[6]

As with Scottie, Jack's doubts about the woman seem bound up with his need not to be victimized by other men, such as those involved in the political (Burke) or financial (Manny) conspiracy against McRyan. "I'm sick of being fucked by these guys!" Jack tells Sally, as his compassion for her as a fellow victim gives way to his desire to use her in a plan to prove the conspiracy. After wiring Sally and sending her to the meeting with the man who ends up being her killer, Jack cynically dubs her screams into the slasher porn film he is mak-ing solely for the money. In profiting from Sally's dying screams, Jack seems little different from Manny, who had sold photos of Sally as she was sinking to what could have been her death in the car with McRyan.

There are also peculiar connections linking Jack and Burke that work against Jack's attempts to establish himself as the hero in opposition to the villain. We have noted the sense in which Jack, recording sounds in the park for use in his slasher film about a voyeuristic killer, is himself a kind of audio voyeur, intruding with his phallic/shotgun microphone upon some lovers. Of course, Jack is ostensibly just doing his job as a soundman and not emotion-ally involved. His interest in the sounds of sex and death, such as those of the lovers or of the woman being stabbed in the shower in *Coed Frenzy*, is purely technical—or is it?

Burke, too, is supposedly just doing a job, voyeuristically stalking and stab-bing women so that when he kills Sally, her death will appear to be merely one in a series of sex-murders rather than a political cover-up—but is he really so dispassionate? Stalking his first victim in a fish market that adver-tises "CLAMS" in the window, Burke grabs an ice-pick next to a dead fish on the left side of the screen, while on the right can be seen his female prey. Male disgust at the female sex has sometimes been expressed in terms of its "fishy" smell. Soon after, Burke kills the woman by rolling around on top of her down the side of an excavation site and, while breathing heavily, by stab-bing her repeatedly with the ice-pick—a lust-murder that seems to punish her for arousing his desire. "She made me do it," Burke later tells the police by phone, with deep emotion in his voice but a totally blank look on his face. Consciously, Burke is merely impersonating a sex-murderer as part of his job as a political operative, but the impersonation reveals an unconscious truth about his emotional involvement in these lust/disgust killings.

Later, after watching a prostitute give a blow job to a sailor, Burke pretends to be her next client, stalking her to a restroom where, instead of receiving oral sex, he strangles her with a wire. The red-haired hooker in her red dress stands out against the white tiles and toilet in the restroom stall; in Burke's eyes, her sexuality defiles the purity of the room. As he garrotes her, toothpaste foams near her mouth (she had been brushing her teeth), and her legs kick spasmodically as Burke punishes her with a sexualized death for the blow job she gave.

Of course, Jack—unlike Manny, who attempts to rape Sally, and unlike Burke, who stabs women—does not have sex with her or any other women in the film. Jack seems more interested in his job, in his sound equipment, than in sex, but could his profession as an audio voyeur be a cover for his prurient interest, much as Burke's job is for *his* lust? Rather than making him out as the pure hero, Jack's abstinence is a problematic sign of repression. It is as though he avoids sex—or expresses his desire only indirectly through his sound equipment—because he, too, has a problem with women, as when he turns contemptuously on Sally for having "prostituted" herself in the com-promising photos. Jack *can't* have sex with Sally because he is afraid that, in reaction to her sensuality, his desire might turn murderous. This potential similarity between Jack and the killer is implied in the film-within-the-film, *Coed Frenzy*, when a campus security guard, ostensibly there to protect the coeds, stands leering at them from outside a window and is then stabbed by the knife-wielding killer. Even the security guard is a voyeur and potential sex-murderer, punished for his lust by the actual sex-murderer from whom the security guard failed to differentiate himself.

Jack's struggle to differentiate himself from Burke runs into similar trou-ble. Following Sally's screams, which he hears from the bug with which he has wired her, Jack makes a heroic run to rescue her, but he arrives too late. Why? Jack's run is presented in slow motion, as if he were fighting against something that compromises his ability to save her. Could it be that Jack does not have enough faith in Sally's or his own goodness and that this psychological weakness slows him down, fatally impairing his capacity to arrive in time to rescue her?

When he does finally get there, Jack prevents Burke from stabbing Sally by bringing Burke's hand with the ice-pick down into Burke's chest. Since Jack is standing behind Burke during this action, it looks as though Jack is also stabbing himself. In this way, Jack attempts to kill the "Burke" within him, to destroy the lust-murderer inside himself so that his own potentially murderous desire will not hurt women in the way that Burke's has. Jack's implied self-stabbing suggests at least some degree of recognition that his failure to save Sally is partly due to his own compromised character, his too-close connection with repressed voyeurs like Burke, leading to an inability to establish his own goodness in time.

Jack's connection with Burke can also be seen in the "wire" motif that links them. Back in the days when he worked for the police force, Jack wired an informant as part of a sting operation, but when the bug was discovered by the mobster who was the target of the sting, the informant was killed by being hanged with Jack's wire around his neck. Despite Jack's remorse over the death, his own egotistical belief in his technical prowess and his own obsession with proving the conspiracy lead him to persuade Sally to wear a wire when she goes for the meeting with the TV reporter who turns out to be impersonated by the killer Burke.

In the scene where Jack is on the phone with Sally convincing her to go, we cut from the conversation to a shot of Burke listening to it on a tape recorder, for he has bugged Jack's phone, thereby gaining the information that will allow him to impersonate the TV reporter. Burke thus uses a wiretap to thwart Jack's plan to wire Sally. How different is Jack really from Burke, when both men use wires that endanger others to further their own ends? We cut back from Burke to Jack in phone conversation with Sally, which is now presented as a split-screen with Jack on the left, persuading her to go along with his plan, and Sally on the right. A split has opened up between Jack and Sally, as Burke intervenes between them, listening in, but also as the "Burke" within Jack divides him from Sally, persuading her to endanger herself in furtherance of his own ends. Like the other female victims, Sally is strangled by Burke with a metal wire that he pulls from his wristwatch, but in a sense Sally is also strangled by Jack's wire—by his sending her to that meeting wired with a bug that allows him to hear her but not to save her in time, just as he was unable to save the informant before.

Blow Out did not fare well at the box office. One reason for this may have been the lack of a romance between Jack and Sally when, as De Palma ruefully

admitted, "that's what the public expects, it seems, when you have John Travolta and a pretty girl."[7] "How can you put John Travolta and Nancy Allen
together in a movie [and not have a romance]?" was Allen's comment. "Everybody's going to be expecting *hot stuff* like they had in the car scene in *Carrie*."[8]

Another reason for the film's box-office failure was almost certainly its
tragic ending. According to De Palma, "When I showed it to the executives,
they were like—'cause the ending's so shocking—they were like, 'Oh, my God,
what a downer this is!'";[9] "I'll never forget when the distributor saw it, they
almost had a coronary."[10] "How can John Travolta [Jack] not save the girl?"[11]
asked Allen, noting that audiences had certain expectations of Travolta, who
by that time had become a big star, which the film failed to meet. She, editor
Paul Hirsch, and producer George Litto lobbied De Palma for a happy ending. As Litto recalls, "I always felt that the girl should be saved in *Blow Out*
and they should go see *Sugar Babies* [the Broadway musical that Sally wants
to attend with Jack], but [De Palma's] view was different, and the film still has
many admirers that way. But I was a firm believer in the Hitchcock concept:
you meet two people you like; they get into jeopardy; and you root for them
to extricate themselves safely."[12]

De Palma has noted that Jack "finds himself in the same situation as Cary
Grant in Hitchcock's *Notorious*: after having thrown the girl [Ingrid Bergman]
into the arms of a murderer, he wonders, 'My God, what have I done?'"[13] Grant's
character even has the same ambivalence about the Bergman character's overt
sexuality as Jack does about Sally's; it attracts him but also makes him suspect
her of being a kind of prostitute. Yet Grant succeeds in rescuing Bergman, carrying her in his arms away from her would-be murderer, whereas Jack fails,
able only to hold Sally's lifeless body in his arms after Burke has strangled her.
De Palma's darker vision, his distance from Hitchcock, can also be seen in the
fact that celebratory fireworks go off behind Jack and Sally as he cradles her
corpse—an ironic allusion to the romantic scene in Hitchcock's *To Catch a
Thief* where Cary Grant's embrace of Grace Kelly is backgrounded by exploding fireworks. (Interestingly, the novelization of *Blow Out* not only features a
romance between Jack and Sally but also a happy ending in which he saves her
in time.)[14]

In addition to the links with Hitchcock, *Blow Out* has connections with De
Palma's own films. As early as *Murder à la Mod* (Manny watches a scene from
this film on TV in *Blow Out*), De Palma explored the idea of three male characters—like Jack, Manny, and Burke—who are all to one degree or another
implicated in the ice-pick murders of women. In De Palma's original treatment for *Blow Out*,[15] the character of Jack is called Jon—the same name as the
Robert De Niro character in *Greetings* and *Hi, Mom!*, whose "peep art" camerawork, like Jack's audio voyeurism, implicates him in lustful and potentially

murderous attitudes toward women. Jack, a tech geek, is like a grown-up version of Peter from *Dressed to Kill*, who failed to save his mother, Kate, from the killer and whose own dark desires then compromised his ability to save Liz (Nancy Allen). In *Blow Out*'s original treatment, the character of Sally (played by Allen) is called Kate and, as we know, Jack fails to save her.

Of course, De Palma himself is something of a tech geek, like his surrogates Peter and Jack. (De Palma got the idea for a film about a soundman while he was doing the sound mix for *Dressed to Kill*. Another inspiration for *Blow Out* was fellow director Francis Ford Coppola's film about a sound technician, *The Conversation*, itself based on Antonioni's *Blow-Up*.)[16] We have already noted how Jack's involvement with his own work, as well as his technician's obsession with using a wire to prove the conspiracy, contributes to Sally's death and serves as an object lesson for De Palma regarding his own tendency to cut himself off from the world and from human relationships when he is working on a film. Actual soundman Jim Tanenbaum described how "withdrawn" De Palma was while working on *Blow Out*: "He was wearing a Sony Walkman when we were shooting, but the bleed from the ear pieces was not acceptable so he had to shut them off."[17] Like Jack, who struggles to move beyond immurement in his tech world and make human contact with Sally, De Palma has encountered a similar challenge in his own life. "He appears to be aloof and caustic," says Allen (De Palma's wife at the time), "but there are always these two big soulful eyes. I saw a sensitive, vulnerable man who needed me."[18]

De Palma was sensitive to Allen's concern that she not be typecast in "hooker" roles, like the ones she had played in his two previous films—"We both agreed that she should follow up *Dressed to Kill* with something other than another prostitute"[19]—but he went ahead and cast her in just such a part again in *Blow Out*. (Granted, this was at Travolta's urging, but De Palma didn't have to consent to it.) Although Allen is "severely claustrophobic and Brian knew that,"[20] the part of Sally requires her to be "trapped" in the McRyan car while it fills up with water. De Palma was empathetic—"It's like the scariest moment in my life putting my wife in that car"[21]—and made sure that she could see the escape route, donned scuba gear himself to be with her underwater, and offered to shoot the scene with a body double for her instead. Nevertheless, to realize the project that was in his head as director, De Palma did put his wife in a fearful situation involving some danger. As Allen described it, "The car started filling up really, really fast with water, so any panic that you see, yeah, there's not much acting going on; there was real sheer terror."[22] De Palma had to admit—somewhat facetiously but also half-seriously—that this was "not the best thing for a marriage, I can tell you!"[23]

We recall that, as part of his plan to prove the conspiracy, Jack endangers Sally by sending her to meet with the man who turns out to be Burke. In directing the scenes where Burke is manhandling the screaming Sally, De Palma "kept saying, 'be rougher, be rougher!' and Lithgow [Burke] would say, 'I don't want to hurt her,'"[24] according to Allen's account of the filming. "Brian kept saying, 'No, I really want you to throw her around.'"[25] It would be interesting to know how De Palma felt when he added his own wife's scream to the *Coed Frenzy* soundtrack—"In fact, it is Nancy's scream that we dub into the girl's voice at the end of the movie"[26]—just as Jack uses the terrified Sally's scream as the voice of the coed being stabbed in the shower.

The commercial and critical failure of *Blow Out* crushed De Palma. Apart from a rave review from the *New Yorker*'s Pauline Kael ("De Palma has sprung to the place . . . where genre is transcended and what we're moved by is an artist's vision"),[27] most critics dismissed *Blow Out* as if it were *Coed Frenzy*, the kind of cheap genre film that De Palma was trying to mock and move beyond: "It's an unusual film, full of meaning and very carefully constructed, but it didn't do well. I was stupefied when critics said it was a bad suspense and horror movie. Nobody understood it."[28] The fact that the film recouped only $8 million of its $18 million investment didn't help. "When you make a movie like *Blow Out* and the movie makes 20 cents, you're verboten," De Palma said. "Forget it. Despite Pauline Kael, despite anybody. You can't get a job."[29]

CHAPTER 15

Scarface (1983)

Following the poor performance of *Blow Out* at the box office, De Palma decided to switch genres, explaining, "I'd just made a very difficult, very unsuccessful picture, *Blow Out*. I kind of wanted to move into a different world. I was hoping to make a more commercial picture by making a gangster picture. I'd never done one before."[1] Besides, he added, "I get tired of making these Brian De Palma movies. You get tired of your own obsessions, the betrayals, the voyeurism, the twisted sexuality. I've made a lot of movies like this, so you're glad to get out there with those Cuban . . . gangsters. It gives you a little relief."[2]

Scarface is set in 1980, and Tony Montana (Al Pacino) is one of the Cuban evacuees who journey to Florida as part of the Mariel Boatlift when, along with many law-abiding citizens, Fidel Castro also unloaded some criminals from his jails. Our first view of Tony is of him being interrogated by U.S. immigration officials. According to cinematographer John A. Alonzo, "Instead of using this big, wide crane shot to introduce the character, [De Palma] introduces [Tony] in close-up, sitting in a chair, and he had the camera roll 360 degrees all the way around him . . . he was introducing that face to the audience,"[3] so that the viewer felt "this Latin machismo coming out of this man with a scar on his face."[4] Even as Tony is the object of suspicion and ridicule by his interrogators, the camera's circling suggests that—in his mind, at least—he is already holding court, lording it over his underlings.

Tony's bravado is overcompensation for his weakness; he is macho *because* of that scar, making a strenuous claim to power to avoid being wounded again. As he tells the immigration officers, "There's nothing you can do to me that Castro has not already done." William Schoell argues that, in displaying Tony's "insolent pride," Pacino "clearly put some of himself in the role, remembering early insults to his background, height, ability."[5]

When Tony is asked how he learned English, he tells the agents that it was from "the movies. I learn. I watch the guys like Humphrey Bogart, James Cagney. They teach me to talk." Tony's gangster pose is thus a performance modeled on movie gangsters; his is a macho act designed to make him feel bigger and stronger than he, or any man, actually is. Likewise, Pacino's grandiose act as Tony is modeled on Paul Muni's over-the-top performance as Tony in the original 1932 gangster movie of *Scarface*: "All I wanted to do was imitate Paul Muni. His acting went beyond the boundaries of naturalism into another kind of expression. It was almost abstract what he did. It was almost uplifting."[6] Though Pacino admits that "I'm not the way Tony Montana is at all," he adds, "but who doesn't want to be fearless?"[7]

Foolhardy and insane as it may ultimately be, there is a strong attraction to Tony's boundless bravado and his vaunted indomitability—an attraction and a repulsion. When we imagine ourselves being as empowered as Tony, we find his "forceful" and "violent" character "totally captivating,"[8] as De Palma says, but the lack of any limit to Tony's destructive power is also terrifying and repellent. According to Pacino, "The picture had a fire to it. That was part of Brian's concept, to do everything in an extraordinary way—to have the violence blown up, the language blown up. The spirit of it was Brechtian, operatic."[9] Tony's performance is "operatic" in the sense of being larger than life, a great fearlessness and force that we are tempted to identify with, but his macho pose is "Brechtian" in the sense of being ridiculously overblown, a mere pretense of power, an act of fearful destruction toward others that won't save himself but in fact only hastens his own demise. As Pacino scholar Karina Longworth explains, "In this case, 'Brechtian' means that Tony Montana was not intended to be a character that the audience identified with, but instead looked at from an emotional remove."[10]

Soon after proving his manhood by sticking a knife in the belly of Rebenga, one of Castro's former allies, Tony faces an extreme challenge to his machismo. At gunpoint, he is forced to watch as his friend Angel's arm and leg are cut off with a chainsaw when the man is tied to a shower rod in a motel bathroom by some Colombians as part of a drug deal gone bad. As a *New York Times* critic noted, "The most exquisite example of the De Palma touch is the chainsaw-in-the-bathtub scene, with its voracious blade, its grinding noise and gouts of blood. Indubitably an effective scene, if effectiveness be measured by one's desire to turn away from it."[11] Indeed, De Palma acknowledges *our* desire to turn away from the gruesome scene by having his camera move out through a window and crane down to the street below, where Tony's friends Manny and Chi Chi are seated outside in a car, oblivious to the violence occurring inside the motel, much as Hitchcock in *Frenzy* moves *his* camera down the stairs and out into the street where passersby are unaware that a man is raping and murdering a woman in one of the rooms inside. In both cases, the obliviousness of outsiders serves to emphasize the victim's terrible helplessness, with potential aid so close yet out of reach.

The allusion to *Frenzy*'s rape-murder also suggests the almost sexual violation that the chainsaw's cutting represents, the "emasculation" of Angel while Tony is forced to look on helplessly. Interestingly, De Palma once said that "the most violent scene I ever saw . . . was in *Deliverance*,"[12] referring to the scene where Bobby (Ned Beatty) is raped, and Ed (Jon Voight) is compelled to watch while unable to do anything. It is also noteworthy that De Palma, in defending himself against critics "reproaching him for the loads of violence, the sadism"[13] in scenes like the one with the chainsaw, has said that "you don't have to look at it. Nobody had to go and see *Scarface*. Nobody held a gun to anybody's head."[14]

With a gun held to his head, Tony *does* have to look at it. Tony thus joins the long list of traumatized witnesses to violence in De Palma's films, including Grace in *Sisters*, Sue in *Carrie*, and Liz in *Dressed to Kill*. It is no accident that many of these witnesses are women, for suffering the shock of a traumatic sight can have a feminizing or disempowering effect, especially as one tends to empathize with the violated victim. Once again, we are reminded that the young De Palma was a witness to amputations performed by his surgeon-father: "When I was, like, 16, 17, I saw him do a lot of bone surgery, amputate legs. . . . You *do* see a lot of blood when people operate";[15] "That influenced me in the sense that I have a very high tolerance for blood. Things that shock other people don't shock me."[16] Tony tries to respond with similar macho fortitude, maintaining a blank face at the sight of his friend Angel's gorily amputated arm and leg. Just as soon as Tony is able to turn the tables on his chainsaw-wielding assailant, he pumps a series of bullets into him, gunning him down in the street in front of shocked witnesses. Now Tony is the one doing the violating, traumatizing others.

Tony's machismo involves him in an Oedipal rivalry with his older boss, Frank (Robert Loggia), over that man's girlfriend, Elvira (Michelle Pfeiffer). Tony first sees Elvira when she is displayed to him by Frank; Tony wants her because she is his boss's possession, a sign of superior wealth and power. The blonde Elvira descends from on high in a glass elevator; she is like an angelic doll in a toy-store box that Tony wants to buy and own. Wearing a sexy backless dress, she is turned away from him in the elevator, much as later, while dancing at the Babylon Club to the song "She's on Fire," she has her back to him. Coming from a wealthy and cultured Baltimore background, Elvira is of a higher class to which Tony aspires, making her inaccessible and all the more desirable.

Unlike his friend Manny, whose adolescent attempts to pick up women by flicking his tongue at them at least suggest a willingness to please through oral sex, Tony takes the more macho approach, arguing that if you "get the money" and then "get the power," you will "get the woman." Believing that "this town [is] like a great big pussy just waitin' to get fucked," Tony tells Elvira that "you got a look in your eye like you haven't been fucked in a year." Seeing Frank as "soft" because "the booze and the *concha* tell him what to do," Tony determines that he will be harder than Frank, eventually shooting him and taking over his woman.

Although part of what excites Tony about Elvira is her defiant spirit, which perhaps reminds him of his own, he breaks that very spirit by taking possession of her. "She's a tiger; she belong to me," he thinks, and after they are married, he keeps her "caged" and on display in his mansion, like the tiger he keeps tethered on the grounds of his estate. Notably, Tony and Elvira are never shown making love—or even having sex. Instead, as soon as he "owns" her as his wife, she seems like a broken doll, with only occasional flashes of defiance, and he treats her coldly, like a sex object, one of his possessions.

As Pfeiffer (Elvira) has said about acting with Pacino in *Scarface*, comparing his treatment of her on that film to their later work together on *Frankie and Johnny*, "He was much more introverted and much less accessible [on *Scarface*]. I tell him things he did, and he can't believe it. He says: 'I did *not* do that.' And I say: 'Yes, you did. And you did *this* . . .'"[17] According to Mary Elizabeth Mastrantonio (who played Tony's sister Gina), "I was shy and so was Michelle. It was a man's world and all these people with greasy hair and these big guns. We girls didn't know why we were there."[18]

De Palma joined with Pacino in this cold isolation of Pfeiffer. As Steven Bauer (Manny) has said, De Palma "made Michelle feel like a scared, lonely little girl in a world of men. He did the right thing [for her performance], but it was hard to watch. That poor girl was always alone, always on edge, very vulnerable, brave but alone in her performance";[19] "She was intimidated and it worked for the character and he kept her off balance. . . . Really fragile and Brian didn't do anything to help that."[20] For costume designer Patricia Norris, De Palma's coldness was a bit too much like Tony's, and De Palma's and other men's attention to Pfeiffer's sexy attire was too close to Tony's sexual objectification of Elvira: "He [De Palma] was tense a lot of the time; he could be cold and rude, dismissive. . . . the only clothes he was interested in were the women's clothes, Michelle's clothes. He and [producer] Marty Bregman both. They wanted a lot of input in how she should look—it was more than a little creepy, if you ask me. I'd overhear them arguing about how she should be dressed, how sexy, how much skin they wanted her to show."[21]

Pfeiffer herself said that "I was objectified" by De Palma: "If there was one hair out of place . . . I remember once I had a bruise or something on my leg, and he made me go back and take off my pantyhose and have makeup put on because he could see an imperfection."[22] However, Pfeiffer later seemed to imply that De Palma was *exposing* Tony's reduction of her to a sex object more than he was objectifying her himself: "Sometimes . . . by playing an object you can actually say more about objectifying women than if you play somebody of strength. I felt that Elvira in *Scarface* was a complete object. She was a hood ornament, like another Rolls-Royce or something, for both of the men [Tony and Frank] that she was with. I felt that by playing something that mirrors someone's life in that way, I could make a kind of feminist statement. It depends on the way in which it's presented. If you're glamorizing or glorifying it, then I object to that."[23] Perhaps it could be said that, in *Scarface*, De Palma was revealing his own tendency toward sexual objectification in an attempt to gain some critical distance from it.

Much as Tony's marriage to Elvira disintegrates by the end of the film, so De Palma's to actress Nancy Allen fell apart. They were divorced around the time of *Scarface*'s release. Allen was reported to have said that "the pressures of his work in filming *Scarface* have contributed to their difficulties,"[24] and, as noted in the last chapter, De Palma himself has admitted that work for him can become an "obsession" to the exclusion of all else: "When I'm making a film, nothing else matters to me. . . . I no longer pay any attention to my wife or my children and sometimes I've lost everything because of it."[25] Tony becomes another one of those Howard Hughes-like characters, like Swan in *Phantom of the Paradise* or Childress in *The Fury*, whose "megalomania" fascinates De Palma because it allows him to reflect upon the dark side of himself: "Those people want everything to be an extension of their own reality. I can identify. Making movies is a lot like that."[26] According to De Palma, "My characters create a reality to which others must conform. It's a little bit like what I myself do when I direct a film."[27] Did De Palma bring too much of what he calls his characters' "god complex"[28] into his own marriage to Allen, making it more one of director to actress than of husband to wife? "Problem is you start to feel like a manipulative mind-fuck," he has said, adding that "the director has to stand behind the camera,"[29] rather than carrying that one-sided power relationship over into personal life.

Tony's god complex is on display in the scene where he sits at a round table, his image reflected in multiple mirrors, looking out at and lording it over all the patrons at the Babylon Club. But this image of unlimited power is only an illusion, a hollow pretense like that of the fat-suited clown who is shown as ridiculously puffed up with pride, performing his act in front of Tony. Tony's overreaching pride, his desire to possess Elvira, has prompted Frank to send two hit men to gun him down, and as they fire, their bullets drill into the fat suit of the clown standing in front of Tony as if to foreshadow the puncturing of his pretense. Right before the shooting, a reflection of De Palma's own face can be seen in the mirror behind a reflection of Tony's head, as if to implicate the director himself, with his own god complex, in Tony's hollow hubris and consequent downfall.

After escaping Frank's attempted hit, gunning *him* down, and taking his woman, Tony laments that the image of the wealthy, powerful man is hollow and not what it was projected to be: "Is this it? That's what it's all about . . . eating, drinking, fucking, sucking, snorting? Then what? . . . You're fifty. You got a bag for a belly. . . . You're eatin' this fuckin' shit and you're lookin' like these rich, fuckin' mummies in here [the upscale restaurant where Tony is dining]." In a rare moment of insight, Tony seems to realize that he will become—has become—that clown with "a bag for a belly." In acquiring Frank's wealth and woman, Tony has not found fulfillment but merely an empty display. Having reduced Elvira to an object, he cannot find love with her as a person. Having displaced the father figure Frank, Tony has merely set himself up to be killed by another foolish, grasping "son" like his former self.

Like Tony, De Palma has been envious of other men. Speaking of the time before his first hit, *Carrie*, he admitted, "Frankly, by then I was more than ready for big-time success. All my best friends in the business—Marty Scorsese, George Lucas, Steven Spielberg—had already made it in a huge way, and there was I, after eight or nine pictures, still struggling."[30] And yet De Palma was soon to discover that "in this business success can be even more destructive than failure, because it can isolate you and leave you surrounded by film people talking about deals and budgets and percentage points, and soon you yourself begin to forget what you want to do. Because you have some big star and a terrific deal, you forget to worry about whether this is a movie you really should make."[31] Here, De Palma is referring to Kirk Douglas and *The Fury*, a project on which the prospect of great remuneration and renown—the idea of being a big shot—compromised his own artistic values, much as Tony's desire for wealth and fame went to his head. Later, after the relative failure of *Blow Out*, De Palma was again tempted to make a movie for the money (he almost agreed to direct *Flashdance*), calculating that this would then allow him to finance the pictures he really wanted to make.

To some extent, *Scarface* itself represents this temptation ("I was hoping to make a more commercial picture"),[32] but Tony is also an object lesson in the isolating and soul-compromising effects of greed, as if De Palma were simultaneously giving into and fighting off his own money-grubbing tendencies by making this film. When asked about the fortune George Lucas has made on the *Star Wars* films, De Palma's reply was: "Who cares? After you've made a couple of million dollars, who cares about $50 million more? That's what I think is the sickness of this business. People get into this money-power game. And to what purpose? It doesn't help them creatively."[33] Indeed, *Scarface* seems expressly designed to show what happens when one gets into the "money-power game."

While Tony's life of greed, violence, and drugs is repellent, at least he is upfront about it, unlike the "respectable" members of society who secretly profit from his illegal activities and who snort his cocaine behind closed doors. As he tells off the upper-class diners at the restaurant, "You need people like me so you can point your fuckin' fingers and say, 'That's the bad guy.' So, what that make you? Good? You're not good. You just know how to hide, how to lie." The wealthy diners' hypocrisy can be compared to that of the Hollywood Establishment, which snootily disparaged the film for its depictions of excessive drug use at a time when so many in the film community were themselves doing drugs. As Scorsese said at *Scarface*'s premiere, "Hollywood's going to hate this film. It's about *them*."[34] According to Bregman, "Scorsese was right. Hollywood did hate it, *hated* it. We were looked at as though we were dragging filth into their living rooms," despite the fact that "there was a bowl of white powder as you entered" the "house parties of some senior executives" at that time.[35] "They've got the piles of cocaine on the table at parties that are every bit as big as the one Pacino [as Tony] had," said De Palma.[36]

In addition to dealing drugs, Tony commits violence—such as knocking off his competitors—in order to make more money. Another form of hypocrisy that De Palma takes aim at involves the media who criticize *him* for depictions of violence in *Scarface* and then turn around and use clips from his film on TV shows or descriptions of its violence in articles in order to sell more TV commercials or newspaper ads. Notice the segue that De Palma makes here between Tony and himself: "It's easy for everybody to point their finger at [Tony] because he's the obvious bad guy, but they're all bad guys. They need bad guys like him for them to point their fingers at. But at least he's honest, even in his evil, and that goes back to, like, television commentators accusing you of making money making violent movies. . . . I'm of course attacked on this many times [with them] saying, 'Well, you're just using violence to make money and you're pandering to the worst aspects of the human character in order to make more and more money.'"[37] But, as De Palma knows from his many appearances over the years on TV talk shows on which he has been pilloried for profiting off the violence in his films, "they can have us talking, they can show all the violent sequences from our movies, and of course say, 'They're morally reprehensible, we're embarrassed to have them on air, but please keep watching!' And at the same time, we're just used as a product [to sell TV ads]."³⁸

De Palma's upfront and hyperbolic depiction of Tony's excessive violence both sells and satirizes the myth of macho power. When an army of assassins sent by a rival drug dealer swarms around Tony, he taunts them by saying, "Say hello to my little friend"—an ironic reference to the massive weapon between his legs, the M16 assault rifle with its M203 grenade launcher that he shoots to blow away a bunch of his attackers. We identify with the desire for omnipotence represented by Tony's gargantuan gun, even as its ridiculous size distances us from him, exposing him in all his macho absurdity. "You think you kill me with bullets? I take your fuckin' bullets!" he brags, still standing after receiving multiple rounds of fire, but neither his big gun nor his bravado can save him from the self-destructive consequences of his own greed and violence, as a double-barreled shotgun blast from one of the assassins brings him down.

De Palma may profit from violence, but his similarity to Tony is countered by a satiric style that punctures his main character's mythic pretensions and reveals his machismo to be hollow, a mere performance of power—in imitation of movie gangsters—that neither fulfills nor fortifies the self against feelings of emptiness or against the revenge of rivals as greedy and overreaching as he is. The film's style, with its garish neon colors, sweeping camera moves, and pulsing electronic soundtrack, is as hyperbolic as Tony's frantic greed and macho bravado. Asked about the moral of *Scarface*, De Palma described it as being that "capitalism works only when tempered by a very strong moral order. There are good and bad ways to make money, and money is not an end to itself. That's a recurring theme in my movies."³⁹

"If you're a filmmaker dealing with millions of dollars, you've got to be a capitalist," admits De Palma, indicating that his films must make money, but he adds that "you've got to be able to deal with the money, and hopefully, hold your aesthetics safe from the capitalistic system affecting it";⁴⁰ "I think I live in a very greedy world, but there are certain things I wouldn't do—and I'm the one that's attacked constantly."⁴¹ Interestingly, there are also certain things that Tony won't do, despite the fact that critics have attacked him for his unlimited violence in the interests of greed. In the scene where Tony is expected to help detonate a bomb under a car, he won't do it because the vehicle contains not only the enemy who is his target, but also the man's wife and children. "What do you think I am?" Tony asks his accomplices and himself in a rare moment of self-recognition in which he looks at his own image in the rearview mirror. "You think I kill two kids and a woman? Fuck that! . . . Two little kids in the car. This is so bad."

This scene recalls Hitchcock's classic definition of "suspense," which he exemplified as a movie moment where there is a "bomb under the table and the public *knows* it"[42] and must wait in excruciating fear for the characters that it might go off. We are reminded that, in his film *Sabotage*, Hitchcock had a bomb go off on a bus, killing the young boy who had been unwittingly carrying it. Hitchcock later regretted his directorial decision to have the boy explode, calling it a "grave error."[43] In a sense, De Palma corrects that error by not having the car bomb kill the children. He deploys Hitchcockian suspense with the bomb under the car but decides that there are certain things he himself won't do, such as having children explode, much as Tony decides that *he* won't detonate the bomb with the kids in the car. It is one moment when both De Palma and Tony hold their morals safe from the capitalistic system surrounding them. (Later in his career, in *The Untouchables*, De Palma *will* show a little girl blown up by a bomb. As we shall see, this is a film that, while seeming to draw a firm distinction between good and evil, actually blurs the line between them quite a bit.)

Upon its first appearance, *Scarface* was not especially successful with the public or the press. As De Palma noted, "The critics didn't like *Scarface* because the film was too cynical, brutal, violent, exaggerated."[44] "Believe me, you didn't want to be around for the preview of *Scarface*," he said, or for "the opening. People were outraged—you saw people running up the aisle. I remember the opening-night party, I thought they were going to skin me alive."[45] Rex Reed of the *New York Post* wrote, "The violence is endless, the four-letter words take the place of the English language . . . the decadence and perversion drown everything in a vicious grunge. When it's over, you feel mugged, debased, like you've eaten a bad clam."[46] Even Pauline Kael, normally a stalwart supporter, argued that "the scenes are so shapeless that we don't know at what point we're meant to laugh. . . . The picture is peddling macho primitivism and at the same time making it absurd."[47] An expensive studio production, the film did little more than recover its initial cost ($25 million). However, as time went on, the movie became a massive cult hit, raking in the money on rerelease and on video rentals and sales. Critics began to appreciate the film for its stylized representation of the 1980s drugs-and-guns culture, and the controversy over its morality fueled much debate. As Ken Tucker succinctly put it, "One man's harsh-critique-of-crime is five others' *wow-look-at-those-guns-I-can-do-that-too!*"[48]

But this re-evaluation of *Scarface* was still several years away. In the meantime, De Palma was stuck with the feeling that his attempt at a gangster epic had not been a hit—and certainly not as successful as his friend Francis Ford Coppola's *The Godfather*. So it was only natural that De Palma would return again to what he knew best: the horror suspense thriller. Having stirred up controversy with the violence in *Scarface*, De Palma was ready to provoke similar outrage over sex in *Body Double*. "Yeah, there was a certain amount of

'You think *Scarface* was trouble? I'll show you trouble,' in my attitude going in to *Body Double*," De Palma admitted. "But it was also an idea I'd had in the back of my head for years, well before *Scarface*. I knew I wanted to eventually do something about sexual duplicity in the context of the sex film, the porn business."[49] The result was a movie that would draw more negative critical fire than any other De Palma film, before or since.

CHAPTER 16

Body Double (1984)

Body Double begins with Jake (Craig Wasson) attempting to act his part as a vampire in a low-budget horror movie. Lying in his coffin, he bares his fangs but then freezes, unable to bite or to rise from his resting place due to an attack of claustrophobia. The film's director, Rubin (Dennis Franz), and his male assistant are witnesses to Jake's inadequacy. Later, in drama class, Jake relives a time from his childhood when, while playing a game of Sardine with his two older brothers, he ended up jammed behind a freezer and unable to move. "They'll laugh at me for getting stuck behind the freezer and for crying out for help," Jake recalls thinking at the time, even as his actor friends Sam (Gregg Henry) and Billy look on at Jake's current humiliation, his being frozen in acting class just as he was as a boy in front of his two big brothers.

For this immobility rooted in a sense of inferiority, De Palma has drawn on his own past when he himself, playing Sardine with his older brothers Bruce and Bart, hid behind a refrigerator and could not get out—"A particularly humiliating experience" in De Palma's memory "because I had to call out to my brothers for help."[1] We have already noted De Palma's feelings of inferiority to—and his years of rivalry with—his big brothers, particularly Bruce, whose prowess when they were growing up together always seemed to exceed young Brian's. To be rendered passive through an inability to act can be experienced as emasculating or "feminizing," and it is interesting to note that De Palma has given his male character Jake the same immobilizing condition—claustrophobia—that his wife, Nancy Allen, had and that she suffered from while shooting the underwater scene in *Blow Out*.

After work, Jake stops at a Los Angeles fast-food stand, Tail o' the Pup, where he sees a man feeding a woman a hot dog. After buying his own hot dog to feed his girlfriend Carol, Jake drives to her house, where a sign reading "Jake ♥ Carol" and a photo of her with her arms around Jake and a cuddly dog suggest that he feels secure in his romance with her. But this security is undermined when some whimpering from the actual dog alerts Jake's ears to strange sounds coming from the bedroom, which turn out to be the orgasmic cries of Carol in bed with another man. (Ironically, Carol had been holding up the dog's ears in that cute photo.) Carol is not the faithful sweetheart he thought she was but instead more carnal and duplicitous, and the feckless Jake has had his "hot dog" replaced by another man's (much as he soon finds out that he was also replaced on the movie shoot by a vampire-actor with more bite). "Christ, I keep seeing it," Jake laments; "Carol lying there; her face was glowing" with illicit pleasure, with sensual enjoyment of another man she chose as superior to him.

Now loveless, homeless, and jobless, Jake accepts a house-sitting offer from his friend Sam, who takes him to a Hollywood Hills building shaped like a mushroom head atop a tall stalk (actually, architect John Lautner's "Chemosphere"). This phallic structure overlooks the valley where, every night in a curvy house down below, a woman does a sexy dance in the window, which Sam encourages Jake to watch through a telescope. At first feeling somewhat inhibited in his watching by Sam's presence (perhaps due to an inferiority complex), Jake freely indulges in his scopophilia once the other man is gone, growing excited by the sight of this woman whose dance includes undressing, donning some jewels, and then stroking herself. From his round, observation tower-like room with its panoramic view, Jake is in the perfect perch for a voyeur, like Swan's seat in the balcony overlooking his theater in *Phantom of the Paradise* or Tony's circular table from which he surveyed the Babylon Club in *Scarface*. (Jake's room also has a rotating round bed from which he can watch porn on TV, similar to Swan's "vinyl record" waterbed and Tony's circular bubble bath.)

However, Jake's voyeuristic satisfaction in being able to take sole possession of the woman in the window is disturbed when he notices what appears to be an "Indian" working on a satellite dish nearby and ogling the woman as she does her sexy dance. De Palma describes this man as a "macho Indian" and claims to have gotten the idea for the character when he heard that there were Native Americans who could "work at great heights without being scared."[2] The non-acrophobic "Indian" seems more macho than claustrophobic Jake, who feels bested again by another man, much as young De Palma himself often felt inferior to big brother Bruce. (The prominent birthmark scar on Bruce's face suggests a link between him and the scar-faced "Indian.") Furthermore, the "Indian's" leer at the woman in the window makes Jake, who is also watching her, fear that his own desire may be ugly and bestial; the sight of the "Indian" confronts Jake with his own dark side, his own worst impulses.

The next day, when Jake sees the "Indian" follow the woman in her car to a Beverly Hills shopping mall, Jake follows her, too. Jake stands outside the window of a clothing boutique and watches the woman try on some panties, her undressing barely visible through the curtains of a changing room. When it becomes apparent that the "Indian" is also watching her from a window on the other side of the shop, Jake walks around to that side. The "Indian" has fled, and Jake is now standing where the other man stood, peering in the window, with a saleslady staring back at him, her face accusing him of being a Peeping Tom. Indeed, how different are Jake's prying eyes from the "Indian's"? Does Jake desire to protect the woman from the other man or to possess her himself?

Jake sees the woman inside a glass elevator. We recall that, in *Scarface*, Tony's first sight of the angelic Elvira was of her descending from on high in a glass elevator. Spotting the "Indian" running toward her, Jake gets into the elevator with the woman, but just as he is about to speak to warn her, other people crowd in and he is paralyzed by claustrophobia. Unlike the crudely brash Tony, Jake is unable to summon up the courage to act with a woman when others are present; he fears that they might see him fail with the angel of his dreams.

Later, having followed the woman to a beach, Jake does start to warn her: "Someone's following you." "I know," she says and smiles at *him*. "No, it's not me. I—" Jake begins to reply, but as he stands there unable to speak, the "Indian" runs by and grabs her purse. Confused about his own intentions, by the thought that he may have followed her because he has the same nefarious desires as the "Indian," Jake freezes. Having rendered himself impotent so that he cannot hurt her, he is also unable to help save her from the man who definitely does want to do her harm. Jake chases the "Indian," but as they enter a tunnel, Jake is immobilized, unable to prevent the "Indian" from pillaging the woman's purse. Because Jake fears that he himself would like to take this kind of violent possession of her, he paralyzes himself, but in the process of ensuring that he does not become a villain like the "Indian," Jake becomes a passive victim, a helpless child. It is the woman who saves him, helping Jake to stand and walk and leading him out of the tunnel, much as a mother might help a boy.

Standing in the daylight outside the tunnel, Jake "slowly, tentatively" moves toward the woman, beginning a kiss that "extends," becoming "more forceful and passionate"[3] as the camera turns in ecstatic circles around them. As De Palma describes it, "I pulled the stops out for this huge, romantic kiss,"[4] for this moment that is "both erotic and romantic": "Jake gathers up her skirt— Revealing the thinnest, sheerest garter belt and silk stockings . . . Opens her blouse to a lacy bra . . ."[5] At least in this one moment, Jake seems able to act without fearing that his desires will become rapacious. Having vacillated between villain and victim, between attacker and child, Jake is here able to find a happy medium where he can be a man without manhandling her; he can undress his lacy angel without stripping her like a whore. He may have failed to prevent the purse-snatching, but he did *try* to stop it and to recover the woman's valuables, and so his "good boy" behavior is rewarded with the woman's loving attention, which gradually moves toward passion.

But serious doubts remain. When she breaks off the kiss, saying, "I can't do this," does it make him feel as though he has imposed himself on her? Later, back at his hillside house, Jake imagines phoning her to say, "Maybe you remember me. I'm the guy that almost fucked you at the beach today." Jake's joke, crude and awkward, betrays an underlying fear that he acted like a brute on the beach with her. When Jake then looks through his telescope at the woman's house below and sees the "Indian" inside stealing her jewels from the wall safe and then watching her undress in an adjoining room, Jake calls to warn her, but the ringing phone brings her into the room where her attacker is, and as she picks up the receiver, the "Indian" wraps the phone cord around her neck and uses it to strangle her. It is as though Jake's phone call makes him complicit in the woman's attack, which is again a sign that he is having trouble dissociating himself from the "Indian" who desires to plunder her.

Jake races to her house, yet seems to take forever to get there, as if he were somehow held back by self-doubt regarding the role he would play when he arrives—loving protector or voyeur and violator? When Jake finally does arrive, he is too late. As the "Indian" uses a phallic drill to penetrate the woman's supine body on the second floor, the bloody drill-bit bores through the floor, which is the ceiling above where Jake is lying on the first floor where he himself is bitten bloody by a vicious guard dog. Jake's compassion for the woman's suffering is signified by the fact that they are both bloody victims, with Jake being attacked in the same supine position right below her. Having failed to dissociate himself from the villain's rapacious desires in time to save her, Jake ends up becoming a passive victim just like her.

The murdered woman—the woman Jake followed to the shopping mall and kissed on the beach—was Gloria Revelle (Deborah Shelton). However, the woman he had watched doing a sexy dance in the window was Holly Body (Melanie Griffith). Sam, who turns out to have been Gloria's husband, had hired Holly to give her performance in order to lure Jake into witnessing Gloria's murder by an "Indian," who was in fact Sam in disguise. With Jake pinning the crime on the "Indian," Sam could get away with murdering his wife.

Jake first begins to suspect the deception when, in despair over the loss of Gloria, he is watching porn on TV and discovers a woman doing the same sexy dance he had witnessed in the window. The dream girl he fell in love with (the "reve" in Gloria Revelle means "dream") turns out to have been a body double, a kind of Hollywood act (by Holly Body). (The duped Jake is similar to Denis in *Home Movies*, who discovered that the woman he had been watching undress in a window was in fact the movie image of an actress projected onto a screen in order to fool him.) In retrospect, perhaps Jake should have seen that his "sparkling vision of flesh and diamonds"[6] was more porn queen than angelic star, more reel than real, for the sex-starved housewife wearing jewels and high heels is a common adult film scenario.

This split between flesh and fantasy, between porn performer and legitimate actress, was also evident behind the scenes of *Body Double*. Partly owing to his struggle with the MPAA ratings board over *Dressed to Kill* and *Scarface*, De Palma had originally spoken of making *Body Double* as the first mainstream X-rated film: "If they want an X, they'll get a *real* X. They wanna see suspense, they wanna see terror, they wanna see SEX—I'm the person for the job. It's going to be unbelievable";[7] "I think it's about time to blow the top off the ratings."[8] However, despite his desire to claim his right to free speech and artistic freedom, De Palma realized that "no major company would finance or distribute"[9] an X-rated movie, so when the ratings board demanded cuts to *Body Double* in order to make it a "legitimate" Hollywood film, he complied.

For the role of Holly Body, De Palma had trouble finding a Hollywood actress because the part required doing a masturbatory window dance. "I tried to get a lot of people to test for the part," De Palma said, "but I couldn't get many because of the nature of this material. I talked to everybody that was interested in it, and I said that there's going to be a lot of nudity in this, don't do it if you're uncomfortable"[10]—and everyone was! According to Melanie Griffith (Holly), De Palma told her that he was "probably going to have to use a real porno queen because no *real* actress would do this."[11]

So De Palma turned to adult film star Annette Haven, who had featured in such titles as *Bodies in Heat*, *Coed Fever*, and *Dracula Sucks*, but although she had "a terrific body,"[12] Haven as a veteran of the porn business could not project the sense of tender innocence and playful desire for love that were needed for the role. After "all her experience in making porn films, I think she had lost her ability to flirt," De Palma said,[13] and Craig Wasson (Jake) commented that, as a result of Haven's having had to defend herself so many times against charges of immorality, "she's built up a shell and you could feel it while rehearsing for the role. . . . That's why she lost the part."[14]

Griffith got the part for her ability to seem "vulnerable" like "Marilyn Monroe,"[15] along with her willingness to strip in a window in front of strangers. (Ironically, Griffith had originally tried out for a part in *Carrie* but lost the role because she wouldn't kiss a stranger. De Palma "wanted me to kiss [a] guy that I didn't know," Griffith recalled. "I said I didn't want to do it. Brian simply told me to get out. I said fine, goodbye and that was it!")[16] Working with Haven, Griffith modeled her sexy window dance on one of Haven's actual porn routines. Thus, Griffith is Haven's body double, much as Holly is Gloria's. And, as director of *Body Double*, De Palma in a sense "doubles" as a porn director: "The adult film actress [Haven] and Melanie rehearsed the masturbation scene that she does with the jewelry in her bedroom, and I first worked with putting a video camera outside my bedroom window in my house. I had rented a house on the top of Mulholland Drive. . . . This became a legend in Hollywood because a rumor went out that I was having actresses come up to my house to masturbate."[17] Later, De Palma noted, "My editing office for *Body Double* was right across the street from the Pussycat Cinema on Broadway."[18]

To find his "angel in the window"—the woman he thought was Gloria but was thereafter revealed to be porn star Holly Body—Jake himself auditions for and takes a job acting in a porn film. (In this, he is like Jon in *Greetings*, who tries to move beyond merely watching the woman of his dreams through a window by setting up a camera to film him entering her apartment and making love with her. In De Palma's original treatment for *Body Double*, the character of Jake was called Jon.) Acting in a porn scene, Jake looks into a mirror and sees reflected there an image of Holly performing her sexy dance routine, reminiscent of his idealized view of her earlier when she danced in the window. Jake, wearing glasses and dressed in a preppy sweater, is the innocent boy, open-mouthed in worshipful adoration of the wonderful woman he sees. "I like to watch," he says.

However, his words are also those of a sleazy voyeur, and Holly's reply is from the porn script: "Makes me hot. . . . Why don't you come over here and I'll show you how hot?" As she pulls him lasciviously toward her, the mirrored door swings around to reveal a camera crew filming the shot: Jake's angelic Holly is shown to be open to any man's gaze, making her a kind of whore selling (the image of) her body to everyone, not reserving it exclusively for him. Indeed, rather than the soft negligee and shining jewels that Holly wore in her window dance for Jake, she is now garbed in black gloves and studded leather, coming at him crude and hard.

And yet as Jake kisses and embraces her, the camera swirls in 360-degree turns around them, and Jake visualizes holding Gloria in his arms again on the beach. The same swirling camera, slow motion, and romantic music continue when Jake's mind returns to the reality that it is Holly he is holding. It is as though Jake were trying to recapture the romantic adoration of his angel, the time before she was revealed to be a "deceiving whore." Can he believe in a woman again—and in himself as the kind of man who is something other than a furtive voyeur or a lustful penetrator? The answer would seem to be no, for the porn scene ends with Jake thrusting into Holly's body up against a phallic column, while the sleazy song we hear about "when you wanna come" makes an explosive sound. But in fact there is some reason to hope, for not only do Jake and Holly end the scene in a laughing and affectionate embrace, but they departed from the porn script by not having Jake withdraw from her for the "cum shot." This moment of real intimacy displeases the director, who wants only to give porn's voyeurs the fragmented body parts they paid to see.

Interestingly, this porn director is played by Al Israel, fresh from another kind of body-fragmenting performance as the chainsaw-wielding killer in *Scarface*. De Palma himself has described directing porn films as being "like surgery, very mechanical and unsexual."[19] When he was directing Griffith in a (fake) trailer for a (fictional) porn film, De Palma was "so respectful" that he "wouldn't look" at her; instead, he turned "beet red" and then was quickly "out the door," according to Griffith's account.[20]

Once Jake has seen his angel acting in a porn film, once his romantic vision of her is revealed to have been a paid performance, can he ever love or trust her again? And once he himself has behaved like a prurient voyeur and then gotten into the act as a thrusting porn stud, can he ever regain a sense of his own innocence and capacity for tenderness? Jake's doubts about Holly's and his own identity will continue right on through the end of *Body Double*. Pretending to be a porn producer with slicked-back hair, he would seem to want to degrade her further by hiring her for his own sleazy film, but then he compliments Holly on her smile rather than her body, as if responding to her as a person and potential love interest. However, this show of affection is also part of Jake's own deception, for he wants to get her to trust him enough that she will reveal her part in having deceived him, along with the name of the man (Sam) who paid her.

After luring Holly back to his hillside house and its round bed, Jake seems ready to use it as a casting couch, as if to treat her like the whore he fears she is. But when *she* throws herself at *him*, exclaiming about the bed that "we had one of these in *Star Whores*," he is taken aback, seeming to feel that she—and he himself—are better than this. Jake admits that he isn't a film producer and confesses that he was the one watching her sexy dance in the window. After confessing that he's a liar and a pervert, he expects her to believe that he is now a good, truthful man and that Sam is the villain. No wonder she calls Jake a "sick" "weirdo" and runs away from him in fear.

Indeed, what kind of man is Jake? Seeing that Sam (in his "Indian" disguise) has kidnapped Holly, Jake follows them to a plot of land near a reservoir. Jake has seen Sam knock Holly unconscious with a phallic car jack, much as Jake was present earlier when Sam used the power drill on Gloria. Back then, perhaps because of an identity crisis over whether he was too much of a brute like Sam, too susceptible to his own rapacious impulses, Jake did not act quickly or resolutely enough and was unable to save Gloria. Will the same thing happen this time with Holly?

We know that Jake is fighting a certain amount of contempt for Holly for having deceived him with her sexy angel act when she was in the employ of another man. (In an earlier version of De Palma's script, Holly was even guiltier: not only was she paid to strip, but she was actually in on Sam's plot to kill his wife and make Jake the alibi witness.) Jake's girlfriend, Carol, deceived him with another man, and Jake had to leave the house, since it was hers. Sam's wife, Gloria, was also having an affair, and the jewels and probably the house were both hers, since she was rich. How different are Jake's feelings toward women from Sam's? Is Jake, too, tempted to view them as whores "deserving" of sexualized violence as a way for the men to punish and take repossession of them forever? The fact that Sam is not only Jake's adversary but also his alter ego is suggested by their strangely similar clothing, with Sam garbed in a blue coat and brown trousers and Jake wearing a brown leather jacket and blue jeans.

Jake spends a very long time watching Sam dig a grave and slide the unconscious Holly into it. Does Jake hesitate to save Holly because at some level he senses that Sam's rage at her is his own? Some part of Jake shares the desire to have Holly unconscious and at his mercy. To counteract that nefarious desire, to make sure that he himself doesn't do to Holly what Sam is doing, Jake hesitates; he watches; he hides behind a water tank and then behind the back of Sam's truck, approaching slowly, trying to define his own identity as a hero or a villain. But in his hesitation, not only is Jake almost too late to save Holly, he also opens himself up to becoming, like her, a victim. A rack focus takes us from Sam's face to the dog in the back of his truck, which begins viciously barking at Jake. Sam pulls Jake into the grave, strangling him and pushing his body down until it lies alongside Holly's, both of them dominated by the villain as Jake and Gloria had been during Sam's drill attack. Jake lies in the grave, immobilized by claustrophobia—that is, by paralyzing self-doubt. Can he resolve his identity crisis in time?

Jake acts, grabbing the spade end of Sam's shovel, struggling with Sam for control of the phallic implement and using it to pull himself out of the grave. It is as though Jake is trying to take on the villain's aggression and turn it against him. The dog that had earlier menaced Jake now leaps at Sam, taking him down into the waters of the reservoir. The dog becomes a symbol of how Jake seems to have channeled his rage away from the woman (as a "deceiving whore") and away from himself (as a voyeur and potential violator) and toward the man who actually committed the crimes against Gloria and Holly. The dog De Palma used for his film is the same white German shepherd (and lookalikes) that he saw in Samuel Fuller's *White Dog*. In Fuller's film, a dog that has been trained to attack black people is retrained to attack whites. Perhaps this is where De Palma got the idea of having the dog as a symbol of Jake's rechanneled aggression.

Yet Holly's response to Jake's actions can lead us to doubt his heroism. Although her attitude toward him is partly played for laughs, her accusations are unsettling. When Jake says, "I'm saving you," Holly's reply is to ask "from who?" Having been unconscious during Sam's digging of the grave and Jake's vanquishing of Sam, Holly wakes up in the hole to see no one but Jake standing above her grave. But Holly's question points to Jake's psychological complicity in the crimes against her, his own fear that *he could have been Sam*, doing what Sam did to her. Holly accuses Jake of being a "necrophiliac" ("unconscious is good, but dead is better, right?"), and the charge comes uncomfortably close to pinpointing the rapist's rage to punish and repossess her that Jake has felt.

Jake stretches out his hand to help Holly out of the grave, but she, afraid of him, won't take it. Jake thus becomes another in a long line of De Palma heroes and heroines whose ability to help the victim is compromised by their own complicity with the villain. Think of Jack when Sally reaches out to him in *Blow Out*; Peter unable to comfort Liz in *Dressed to Kill*; Sue gripped by Carrie's outstretched hand in *Carrie*; or Grace as Phillip reaches out to her in *Sisters*. When Holly won't take his hand, Jake drops his outstretched arm in frustration and turns away from her and toward the rushing reservoir waters that carried Sam away. Is Jake still torn between the roles of hero and villain, caught between Sally in the grave, who fears his "help," and Sam in the water, who represents the villainy in Jake that he may not have entirely vanquished?

The film's coda is similarly equivocal. Jake is back on the set of the horror movie, having been rehired as the lead actor since he has overcome his claustrophobia, able now to rise from his coffin (as he did from the grave in the preceding scene). There are signs of Jake as a new kind of man, more "feminine" and sympathetic to the female victim. In his vampire role with spiky blond hair and a black leather outfit, Jake looks remarkably like Holly in the porn film. He is also "feminized" in being the object of the camera's gaze, a fact emphasized when make-up girls touch up his hair and powder his face. When the actress he is supposed to attack tells him that her breasts are sensitive due to her period, Jake appears to take care not to be too rough with them. His could be described as a gentle clawing or a tender mauling.

And yet Jake's act is one where he sinks his teeth into a woman's throat, penetrating her and causing blood to run down her body. How different are Jake's gory fangs from Sam's bloody drill? Jake's actions as a new kind of man are not that far from those of the old kind of rapist. Moreover, Jake is acting in a sleazy horror movie whose softcore scenes link it to porn films. Jake's vampiric attack on a nude woman in the shower (called "The HOOKER" in the screenplay)[21] appeals to the same voyeurs who get off on seeing sexualized violence against "slutty" women in porn.

Indeed, the director of Jake's horror movie, Rubin, seems to be a particularly unsavory type. Assigned the last name of the voyeuristic Jon from *Greetings*, Rubin is portrayed by Dennis Franz, who has not only played sleazy characters in previous De Palma films (*Dressed to Kill* and *Blow Out*) but is actually imitating De Palma himself in *Body Double*, copying his mannerisms and wearing his customary "directing outfit," a "green jacket."[22] That De Palma would cast a sleazy voyeur as his own representative in the director's role speaks to his ability to critique some of his own proclivities, and it suggests an awareness of the crude violence underlying the seeming humor of Jake's role as a "sensitive" vampire.

It is interesting that both *Body Double* and *Blow Out* end with the male protagonist giving a cheap horror film director what he wants: a phallic attack on a woman in the shower. We see how the scream in *Coed Frenzy* (the film-within-a-film in *Blow Out*) is created by dubbing Sally's dying cries into the shower victim's mouth as she is knifed. We also see how the shower attack scene in *Vampire's Kiss* (the film-within-a-film in *Body Double*) is created by cutting together two separate takes, the first a head shot of Jake biting into a woman's neck, and the second a below-the-neck shot of a body double's breasts with blood running down them.

While ostensibly the scene in *Blow Out* is tragic, whereas the one in *Body Double* is comic, both can be understood as critiques of sexualized violence toward women. When Sally's dying screams are used in a slasher/porn film, this not only trivializes her death but also makes it a turn-on for sadistic voyeurs. In separating Sally's voice from her body, the filmmakers do violence against her as a whole person. Similarly, when in *Body Double* one woman's "very pretty" face is separated from her body (because the latter "leaves much to be desired") and when another woman's "perfect breasts" are separated from her face (which has been deemed "rather homely"),[23] the cut-together result may seem ideal, but two real women have been fragmented, parts of them discarded, and their integrity violated because they do not live up to some male-defined standard of outward beauty. Earlier, with *Dressed to Kill*, we saw how De Palma used a younger body double for Angie Dickinson in the shower scene, and another woman's voice for Dickinson's orgasmic cries in the taxi scene. Could *Blow Out* and *Body Double* show De Palma having second thoughts about—and returning in a self-critical spirit to—such scenes where a male director "fragments" his female stars?

It should come as no surprise that *Body Double*, more than any other film De Palma has directed, brought on accusations of misogyny. A particular target was the "driller killer" scene, which Stephen Prince, an expert on violence in the cinema, identified as "the decade's ghastliest sequence of sexual slaugh-ter in a mainstream film."[24] Prince believes that "this appalling sequence has sexualized its violence so that it becomes difficult to find an acceptably moral point of view on the carnage. As in *Dressed to Kill*, the violence becomes a punitive response directed at a woman because of her sexuality."[25] According to Charles Derry, "The violence is so extreme, the defilement of Gloria so great, that it is very difficult for audiences not to respond to the scene as a misogy-nist attack, by De Palma himself, on all women."[26] Margo St. James argues that "even if we swallow . . . [De Palma's] assertion that he 'likes women,' it's hard to imagine him liking them for any reason other than to put them into his films as victims. And particularly his penchant for offing the Bad Girls."[27] Ann Snitow warns that "De Palma had better watch out: Sexual violence is a dan-gerous theme because it is so charged for everyone. If he doesn't keep making discoveries about his obsessions (as his mentor Hitchcock always did), his painfully suggestive bloodlettings will become mere special effects. A success-ful sexploitation director can coast on received ideas about what was once his own nasty, interesting soul and stop telling us anything about the nastiness, the soul, or the place where they meet."[28]

Does Sam commit phallic violence against Gloria, using that drill to pun-ish her for her sexual infidelity and to take repossession of her, once and for all, as his own? Yes. Is Jake tempted by the same nefarious desire to attack Holly, to punish her for deceiving him with her sexy angel act when she was in fact being paid to do it by another man and "whoring around" in porn films? Yes. But the drama of the film lies in Jake's attempts to differentiate himself from Sam's lustful rage toward women, and it is De Palma who has scripted and directed this drama (along with many others like it: *Blow Out*, *Dressed to Kill*, *Greetings*, and all the way back to *Murder à la Mod*). Does it seem likely that De Palma is himself prone to the same misogynistic attitudes as his male characters? Very. But it seems equally likely that his films are attempts to bring to consciousness and critique these attitudes.

Like his characters, De Palma is torn between acting out his nefarious desires (they *are* acted out in his films) and exposing these problematic desires as being misogynistic (they *are* revealed as such in his films, which comment self-reflexively on their heroes' disturbing similarity to the villains). Asked whether he accepts "the feminist view that men learn from movies how to assault and rape women," De Palma replied, "I subscribe to the Aristotelian theory. I believe that movies purge you of these emotions."[29] Is not *Body Dou-ble* Jake's—and De Palma's—attempt to purge himself of lustful rage toward women? By making films about his characters' propensity for "offing the Bad Girls," De Palma *is* revealing "his own nasty, interesting soul" and "making discoveries about his obsessions"—discoveries which hopefully will help him to become a new kind of man. However, De Palma is honest in bringing *Body Double*'s protagonist to an equivocal end: it's by no means clear that Jake is a new kind of man when he acts in that vampire film. But what *is* clear is that he made the attempt to separate himself from Sam's punitive prurience and to side with Holly, to believe in his own capacity for tenderness and romantic devotion.

Beyond charges of misogyny, *Body Double* also led to perhaps the fiercest criticism of De Palma as a plagiarist of Hitchcock. "Brian De Palma is back to offend women, the memory of Alfred Hitchcock, anti-violence proponents and anyone with an ounce of sense," wrote Jimmy Summers.[30] Noting that "the distinction between rip-off and homage is sometimes stretched a bit thin in De Palma's films," Peter Rainer referred to *Body Double* as a "bargain-bin *Rear Window*,"[31] and Richard Corliss wondered, "Is this his third remake of *Vertigo*?"[32] Even Pauline Kael, normally one of De Palma's staunchest supporters, wrote about *Body Double* that its "big, showy scenes recall *Vertigo* and *Rear Window* so obviously that the movie is like an assault on the people who have put De Palma down for being derivative. . . . these big scenes have no special point, other than their resemblance to Hitchcock's work."[33] It seems that the only reason the film, with its attack on a woman in the shower, wasn't accused of stealing from *Psycho* was that critics were too busy trashing it for thieving from other Hitchcock films, though Scott Ashlin charged that "*Body Double* may devote most of its energy to copying *Rear Window* and *Vertigo*, but . . . this is a *Psycho* rip-off all the way."[34]

Body Double does indeed follow Hitchcock's films very closely, even to the point of its seeming to be their cinematic "double," but by considering the moments when De Palma's film makes a significant *departure* from Hitchcock, we can recognize that the younger director is innovating upon—and not just slavishly imitating—the Master. When prurient Jake looks through the telescope at Holly (who he thinks is Gloria) disrobing in the window, he is like Norman (Anthony Perkins) in *Psycho* peering through a peephole while Marion (Janet Leigh) undresses. When Sam kills Gloria with a drill and then almost murders Holly, it is as though he is acting out Jake's darkest desires, his impulse to punish women for their overt sexuality. Similarly, when Norman's "mother" knifes Marion in the shower, the "mother" (who is actually one side of schizophrenic Norman himself) is punishing Marion for her display of nudity. Though Norman tries to be different from his "mother," he cannot; she has already taken over his mind.

But Jake seems to have more success differentiating himself from Sam and his misogyny. Although Jake is tempted to hate Holly for being a "deceiving whore," he also tries to play out a romantic scene with her on the porn film set, and instead of taking revenge on her for her deception, he directs his anger at Sam, who victimized them both, and in the process saves Holly from being murdered. Still, Jake's character remains in doubt at the end: the vampire act in which he sinks his fangs into a "hooker" in the shower is not that far removed from Norman's knifing of nude Marion in the shower.

De Palma's self-reflexivity, his calling attention to the fact that Jake is acting in a movie, makes us aware of our own voyeurism and our own prurient-punitive enjoyment of violence against women. Hitchcock used a body double for Janet Leigh in *Psycho*'s shower scene, but De Palma *calls attention to* his use of a body double in the film-within-a-film, making us cognizant of our desire for "ideal" female beauty—a desire that entails a raging disappointment and a sexualized anger at women who are then treated like whores when they fail to live up to that "ideal." (De Palma tried to cast Janet Leigh's daughter, Jamie Lee Curtis, in the role of Holly, but when this wasn't possible, he chose Melanie Griffith, daughter of Tippi Hedren, who had starred in Hitchcock's *Marnie* and *The Birds*.)

In *Rear Window*, Jeff (James Stewart) watches a scantily clad dancer he calls "Miss Torso" practice her routine in an apartment across the way from his. Later, he sees his beloved Lisa (Grace Kelly) menaced in another apartment by Thorwald (Raymond Burr), a man who has murdered and cut up his own wife. Thorwald acts out Jeff's latent aggression toward Lisa and women in general, his tendency to sexually objectify their body parts, to fragment them, in a prurient-punitive way. But this dark side of Jeff's character—his connection with the villain—is merely suggested in *Rear Window*, and it is only hinted that Jeff's broken leg in a cast, which immobilizes him and keeps him from acting to save Lisa from Thorwald, may be the sign of a psychological conflict within Jeff, of his struggle between wanting to save and desiring to kill her.

In *Body Double*, Jake peeps at "Gloria" (actually Holly) as she does her masturbatory dance in the window. His eyes are glued to her body parts, so he doesn't notice her face; if he had, he would not have been duped by Holly as Gloria's "body double." Thereafter, Jake is peeping again when he sees Gloria menaced by the drill-wielding "Indian" (really Sam in disguise, murdering his wife and setting up Jake as an alibi witness). De Palma goes beyond Hitchcock in making Jake's voyeurism much more incriminating than Jeff's. As a police detective tells Jake, "You're the real reason Gloria Revelle got murdered. If you hadn't been so busy getting off by peeping on her, if you'd have called the police about your blood brother, the Indian, Gloria Revelle would still be alive." De Palma highlights the extent to which Jake is the villainous Sam's "blood brother": both men are sexually enraged at women for being "deceiving whores." And unlike with Hitchcock's Jeff whose affliction is physical (a broken leg), De Palma gives Jake a psychological condition (claustrophobia) which strongly implies that there is something going on in his head that keeps him from acting quickly or resolutely to save women, as in the scene where he arrives too late to protect Gloria from Sam's drill, or in the scene where Jake keeps hesitating—hiding and watching—as Holly is being buried alive by Sam.

Yet, perhaps because Jake himself is more aware of his faults than Jeff, Jake feels guiltier and does finally take action: he approaches, confronts, and does battle with Sam in the end, thereby saving Holly. By contrast, Jeff seems less self-aware and less proactive in his final scene with Thorwald. It is Thorwald who approaches and confronts *him*, and Jeff fights to save himself more than Lisa. Whether Jeff recognizes his own complicity in Thorwald's crimes, whether Jeff's character has changed much at all by the end, remains unclear.

In *Vertigo*, Scottie (James Stewart) secretly observes and follows the woman of his dreams, "Madeleine" (Kim Novak), but his acrophobia renders him unable to save her from falling off a tower. Scottie discovers that "Madeleine" was really Judy (also Novak), who had been hired by Gavin to impersonate his wife (the real Madeleine) so that Gavin could kill her and throw her off the tower but make her death look like a suicide to Scottie, who would thus serve as an alibi witness. In one of the film's early scenes, before Scottie's belief in the ideal "Madeleine" has been shaken, he sees her reflected in the mirror of a florist's shop, looking as perfectly beautiful as the flowers. Jake, too, sees Holly reflected in a mirror, a vision of perfection doing the same sexy dance she did as his "angel in the window." However, this mirror is on a porn film set, and as the mirrored door swings around, a camera crew is revealed, reminding Jake that Holly is really a porn actress hired by another man to deceive him.

If Hitchcock shows that Scottie has been duped by his belief in the ideal woman, De Palma takes this revelation one step further, showing not only that Jake has been fooled, but that we in the movie audience have been, too. "*Body Double* was a kind of meditation on the idea in *Vertigo* where you create an elusive, beautiful, evocative woman character," said De Palma. "That's what we do as directors all the time in movies: we create these feminine illusions. . . . We set it in the world of movies as a kind of Brechtian device where you're saying, 'This is about the creation of illusion. Do not believe what you see. Don't be sucked in by the emotion and the illusion because you're being set up to be twisted and turned and manipulated to believe what I want you to believe.'"[35]

Despite some struggle to accept Judy for who she really is, Scottie cannot move past his vision of the perfect "Madeleine" and he attempts to impose this vision on Judy, forcing her to dress and walk like his "ideal" of feminine beauty, even when it visibly pains her to do so. Jake, too, is greatly disillusioned when his angelic "Gloria" is exposed as having been porn star Holly putting on an act, but unlike Scottie, Jake makes significant progress toward finding his feminine ideal in the real woman. Perhaps because he does not dichotomize females to quite the same extent as Scottie, for whom women are either the ethereal "Madeleine" or the crudely earthy Judy, Jake seems more able to see the romantic and the erotic as combined in one woman, as when his tender, tentative kissing of Gloria turns passionate on the beach, or when his sex act with Holly in the porn film involves emotional and not just physical closeness. It is worth remembering that Jake's "angel in the window" already had a sensual component as she did her masturbatory dance; his fantasy of her already incorporated flesh to some degree. For this reason, Jake does not try to force Holly to conform to some angelic stereotype, as Scottie does with Judy.

Scottie also fails to get beyond his sexualized anger at Judy for having deceived him by pretending to be his dream woman, "Madeleine." He shakes and manhandles her in a bitter parody of a loving embrace, taking violent repossession of her after she has been with another man (Gavin). He drags her up to the top of the tower where, confronted with his anger and her own guilt over having deceived him, she slips or jumps to her death. Scottie's acrophobia or identity crisis is cured, but only by his becoming like the villain, Gavin, who threw his own wife off the tower. By contrast, Jake works to overcome his villainous tendency to despise Holly for being a "deceiving whore." Jake tries to resolve *his* identity crisis, dramatized as his claustrophobia, not by siding with Sam and his misogynistic rage, but by empathizing with Holly, who like Jake has been victimized, and by turning his own rage against Sam, knocking him into the reservoir and saving Holly from being buried alive.

At the end of *Vertigo*, Scottie stands at the edge of the tower, looking down at Judy's dead body. If he feels empathy for her now, it is too late. In the finale of *Body Double*, Jake stands at the edge of the grave, holding out his hand to Holly, and at the edge of the reservoir, where Sam's body was washed away. If Holly won't take Jake's hand because she is still afraid of him, if Jake continues to have doubts about his own character, at least Holly is still alive; Jake is actively trying to help her; and the worst villain, Sam, is dead.

Bringing in about $1 million less than it cost ($10 million), *Body Double* was not a success at the box office. Right after *Scarface*, Columbia Pictures had signed De Palma to a three-picture contract that included his own office. *Body Double* was the first movie made as part of this deal. However, after that film flopped, the studio tore up his multi-picture contract and asked him to vacate his office. What would De Palma do now? "Following the failure of *Body Double* and the virulent attacks from feminists, I wanted to distance myself from the Hitchcock thriller," De Palma explained. "I had to re-invent myself."[36] What could be more distant from an erotic thriller than a gangster comedy called *Wise Guys*? "This time," De Palma said, "no one can accuse me of ripping off Hitchcock."[37]

CHAPTER 17

Wise Guys (1986)

As a gangster comedy, *Wise Guys* is best appreciated as a happy alternative to *Scarface*, a wish-fulfillment fantasy in which things that went wrong in that film—and in De Palma's life—now go miraculously right. Harry (Danny DeVito) and Moe (Joe Piscopo) are small-time mobsters who live side by side in houses under a New Jersey expressway. Moe thinks that everyone has forgotten his birthday, even his own mother, and we recall that the lack of birthday celebrations in the De Palma household was a sore point for De Palma himself, who wondered about his mother, "How could she forget her own son's birthday?"[1] However, it turns out that Moe's mother and his friends have merely been pretending to forget, the better to surprise him with a big birthday party.

Harry and his young son are both introduced wearing snazzy gangster suits and saying to their reflections in mirrors, "You talkin' to me?!" The small-fry Harry, Jr., wants to be a tough guy like his father, the diminutive Harry, who himself is trying to live up to the movie image of a tough guy, which is also what Travis Bickle (Robert De Niro) was trying to do when he spoke these lines into a mirror in *Taxi Driver*. (De Palma may also be poking fun at *Taxi Driver* writer Paul Schrader for imitating *him*, because Travis's lines are very like the dialogue spoken by Jon [Robert De Niro] when he is rehearsing a tough guy persona in De Palma's *Hi, Mom!*)

Harry and Moe both look up to crime boss Castelo (Dan Hedaya), a mid-level mobster whose pretensions to power are parodied by mock *Godfather* music and by a painting of a gentleman on horseback (like the one that "big shot" wannabe Harry Flowers displays in the gangster film *Performance*). Though Harry and Moe seek his approval, godfather Anthony Castelo is cold and distant toward them, much as De Palma felt that his own father, Anthony, often behaved toward him and his brothers. Castelo, surrounded by his "wise guy" cronies who bustle about and hop to in performing his every command, could be seen as a comic version of De Palma's own doctor-father: "His sons, who occasionally visited him at work, remembered him as a general, marching through the hospital followed by a trail of functionaries—nurses, residents, medical students—all there to do his bidding," reports Julie Salamon.[2] To test whether his car has been wired with a bomb, Castelo makes Harry turn the ignition, and De Palma emphasizes Moe looking on, unable to help his friend who could be blown up. "At our house," De Palma said, "when I would see my parents . . . laying into my brother Bart, I couldn't intervene and I felt powerless."[3]

De Palma has also described "the family as a structure involving manipulation and destruction of the individual."[4] Castelo takes these traits to the extreme in his Mafia "family": pulling Harry and Moe aside for separate conversations, he gives each a secret contract to kill the other, thus manipulating both toward their literal destruction. The two friends are pitted against one another to please the godfather. "I love you more than I love my own brother," Harry tells Moe—though Moe almost pushes him in front of a truck and Harry almost shoots Moe in the head. De Palma recalled that "my brothers and I grew up in a competitive atmosphere: it was about who would be the best, twenty-four hours a day! . . . When I think back on it, this competition existed only because my parents were there to stir it up."[5]

In fear for their lives if they don't kill each other, Harry and Moe hightail it to Atlantic City, where they use a mob credit card to put themselves up in a luxury hotel suite. Living the high life and pretending to be the big-time gangsters they'd always dreamed of being, Moe soaks in a circular bubble bath with a girl for company, while Harry indulges his appetite, claiming, "I could eat a horse." We recall that Tony in *Scarface* sat in a similar bath; he had actually achieved success as a gangster, but his bloodthirsty rise to power ("I could eat a horse," he had said) alienated his wife, so she would not join him in the tub. Harry obtains money from his grandmother to pay back the mob and puts the bills in a cake box—one with happier associations than the birthday cake box in *Sisters* which was linked to the knife used to suddenly stab a man. In a sense, though, Moe too gets a nasty surprise, for when Harry presents him with the cake box, he says that he plans to gamble the money rather than pay it back, thus risking both their lives. To stop Harry, Moe pulls a gun on him and, in the ensuing struggle, Harry is shot and apparently killed. Similar to *Scarface*'s Tony when he shot his best friend, Manny, and felt suicidally guilty afterwards, Moe is inconsolable at the death of his partner. He returns home and dejectedly climbs the stairs, like Carrie after her disaster at the prom. Moe hangs himself from a lighting fixture, but Harry, who has merely faked his death, arrives in time to save Moe from strangulation—unlike Jack in *Blow Out*, who fails to save the police informant he had wired.

To ensure their freedom from the mob, the two friends plot to fake Moe's death too, but they must flee before getting a chance to ignite a gas explosion because Castelo arrives with his entourage of cronies. As these men hasten to do the godfather's bidding and light his cigar, they inadvertently blow up their boss. Pauline Kael has criticized the ending of *Wise Guys* for being too lightweight: "Although the two underdogs [Harry and Moe] come out on top, the picture doesn't have any real emotional payoff, because they don't get their revenge consciously. These two frightened clowns don't get to release their anger."[6] But *Wise Guys* isn't *The Fury*, where Gillian directs her tele-kinetic rage at Childress and causes him to explode in the end. The whole point of *Wise Guys* as a wish-fulfillment fantasy with a truly happy ending is that Castelo dies (in a sense, self-destructs) without Harry or Moe being responsible for his death. They are free of the mob *and* guilt-free for how they got there. When Harry and Moe go on to open up a delicatessen together, it seems like some version of a dream De Palma might have had for himself and his brothers. Indeed, at least Brian and Bart, once free of their competi-tive family environment, did go on to collaborate on several films (*Hi, Mom!*, *Obsession*, *Femme Fatale*).

De Palma hoped that *Wise Guys* would be a hit. Producer Aaron Russo described the film as "*Laurel and Hardy Meet the Godfather*,"[7] which sounds like fun. But the film returned only $8.5 million on its $13 million dollar investment. The fact that it was a gangster comedy—another mixed-genre film—may have been part of the problem. De Palma believed that audiences were confused about the kind of picture it was supposed to be, so they stayed away. "The same thing happened to me," he said, "with *Phantom of the Para-dise*"[8]—his musical comedy horror film.

Nevertheless, with *Wise Guys* De Palma proved to the studio that he could be a "team player." The film was completed on time and on budget (both *Blow Out* and *Scarface* had exceeded their projected budgets). Furthermore, the film was noncontroversial, showing that De Palma could make a truly main-stream film. This would lead to *The Untouchables*, a serious gangster film that would become one of De Palma's biggest box-office hits.

CHAPTER 18

The Untouchables (1987)

Set in Prohibition-era Chicago, *The Untouchables* shows Treasury agent Eliot Ness (Kevin Costner) and his handpicked band of incorruptible men—veteran cop Malone (Sean Connery), rookie Stone (Andy Garcia), and accountant Wallace (Charles Martin Smith)—pitted against mob kingpin Al Capone (Robert De Niro). But sometimes, as De Palma has indicated, the film may seem less like "a gangster movie" and "more like a *Magnificent Seven*"[1] (the John Sturges Western). According to location manager Eric Schwab, De Palma told him that "this is a Western. Good guys. Bad guys."[2] Hence, the rather improbable scene set in a Western landscape where the Untouchables mount horses and ride four abreast, making a magnificent charge with their shotguns in order to intercept some mobsters smuggling liquor across the Canadian border. This scene is spoofed in "The Unwatchables," a *Mad* magazine parody of *The Untouchables*, where observers wonder "how four city guys can suddenly ride horses like rodeo champions."[3] Andy Garcia (playing Stone) tried to convince De Palma that this scenario was unlikely—"Brian, my character has never been on a horse. This guy's from the Southside of Chicago"[4]—and Charles Martin Smith (Wallace) notes that he and his fellow actors were similarly unskilled: "We had trouble trying to ride—we're not any of us great riders—four abreast close enough so the camera can get the shot."[5] But De Palma filmed the Old West-style scene anyway, and it became a favorite with audiences of the picture. The Untouchables' heroic charge astride their steeds gives them a mythic stature as the classic American good guys against the evildoers.

Still, the most intriguing aspect of De Palma's work—and *The Untouchables* is no exception—is when he explores the blurred line between good guys and bad guys, or the split within the self between good and evil. The nerdy accountant Wallace is a paper-pusher trying to get Capone on tax evasion, but during the Canadian border raid, Wallace gets to fire directly at the bad guys, and when his shotgun runs out of bullets, he uses it as a battering ram to charge and knock out his adversary, afterward sneaking a drink of forbidden liquor from a bullet-ridden barrel. The look of triumphant satisfaction on Wallace's face says it all: fighting the gangsters has unleashed the "gangster" within him—the killer and the drinker. The diminutive accountant has become a "big shot" through violence; no need to worry anymore about the fine points of tax law.

The rookie Stone changed his name from Giuseppe and joined the force so that he could prove he's not a lawless killer like Capone or the other Italian gangsters. "It was my idea to make Stone Italian," De Palma said. "In the original script he was supposed to be Polish. But I didn't want to make a one-dimensional movie about the cops against the wops."[6] By making Stone Italian, De Palma turns this character's battle against the mob into a psychodrama as well, an attempt to differentiate himself from what is perceived as a dark ethnic heritage. Stone's role as a sharpshooter thus figures his desire to hit his target exactly, to shoot only the bad guys, for if, in the process of going after them, he also shot some good guys, how different would he be from the indiscriminate killers he is hunting? Interestingly, prior to De Palma's film, Andy Garcia had just finished playing a gangster named Moldonado in *8 Million Ways to Die*, and before being cast as Stone, Ness's right-hand man in *The Untouchables*, Garcia went up for the opposite role—that of Nitti, Capone's lieutenant and chief enforcer.

As for the veteran cop Malone, he initially appears rule-bound, chiding Ness for littering, and deathly afraid, refusing to help fight the gangsters because doing so would endanger his life: "That's the thing you fear," he tells Ness. "I just think it got more important to me to stay alive." Yet what Malone really fears is his own deep-seated desire to break all the rules, his own underlying death wish. What Malone fears is that he is *too like* Capone.

When Ness says that he is prepared to do "everything within the law" to get Capone, Malone replies, "And *then* what are you prepared to do?" Malone has taken Ness to a church for this conversation, but while Ness is holding his hands as if in prayer, Malone seems to be getting a dark enjoyment out of flouting Christian precepts. He challenges Ness: "You want to get Capone? Here's how you get him: he pulls a knife; you pull a gun. He sends one of yours to the hospital; you send one of his to the morgue." (It was Sean Connery [Malone] who suggested setting the scene in a church because his character's speech has "a sort of eye-for-an-eye quality"[7]—or, rather, two eyes for an eye, since it is one of ever-escalating violence.) Malone *enjoys* taking an axe to the door of some bootleggers (though he keeps a bottle of booze hidden at his home).

There is a gleam in Malone's eye as he props up the corpse of a gangster, pretending the man is still alive, and blows out his brains in order to terrify a mob informant into talking. Ness had killed this gangster in self-defense but feels terrible about it. "Would you rather it was you?" Malone asks, and then takes grim pleasure in assuring him that "you've done your duty. Go home and sleep well tonight." It is Malone who fears that he will sleep well—too well—after all his killing, and Malone who is terrified of where his own lack of restraint will lead. He is both terrified and overjoyed, knowing that the road of violence is taking him toward a death which, deep down, he desires and feels that he deserves for what he has done. "What the hell, you got to die of somethin'!" he says, before charging hell-bent at the gangsters with his shotgun. (Given the extent to which, in fighting Capone's gang, the Untouchables are also fighting the dark side of themselves, it is interesting that, in the scene where Ness and Wallace aim their guns at what they fear are gangsters in an approaching car, the vehicle turns out to contain Stone and Malone.)

Ness's insistence that the men working with him "must be pure" and not drink *any* liquor indicates that he is desperate to differentiate himself from the bootleggers. His absolute prohibition suggests an internal weakness, as if he feared that imbibing one drop would make it impossible for him to stop. The overzealousness of Ness's temperance crusade makes him seem like a matronly teetotaler to the men.

When Ness's first liquor raid is a bust, revealing umbrellas inside boxes instead of bottles of booze, a photographer snaps a picture of the humiliated Ness holding a dainty umbrella—a photo that later makes the front page with the caption "Eliot Ness (Poor Butterfly)," likening him to the forlorn and suicidal girl of Puccini's opera. Every night before bed, Ness gives his daughter "butterfly kisses" (they flutter their eyelashes close together). Right before the raid, Ness commented that it's "nice to be married" and read a note from his wife that said, "I am very proud of you"; Ness's rallying cry for the raid is "Let's do some good!" After the raid's failure, Ness stares at the newspaper photo of himself as "Poor Butterfly" and crumples up his wife's note, throwing it away. A family man, Ness is "feminized" by his connection to his wife and daughter. They are what he fights for, but they also threaten to make him weak—too softhearted, too purely good. When the newspaper is brought to Capone, he smokes his big cigar while chuckling over the "feminizing" photo of Ness as "Poor Butterfly."

Another time, when Ness is bringing a present home for his daughter, Capone's enforcer, Nitti, is waiting with a warning for him: "Little girl's having a birthday, huh? Nice to have a family. A man should take care, see that nothin' happens to them." Ness is being a good father and celebrating his daughter's birthday (in the way that De Palma wishes his own birthdays had been celebrated), but Ness's love for his family makes him vulnerable to attack by Capone. Ness rushes into the house, at first seeing nothing but a Raggedy Ann doll in his daughter's bed (which is all that Michael saw when his daughter had been kidnapped in *Obsession*), but then realizing that his daughter is present on the other side of the room. Bundling his wife and child off in a car, "hiding" his "feminine" weakness, Ness attempts to assert himself, charging on horseback with his shotgun during the Canadian border raid and then, back in a Chicago hotel lobby, punching out one of Capone's henchmen and moving to pull a gun on Capone himself before being restrained from doing so. "If you were a man, you woulda done it now!" Capone taunts him, explicitly targeting Ness's lack of masculinity.

The closer Ness moves toward committing "manly" violence in his fight against the mob, the more he becomes like the very gangsters he was trying to protect women and children from. This division within Ness—the increasingly blurred line between hero and villain—can be seen in the bravura sequence that takes place on the marble steps of Chicago's Union Station. Although it was inspired by the famous Odessa Steps sequence from Eisenstein's *Battleship Potemkin*, De Palma brings his special motive for crosscutting, his own unique interest in the "split self," to his version of the scene: "You always have to try to find something that you can bring your particular sensibility to, like the shoot-out on the stairs in *The Untouchables*, when you're working in a genre piece," he has said.[8]

Originally scripted as a chase sequence that would have involved expensive helicopter shots of moving trains and a crash, the scene was changed at the last minute when funding fell short, and De Palma had to throw together something on the fly, improvising (without storyboards and based solely on his memory of the Eisenstein film) up to fifty setups a night over a period of five nights. "It was Brian at his best," producer Art Linson recalled. "He just sort of said: 'OK, guys, we've run out of money. So give me a staircase, a clock, and a baby carriage.'"[9] If that wasn't enough of a challenge, the scene also had to be very carefully blocked out and shot because the majority of it is presented in slow motion, not just to ratchet up the suspense but more importantly to convey Ness's psychology. According to De Palma, "The reason for the slow motion was that I also had to slow down the emotional journey of [Ness's] character ... in order to study his behavior and his reactions."[10]

Ness has gone to the train station in order to nab a mob bookkeeper before henchmen can hustle him out of town. While waiting, Ness helps a mother drag a baby carriage with an infant in it up the station's marble steps. Some gangsters arrive, but at first "they don't recognize" Ness "because he looks like a family man," as De Palma explains the scene.[11] However, as Ness reaches the top of the steps with the mother and the baby carriage, he senses that, behind his back, one of the men has begun to eye him suspiciously. (This is the henchman that Ness punched earlier.) "Ness turns, pulls his gun from his trenchcoat with his right hand. He's still holding onto the carriage with his left."[12] Ness points his gun at the henchman and, when this man reaches into his coat for his gun, Ness shoots him. Ness then turns again, letting go of the baby carriage, and "as he rotates to shoot" another gangster before the man can shoot him, Ness "bumps the carriage. It starts to roll."[13] The mother puts her hand on Ness's shoulder, trying to get him to stop the carriage, but he pushes her aside, continuing to fire his shotgun at the gangsters who are firing at him. The carriage begins to bounce down the staircase steps, with the infant caught in the crossfire of the shoot-out between the gangsters and Ness.

It is interesting that De Palma's description of the scene (the part in quotes above) seems to stress Ness's *inadvertent* endangerment of the infant, noting only that he "bumps" the carriage "as he rotates to shoot." De Palma neglects to mention that, before this, Ness actually lets go of the carriage, or that, after the carriage starts to roll and the mother tries to get his help, Ness pushes her aside. (It is also the case that Ness shoots the first henchman before the man has pulled his gun.) The scene itself seems to implicate Ness as being rather more aggressively and willfully involved in the violence that threatens the child than De Palma's recounting of it would indicate. Given Ness's blasting away at the gangsters with his shotgun, there is a certain irony to De Palma's noting that "because [Ness] looks like a man with a family, the gangsters don't [at first] recognize him." In terms of the way the scene plays out, with Ness giving as good as he gets when it comes to gunfire, his status as a "family man" is in some doubt. (It is almost as if the "family man" behavior acts as camouflage for the violent man that is about to break out.) Does Ness tip with a little too much grim satisfaction toward "manly" violence in this scene, thereby endangering a mother and an infant who could be his own wife and child? (In fact, this shoot-out between Ness and the gangsters was originally envisaged as occurring on the stairs of the hospital in which Ness's wife had recently given birth to a son, in which case the family caught in the crossfire *would* have been Ness's own wife and child.)

Of course, Ness is presented with a terrible dilemma, drawn out in all its excruciating detail by the slow motion: if he shoots at the gangsters, the child could die, but if he rescues the baby carriage, the gangsters could shoot Ness himself. Ness's attention is divided between firing at the mobsters and racing down the stairs in an attempt to rescue the runaway baby carriage. This division reflects the split within Ness between family man and man of violence. How will he resolve this dilemma? According to De Palma, Ness "decides to go after the baby—even though there's a guy at the bottom shooting up and a goon at the side shooting across."[14] This description makes Ness out to be rather more decisive and, by implication, more successful than he actually appears to be at this point in the scene. Yes, Ness runs down the steps, but his progress toward reaching the carriage is considerably slowed by his continuing exchanges of gunfire with the gangsters. The fact is that he keeps firing rather than determinedly running for the baby carriage. The crossfire also mortally endangers the child, whose carriage is hit by bullets more than once. (Granted, if Ness did not return fire, he could have been killed and then the baby could have died anyway.)

Ness keeps shooting, eventually running out of bullets. He stands there impotent and defenseless, with the gangsters about to kill him, while the baby carriage, which he was not sufficiently determined in running after, is still beyond his reach. For a moment, it appears that his decision to continue firing, to be a man of violence, will result in his own death along with the child's.

It is at this point that a certain wish-fulfillment fantasy intervenes, as if Ness could somehow split himself into two people. Rather than remaining tragically alone, a violent man shot down and unable to save the child, Ness is suddenly joined by Stone who, acting as his right-hand man (as if the two were somehow one), tosses Ness a gun so that he can shoot the gangster before being shot. Stone also uses his foot to stop the runaway carriage so that Ness can grab the other end of it, securing the child. This is the first—but not the only—time that the film will imagine an easy way out of Ness's dilemma, fantasizing that he can have his cake and eat it, too: be a man of violence *and* a family man, as if the former did not impinge horribly on the latter. (In this light, it is interesting to note an on-set anecdote. Needing to get the sixteen-month-old baby in the carriage to laugh at the end of this scene, De Palma recalled that "we had Kevin Costner [Ness] wave a rattle. No go. Then [the infant's actual] father—up in the top of the frame—fired off a gun. And the baby gave us a beautiful laugh.")[15]

After Malone has been killed by Capone's lieutenant, Nitti, Ness chases the man up to a courthouse rooftop, where Nitti ends up dangling off the side on a rope. Standing at the roof's edge with his gun pointed down at Nitti, Ness is torn between phallic dominance and "feminine" demurral, between blowing the villain away and saving him so that he can stand trial. Ness's finger is on the trigger, but after closing his eyes (to access his conscience?) and then looking upward (at heaven?), he acts to save Nitti, pulling him up to safety. However, when Nitti brags about beating the rap (he has a note of support from the city's mayor) and then gloats over the murder of Malone ("Your friend died screamin' like a stuck Irish pig!"), Ness shoves him off the roof and he falls screaming to his death. In a moment of unrestrained "virile" fury, Ness puts personal revenge before institutional justice, the certainty of violence before a shaky faith in the system or in the power of goodness or God. To defeat a murderer, Ness has become one, pushing aside all civilized scruples to shove a man off a roof, much as he had earlier pushed aside the mother in the train station in order to blast away at the gangsters.

And once again the film indulges in a fantasy that Ness can act like a vicious gangster but not be one, that he can commit such violence and at the same time be *right*. "There is only one way to deal with such men [as Nitti and Capone]," Ness tells a judge, "and that is hunt them down. I have. I have forsworn myself. I have broken every law I swore to defend. I have become what I beheld and I am content that I have done right." Although there is a hint of shame and remorse in his voice as he begins this speech, Ness sounds more and more determined and self-justifying as he goes on. It is a rousing speech in defense of "righteous violence," and it takes the easy way out of a serious dilemma posed by Ness's behavior: he need not worry, for his personal revenge *was* just; his unrestrained violence *was* good. He can act like the villains but still be a hero because . . . well, because he just *knows* he is right.

Fortunately (in terms of the film's having some moral complexity), Ness does seem to worry in the end. True, triumphant music plays as Ness is congratulated for having defeated Capone and his organization, which Ness accomplished by shoving Nitti off a roof and by blackmailing a judge in order to coerce Capone's lawyer into entering a guilty plea. But then the music turns melancholy as Ness looks at a photo of the Untouchables, including Malone, and shakes his head, muttering, "So much violence." Is Ness merely lamenting the death of his friend, shot by Nitti by order of Capone, or does Ness's very general reference to violence include his own—a sadness over the rooftop retribution he took against Nitti, the blasting away he himself did at the train station? If the result is so much death, could it be that Ness's violence wasn't simply "right"? (Adding to this question is the announcement that Prohibition has been repealed. What was all that fighting really for?)

And, if the violent man can be the family man, why does Ness pack up all his things, including his gun, and quit the force in the end, saying, "I'm going home," and leaving Stone to carry on the fight? It is as though, disturbed by his own increasingly gangster-like behavior, Ness feels that he must put away his gun entirely if he wants to try to become a family man again. Thus, the movie, having brought the loving protector and the vicious killer together in a fantasy fusion in the train station sequence where Ness and Stone were joined, now splits the family man and the violent man at the end, with Ness going home while Stone stays to fight.

We have seen that the more Ness gets embroiled in combating Capone, the more he becomes like him. Both men manipulate the justice system: Capone bribes a jury, and Ness blackmails the judge. Both men, in their unrestrained violence, break the law: Capone has Malone gunned down by Nitti, and Ness kills Nitti by shoving him off a roof. "You can tell Capone that I'll see him in hell," Ness says at one point, as if at some level he suspects they are both going there. And both men view their contest as a kind of macho oneupmanship, using boxing metaphors and celebrating a triumph by smoking a big cigar, as Capone does after Ness's first failed raid ("Poor Butterfly"), and as Ness does after a successful bust of Capone's liquor warehouse. Bit by bit as the movie goes on, "good guy" Ness comes to resemble "bad guy" Capone.

Curiously, Capone himself claims to be a good guy. He puts on the front of a model citizen and a respectable businessman, posing for press photos and maintaining that he is "a peaceful man." He also claims to be a family man, taking offense when Ness insults him in front of his son. He pretends to believe in the law, crying foul ("Your Honor, is this justice?") when Ness blackmails a judge in the case against him. Capone's "good guy" act is, of course, a sham, but it is a sham that exposes the increasing hollowness of Ness's own performance. Ness, too, poses in front of the press, vying for good publicity. Ness claims to stand for peace, aiming to stop "the flow of illegal liquor and the violence it creates," while himself committing greater and greater violence. Ness, the family man, packs away his wife and daughter and pushes aside a mother with a baby carriage in order to blast away with his gun at the gangsters. To obtain justice, Ness shoves an unarmed man off a courthouse roof and blackmails a judge.

In thinking about the characters of Ness and Capone, we should ponder the actors who play them. When young Kevin Costner was first considered for the role of Ness, De Palma was "worried Costner did not have enough star power to ensure a hit," according to producer Art Linson.[16] Then the legendary Robert De Niro was cast in the opposite part as Capone. Would Costner be able to stand up to him? Costner's view of Ness is that initially he presents as "stupid" and "naïve" but then he comes on "real strong" and "very violent."[17] "I really like the gun play in the movie," Costner added. "I like guns and I feel very comfortable with one in my hand."[18] It is revealing that Costner considers the peaceful, law-abiding Ness from the first part of the movie to be "stupid" and "naïve"; he prefers the later Ness, whose violence Costner equates with strength and enjoys acting out. But physical strength can be moral weakness.

Certainly, Capone, as portrayed by De Niro, is both powerful and immoral. The film begins with an overhead shot of Capone in a throne-like barber's chair surrounded by minions giving him a shave, a manicure, and a shoeshine, while members of the press fawn over his every word. In describing this opening shot, De Palma has said that he wanted to "make Al Capone like Louis XIV. He's the Sun King. . . . Everybody sits and waits for the master, the man of power, the man that runs the world, the god that's at the center of the universe."[19] Later, the camera adopts a similar high-angle shot when Capone takes a baseball bat to the head of one of his cronies, thus deploying violence to ensure his regal mastery over them. De Niro had his hairline raised, gained twenty-five pounds, and wore a latex bodysuit so that he could better impersonate the balding Capone, bloated with his own power.

It was De Palma himself who "kept on pushing" to cast De Niro because of his own "long relationship with him."[20] Indeed, a young De Niro had played naïve characters who were De Palma surrogates in the director's films from the 1960s, *The Wedding Party*, *Greetings*, and *Hi, Mom!* Now, in *The Untouchables*, De Niro would play a powerful father figure, one that was as imposing and manipulative as De Palma considered his own father (Anthony) and his older brother (Bruce) to be. (We recall that Anthony, a surgeon, was often surrounded by medical students and staff to do his bidding, and Bruce, a physicist and inventor, had a cult of followers.) Aware of his own manipulative power as a director, De Palma has long sought to avoid ending up like his father or older brother, much as Winslow was in danger of becoming like Swan in *Phantom of the Paradise*, Robin like Childress in *The Fury*, or Tony like Frank in *Scarface*. Now, in *The Untouchables*, De Palma shows Ness to be at risk of becoming like Capone. Linson's description of De Palma indicates that he can have a fearsome presence like Capone: "He is large, abrupt, and seemingly stern. You are instantly given the feeling that if he hasn't yet scared the shit out of you, he eventually will." Linson notes that De Palma is reported to have "thrown the producer [of *Wise Guys*], Aaron Russo, off the set and off the picture"[21] when Russo ventured a suggestion about a shot setup.

Given the scene where Capone takes a baseball bat to a man's head, it is interesting to consider De Palma's use of baseball as a metaphor: "Don't forget, in Hollywood, three strikes and you're out," he told Linson,[22] referring to the fact that his previous two films, *Body Double* and *Wise Guys*, had failed at the box office, so *The Untouchables* was his last chance "at bat." "With the poor outcome of his last two pictures still lingering," Linson explained, De Palma "was in no mood for compromise. He was standing at the plate with two strikes. He wanted to take a full swing."[23] In the event, taking a full swing meant that De Palma "threatened to quit if [studio executives] didn't hire De Niro"[24] for the role of Capone, even though hiring him would cost considerably more money and thus increase the studio's risk. Linson told the executives: "Think of it, when Bob De Niro kills somebody with a baseball bat, with Brian directing, it will never be forgotten."[25] And indeed it never was: because of the way De Palma filmed the scene, including the overhead shot at the end to magnify Capone's supreme dominance, this "full swing" remains disturbingly memorable.

The Untouchables was both a critical and a commercial smash hit. It launched Kevin Costner's career and garnered a Best Supporting Actor Oscar for Sean Connery. For its $20 million investment, it earned $76 million domestically, $186 million worldwide. The film's success put De Palma in the position of being one of Hollywood's A-list directors. What he chose to do with this financial clout was very brave. Rather than merely making a sequel to *The Untouchables* or some equally remunerative mainstream film, he decided on a risky venture: shooting a war movie. The result, *Casualties of War*, would be one of his finest films—and one of his biggest box-office disappointments.

CHAPTER 19

Casualties of War (1989)

Based on an actual 1966 incident first reported in a 1969 *New Yorker* article, *Casualties of War* tells the story of a squad of American soldiers during the Vietnam War who kidnap, rape, and murder a Vietnamese peasant girl, Oahn (Thuy Thu Le). Of the five-man squad—Meserve (Sean Penn), Clark (Don Harvey), Hatcher (John C. Reilly), Diaz (John Leguizamo), and Eriksson (Michael J. Fox)—only Eriksson refuses to participate in the rape and murder, and it is he who brings charges against the men in the end.

Early in the film, during a night patrol, a mortar explosion causes Eriksson to be trapped in a hole above an underground Vietcong tunnel, with his torso above the earth and his legs dangling below—"stuck . . . like . . . Winnie-the-Pooh," a comrade later comments, making light of the event which is actually terrifying at the time. Unable to move, Eriksson has to cry out to his fellow soldiers for rescue: "Help me! Somebody, help! . . . Sarge, help me, I'm stuck!" Here, De Palma revisits the "particularly humiliating experience" from his childhood where, having gotten stuck behind a refrigerator, he "had to call out to my brothers for help."[1]

Unseen by the struggling Eriksson, a Vietcong guerilla fighter with a knife between his teeth is crawling toward him in the tunnel below. De Palma said that he "wanted to get across the idea that the enemy could be right underneath you and you wouldn't know it."[2] The director's instructions to Michael J. Fox (playing Eriksson) were "think *Jaws*,"[3] referring to the opening of that film where a young woman goes skinny-dipping in the sea, unaware of the shark moving ever closer to her legs dangling below the ocean surface. De Palma's tunnel scene, which was his own idea (the real-life incident involved a tree falling on Eriksson), is not only a (rivalrous?) tribute to his friend Steven

Spielberg, it also has implications for the way we think about the characters. Occupying a position similar to that of the vulnerable woman, Eriksson is "feminized," even more so given that his legs are at risk from the VC knife, while the VC fighter, through his analogy to the shark, is made out to be a subhuman monster. If this is indeed a racist depiction of the Vietcong—consistent with how one side often views the other, the enemy, in wartime—we should note that, later in the movie, De Palma films the American soldier Diaz in essentially the same way, holding a knife and crawling toward Oahn, intent on killing her with it. Thus, the Americans can be as shark-like as the Vietcong. (It is also worth noting that, still later in the film, Eriksson himself volunteers to be a "tunnel rat.")

At the same time that we see Eriksson being menaced by the crawling VC in the tunnel below, we also see Eriksson's superior, Sergeant Meserve, running above ground to rescue him: "It's basically intercut with Meserve moving toward Eriksson and the VC moving toward Eriksson," De Palma said, "and they both arrive at the same spot, one above and one below the earth. And Meserve pulls him out just as the VC takes a swipe at his feet"[4] with the knife. Here, there seems to be a clear distinction between earth and sky, burial and freedom, killer and protector. Meserve saves Eriksson's legs from the enemy. Just before the rescue of Eriksson, another soldier had had his arm blown off and was crying out for it; Meserve comforted this man by handing him a tree branch, as if restoring his arm to him.

But after Meserve has pulled Eriksson to safety, Meserve pushes him aside and blasts away at the VC fighter, who has appeared in the hole where Eriksson was just moments before. As Meserve fires his big gun, screaming wildly, he is seen in a skewed, low angle from Eriksson's shocked point of view on the ground, looking up at his superior as the man empties his weapon into the VC. Eriksson looks none too sure about his power-mad sergeant's ability to tell friend from foe. When Meserve then reaches out an arm to pull him to his feet, Eriksson appears relieved not to have been the one being blown to bits. Later, Meserve will threaten to shoot Eriksson if he doesn't rape Oahn and if he doesn't kill her.

De Palma has described Meserve as a "father figure"[5] to Eriksson and the other men, and in Eriksson's uncertain attitude to his sergeant's phallic power, we can see something of the young De Palma's ambivalence toward his own father. We recall that as a teenager De Palma regularly witnessed his father perform surgery, including the amputation of arms and legs, and that, on one such occasion as "I was standing right next to him in front of the operating room table," "he cut off a patient's leg and then gave it to me!"[6] The father's power can be used to take or to give, to amputate or to restore. Positioned between his father and the patient, the young De Palma is like Eriksson, halfway between Meserve and the VC. The father's knife is meant to save, to restore health, but what if that kind of power got out of control, if that sort of violence were turned on De Palma himself? Meserve, who restores the "arm" (as a branch) to the wounded soldier and who lifts Eriksson to safety, uses his gun to kill the VC fighter and then later threatens to shoot Eriksson.

After saving Eriksson in the tunnel scene, Meserve and his platoon find rest at what seems to be a friendly village, but as the sergeant is standing with his longtime friend, Brownie (Erik King), a sniper bullet strikes his buddy in the neck. Holding his bleeding friend, Meserve is a helpless witness to the man's dying. Afterward at base camp, while the other guys in his squad are shown in conversation at screen left, Meserve sits apart from them on the right, using a mirror to shave with a straight razor. His hand shakes and he checks his neck for a cut, as if he felt a physical connection to his buddy's neck wound. Traumatized by Brownie's death, Meserve now reacts against the danger of becoming a victim like his friend by wielding that razor with a coldly steady hand, determined to take control and be a victor. In this scene of Meserve looking at himself in the mirror, we see him try to resolve the split within him between victim and victor by closing off all feeling and weakness so that he can be armored with a hardened will. It is here—in his grief over his friend's death, in his anger at the supposedly friendly Vietnamese who harbored a sniper, and in his desire to be victorious and not a victim—that Meserve begins to go crazy, losing track of the difference between whom he should save and whom he should kill, and eventually turning his violence toward Oahn and Eriksson.

Through Meserve as a disturbed and disturbing father figure, De Palma may be trying to imagine the traumatic effect that the witnessing of war could have had on his own father, who served for three years on a hospital boat in the Pacific during World War II, "following combat troops and collecting the casualties, a horrifying assortment of mangled bodies."[7] Sometimes there were injured men on whom his father would operate. According to De Palma, "One time—I'll always remember it—he told me about a guy who didn't have legs anymore; he was flailing his stumps."[8] Meserve sees the soldier screaming for his lost arm and can only provide him with a branch. Meserve sees Brownie dying from his neck wound and cannot staunch the blood. This last sight— the death of his close friend—is one casualty too many for Meserve, pushing him over the line into lawless violence and personal revenge (as the sight of Robin's death does to Gillian in *The Fury*, and as the witnessing of Malone's death does to Ness in *The Untouchables*). After seeing Oahn's bloody body and after almost being killed himself, Eriksson regains consciousness in a hospital filled with screaming, injured soldiers, including a man who is flailing two stumps instead of legs. Eriksson's challenge is to maintain his compassion for the victims without hardening in fear that he will become one or turning his gun on others in revenge. As for De Palma, he has said that "I think I was lucky I didn't go to Vietnam. . . . Maybe it would have given me an understanding of some things I only understand second-hand. But I think you'd be so horribly scarred by it."[9]

Driven half-crazy by the war, the vengeful, domineering, and indiscriminately violent Meserve is definitely the villain of the piece. As seen in the shaving scene, Meserve is increasingly separated from the rest of humanity, hardened against compassion by the death of his friend, Brownie. Sean Penn (playing Meserve) replicated this emotional remove by remaining apart from the other actors: he was "real aloof through the whole shoot. Didn't party with the rest of us, wouldn't even say hello," reported John Leguizamo (Diaz).[10] De Palma noted that Penn "never associated with Michael J. Fox [Eriksson] . . . which created a tremendous amount of tension between them when we were shooting,"[11] and producer Art Linson agreed: "There was definitely a tension. Sean kept his distance from Michael—treated him like he was shit, in fact."[12] According to Linson, this was Penn's way of striking fear into Fox, but also of hardening his own heart: "Sean had to be a terrifying presence to Michael, and he didn't want to let Michael off the hook any more than he wanted to let *himself* off the hook. I don't think that he wanted to deep down *like* Michael and have any of that affection creep into his performance. And it could have been even more interesting than that, which is: he didn't want any of the fear that Michael might have had in him to not be in Michael's performance."[13]

Playing the domineering Meserve, Penn may have let his own violence get a bit out of hand. Leguizamo said that "there was one scene I didn't like doing over and over. The one where Penn, playing the rogue sergeant, slaps me around for not wanting to help gang-rape the Vietnamese girl he's kidnapped. Because Sean Penn doesn't believe in staged combat. He's too method for that shit. When Sean Penn slaps you, he really wallops you. It was no joke. By the thirteenth take my face was beginning to swell up so badly I couldn't even say my lines clearly."[14] Leguizamo pleaded with De Palma not to have to do the scene again, but the director wanted more: "I don't know," Leguizamo said, "but I think Brian was getting off on it. 'Just one more take.' He smiled. 'You're doing great. It's so believable. No really. Just a few more angles and we'll have it.' I could swear he smirked at one of his assistants. So we did another take, and Penn really laid into me. I was seeing stars."[15] (Shades of De Palma insisting on multiple takes of Betty Buckley slapping Nancy Allen—"*Hit her harder!*"[16]—on the set of *Carrie*.)

Meserve's psychological and physical domination of his men to get them to rape and murder Oahn, along with his own leading role in these crimes, is reprehensible and inexcusable. But we miss something important about his character if we fail to see that this is a hardened killer who is still struggling with some remnants of feeling and conscience, that this is a villain who still remembers what it was like to be a hero. It is interesting to note that writer David Rabe originally had Sean Penn in mind for the role of *Eriksson*: "Frankly—though I'm very fond of Michael J. Fox's performance—I was always thinking about Sean for Eriksson. I was thinking about the working-class quality Eriksson should have, and I felt having Sean there would be like Brando in *On the Waterfront*, that kind of presence at the core of the movie."[17] Would Eriksson have gone over the edge like Meserve if he had spent as much time in Vietnam and witnessed as many horrors as Meserve had? Linson believes that "Sean's performance made it clear that Meserve was just as much a victim of Vietnam as a man of intrinsic menace."[18]

After the abduction of Oahn, Eriksson tells Meserve that he thought the sergeant had only been kidding about his plan to "requisition ourselves a girl—a little portable R&R," but Meserve replies, "I was serious as a heart attack." This statement suggests more than just Meserve's grim determination and his knowledge of the gravity of what he has done. It also implies some awareness of motive—after the death of Brownie, he is hardening his heart against *all* Vietnamese, even the ones he is officially there to protect—and some understanding that his own lack of compassion will kill him, that it constitutes a moral death. After the men rape Oahn, Clark dismisses her as less than human by asking, "When was the last time you had a *real* woman, Sarge?" But Meserve's answer—"She was real; I think she was real"—indicates that at some level he realizes the violation of humanity he has just committed. Note that Penn speaks this line solemnly, almost forlornly. Of course, the point of taking revenge—as Meserve is doing on Oahn for the death of Brownie—is lost if there is no sense of violation, if the victim is viewed as subhuman. But Meserve also seems to have a sense of the severity of his actions—certainly more of a sense than the insanely sadistic Clark, the mentally challenged Hatcher, or the scared-witless Diaz.

Speaking to Eriksson, Meserve recites his own version of Psalm 23, "The Lord Is My Shepherd": "Yea, though I walk through the valley of evil, I shall fear no death, 'cause I'm the meanest motherfucker in the valley!" A faith in goodness and God didn't save Brownie, and Meserve fears it won't save him, so he has replaced it with a belief in the power of his own hard will and capacity for violence. (Before raping Oahn, he grabs his crotch and calls it "a weapon.") Yet Penn delivers his prayer to power with more than a hint of sadness and desperation, as if mourning his loss of faith and half-realizing that violence may save his skin, but a lack of compassion has damned his soul.

"You probably like the army, don't ya, Eriksson?" Meserve says. "I hate the army." This is tantamount to a confession that Meserve knows that war has ruined him. Earlier, speaking to his squad, Meserve had said that "we all got weapons. Anybody can blow anybody away, any second, which is the way it ought to be." In Penn's acting of this scene, Meserve has a strange look on his face during this speech, half-menacing and half-ironic, and he ends it with a crazy grin. One part of Meserve wants to believe that the more armed and armored they are, the more weaponized and hardened, the greater their strength will be, but another part of him senses that this is crazy: the macho displays and the proliferation of firepower have led to a pervasive paranoia that has replaced fellow feeling with fear and violence. Not only can the Americans no longer tell Vietcong from Vietnamese "friendlies," but the distinction between friend and foe within their own squad has broken down as aggression gets out of control. "It showed that we were over there basically fighting ourselves instead of the enemy," De Palma said, "that to boys of that age the whole world of this strange land must have been like being on a different planet where values can get turned upside down."[19]

If the villainous Meserve is not pure evil, given that he is still troubled by a residual conscience, then neither is Eriksson—ostensibly the moral opposition to Meserve in the film—an unalloyed hero. Having refused to rape Oahn, Eriksson nevertheless stands wide-eyed while Meserve drags her kicking and screaming into the hootch, rips off her pants, and climbs on top of her. Meserve looks back with a grin at Eriksson, inviting his voyeuristic complicity by saying, "You gonna watch?" From this moment on, except for one quick backward glance, Eriksson separates himself from the group, keeping his eyes resolutely turned away while, behind him, each member of the squad takes a turn with the Vietnamese girl. Remaining motionless, Eriksson does not intervene to stop the assault. It is as though, in order to avoid complicity with the rapists, he overcompensates by rendering himself impotent, by becoming totally inactive.

It is true that the squad has offered him no position to occupy besides that of macho victor or feminized victim. Meserve says that if Eriksson won't take his turn with Oahn, maybe it's because he's a "queer" or a "VC sympathizer." Meserve puts his rifle barrel in his own mouth and mimes sucking it off, implying that being gay is a death sentence, and he warns that if the guys can't count on Eriksson's loyalty, one of them may "accidentally" shoot him. If Eriksson won't join the men in assaulting Oahn, then they'll treat him just like her: "Maybe when I'm done humpin' her, I'm gonna come hump you!" Meserve tells him. The one time that Eriksson appears close to making a move to stop Meserve from beginning the rape, Eriksson is dissuaded from doing so by Clark's knife near his throat and by Hatcher's rifle pointed at him. He then walks away, letting the gang rape go on.

If the threat of imminent phallic violence directed at his person provides one explanation for why Eriksson did not move to save Oahn from the rape, this reason cannot be offered in his defense when he fails to rescue her later. With all the other men in his squad away from the hootch, Eriksson is left alone with Oahn and sees, for the first time since the rape, the extensive damage that has been done to her body and her face. At first, he can barely look at her, so sympathetic does he feel with her wounds and so guilty about having turned away before and having abandoned her to the men's predation. But eventually, seeing that she is not only injured but sick, he moves compassionately to comfort her. Interestingly, Michael J. Fox himself "got really sick" during the shoot, and while in the hospital he had a dream in which he imagined himself experiencing a very female kind of suffering: "I think that the only way my brain could process the amount of pain my stomach was in was to let me have a dream that I was giving birth."[20] Eriksson bonds with the Vietnamese girl to the point where he decides that *they* cannot bear any more pain— "I'm gonna take you out of here, okay? You, me, we go"—and he resolves to return her to her mother.

But then comes a moment of hesitation when, as they are leaving, he thinks not of her but of himself, of how other men (the army) would punish him for desertion: "He again tries to help her," De Palma says, "but he doesn't move fast enough, and he's afraid he's gonna be court-martialed for being a deserter, so again he sort of doesn't do the heroic thing, which ultimately leads to her death."[21] Like Jack trying to help Sally in *Blow Out* and like Jake trying to help Gloria in *Body Double*, Eriksson is too slow to act. He is unable to become a new kind of man, to occupy a position between feminized victim and rapacious victor.

As a result of his hesitation, Eriksson and Oahn are unable to escape before Clark returns to collect them from the hootch and take them to the rest of the squad, who are hiding out near a mountain bridge and surveilling the enemy on the other side of a river below. When Diaz, acting on orders from Meserve, is about to kill Oahn, Eriksson creates a distraction by shooting at the Vietcong, forcing the members of his squad to defend themselves by returning fire when the enemy starts shooting back at them.

However, a split-diopter shot[22] shows that, while Eriksson is firing at the Vietcong in the right foreground of the frame, his head is turned away from Clark, who, in the left background, uses a knife to stab Oahn. This shot shows the fatal consequence of Eriksson's having *turned away from Oahn*, first during the rape and then afterward when they were alone together at the hootch. Because he didn't "do the heroic thing" and rescue her, she ends up dead. Moreover, the shot shows the split within Eriksson that has caused his hesitation, for while one part of him very much wants to do the right thing, to fire upon the true enemy, another side of him is tempted by voyeuristic complicity and by lustful rage toward all the Vietnamese "friendlies" who seem to have betrayed them. This dark side of Eriksson is tempted to feel the same way Meserve and Clark do—that all Vietnamese women are "VC whores" who deserve to be punished with rape and murder. (The real-life Eriksson commented about the men in his squad, "They were among the ones—among the few—who did what everyone around them wanted to do."[23] We recall Jon at the end of *Greetings* who, as a soldier in Vietnam, is tempted to leer at or to shoot a Vietnamese girl.)

Although set in Vietnam, *Casualties of War* was filmed in Thailand, and for this climactic scene, De Palma used the very bridge that featured in one of his favorite films, *The Bridge on the River Kwai*. The split within Eriksson can be compared to a similar conflict inside that film's protagonist, Colonel Nicholson (Alec Guinness), who also struggles with divided loyalties. On the one hand, he wants to save the bridge that he and his fellow prisoners of war built, but this feat was accomplished in aid of the enemy war effort and against the interests of his own side, so on the other hand, he feels a loyalty to the Allied cause and its imperative to destroy the bridge. Eriksson believes he should be loyal to his fellow squad members and he is assailed by the same moral confusion they experience in Vietnam regarding who is friend or foe, but his empathy for Oahn's suffering pulls him toward siding with her against his own men.

When, having been knocked to the ground by Meserve, Eriksson looks on helplessly while his sergeant and the other men shoot multiple rounds into her, it is not only a human being he watches die but also the men's humanity, as American soldiers kill someone they were there to protect, and thus destroy their own humane purpose in this war. Similarly, when U.S. helicopters bomb the Vietcong on the riverside below, the explosions also kill Vietnamese civilians and cause a U.S. gunboat to catch fire, consuming those American soldiers as well. De Palma says that he meant to show "the irony" that "they blow up themselves. It's like you're capsulizing the absurdity of this war, because again this is a war with no moral borders to it or moral lines. It's all kind of gray."[24] When the bridge is blown up at the end of *The Bridge on the River Kwai*, it also shows the futility of war.

Eriksson brings charges against the men in his squad, who are convicted, but as they leave the sentencing hearing, Meserve whispers something in Eriksson's ear. We do not hear what is said, but Eriksson remembers his captain's warning that, once the men have served their time and are let out, they will be "lookin' for a little payback!" (De Palma recalls that Penn actually whispered into Fox's ear, "I screwed your wife many times and now it's gonna be your turn.")[25] In the "nightmare ending"[26] originally considered for the film, Eriksson imagines the men invading his home back in America to get at his wife and daughter (much as Ness fears that Capone will attack his wife and daughter in *The Untouchables*, and as Michael fears that his family will be taken in *Obsession*). While Meserve has his "arm around Eriksson's neck, the knife at his throat," the sergeant and Clark discuss whether to take the wife or the daughter, repeating the same dialogue they used—"Take the pretty one"[27]—during the abduction of Oahn. Then, with Eriksson as witness, "the rape begins again, this time with his wife as the victim."[28] Figuring both a fear of revenge and a haunting sense of guilt over his own failure to save Oahn, this nightmare shows Eriksson's almost total identification with the passive female victim.

By contrast, the ending that De Palma actually chose for the film puts Eriksson in a very different light. On a streetcar back in the U.S., he sees a young Vietnamese woman who reminds him of Oahn (played by the same actress, Thuy Thu Le). Eriksson's furtive gazing at her makes her uncomfortable, as though she fears that this strange man might be about to accost her. Once again, we are reminded of Eriksson's difficulty positioning himself as something other than a voyeur or an aggressor, his struggle to find a new kind of male role different from the one enacted by the men in his squad.

Then, when she exits the tram, leaving her scarf behind, he runs after her to return it. Earlier in the film, when Oahn was being abducted, Eriksson saw her mother run after her to give her her scarf, so by repeating this gesture, he is enacting a maternal role and, in a sense, bringing "Oahn" back home to her mother in the way that he started—but ultimately failed—to do when he had the chance to rescue her. Realizing that this gesture is way too little, way too late, Eriksson can barely look at the woman, though he tries to, glancing at her, then turning away, then looking at her again. When she asks, "You had a bad dream, didn't you?" he says, "Yes," and looks down, overcome by guilt. But when she then eyes him compassionately, saying, "It's over now, I think," he raises his eyes slowly and is able to look directly at her face. She smiles, says goodbye, and walks away, and his eyes follow her for a time. He then looks briefly upward, his face in partial sunlight, and walks away, half-smiling, while the camera cranes up and a female choir is heard on the soundtrack.

This, which De Palma calls the "redemption ending,"[29] proved controversial with the critics. Cynthia Fuchs scoffed that "the film's unconscionable finale hoists Eriksson to ethical heaven,"[30] and Elliott Gruner charged that, "whatever atrocity the U.S. soldiers committed, by the end of the film the male hero can dismiss it as merely a 'bad dream.'"[31] Screenwriter David Rabe said that he wrote the "you had a bad dream" line "under duress."[32] With this understated line of dialogue, De Palma was probably trying not to push too hard for emotion, but the unfortunate consequence is that it could be seen as trivializing the deaths of thousands of Vietnamese like Oahn, which is surely not what he intended. As for the female choir, while it could be accused of sappy sentimentality, the fact that the chorus sings the same musical theme heard during the tragic moments of Oahn's rape and murder gives it the weight of mourning as well as a ray of hope. Editor Bill Pankow called the choir "sad and yet somewhat hopeful," arguing that "it evoked so many of the souls that were killed in this war and yet it helped us feel like we were rising above it and changing."[33] It is also worth pointing out that De Palma thought of the young Vietnamese woman as emblematic of a strength to survive that could serve as an example to Americans: "What I wanted to show was: the Vietnamese recovered; what's our problem? Because many Vietnamese came here, started new lives, they managed to go on. . . . I wanted to have that feeling at the end of this movie, that this terrible nightmare had happened but you cannot let this wound not heal; you've got to move on."[34]

De Palma has described the Vietnam War as "the scar which refuses to heal," and he has compared traumatized veterans like Eriksson to "an abused child—the damage from the abuse never goes away and years later the child is still damaged."[35] Continuing the analogy between war and child abuse, De Palma said that "it's a little like how I see our childhood. It can have a bad influence on our adult conduct. Your parents have communicated neuroses to you, which lead you in turn to be destructive. But at a certain moment you have to be able to wipe the slate clean and say, 'Okay, I get it: they did a very bad job taking care of me, but am I going to spend the rest of my life punishing and destroying myself, or am I going to move on?'"[36] De Palma may be thinking of his own father, who saw such horrible things during the war and whose parenting of De Palma himself left so much to be desired—a relationship that the director seems to have mapped onto the one between the father figure, Meserve, and Eriksson, the young recruit. If De Palma gave *Casualties of War* a "redemption ending," it was because he needed to believe in the possibility of overcoming trauma, of moving on, of becoming a different kind of man than the father—for Eriksson and for himself: Eriksson "shouldn't hold it against himself for his entire life";[37] "I couldn't stay haunted by this story for the rest of my life."[38]

Of course, the Vietnamese woman who speaks to Eriksson at the end is not Oahn, and her words refer only vaguely to "a bad dream." The fact that he sees her as some kind of "forgiving angel" says more about his need to be forgiven than it does about any actual absolution. In a sense, this happy ending—that he can look her in the face again, that he can raise his face to the sun—is the wish-fulfillment counterpart to the guilty, haunted, "home-invasion" alternative; it is the dream version of that "nightmare ending." Interestingly, De Palma had actress Amy Irving dub the voice of the Vietnamese woman. The practical reason for this was so that she would not sound too much like Oahn since, though played by the same Vietnamese actress, she is supposed to be a different person. But, in *Carrie*, Irving played the character of Sue, who remains horribly haunted in the end by her inability to save Carrie. Having Irving be the voice of the angel that forgives Eriksson for his failure to save Oahn is almost like having Sue forgive herself. It suggests that, through his protagonists, De Palma may be striving to move on—from nightmare to redemption.

Casualties of War was De Palma's bid to make a serious film on an important subject that he cared deeply about. Some critics responded with approbation. The *Nation*'s Stuart Klawans noted that "*Casualties of War* has one virtue that is lacking in every other Vietnam War film I've seen: It makes you look at the face of the 'enemy' [the Vietnamese girl Oahn] for a good long time."[39] Indeed, De Palma claimed that "this was the first war movie with a woman as the pivot."[40] Pauline Kael wrote that "this movie about war and rape—De Palma's nineteenth film—is the culmination of his best work. In essence, it's feminist."[41]

But the film's showing at the box office was deeply disappointing, making back only $18.6 million of its $22.5 million cost. De Palma speculated that the failure of his film might have been due to the fact that "Michael J. Fox was considered a comedy star at the time," so the public wasn't willing to accept him in a serious drama. De Palma also felt that *Casualties of War* could have been overshadowed by "other Vietnam movies"[42] released in the late 1980s—*Platoon*, *Full Metal Jacket*, and *Born on the Fourth of July*—which may have given moviegoers a kind of war fatigue by the time of his film's release. Perhaps De Palma's film, despite its redemption ending, was just too tragic and sorrowful for most audiences to bear. "*Platoon* was such a success . . . because [Oliver] Stone's film ended much like a western where the good guys triumph over the bad," De Palma said. "Things didn't go that way. Everyone lost in Vietnam"[43]— a pervasive sense of loss emphasized in *Casualties of War*. "My darkest films," De Palma added, referring to *Blow Out* and *Casualties of War*, "have never been successful."[44]

Casualties had not yet been released to theaters when the studio offered him *The Bonfire of the Vanities* to direct. If the poor performance of De Palma's war film had been known, he might not have been offered this big-budget movie. Perhaps, though, that would have been just as well, since *Bonfire* would turn out to be the most high-profile disaster in this director's career.

CHAPTER 20

The Bonfire of the Vanities (1990)

The Bonfire of the Vanities recounts the fall of Wall Street bond broker Sherman McCoy (Tom Hanks). Pulling in millions, ensconced in a posh Park Avenue apartment, Sherman thinks he is "impervious, untouchable, insulated by wealth and power—a Master of the Universe." But after one wrong turn into a Bronx ghetto results in his Mercedes accidentally backing over a black youth, Sherman finds himself the object of an onslaught by reporters, politicians, and the police. In one scene, an overhead shot shows Sherman reigning supreme as a Wall Street power broker: seated at his desk, he has his shoes shined while sweet-talking an investor on the phone. A similar overhead shot presented mob kingpin Al Capone in his barber chair getting a shave and a shoeshine while talking to reporters in The Untouchables. But, in Sherman's case, the camera cranes down to the floor to reveal a newspaper headline about the scandalous hit-and-run accident, presaging Sherman's own fall from the great height of his wealth and power. Reading the headline rattles Sherman, and the panic in his voice spooks the investor, blowing a $600 million deal. As the scandal grows, Sherman will lose his job, his wife, his mistress, and his home, and he will turn to alcohol.

The scene of Sherman's arrest marks his nadir. First handcuffed and forced to undergo a perp walk, he then has his mug shot taken, is strip-searched and fingerprinted, and gets thrown in jail where he encounters cellmates who are not from the upper echelons of society. For this pivotal scene, De Palma drew upon the memory of the one night he himself had spent in jail. He was twenty-three; his girlfriend had left him; he got drunk and lost all his money in a poker game. Not knowing how to get home, he stole a motor scooter and ran some red lights. When a cop pulled him over, De Palma knocked him down and tried to drive away, but the policeman pushed the scooter over. De Palma ran, and the cop shot him in the leg. After being treated at a hospital with a police guard at the door, De Palma spent the rest of the night behind bars with other accused criminals waiting for arraignment. "I understand that moment Sherman has very well," De Palma said. "When you're brought up as a middle-class kid from Philadelphia, you've gone to private schools and Columbia [University], and suddenly you're in the tank? Whoa! You're in there with people you've sort of read about in the newspaper. And you realize you're just one [of them], and everybody is equal before the law."

De Palma added, "Anyone who's spent a night in the Tombs, which I've had the *privilege* of doing . . . You get it real fast."[1] Here, "privilege" is being used both sardonically *and* seriously, for the point is that, undesirable as it may seem, it *is* a privilege for the privileged class—like Sherman, like De Palma—to have the insulation of wealth and power taken away, to be touched by some of the suffering that the less advantaged—those who live at the bottom of the social heap—are exposed to every day. Sherman "lives in a protected world," explains De Palma, but he "comes to realize that there exists another reality, a very different one, whose existence he did not suspect."[2] (Interestingly, De Palma's mentor, Alfred Hitchcock, also spent a very brief time in jail when he was a boy, an event which may have contributed to his sympathetic depiction of outcast and accused individuals in his films.)

Before Sherman is made aware of his own limits, his own susceptibility to suffering, he indulges his boundless ego. De Palma described him as "a guy who thinks he has the power to do whatever he wants."[3] Though blessed with a wife, Sherman says of himself, "I am a Master of the Universe. I deserve more." According to Tom Hanks, Sherman "thinks he's hip enough to have a mistress on the side and conceal it from his wife."[4] But when he is caught cheating and when the scandal of the hit-and-run accident breaks, Sherman finds that both women deny him solace. If neither his wife nor his mistress provides him with the love he seeks in his time of need, it's important to understand the extent to which he has brought this on himself, for these women are merely living out the roles in which he has trapped them.

He married Judy (Kim Cattrall) in order to have a trophy wife, the perfect spouse to show off to high society, so he should not be surprised if she focuses more on her image than on him. Reflected in a mirror as she works out on an exercise machine, Judy is more concerned about his adultery's harm to her image than she is about their relationship: "I don't want to be this person. I am thin. I am beautiful. I do *not* deserve this." If she considers him inferior to his father, her judgment is based on the same "blue-blood" values that Sherman married her in order to maintain. When she refuses his request to forgive him for the well-publicized scandal, saying, "I suppose I can forgive anything but not television," and when she tells him she's leaving him but "after the party . . . we have guests," she is only saving face and keeping up appearances in exactly the way she has always been expected to do—by people like him.

On Sherman's Wall Street desk, next to the family photo of Judy, himself, and their daughter, there is a handwritten note from his mistress, Maria (Melanie Griffith). On the one side is his wife, and on the other, his mistress. The first is for show, and the second is for sex. Having assigned Maria the role of sexpot, Sherman should not be surprised when all she wants to do is make love rather than give him the true love he needs. When he tries to tell her about his troubles, she says, "Don't you want a little poontang first?" This is all he has ever wanted from her before. When he is concerned that they may have hit someone with the car, Maria tells him, "Don't think, Sherman. Just fuck." Rather than listen to him about the car accident or his lost job, she performs a striptease and seduces him into sex. On the wall of the apartment that is their trysting place, there is a painting of a nude woman looking at her reflection in a mirror. Maria is like this woman, merely conforming to the image of "the mistress," which is how she has been regarded.

Actress Melanie Griffith had a similar problem with being typecast in such one-dimensional roles: "Here's this bright, sensitive woman who always ends up in movies with her clothes off, saying, 'Fuck me,'" De Palma said. "It's that old problem. She wants to be treated as more than that, but then when she sees she is treated like a sex object she goes with it."[5] We recall that Griffith also performed a striptease as Holly in *Body Double*. Interestingly, Michelle Pfeiffer was originally considered for the role of Maria. Pfeiffer had played Elvira in *Scarface*, a woman who is at first Frank's mistress and then Tony's wife, who moves from being lusted after as a "whore" to being put on a pedestal as a wife and potential mother, much as Sherman's women are split between Maria the mistress and Judy the wife and mother.

Judy and Maria both abandon him in his time of trial, and Sherman has only himself to blame. But he does receive support from an unexpected source: his father. For years, Sherman has suffered from the feeling that he is not the man his father was, a legendary "lion" at a respected New York law firm. He has chafed under his father's disapproval of his job as a bond broker, hearing the old man make such comments as: "Of course, in my day, there was some integrity to it. Now it isn't about anything, is it? Except the money." So, when his father shows up at his door, Sherman expects to be taken to task for his shortcomings, but instead the patriarch offers him, haltingly but unmistakably, his total love and support: "I came here to—I don't know how to do this. You didn't call. We wanted to help. I came to say that we are here for you, and that you are our son and that we love you. We, uh, I don't mean we. I mean I. I love you. That's all."

De Palma's own father, Anthony, had trouble conveying affection: "He wasn't the kind of man who could easily express what he felt. It was very difficult for him to talk to me."[6] Anthony, a respected surgeon, had hoped that his son would follow in his footsteps by entering a scientific field like medicine or physics. (Did the father see filmmaking as something merely trendy and commercial, much as Sherman's father views bond trading?) As we have noted, when De Palma neglected his college studies in order to pursue an interest in directing, he met with strong disapproval from his father: "My father and I got into a big argument about what I should be doing with my life. He thought I should be spending my time getting out of college instead of running around making movies, and I ultimately told him I was going to make movies whether he liked it or not and he stopped supporting me after that."[7] In the reconciliation scene between Sherman and his father, De Palma seems to imagine the love and acceptance he had always wanted from his own father, the words of approval he wishes he himself could have heard.

The strongest connection between De Palma the director and Sherman the bond broker is that they are both men of great power, deal with vast quantities of money, and oversee an army of workers below them. If people perceive Sherman as a "Master of the Universe," De Palma is regarded as "godlike,"[8] according to Griffith. "A lot of people kind of fade away from him because he's Brian De Palma," Bruce Willis said. "He's treated with a lot of respect and a lot of awe."[9]

For years, as we saw in previous chapters, De Palma has been making movies about characters who "have a god complex," who "literally take themselves for gods."[10] He mentions Swan in *Phantom of the Paradise*, Tony in *Scarface*, and Meserve in *Casualties of War*, along with Sherman in *Bonfire*. And De Palma has been very much aware that these characters, who "live surrounded by a court which venerates them" and who "create a reality to which others must conform,"[11] are not so different from a film director: "I can identify. Making movies is a lot like that."[12] The risk is that a Hollywood director can become money- and power-mad, thinking only about profit and prestige—"How big is the budget of your movie? How big will it open? Who is the star?"[13]—and forgetting about artistic or humane values. The "American film industry and the importance of directors are often linked to the big studios," De Palma has said. "The director is now God and the driving economic force, so there are no more limits, no more barriers. And the result is excess—like those unbelievable castles of mad emperors. It can happen to any one of us."[14] "For these men, for these Masters of the Universe . . . there were no limits whatsoever," the narrator of *Bonfire* says about Sherman, repeating what De Palma has said about overweening directors.

Given that De Palma made *The Bonfire of the Vanities* as a warning against Sherman's kind of megalomania, there is considerable irony in the fact that the film itself came to be perceived as a sign of 1980s exorbitance, the product of an out-of-control director. According to Julie Salamon, "this movie . . . had become a metaphor for everything that was wasteful and rotten in modern moviemaking. . . . De Palma's film had become *the* film to hate because of its excess."[15] Rumors circulated that studio executives were unable to control De Palma's spending, much as in *Bonfire* when Sherman is criticized for "profligate wasting of himself and others." Before the film's release, *Newsweek* predicted that "*Bonfire of the Vanities* will bomb";[16] "The wrath of heaven is at hand," Sherman is told, and "its justice will not tarry. I see the deadly thunderbolt poised above [your] head." "What makes this movie the one everyone wants to see fail?" De Palma wondered. "I've never seen them . . . so gleeful for the fall."[17] Following a preview screening, critic Joel Siegel said, "This is not just a bad movie, this is a failure of epic proportions—*Ishtar* of the Vanities,"[18] and an *American Film* magazine poll later rated it the worst movie of the year. The film bombed at the box office, bringing in only $15.7 million on an investment of $47 million.[19]

Yet De Palma, like Sherman, would come to believe that power, profit, and social reputation are ultimately of little importance. One should hew to more lasting values and not put too much stock in what people say, for social opinion is fickle and likely to turn at any moment. "You're just dinner," Sherman is told in the movie. "Don't you get it? A week from now, a month from now, these people aren't even going to remember what they ate." De Palma uses remarkably similar words in speaking about his own situation regarding the movie's failure: "The media and the critics just gobble us up and forget about what they had yesterday. . . . It's a big deal for about thirty seconds, and they move onto somebody else."[20]

Of course, De Palma has known failure before: after the success of *Greetings*, he was fired from *Get to Know Your Rabbit*, his first Hollywood film. After *Dressed to Kill*, *Blow Out* bombed at the box office, and *The Untouchables* was followed by the disastrous *Casualties of War*. There would be other successes (*Mission: Impossible*) and failures (*Mission to Mars*) to come. Years later, thinking back on *The Bonfire of the Vanities*, De Palma would say, "In my career, I've been burned down to the ground about every 10 years. Finished! And somehow I've managed to rise up out of the ashes."[21]

De Palma's comeback would involve a return to the genre in which he feels most at home: the suspense thriller. "I wanted to make movies because I had strong visual ideas, and I wanted to make movies based on those visual ideas," he said. "That's how I started making movies and that's where I'm going to try to return to."[22] As we'll see, De Palma also goes home in another sense, because *Raising Cain* turns out to be very much about his own family, present and past. And there is a dual tribute in the film's title that is worth noting: a nod to Orson Welles (*Citizen Kane*), one of De Palma's directorial mentors, and a shout-out to the film critic who has been his biggest supporter through good times and bad, Pauline Kael (who wrote the essay "Raising Kane").

CHAPTER 21

Raising Cain (1992)

Carter (John Lithgow) is a child psychologist who is taking time off from his practice in order to remain at home and observe the growth of his daughter, Amy. De Palma has said that "I got the idea because a friend of mine, a child psychologist, had a little girl and got obsessed with her and decided to quit his job and stay home and study her and write a book about it."[1] But De Palma himself had recently become a father for the first time, and he filmed *Raising Cain* within a five-minute radius of his house in northern California ("We practically shot in my backyard")[2] in order for him to be near his wife, Gale Anne Hurd, and their newborn daughter. The film's opening credits—"Produced by Gale Anne Hurd" and "Written and Directed by Brian De Palma"—occur over a shot of Carter comforting Amy in her little bed. Perhaps this film shows De Palma thinking about what it would be like to be a stay-at-home dad and what kind of father he would be.

Another important influence on *Raising Cain* was Michael Powell's film *Peeping Tom*, in which a psychiatrist subjects his young son to a series of cruel experiments in order to study the boy's fearful reactions and document them on film. The abused then turns abuser when the son grows up to become a killer of prostitutes, filming the terror on their faces as he stabs them with a spike affixed to his camera's tripod. Carter's father, Dr. Nix, was a child psychologist who, according to a colleague, "traumatized his own son, then over the years he observed the effects." Will Carter become like his father (both are played by John Lithgow), doing psychological damage to his daughter in the process of studying her in the interests of science, much as his father did to him?

De Palma has long been fascinated with powerful doctor-fathers whose influence proves destructive, as we have seen with Dr. Emil Breton in *Sisters*,

Dr. Byrd in *Home Movies*, and Dr. Elliott in *Dressed to Kill*: "It's always the idea of the mad genius, who works for the benefit of humanity but creates a monster in the process."[3] We know that De Palma had a troubled relationship with his own doctor-father, Anthony, who had him witness bloody surgical operations when he was in his teens. Is De Palma concerned about whether he will be the same kind of father that Anthony was? "Becoming a father has brought back my own childhood," he has said, noting that, when he looks at his daughter, "it's myself that I see" and "I relive it all once again."[4]

Dr. Nix is a genius, and Carter greatly admires him, noting that his father is "one of the most visionary men in his field" and that he "wrote the book on child development," *Raising Cain: The Creation and Evolution of the Multiple Personality*. Similarly, De Palma's father, one of the country's most respected orthopedic surgeons, authored many of the standard texts on the subject, such as *Diseases of the Hip in Children* and *Genetics of Congenital Deformity*. Despite his father's good intentions, however, he was often cold and distant, and he did not always have a positive effect on his son, such as when, after amputating a patient's leg, he handed the bloody limb to the teenage De Palma, which seemed to instill in him a fascination with gore. Similarly, while Carter's goal may be to love his daughter and ensure her healthy upbringing, he finds himself studying her with a clinical eye, observing her every move with the aid of a video camera and planning to write a book about her, much as his father did to him.

If Anthony was often an absent father, spending most of his time at work, De Palma resolved to be much more of a presence to his child, and the character of Carter seems to be the director's way of imagining the life of a stay-at-home dad, including the anxieties attendant upon this new role. In one scene, Carter gets a lustful look on his face, unzips his fly, and climbs into bed behind his wife Jenny (Lolita Davidovich), feeling her up. "How horny we are," she says appreciatively, but then cries out, "Ow, you're hurting me!" when he gets rough. Just as he is pulling her into a passionate kiss with one hand around her neck, he hears Amy on the baby monitor and goes to tend to the child. This scene shows Carter torn between two extremes, the conquering lover and the asexual dad. It is as though he can't find a way to be both a husband and a father. As John Lithgow said, De Palma "takes the concept of the new-age dad and throws it into a blender. He's sort of plumbing the depths of the hidden conflict there."[5] Later, when Jenny's friend Sarah comments that Carter is "the perfect man" for his willingness to spend so much time with their daughter, Jenny scoffs, "The perfect man? Yesterday, out of the blue, he started to make love to me and then stopped when Amy started to cry."

Instead, Jenny turns to Jack (Steven Bauer), a man who, desiring her and unencumbered by a child, makes love to her in the bower of a public park.

As it happens, Carter ends up witnessing this little tryst from a hiding place behind a tree. While one part of him weeps and nearly faints at the sight of his wife's infidelity, another part of him licks his lips voyeuristically, ogling the scene like a Peeping Tom, and plots to kill Jenny and frame Jack for murder. Unable to reconcile the asexual dad and the conquering lover, Carter psychologically splits into two personalities, one of them the sensitive "house husband" (Carter) and the other an aggressively dominant male (Cain). It was his father's traumatic experiments on him as a boy that first prompted Carter's multiple personalities to materialize, but shocking sights like that of his wife's adultery can still trigger the split in the present.

Moreover, Carter's father is still alive—not only in Carter's head, but in actuality—and has been ordering his son to bring children to him for more experiments. When Carter is not up to the task, the "Cain" side of him takes over to perform it. In one scene, new-age dad Carter befriends a mother named Karen at a playground. After some companionable conversation with her in a car, he chloroforms her so that he can abduct her son to take to his father. However, Karen's head flops down onto the car horn, alerting some male joggers who are coming up from behind, suspicious about what is going on. The "Cain" side of Carter "appears" in order to have him fake a romantic moment with Karen in order to throw off their suspicions: "What do you think you look like, killer? Come on, kiss her." This scene figures the split within Carter: associating masculinity with rape, he cannot kiss because he is afraid that doing so will kill. Rather than risk being too overbearing, he neuters himself, becoming passive, impotent Carter (one extreme), while Cain is let loose to express murderous lust (the other extreme).

To put it another way, sensitive Carter identifies with the female victim, whereas tough-guy Cain—who sports a leather jacket, wears dark glasses, and smokes and drinks heavily—plays the macho aggressor. For example, the film places Carter and Jack's wife, Emma, in similar positions. Just as Carter sees Jenny and Jack commit adultery in the park, so Emma, when she is dying of cancer, sees Jenny and Jack kissing near her hospital bed. The shock of what Emma sees causes her death, much as Carter is sickened, nearly faints, and has to go home to sleep after what he witnesses.

Carter's identification with the wronged woman can be compared to De Palma's sympathy for his mother. We recall that, after learning of Anthony's adultery, De Palma's mother took an overdose of pills and had to be rushed to the hospital by her son, where she almost died. Out of compassion for his victimized mother, De Palma attempted to gather evidence for a divorce, which is what led him to burst into his doctor-father's office to discover him and the nurse with whom he had been having an affair. De Palma and his mother were thus in league against his father and the nurse in their adultery, much as

Carter and Emma are linked in opposition to Jack and Jenny in their adultery. At the same time, though, we also know that De Palma took a knife to his father's office and broke through a glass door in order to confront him about his illicit liaison, with the terrified nurse cowering in a closet. De Palma thus acted with masculine aggression, of the kind that the "Cain" side of Carter takes to an extreme when he knifes a flirtatious babysitter (a substitute for his "whorish" wife) and then tries to smother Jenny with a pillow.

Carter and Cain are like brothers competing to see who can best please their father, Dr. Nix. Carter has become a child psychologist like his father, is studying his own daughter, and attempts to kidnap children to further his father's experiments. As Dr. Nix's former colleague remarks about Carter (who is, of course, also called "Dr. Nix"), "Same name, same face. . . . It's uncanny—he looks exactly like his father." But Carter always seems to fall short of his father's expectations. "Poor schmuck," Cain calls him, stepping in when his "brother" fails to pull off a kidnapping: "Carter's an amateur. He panicked."

It is Cain who more strenuously strives to live up to the "ideal" set by his father, but in doing so, Cain can go overboard, exhibiting not only a crazy genius like his father's but a madness that seems out of control. For this reason, despite Cain's attempt to imitate him, he does not win his father's approval. "I know you," his father tells Cain. "Carter weakened and you stepped in. We all know your tough-guy act, but we don't need a loose cannon here. . . . You're nothing but a cheap hoodlum." "I am what you made me, Dad" is Cain's reply, an angry retort but also a plaintive admission that he is only trying to match his father's image, to be recognized as a worthy son. "Where would I be without you?" Cain asks, and when his father answers that "you wouldn't exist," Cain says, "That's right. But I do exist, don't I? I'm that fucked-up experiment of yours that just won't go away."

Here, De Palma presents, in exaggerated form, a version of his own childhood alongside his older brother, Bruce, as they were raised by their doctor-father, Anthony. Asked in an interview about *Raising Cain* why he is so interested in twins, De Palma said, "It all has to do with sibling rivalry," and he noted that he was "very competitive with my brothers."[6] Like Carter and Cain, Brian and Bruce were rivals for their father's affection. One of the earliest examples of Brian's vying for attention was when, as a young child, he would bang his head against his crib so that it would hit the wall, not stopping until his father heard the booming sound and came in to comfort him. (We recall Carter comforting Amy in her little bed.)

Brian and Bruce each tried to outdo the other in virtually everything they attempted, both trying to live up to the ideal set by their father in order to win his approval. Following Anthony's example of success in the medical-scientific profession, both boys competed in science fairs, but Brian always felt that Bruce's accomplishments outshone his own in their father's eyes. When his brother decided to study physics in college, Brian originally set his mind on doing the same thing. However, theater and film beckoned him instead—choices which his father did not recognize as worthy. By contrast, Bruce went on to become the inventor of what he claimed to be a perpetual motion machine; he also took psychedelic drugs. Bruce can be said to have taken the example of his father's great brilliance to an extreme, becoming a crazed genius.

Brian's other brother, Bart, though also someone he competed with, seems more often to have been a fellow sufferer whom he felt compassion for as a victim. For example, we noted earlier that De Palma has said that "seeing Bart upset over my mother being torn up [over the father's adultery] and being too small to do anything about it, that had an impact on me." Years later, as an adult, De Palma "realized that's why I always have characters who can't save people. That's me trying to save my brother."[7] The Bart character in the film is probably Josh, another one of Carter's multiple personalities. Josh is a piti-able figure, a seven-year-old boy who whimpers in fear of his father that "he'll hurt me!" The film thus presents Carter (Brian) imagining himself as hav-ing been split between madly aggressive Cain (Bruce) and pitiably victimized Josh (Bart) as a result of their upbringing by doctor-father Nix (Anthony).

If *Raising Cain* is unusually rich in influences from De Palma's family life, it also makes significant references to his previous films. In one scene, Jenny sneaks into her lover Jack's hotel room to slip a Valentine's Day present into his bedside drawer, but she accidentally leaves a present for her husband Carter instead. This moment is reminiscent of the one in *The Bonfire of the Vanities* where Sherman sneaks out of his home in order to call his mistress but ends up phoning his wife. Both Sherman's and Jenny's "mistakes" could be seen as signs of guilt. While the bad part of them sins, their consciences are telling them that adultery is wrong and leading them to get caught. (Note that Jenny puts the present next to a Gideon Bible—a hint that, if she were a faithful wife, she would be reserving her Valentine's present for her husband and not giving it and herself to a lover. Interestingly, the actress who plays Carter's wife Jenny, Lolita Davidovich, had tried out for the part of Sherman's mistress in *Bonfire*.)

Realizing her mistake, Jenny returns to Jack's hotel room to get the mis-placed present, but this time Jack is there and they end up making love, after which she falls asleep and doesn't wake up again until morning. De Palma has said that he got this idea from his own experience: "I was having an affair with a married woman. She used to come over to my house before she went home, and we would make love. Then one time she fell asleep, and I thought, 'What would happen if I didn't wake her up and she slept through the night?'"[8] While driving home the next day, Jenny hears on the phone from her friend that

Carter had been worried sick about her absence. At this point, Jenny imagines swerving her car to avoid some bikers and running straight into the pointed lance of an equestrian statue, which impales her through the heart. Thus, the guilt-ridden wife fantasizes a terribly just punishment for having broken her husband's heart with her unfaithfulness. Similarly, when wife Kate (Angie Dickinson) in *Dressed to Kill* realizes that she has forgotten her wedding ring in her lover's apartment and resolves to retrieve it, she is slashed with a razor before she can get out of the elevator, as if her guilty mind had brought a terrible punishment upon her for her sin.

Jenny's impalement turns out to have been a bad dream, but when she wakes up, Carter smothers her with a pillow and bundles her into a car, which he drives to a river. This is the "Cain" side of Carter who, virile and vengeful, leered at her before when she was "whoring around" with Jack in the park and now punishes her for that transgression by sinking the car in the river with her trapped in the back: "She doesn't care who she fucks or where she does it. . . . I'm gonna put that two-timing bitch in a box she'll never swim out of." But as the car stalls in its sinking and as Jenny revives, screaming and pounding on the back window to be let out, Cain/Carter seems torn between wanting her to drown and fearing that he'll get caught—and not just because the sun is coming up and he might be seen, but because he knows what he is doing is wrong and that he should be stopped. The scene is similar to the one in *Blow Out* where Jack (John Travolta) sees the car with Sally (Nancy Allen—De Palma's wife at the time) trapped inside as it sinks into the river. Jack wants to save her, but Burke wants the car to go down. And Burke—the dark side of Jack and the killer of "whorish" women like Sally—is portrayed by John Lithgow, who also plays Cain/Carter.

Returning home some time after successfully submerging the car, Cain/Carter seems to catch a glimpse of Jenny on a video monitor: was it she or just his guilty imagination? Here again, Cain would not feel guilty but Carter has a conscience, and they are "squabbling amongst themselves as to which one gets to control the consciousness," as a psychiatrist in the film puts it. Cain/Carter is frightened when he sees Jenny's shoes protruding from a hiding place, but it turns out they are empty. However, as he is reaching to turn on the light, his wrist is slashed by a scalpel, and Jenny, who survived the sinking car and is wielding the knife, threatens to cut his throat, too. Here, we have a repetition of the scene from *Dressed to Kill* where Liz (Nancy Allen) is terrified by what turn out to be empty shoes right before having her throat cut by a razor-wielding killer, but note that *Raising Cain* puts Cain/Carter *in Liz's place*: it is the man who now occupies what was formerly the female position. The fact that Cain/Carter feels guilty about the vengeance he took on his wife, that he imagines being punished for it even before Jenny arrives to actually punish him, marks a significant advance in morality for his character, suggesting that the split in his psyche could be resolved in favor of conscience-stricken Carter rather than remorseless Cain.

Jenny finds out that Carter, when he was still "Cain," abducted Amy and took her to his father, after trying to kill Jenny by sending her to the bottom of the river in a car. In *Obsession*, John Lithgow—as the dark side of that film's hero—plays Bob, who kidnaps a child named Amy; he is partly responsible for her mother's death while trapped inside a car that sinks in a river. When Cain abducts Amy *and tries to kill Jenny*, he exceeds his father's orders, which were only to obtain children for further experiments. In *Blow Out*, when Burke (played by Lithgow) shoots out a tire and causes the car with Sally in it to plunge to the bottom of the river, he is exceeding *his* orders, for his father figure and boss had not instructed him to commit murder.

Cain not only has doubles or alter egos in *Blow Out*'s Burke and *Obsession*'s Bob, but Lithgow has described how, when he was playing his scenes as Cain speaking to his alternate personalities in the film, actor Gregg Henry would sit in, off-camera, so that Lithgow would have someone he could see and talk to. Henry—who resembles Lithgow in having a baby face and receding blond hair—actually appears in the film as Cain's nemesis, good guy Detective Terri, but Henry also played the villainous Sam in *Body Double*. According to Lithgow, De Palma "loves golden, WASPy villains, which is apparently why he hires me all the time—he likes sort of good-hearted, moon-faced people who end up being deeply deranged."[9]

Jenny goes to the motel where "Cain" brought Amy and takes the elevator up to the third floor. As the elevator door opens, Dr. Nix is revealed, pushing a baby carriage and holding Amy in his arms, but also carrying a gun. In *The Untouchables*, Ness (Kevin Costner) was shown in a similar position on the train station steps, torn between protecting the infant in the baby carriage and shooting at the gangsters around him, which endangers the child. While it is tempting to see Dr. Nix as a pure villain, the parallel between him and Ness can help us see that there is more than one side to the doctor. Yes, he has "Cain" kidnap children for psychological experiments which traumatize them, but in his own mind Dr. Nix is doing it for the benefit of humanity; he sees himself as a doctor trying to help children. Thus, when Jenny threatens him with a scalpel in order to get Amy back and when Dr. Nix tells her to put it away because "I don't want you upsetting the child," he is not just trying to manipulate her into disarming herself; the "good side" of him does actually care about Amy's welfare. Like Ness, Dr. Nix is torn between protecting and endangering the child.

As events transpire, "Margo"—who is actually Carter dressed in drag, enacting another one of his multiple personalities—stabs Dr. Nix in the back, causing him to drop Amy over the third-floor railing of the motel. Luckily, Jack is on the street below, but as he runs up to catch her, a pickup truck is backing up towards him, carrying a giant sundial whose spear-like rod is about to impale him and Amy as he receives her into his arms. It is at this point that Dr. Nix, dying on the third floor above, fires his gun downward and the bullet knocks off the tip of the sundial rod, saving Jack and Amy from being speared. Did Dr. Nix, reeling from the stab in the back, just shoot wildly and happen to hit the sundial? Was his firing one last burst of malevolence in an attempt to kill Jack, who was taking Amy from him? Or did some inherent goodness in Dr. Nix prevail in the end, causing him to shoot to save the child? One can certainly decide to believe in the last possibility, but De Palma leaves the matter unresolved.

After this climactic scene, the film's coda is similarly equivocal, and as with the rest of this highly allusive movie, looking at the parallels with other De Palma films can help us get a handle on the ambiguity. With mother and daughter having been reunited, Jenny takes Amy to play in the park. Hearing what she believes to be her daddy's voice, the child wanders off into the woods. When Jenny finds her, Amy insists that her father is present, though there is no one in sight. However, as Jenny bends down to gather her daughter into her arms, "Margo"—Carter in his female persona—appears to be standing right behind her.

Some viewers have seen this coda as positive. After all, Margo is a mother figure who "protects the children," as Josh told a psychiatrist. It was Margo who killed Dr. Nix so that Amy could be rescued at the motel. If Carter (who escaped after the motel scene) has come back as Margo, then perhaps his good side has won out. Or maybe Margo isn't actually present but is instead a figure for the fiercely protective side of Jenny. We recall that (Carter as) Margo did stab Dr. Nix with the scalpel that Jenny was going to use on him to rescue her daughter. Moreover, Margo is revealed when Jenny bends down and then "disappears" again when Jenny stands back up, as if Margo were a force inside Jenny, the maternal protector. Both Jenny and Margo are smiling at Amy, loving her.

However, frantic and frenzied violin music plays when we see Margo, instilling a sense of panic and suggesting that this could be a shock ending. The Josh persona said that when children were threatened, Margo "got real mad," and he fearfully told the female psychiatrist that Margo was "right behind you. Don't look!" Margo stabbed Dr. Nix in the back, and in the film's final shot, she is standing right behind Jenny. If Carter has come back as Margo, what if s/he decides that Jenny is a bad mother and a threat to Amy? (Jenny made adulterous love to Jack in this very park.) Can Carter be counted on to judge what good parenting is?

There is also the possibility that Margo is a split-off personality of Amy herself, as a result of the trauma the child has suffered. Could what happened to Carter be happening to Amy, too? When she hears her father's voice calling her in the woods, it sounds like an echo, as if it might be reverberating in her own head. As Amy runs off in pursuit of the voice, she drops her stuffed bunny—the toy she had held in her arms earlier when playing with a girl who looked as if she could be her twin and who was herself holding a stuffed animal in her arms. In *Home Movies*, Kristina (Nancy Allen) has a split personality which manifests as a stuffed bunny. At the end of that film, Kristina drops the toy and another girl picks it up. The bunny begins to "talk" to this younger girl, as if the schizophrenia were now afflicting her, too. Could the bunny in *Raising Cain* be a sign of a similar split in Amy?

When we first saw Amy, she was clutching another stuffed animal, a teddy bear, as her father comforted her in bed. Throughout the traumatic motel scene, as Dr. Nix carries Amy in one arm and holds a gun in the other, she hangs on to that teddy bear—right up until she is dropped over the railing, at which point she lets it go. Jack catches her in his arms, but the teddy bear hits the ground. Jack replaces her bear with the bunny, much as he tries to be a substitute father to her, but Amy still misses her daddy, which is why she hears his "voice" in the woods. The trauma of losing him seems to divide her psyche, causing her to fantasize that he still exists in some external form somewhere "near" her.

The idea of a stuffed toy or doll signifying a lost loved one—a loss which causes the self to imagine that the person is somehow still there, present in the toy even if absent in real life—can be seen in other De Palma films. At the end of *Sisters*, a Raggedy Ann doll seated near Grace is a reminder of Danielle and Dominique, the once-conjoined twins who, when one died, became a single schizophrenic sister. In *Obsession*, a Raggedy Ann doll symbolizes the child Amy's loss of her mother, from whom she is separated by a kidnapping, much as Amy in *Raising Cain* is separated from hers.

When the elevator doors opened in the motel scene, Amy saw her mother, Jenny, holding a scalpel and ready to use it, and the maternal Margo (Carter in drag) did use it to kill Dr. Nix. As a result of this traumatic experience of the scalpel-wielding mothers she witnessed, Amy's view of mommy is now divided between love and fear, between identifying with her as a protector and being terrified of her as a threat. Like the Raggedy Ann doll in Amy's room, Margo appears to her as a comforting presence, smiling maternally and dressed in what appears to be the girl's favorite color (red), which links her to Amy as a figure the child identifies with. (Amy wore a red coat in the motel scene, and she has on a red sweater in the park scene at the end; Margo wears a red wool coat.) However, red is also the color of violence and blood, related to Amy's newly acquired fear of what mother might do if she "got real mad." This "mad mother" behind (or inside?) her mother Jenny is terrifying and not someone Amy wants to identify with, for then she would have to recognize the potential madness inside herself. "Like father, like son" and "like mother, like daughter": *Raising Cain* explores these influences as dream—or nightmare.

After the big-budget debacle that was *The Bonfire of the Vanities*, De Palma had deliberately made a relatively "inexpensive" film with *Raising Cain* "so that no one could lose money."[10] The movie was modestly successful, grossing about $21 million domestic on its cost of $12 million. Reviews, however, were mixed, with the film subjected to considerable criticism for its complicated structure in which it was increasingly difficult to distinguish reality from dream. Partly as a result, De Palma determined that his next film, the gangster drama *Carlito's Way*, would have a more straightforward narrative. "It's very conventional," he admitted, saying that "otherwise you find you get reviews like: 'it doesn't make any sense,' 'it's ridiculous,' or 'it's laughable.'"[11] But, as we shall see, it was important to De Palma that the film not be *too* conventional. For one thing, he didn't want to do a remake of *Scarface*.

CHAPTER 22

Carlito's Way (1993)

When first approached about making *Carlito's Way*, De Palma had doubts about directing another film starring Al Pacino as a Latino gangster. However, he was eventually persuaded to do the film: "What I liked about it was it was completely different from *Scarface*. Where Tony Montana is cold, calculating and willing to do anything to rise to the top, Carlito is at the other end of the spectrum: he's trying to reform. He slowly gets dragged back into the game."[1] The new film's many references to *Scarface* help the viewer mark the differences separating them. When Carlito returns to the barrio after five years in prison, his pal Walberto asks him if he's "doin' a little memory lane?" before taking him to see Rolando, a drug-dealing colleague from the old days, who wants Carlito to join him in the cocaine business. Since Walberto is played by Angel Salazar, who was Tony's friend Chi Chi in *Scarface*, and Rolando is played by Al Israel, who appeared as Hector dealing coke to Tony in that film, it is as though Pacino as Carlito were literally being pulled back into his former life as Tony. (Of course, Pacino himself is neither Cuban like Tony nor Puerto Rican like Carlito, a fact which is playfully acknowledged when an Italian mobster says about Carlito, "First time I saw this guy, I thought he was Italian! Look at him—look at that face!" and Pacino as Carlito gives a wry smile.)

Tony started out by slaving away at a little food stand called El Paraiso and staring at his boss Frank's wallpaper of a tropical sunset before making it big as a drug kingpin and surveying his domain from the perch of his mirrored booth in a nightclub. Tony, snorting mountains of cocaine in his flashy white suit, took as his motto "The World Is Yours." Emulating movie gangsters ("I watch the guys like Humphrey Bogart, James Cagney"), Tony died in a hail of bullets, his greed becoming his downfall when rival gangsters took him out.

Carlito was a legend in the drug trade, but being sent to prison wised him up about being a wiseguy. Carlito doesn't do drugs and he wears a black suit, as if mourning his previous life of excess and murderous violence. When he sits in a mirrored booth at a nightclub called El Paraiso, Carlito isn't thinking of taking over the world; he is only dreaming of his own small corner of paradise. He hopes to go to the Bahamas with his girlfriend, Gail, and run a car rental business—a future he imagines when looking at a travel poster of a tropical sunset and the words "Escape to Paradise." Like Tony, Carlito is inspired by Bogart ("So here's me in the club, playing Humphrey Bogart"), but in this case it is the Bogart of *Casablanca* who ran a nightclub but dreamed of separating himself from that milieu and escaping with his beloved (Ingrid Bergman). (As a stylistic departure from *Scarface*, *Carlito's Way* has relatively restrained performances, more muted colors, and a somber score.)

Yet has Carlito really grown beyond his former self? Has Carlito truly mastered the lessons that Tony failed to learn? In *Scarface*, upon seeing his sister Gina dancing with a man in the nightclub, Tony exploded in anger, attacking the guy and accusing Gina: "I saw him putting his hand all over your ass!" By contrast, when Carlito sees another man dancing with Gail, he seems content to watch, even nodding his approval. When his friend Dave (Sean Penn) gets riled—"What I don't appreciate is he's got his fuckin' hands all over her ass!"—Carlito remains calm and resists being drawn into the jealousy that Dave is expressing on his behalf. The difference in the way that these two Al Pacino protagonists—Tony and Carlito—handle very similar scenes would seem to indicate that the latter has grown into a more mature version of the former, finally able to control his rage.

But then a very strange thing happens. Carlito—in what at first appears to be a joke but then, as it goes on and on, turns increasingly serious—begins to encourage his friend's anger and to do so in a way which suggests that Carlito is really talking about his own anger: "Well, I think you should tell him what you think" about Gail's dancing with another man, Carlito tells Dave. "I mean, why not get somethin' like that off your chest? It's a terrible thing to carry around with you." Who is carrying this jealous rage around, bottled up inside, if not Carlito? "I will," Dave says, and Carlito keeps pushing: "I think you should." "I will," Dave says again. "Oh, yeah, go ahead," Carlito says. It is only at the very end of their conversation that Carlito backs off and treats it as a crazy idea, perhaps having come to his senses in realizing that it was his own repressed jealousy that was threatening to come out.

When Carlito first got out of prison, he watched Gail from the rooftop of an adjacent building as, in the window across the way, she practiced her dance moves along with the other members of a ballet class. As De Palma described it, Carlito has "an idealized vision of her. She's a dancer, so we introduced her in the most idealized way. It's his fantasy: he's going to paradise with this almost angel."[2] When Carlito later discovers her doing a pole dance in front of the leering eyes of men in a strip joint, he puts on a good front, suppressing his disappointment in her and his jealousy of the other men, but Gail can see right through his pretense of calm and realizes that he is actually sitting there in angry judgment. (Carlito is like Jake in *Body Double*, who is tempted by fury when his "angel" dancing in the window, Holly, turns out to be a porn star.) It is the same jealous rage Carlito felt at the strip joint that threatens to break out at the sight of Gail dancing with another man in the nightclub. Dave is only expressing what Carlito himself feels inside.

Indeed, beneath the appearance of a reformed man, how much has Carlito really changed? It might seem that he accompanies his cousin Guajiro to a drug buy in order to look out for the kid, but their conversation beforehand— "They ain't gonna know me," Carlito says, to which his cousin replies, "You? You're a fuckin' legend, man"—suggests that he is flattered by the prospect of being seen as a "big man" again, after his ignominious time spent in prison. "And the legend, me, I'm walkin' right in with him," Carlito thinks as they go to the buy, and beneath the sarcasm, is there not the sense that he wants his pride back?

As Carlito scopes out the poolroom where the buy is to take place, his experienced eye detects a deal about to go bad and he prepares to take action the way he would in the old days. "I can't resist this—I gotta show you people a shot," he says. What he can't resist is showing off his prodigious skill at violence, which he proceeds to do by knocking a pool ball into a man's forehead and by gunning down all the drug dealers before they can shoot him. "You up against *me* now," he says to them. "You think you're big time? You're gonna fuckin' die big time!" And they do, because Carlito is still a bigger shot than they are. "I don't invite this shit," Carlito muses. "It just comes to me." Really? While it's true that they pulled their guns first, he was the one who went to them—in fact, walked right in, as "the legend."

Aspiring gangster Benny Blanco (John Leguizamo) refers to Carlito as the "J. P. Morgan of the smack business," awestruck by how many men he used to have under him in his drug operation, and Carlito appears flattered: "First time I ever heard that." But Carlito sends back Benny's drinks, keeps women from him, and puts him down in public. "Why you acting like this for?" an associate says to Carlito. "It doesn't make sense you should hate this guy. This guy is you twenty years ago." With Benny, it's as if Carlito had come face to face with Tony, the incarnation of his former self. According to De Palma, "Carlito hates [Benny] because that's who he was and he doesn't want to be that guy anymore, you know, a ruthless, ambitious guy that's tough as nails. He's not that guy anymore, but when he sees him, it enrages him."[3] Where does the rage come from if not from a desperate attempt on Carlito's part to suppress the ruthlessness in his own personality that Benny reminds him of and calls out?

Ironically, by trying so hard not to be his former self, Carlito becomes that very thing. The rage with which he pushes Benny away looks an awful lot like that same old rage for dominance that Carlito exhibited before. This rage becomes the avenue for Carlito's old self to emerge once again. When asked by Benny if he remembers him, Carlito replies, "Maybe I don't remember the last time I blew my nose, either. Who the fuck are you I should remember you, huh? What, you think you're like me? You ain't like me, motherfucker. You a punk. I've been with 'made' people, connected people. Who you been with? Chain-snatchin', jive-ass, *maricón* motherfuckers. . . . If I ever see you again, you die." The reference to blowing his nose implies that Benny is something that Carlito is trying to expel from inside himself—that ruthless desire to be a big shot. But in the process of being expelled, that desire actually surges back, for what Carlito does is make himself out to be a big shot while simultaneously belittling Benny's manhood. Carlito becomes the kind of macho braggart he hates, and thereby incites the very violence from a rival male that he was supposedly trying to avoid. Indeed, it is Benny who will shoot Carlito in the end.

Even Carlito's relationship with his friend Dave has dark undercurrents that make one doubt whether he is really the "brother" to Dave that he claims to be. Dave, a Jewish lawyer with frizzy hair and a receding hairline, is desperate to counter the stereotype of his being something less than a man. Outwardly, Carlito supports Dave in his efforts to prove his machismo. "Good for him" is Carlito's comment when a waiter informs him that Dave was having sex with a woman named Steffie in the nightclub bathroom, and when Benny tries to claim Steffie for himself, Carlito defends his friend's "claim" to her: "Steffie's with Dave now."

And yet Carlito's remark to Dave—"Faster than a speeding bullet"—about his time with Steffie, although ostensibly a joke, amounts to a slur on his manhood. Again and again, Carlito builds Dave up in ways that include subtle put-downs. Later, Carlito takes a weapon off Dave, seemingly for his friend's protection, but in a way that denies him the virile status he is so desperately seeking. "Give me the fuckin' gun," Carlito tells him. "Since when are you a tough guy? Get yourself killed." Carlito then rubs it in with a remark that he must know Dave will hear as emasculating, which makes one wonder whether, deep down, Carlito is actually more intent on asserting dominance over his friend than on protecting him: "Dave, you are gonna wave that thing at the wrong guy. He's gonna take it from you and bury it up your ass, guaranteed. Now give me the gun."

It is true that Dave makes Carlito complicit in the killing of two mobsters and then betrays him to the district attorney to save his own skin. But what does it say about Carlito's character that he sinks to Dave's level—or below it—and betrays his former friend by setting him up to die? While Dave is recuperating in the hospital after a mob attempt on his life, Carlito offers him advice on how to defend himself, but the gun he hands Dave is empty, for Carlito has secretly removed the bullets. Defenseless, Dave is then shot in the head by a mob assassin. While some may feel that having the betrayer betrayed is poetic justice, it is hard not to see Carlito's last act toward Dave as the culmination of all the ways in which he appeared to support his friend while in fact subtly undermining him. Not only did Carlito disarm Dave, but he as good as shot him himself, as is made evident by a cut from the assassin shooting Dave to Carlito throwing the bullets he took from Dave's gun into the trash.

There's no doubting the pathos of a man like Carlito who, despite his struggles to go straight, ends up being drawn back into the world of crime. This pathos is not lessened—it is even increased—by the realization that, in addition to external pressures, there are also internal forces such as pride, jealousy, and competitiveness that drive Carlito to engage in macho violence again. In his fight to reform, Carlito ultimately loses the battle with gangsters (like Benny) and with the "gangster" in himself.

The film begins where it ends—with Carlito getting shot. As he lies dying, he flashes back over the events in his life that have brought him to this violent demise, including how he belittled and threatened Benny, the wannabe gangster who eventually shoots him. At the film's conclusion, Carlito imagines Gail dancing with their child inside the "Escape to Paradise" travel poster he sees on a wall, and he realizes that he will never be able to join them there. "At the time that I began the film," De Palma has said, "I was going through a personal crisis. In the space of two years, I got married; I had a child; and I got divorced!"[4] Thus, like Carlito, De Palma had envisioned a certain kind of future with his wife and child which was now never going to be, which had eluded him like a mirage.

De Palma continued: "I wasn't able to reconcile my private life and my professional life, whereas the majority of my friends have done so."[5] Like Carlito, who realizes too late that he should have gone with Gail rather than let Dave embroil him again in the kind of work he used to do as a gangster, De Palma has struggled with putting work before family, which may have cost him his marriage. We have already noted his confession that "when I'm making a film, nothing else matters to me. . . . I no longer pay any attention to my wife or my children and sometimes I've lost everything because of it."[6] (Carlito loses Gail, and De Palma loses Gale Anne Hurd, his second wife.) Much as Carlito's life flashes before his eyes, so De Palma was taking stock of his own, thinking of the parallels between himself and his main character: "I was asking myself some questions about my life. It was your classic midlife crisis. In a sense, it was this aspect of the *Carlito's Way* script that attracted me. Because, basically, what is this film about? A guy who just got assassinated and who thinks, 'Shit, I'm dead! How did I end up here?' And he reviews his life to understand the chain of events and to accept what has happened to him. That was my situation at the time. To make this film that conveyed what I was feeling, I had to lay myself bare."[7]

Carlito's struggle to avoid slipping back into his old gangster self, to avoid becoming like Tony in *Scarface*, can be compared to De Palma's desire to escape entrapment in the gangster genre, to avoid just remaking *Scarface*. When Carlito stands before the court to insist that he will not go back to his old ways, it is hard not to hear De Palma himself making the same claim. If we realize that the judge is played by fellow director and old friend Paul Mazursky, who skeptically admonishes Carlito not to be too proud of his newly reformed character ("You're not accepting an award!"), the scene takes on a metacinematic dimension, as if De Palma had been called before a bar of his peers to plead his case.

Certainly, De Palma's last two attempts at respectability—*Casualties of War* and *The Bonfire of the Vanities*—did not win him any awards as a great director. Instead, many critics reviewed those movies as if De Palma were still working within the same cheap thriller genre that he had tried to escape. Frances FitzGerald called *Casualties* a "sado-porn flick" for the "hour of running time (or so it seemed . . .)" that it "devoted to the torture, rape, and murder of the Vietnamese girl,"[8] and Gavin Smith commented, "Maybe what they say is true: De Palma just likes to choreograph women's deaths onscreen—that's all. He can't resist doing it, once again borrowing from his own increasingly withering oeuvre."[9] When De Palma then went on to direct *Bonfire*, a political satire, critics couldn't see him working in this new form. Joel Siegel scoffed at the idea that De Palma, a "director of horror, suspense, and violence,"[10] would make a movie like *Bonfire*, and *New York* magazine ghettoized him as a "gore auteur" who "makes twisty, homage-ridden thrillers and blood-drenched explorations of violence."[11] "There's no vindication here," the judge says, referring to Carlito (and De Palma?), "or absolution or benediction or anything."

Sure enough, soon after claiming to be reformed, Carlito goes with his cousin on that drug buy (a scene which we will consider from a different angle for what it can tell us about De Palma as a director). As Carlito enters the poolroom, his practiced eye scanning every inch of the place, we are reminded of the way De Palma himself will walk a film location, checking out its every aspect. Then, when Carlito tells the drug dealers, "I can't resist this—I gotta show you people a shot," do we not also see, in addition to Carlito's skillful pool-ball shot followed by his gunshots, De Palma's own clever *camera* shots which capture all this complex action? Circling the pool table (so that he can surreptitiously survey the room), knocking a pool ball into a thug's face, and shooting down his opponents, Carlito falls back into his gangster ways—and De Palma returns to the gangster genre. In fact, this violent scene of a drug deal gone awry near the beginning of *Carlito's Way* is strongly reminiscent of a similar shoot-out early on in *Scarface* resulting from a drug buy gone bad. As we noted before, Carlito didn't have to go to the poolroom, but he does.

And when Dave betrays him, Carlito doesn't have to set him up to die by secretly removing the bullets from his gun, but he does. Likewise, De Palma didn't have to film this scene where Carlito takes a low form of revenge on his former friend, but the director did, even changing the scene from the book (where Carlito let Dave live) so that it is better suited to a gangster film. At another point in the movie, Carlito smacks Benny in the head, knocking him down a flight of stairs. "It's like them old reflexes comin' back," Carlito thinks, and much the same could be said of De Palma.

His suspense-thriller reflexes return throughout the extended climax of *Carlito's Way*. The chase scene on a subway train recalls the one in *Dressed to Kill*. The gunfight on an escalator at New York's Grand Central Station recalls the shoot-out on the steps of Chicago's Union Station in *The Untouchables*. And the way that Carlito's superior shooting prowess enables him to single-handedly gun down multiple opponents reminds us of none other than *Scarface*'s Tony, who blew away scores of assassins at the climax of that movie.

If, to some extent, Carlito backslides into being Tony, and De Palma slips into remaking *Scarface*, could this be because it is harder and harder not to be a gangster—and not to make a gangster movie—in the current climate? When Carlito returns to the streets after his stretch in prison, he finds that times have changed. Whatever sense of honor or loyalty there used to be is gone, having been edged out by the one remaining value: selfish profit. "Ain't no rackets out here," Carlito muses after the drug dealers' attempted double-cross in the pool-room, "just a bunch of cowboys rippin' each other off." An old friend of his puts it even more strongly: "These new kids nowadays, man, they got no respect for human life. They shotgun you, man, just to see you fly up in the air."

De Palma has also lamented how Hollywood has changed from the time "when I began making films. The '70s and early '80s were the years of the director. Now, these are the years of the studio heads and the agents."[12] Nowadays, the studios want formulaic genre pictures that can be more certain to yield a big profit, which is increasingly the only goal. Directors are under pressure to make these kinds of films, and those who don't deliver can find that the studio's loyalty is not to them but to the dollar. "I've finally come to realize that your head is always available to go on the block if it makes some kind of business sense," De Palma has said. "You can always be sold out if the price is right."[13]

Returning $37 million domestic on its $30 million investment, *Carlito's Way* was not considered much of a success, but it did well enough to move De Palma at least part of the way back into Hollywood's good graces after the *Bonfire* disaster. This renewed respect—combined with the fact that actor-producer Tom Cruise had loved *Carlito's Way* and wanted to be directed by De Palma—convinced the studio to give him a chance to helm a big-budget spy thriller. Recalling that he "hadn't had a real success since *The Untouchables*,"[14] De Palma decided that it would be a good move for him to make his own kind of movie out of another television series—to "take a TV piece people were familiar with and make something new out of it."[15] The result, *Mission: Impossible*, would be far and away the most financially successful film of De Palma's career. At the same time, the film would give him the chance to further explore his own obsessions. "Espionage is the perfect genre for me," he has said. "I love filming people tracking others or in the middle of spying on others. It's a very cinematic genre: observation, voyeurism, the double life."[16]

CHAPTER 23

Mission: Impossible (1996)

The Impossible Mission Force (IMF) is a team of covert CIA spies. Under orders from their boss Kittridge (Henry Czerny), IMF leader Jim Phelps (Jon Voight) gathers the team, which consists of his wife, Claire (Emmanuelle Béart), Ethan (Tom Cruise), Jack (Emilio Estevez), Sarah (Kristin Scott Thomas), and Hannah (Ingeborga Dapkunaite). Their mission is to prevent a diplomat, Golitsyn, from stealing "the NOC list," which contains the names of undercover U.S. agents, from an embassy in Prague. However, unbeknownst to Ethan, Jim is actually a traitor to his country and the team, for he is using them to steal the NOC list for himself so that he can sell it. As a result of Jim's betrayal, Jack is impaled by spikes in an elevator shaft; Sarah is stabbed with a knife; and Hannah is blown up in a car. It also appears that Jim has been shot and killed, and that Claire dies in the car explosion, but both these deaths are faked (Claire is in on the plot with Jim).

And yet, unbeknownst to Ethan *and Jim*, the entire mission in Prague was an elaborate deception on the part of Kittridge. Suspecting that one of the IMF team is a mole, Kittridge set up this fake mission to flush out the traitor. He had the IMF team shadowed by a second IMF team watching to see which one of them would steal the decoy NOC list. Since Ethan is the only member of his team apparently left alive, Kittridge suspects him of being the traitor, though Jim is the actual mole.

Early in the film, Jim is seated on an airplane and receives a videocassette from a flight attendant: "Would you like to watch a movie, Mr. Phelps?" The video, narrated by Kittridge ("Your mission, Jim, should you choose to accept it . . ."), lays out the Prague mission that the IMF team has been assigned. When the video ends, it self-destructs, causing smoke which Jim "hides" by lighting a cigarette and exhaling more smoke to blend with it. Over this image, we see the words "Directed by Brian De Palma." The scene then dissolves from the smoke-filled plane cabin to a foggy riverbank in Prague, where the mission commences.

In this opening, we may think we see what is going on, but, as hinted by the wisps of smoke and fog, we will realize in retrospect that our view of events was quite hazy. In fact, Kittridge, Jim, and De Palma are all putting up a smokescreen behind which they will practice their deceptions. Kittridge is giving a false assignment to Jim in an attempt to flush out the mole on his team. Jim is pretending to accept and follow that assignment, when in fact he is the mole, planning to steal the NOC list for himself. And De Palma is pretending to start his movie in the same way that every episode of the *Mission: Impossible* TV series began, with a legitimate mission being assigned to trustworthy Jim Phelps, who would oversee his team in taking it to successful completion. But that's not what happens in fog-enshrouded Prague, where the clear plot and the dependable characters of the TV show become increasingly uncertain and unreliable.

Regarding *Carlito's Way*, we have noted De Palma's desire not to direct just another Hollywood genre picture. With *Mission: Impossible*, it is as though he pretends to accept the assignment of bringing the formulaic TV series and its "spy-thriller" clichés to the big screen, while in fact he is a mole within the studio system, "betraying" those conventions by making his own rebellious kind of movie. In the TV series (1966–73, 1988–90), despite all the red herrings and double-crosses, Jim is the father figure whose words can always be relied on. Amid all the danger and deception, the members of the IMF team work together to pull each other out of scrapes. Though the plot takes many twists and turns, and the unexpected happens with regularity, the success of the mission is a foregone conclusion. In De Palma's film, the mission fails and IMF agents actually die. Not only are they unable to rescue each other, but some of them betray their fellow team members. And the fish rots from the head down, with the leader of the team, Jim, as its chief betrayer.

This did not sit well with actor Peter Graves (Jim on the TV series), who commented, "To see him become a traitor to his country, responsible for the death of his entire team at the film's beginning, just seems impossible to me."[1] But this shocking deviation from the trustworthy TV world is precisely De Palma's point. Referring to another beloved TV character, De Palma said that "it's like Perry Mason losing a case. . . . You do the thing everybody thinks you would never do. It's a shell game. Constantly surprise the audience."[2] "I wanted to do the unthinkable, to break the taboo," the director explained. "In the series, the mission was always accomplished; here we're going to kill everyone. It would all finish badly."[3] Ethan, the lone agent still alive after the mission (or so it seems), is not only disavowed by the CIA but himself suspected of being the betrayer. That never happened to an IMF member in the TV series! Like the viewer, he ends up lost in foggy Prague, left wondering what really happened and who is responsible.

As far as the critics were concerned, one of De Palma's worst transgressions against genre norms was the fogginess of his plot, where so many smoke-screens were in play—so many lies and manipulations—that some viewers ended up feeling they didn't have the faintest idea what was going on. Roger Ebert wrote, "I'm not sure I could pass a test on the plot of *Mission: Impossible*. My consolation is that the screenwriters probably couldn't, either."⁴ In its parody of the film, *Mad* magazine picked up on this critical confusion by having Jim receive his mission assignment as if he were De Palma getting his directorial assignment to make the film: "It's . . . totally impossible to understand, understand? . . . Your mission is to take this unbelievably complicated mess and turn it into a major motion picture!"⁵ Later in the parody, when Ethan asks Jim why he betrayed his country as the mole, Jim replies, "Quite frankly, I can't remember why! There have been so many plots and subplots and double crosses and double-double crosses, I just assumed I must be the mole! Who knows—maybe I'm not!"⁶ After reading the reviews, De Palma ruefully admitted that "I became sort of the poster boy for incoherent storytelling."⁷

It is part of the film's dramatic strategy to make viewers feel as shocked and confused as the characters. When Jack, the tech geek, loses control of the elevator's computer system and has his eyes impaled on spikes at the top of the elevator shaft, it is as though *our* eyes have been assaulted. No member of the IMF team is supposed to die; we struggle to believe what we have just seen. One critic of the film complained that, "though we may need to know that Cruise's colleagues are killed at the start, we don't need to see it in such detail or to such effect to follow the story,"⁸ but *seeing* it is the point: this terrible deviation from the safe formulas of the TV series is almost unbearable to watch.

De Palma emphasizes the devastating effect that it has on Ethan, who has a video monitor on his wristwatch that shows his teammate's death from Jack's point of view, through the feed from the micro-camera built into Jack's eye-glasses. When Jack's eyes are impaled, Ethan's watch monitor cuts to visual noise and Ethan himself closes his eyes in sympathy and mourning. Soon after, when Jim is (supposedly) shot by an assailant on the bridge, Ethan—who is again viewing the event on his wrist monitor, this time using the video feed from Jim's camera-glasses—sees the barrel of the gun pointed and fired at him (at the camera, at *us*), visually registering the impact as if he himself were the target, as stressed by the extreme close-up of Ethan's shocked eyes.

Later, however, Ethan comes to realize the extent to which he has been tricked by the video images he saw, and we as viewers have been fooled along with him. When Jim turns up alive in London and sits with Ethan at a train station restaurant, telling him the story he wants him to believe, Ethan reconstructs events in his mind's eye in a way that contradicts Jim's lying narration. For the first time, Ethan takes visual control away from Jim, beginning to imagine events from a wider perspective. Ethan had witnessed the deaths of his IMF team only from one point of view—that provided by his wristwatch video monitor at the particular time. But, during most of the Prague mission, Jim was seated in the control room before a bank of video monitors and thus able to see the operation from multiple points of view, since each monitor showed a different team member's "eyeglass-cam" perspective. As Ethan now realizes, Jim used his superior visual power to dominate the scene, controlling what each team member did and did not get to see and manipulating those images so that they would be interpreted as he wished them to be.

It was Jim who pushed the button causing the elevator to rise and impale Jack's eyes on the spikes. Ethan's watch monitor showed only the impalement, not Jim pushing the button, and all Ethan heard in his earpiece at the time was Jim's lying voice saying that the elevator was out of anyone's control. Now, sitting in the restaurant and hearing Jim lie to him again, Ethan visualizes the truth behind the lie: Jim pushing the button that led to Jack's death.

When Jim left the control room and was "shot" on the bridge, all Ethan saw on his watch monitor was what Jim wanted him to see from Jim's "eyeglass-cam": the gun firing and then Jim holding his hands to his chest, which was covered in blood. What the watch monitor didn't show—and what Ethan now visualizes in retrospect—is Jim smearing fake blood on himself *after* the "shooting" and *before* the sight of his "bleeding" chest. Jim's manipulative use of images is similar to Bob's in *Obsession*, Childress's in *The Fury*, and Sam's in *Body Double*, and the fact that we as viewers are also fooled reminds us of the deceptive beginnings of *Sisters*, *Blow Out*, and *Body Double*, where we are gradually made aware that we are watching images designed to trick us.

When he is seated in the Prague control room before his multiple video monitors, Jim's power to see without being seen makes him seem omniscient and invulnerable, like Swan in *Phantom of the Paradise* or Tony in *Scarface*, with their ubiquitous video cameras. Then, when he fakes his own death, Jim's power only seems to increase, for now he can have eyes on everything while appearing to have no physical presence. However, once he reveals that he is still alive, once he allows Ethan to *see him*, Jim puts himself back in the frame, making him vulnerable to becoming the object of deception and no longer wholly its mastermind. At the end of the film, when Jim thinks that he can kill Ethan and vanish into thin air, Ethan tricks him into being exposed as the villain he is. After making Jim believe that he has the upper hand, Ethan puts on his own "eyeglass-cam" and reveals to the CIA that Jim is still alive and that he is the traitor. Jim is thus framed by the very same video technology he had used to destroy others.

As we have seen, after the Prague mission fails and Ethan is the only one apparently still left alive, he must prove that he is not the villainous traitor or mole. This turns out to be more difficult than our discussion so far has made it seem. At a meeting in a Prague restaurant, CIA boss Kittridge looks meaningfully at Ethan, who is shown in a very close shot, and says, "The mole's deep inside."

Throughout the middle of the film, Ethan is confused about the identity of his two father figures, Kittridge and Jim, and consequently about his own identity which, like a son's, has been defined in emulation of theirs. Kittridge lied to Ethan, sending him on a false mission whose real target was the IMF team and Ethan himself, whom Kittridge now believes is the mole. Could Kittridge be the mole? Later, at another restaurant (in London), Jim will try to convince Ethan that Kittridge is the mole, but Ethan suspects that Jim is lying, that Jim is the mole who had IMF members killed and tried to steal the NOC list during the Prague mission. Kittridge and Jim are both formerly trusted father figures whose words now seem slippery and whose benevolence toward Ethan is in doubt. (Interestingly, both of these older men are associated with watery danger, as when Jim fakes his death, falling into the river, and when Kittridge meets Ethan at a restaurant with giant aquariums. It is also interesting that the son figure, Ethan, uses explosive chewing gum twice: first to blow up the restaurant aquariums when Kittridge threatens to arrest him as the mole, and later to blow up a helicopter carrying Jim, who had tried to saddle Ethan with the blame for being the mole.)

For someone trying to prove he is not the mole who was trying to steal the (decoy) NOC list during the Prague mission, Ethan takes some curious actions. One of the first things he does is to break into CIA headquarters and steal the (real) NOC list—that is, he acts just like a mole! No wonder some critics were confused. Could Ethan, having lost his trustworthy father figures, also have lost his bearings, becoming confused about his own identity?

After pushing the button that sent Jack to his elevator death, Jim knocked over his chair while leaving the Prague control room. Following the failed mission, Ethan goes to this room, picks up the chair, and sits where Jim sat. Ethan then proceeds to use the same computer terminal and the same username ("Job") that Jim used in making plans to sell the NOC list to an arms dealer. Of course, Ethan is only pretending to be Jim pretending to be Job, isn't he?

After having downloaded the NOC list onto a computer disk at CIA headquarters, Ethan performs a sleight-of-hand trick with two identical disks in order to confuse another man, Krieger, as to which is the real disk. The difference between real and fake, agent and mole, becomes less and less clear.

(Interestingly, the two men that Ethan uses to help him steal the NOC list, Krieger [Jean Reno] and Luther [Ving Rhames], are first seen seated on a plane, with Luther leaning forward so that Krieger seems to "appear" from "inside" Luther. Krieger turns out to be a traitor, while Luther is loyal—or so it seems.)

Near the film's conclusion, a man who looks like Jim pulls off a prosthetic disguise to reveal that it is Ethan inside the mask; their two identities appeared as one—confused. If Ethan assumes the place and name of a mole, acts like a mole, and even looks like a mole, should we consider whether he might, in some significant sense, be a mole?

Here, we return to the quintessential De Palma question of whether the hero (Ethan), in addition to fighting the villain (Jim), might himself be internally split between hero and villain, loyal agent and mole. Even before Ethan becomes aware that Jim has betrayed him, Ethan is tempted to betray Jim—with Jim's wife, Claire. Prior to the Prague mission, there is an IMF operation in Kiev, presented by the film as a prologue, during which Claire almost dies. It is Ethan who revives her with an adrenaline shot to the arm, followed by a tender moment with her in his arms. Soon after, we see Jim on the plane, the wedding ring on his finger clearly visible as he looks at a photo of Claire.

The implication that Ethan is tempted to make love with Claire behind Jim's back was even stronger in earlier versions of the film. For example, the shooting script makes the adrenaline injection that Ethan gives to Claire even more phallic by saying that he "jabs the long needle into the . . . woman's thigh." Furthermore, the script has Claire "almost unconsciously slip" her "wedding ring onto her finger,"[9] right before we see Jim wearing his wedding ring on the plane. These more overt indications of adulterous desire were toned down for the finished film because they "took the audience out of the genre," De Palma explained.[10] But it is precisely because they trouble the generic distinction between the hero Ethan and the villain Jim that these illicit desires on Ethan's part are of interest.

When the IMF team is gathered for the Prague mission, there is a subversive undercurrent to Ethan's banter with Jim. First, Ethan complains about Claire's coffee, including the coffee she made in Kiev, implying an intimacy he had with her there—a suggestion not lost on Jim who says, "Hey, take it easy on my wife's coffee, will you?" Then Ethan "jokingly" refers to Jim as "getting soft in his old age"—a coded challenge to the older man's potency. Later in the film, Jim laments that aging agents like himself, who have "a lousy marriage," are viewed as "obsolete . . . hardware not worth upgrading," so he clearly senses the covert threat to his phallic authority presented by Ethan, who acts as a kind of mole in Jim's marriage. (The script has Jim tell a joke to Ethan about a wife who commits adultery with her husband's friend while the husband is away.)

It is no wonder, then, that when Ethan confronts Jim about being the mole in the film's climax, Jim counters with "thou shalt not covet thy neighbor's wife, Ethan." Who betrayed whom? If Jim is a traitor inside the IMF, someone who turned against his own team members, then so to some extent is Ethan, who is at least tempted to—and may actually—betray Jim by sleeping with his wife. It is thus not only an external villain like Jim that our hero Ethan must worry about, but also the enemy within himself, his own illicit desire which could lead him to betray his father figure and friend. Indeed, "the mole's deep inside," as Kittridge warned.

As to the question of whether or not Ethan ever actually sleeps with Claire, the answer remains uncertain, so it is never clear how much of a mole he becomes. Initially, Ethan believes that both Jim and Claire died during the failed Prague mission. Ethan returns to the control room where, guilt-ridden, he hallucinates that Jim has come back from the grave to accuse Ethan of not being there to save him. However, Jim's bloody, outstretched hand becomes Claire's hand on Ethan's shoulder—Claire, who is really there, not a hallucination. Suspicious of Claire, Ethan pulls a gun on her, strips off her coat, and frisks her roughly, then holds her body down under his in bed and interrogates her.

Ethan is violent toward Claire in this scene because he suspects that she might be the mole who got Jim, his father figure, killed. However, Ethan's violence is sexualized, as if he were also secretly acting on his desire for her as he roughs her up. If he is angry with Claire because he thinks she may have played a role in Jim's death, Ethan is also angry at himself because a traitorous part of him wanted Jim dead so that he could have Claire. Ethan's hallucination showed him a dying Jim, who was then replaced by a living Claire who could now be with Ethan. The anger that Ethan feels at himself for his adulterous desire is projected outward as violence toward Claire, something that he takes out on her.

During the break-in at CIA headquarters to get the NOC list, Claire wears a red dress and acts flirtatiously to distract an agent from the infiltration that is occurring right under his nose. Could Claire be doing the same thing to Ethan now, using her body to trick him so that he fails to see the subterfuge occurring behind the scenes? When Ethan gives his sleight-of-hand performance with the NOC list disks, he moves up close to Claire and pulls one disk out from behind her back, as if she had hidden it on her person. The serious fear behind Ethan's joke is that Claire may be using her body to lure and betray him as part of a plot to steal the NOC list. When Ethan tries to envision what really went wrong during the Prague mission, he first imagines Claire pressing the detonator that blew up the car with Hannah in it, but then, in his mind's eye, he replaces Claire with Jim as the culprit. Ethan has his doubts about Claire, but his desire for her distracts him from his suspicions, causing him to see what he wants to believe—that she is loyal to *him* and not to Jim.

But, if Claire can be unfaithful to her husband, doesn't this mean that she could be disloyal to Ethan, too? Even worse might be the possibility that Claire is a kind of double agent moving between the two men—still involved with Jim and only feigning her attachment to Ethan. Ethan's "love scenes" with Claire are thus riddled with doubt about her true character, starting with the very first scene in Kiev where the camera keeps going in and out of focus, struggling to present a clear image of Claire. After Ethan's rough interrogation of her following the Prague mission's failure, he seems to believe Claire when she says she is grieving over Jim (who Ethan still thinks is dead). To comfort her in her grief (and prompted by his own desire), Ethan seems about to kiss her when the scene dissolves, as if throwing a veil of uncertainty over what happens. In a later scene, the two of them are about to kiss but turn their heads at the last minute so that it is not on the mouth. She then almost kisses him on the lips but walks away before doing so, while he traces the place on his lips where her kiss would have been.

Have they not yet made love and are they refraining from doing so out of loyalty to Jim's memory? Or did they have sex before and now feel guilty about it? Just prior to this exchange of repressed kisses, Claire says, "I'm sorry, Ethan," and he replies, "We did what we had to do." Does he mean that, in the extremity of their grief, they were compelled to comfort each other with intimacy—that is, consummate the love they couldn't while Jim was alive? Or is their conversation about regret over *not* having acted on their desire? (Producer Paula Wagner has praised the film's screenwriter, Robert Towne, for his "extraordinary ability to see the layers of something, the complexity of something. He can always come up with that one line of dialogue that makes you wonder, 'What is really going on?'")[11]

Of course, Ethan also hesitates to get too involved with Claire because he suspects her of being a traitor, and once he finds out that Jim is still alive and could be the mole, Ethan fears that she may be working in cahoots with her husband. As Ethan enters a room, his shadow falls over Claire, who is seated in a corner on the floor. Despite the darkness of his suspicion, her face is lit: could she be innocent and trustworthy after all? She reaches out her hand to him, and after a pause to think, he touches it. She draws his hand to the side of her face and then kisses it hungrily, while he looks down at her, his face unreadable before the screen fades to black. Does he resist her and his own desires in this scene, wary that she could be an evil seductress, or does he have sex with her in the darkness, not caring whether Jim, she, or he himself is a traitor, as long as he gets to take what he wants?

The film leaves us uncertain about the degree to which Ethan gives in to his disloyal desire, but the script—more willing to reveal the dark side of the hero—makes it clear that he reciprocates Claire's advances in this scene: "She draws him down by his hand to kiss her. He kisses her again, more fully. She wraps an arm around him and he holds onto the kiss. The room appears to revolve around them." The script is equally explicit about the fact that, in prior scenes as well, Ethan did have sex with her, despite attempts to resist temptation: "They're suddenly, violently in each other's arms, kissing and half-falling onto the converted bed. She suddenly resists. He senses it and pulls away. . . . He rises and goes to the door. He's got his hand on the knob when Claire wraps her arms around him from behind, turns him to her and kisses him, deeply. This time they sink slowly to the bed."[12]

When Ethan disguises himself as Jim at the end, it is to test whether Claire is loyal to Jim or to him. Ethan discovers that Claire has indeed been working with the mole Jim, both of them in it for the money. However, what Ethan ignores is the fact that when Claire speaks to "Jim" (Ethan in disguise) about the money, she is also pleading for Ethan's life: "Listen, Jim, is it such a good idea to kill him? . . . We take the money. Ethan takes the blame." Even after Ethan removes his mask, revealing who he is, and the real Jim appears behind him with a gun, Claire continues to argue for Ethan's life to be spared: "Let's just get the money and get out of here," she says to Jim. Ethan refuses to recognize that, despite all of her deception, Claire is at least partially loyal to him, caring enough to try to distract her husband from killing him.

Ethan wholly rejects Claire, saying, "You've earned it," when he gives her the money, treating her as a whore who only feigned desire for Ethan when her real goal was merely mercenary. Ethan may think that by rejecting Claire so definitively, he is separating himself as a good man from her evil, but it is important to see that, in blaming Claire, Ethan is not only denying his own responsibility for the adulterous desire they shared, he is also *behaving just like the villainous Jim toward her*. Jim, too, regards her as a whore ("Claire was never convinced her charms would work on you, but I was supremely confident, having tasted the goods"), and Jim also condemns her for her disloyalty. When Claire pleads one last time for him not to shoot Ethan, Jim turns the gun on her and shoots her for being unfaithful to him.

As Claire lies dying, this time—unlike in the film's prologue—Ethan cannot revive her. Not only does he fail to save her, but he is metaphorically complicit in her murder, for he repudiated her as a faithless whore in the same way that Jim did. It's probably too much to say that Ethan, when he was still masked as "Jim," would have put a bullet into her himself if the real villain Jim hadn't shown up to do it. No, Ethan is too "good" for that.

In thinking about the character relationships in *Mission: Impossible*, we should consider another spy thriller which De Palma's film resembles in many respects, Hitchcock's *North by Northwest*. In that movie, the lead character, Roger (Cary Grant), is also suspected of being a traitor to his country. When a diplomat is stabbed in the United Nations building, Roger pulls out the knife and is blamed for that crime, which he didn't commit. Similarly, when Golitsyn and Sarah are stabbed outside the embassy in Prague, Ethan ends up with the knife in his hands and he is accused of being the mole. Just as Ethan, suddenly on his own and wanted for murder, struggles with an identity crisis, so Roger, a wrongly accused man on the run, is mistaken for a spy named George Kaplan and must fight to be recognized for who he really is. Like Ethan divided between Kittridge and Jim, Roger is torn between two father figures, one ostensibly good—the Professor (Leo G. Carroll), a director of CIA operations—and the other, evil—Vandamm (James Mason), a traitorous spy. However, the Professor manipulates Roger, keeping him in the dark and risking his life, in order to further the goals of the CIA, much as Kittridge considers Ethan and his IMF team expendable, sending them on the fatal Prague mission, which they don't know is a fake, in order to flush out the mole.

In both movies, the male lead encounters a woman who is at once seductive and suspect. Roger desires Eve (Eva Marie Saint) but doubts her loyalty to him when he discovers that she is the villainous Vandamm's mistress. Her dalliance with Roger may be part of a plot to help Vandamm smuggle a small statue, with a microfilm of government secrets hidden inside, out of the country. Is Eve, like that statue, deceptive, appearing to love Roger while in fact hiding her true mercenary character from him? At an art auction, Roger speaks words to Vandamm that compare Eve to the statue and that accuse her of being a deceiving whore: "I'll bet you paid plenty for this little piece of sculpture. . . . She's worth every dollar, take it from me. She really puts her heart into her work—in fact, her whole body." We recall that, in *Mission: Impossible*, Ethan seems to pull the computer disk, which contains the NOC list of government secrets, out from behind Claire's back, as if she had hidden it on her person. Ethan fears that Claire may have used her body to seduce and distract him, that her love for him may be a front, behind which she is actually working for Jim, with whom she is also sleeping. "You've earned it," Ethan says in handing the money to Claire, implying that she is a prostitute.

Both Ethan and Roger are rough on the female characters, the men's desire being tainted by distrust and jealous anger. However, Roger ends up believing that Eve can be trusted and he saves her from being killed by Vandamm. (It is true that Eve turns out to be working for the good side, the CIA, but one gets the sense that the strength of Roger's love for and belief in her encourages her to act in a way that makes her worthy of that faith and love.) By contrast,

Ethan refuses to recognize that Claire exhibits at least a partial loyalty to him in pleading for his life. Ethan joins the villainous Jim in condemning her as a faithless whore and not only fails to save her, but also must be considered to some degree complicit in her murder, even though it is Jim who actually pulls the trigger. At the end of *North by Northwest*, Roger and Eve are together, like a married couple, on board a train that is taking them on their honeymoon. At the conclusion of *Mission: Impossible*, which also takes place in part on a train, Claire dies in Ethan's arms, for (it is implied) he does not have a faith or love strong enough to revive her. Ethan ends up alone.

Some viewers will see Ethan as having solidified his identity as a hero in the film's finale. He was tempted by—and may even have slept with—Claire, but in the end he excoriates and expels her for her greed and treacherous lust. Ethan also differentiates himself from Jim by revealing him to be the real villain, the mole caught collecting the money when Ethan exposes him, by means of his "eyeglass-cam," to CIA boss Kittridge. The last time we see Ethan, he has been fully reinstated. Indeed, he has been promoted to Jim's old position where, seated on a plane, he is handed a videocassette by the flight attendant containing instructions for the next IMF mission, which he would now oversee. According to spy thriller formula (including the setup for a sequel), this should be a happy ending, with the hero restored to his rightful place and about to embark on the next mission.

Why, then, does Ethan's face appear so troubled, haunted, and wasted? Could it be that, having been lied to and manipulated by Jim *and Kittridge*, having seen members of his former team die or turn traitor, having himself been suspected of being a mole, Ethan finds it hard to believe in the old formulas of trust and teamwork, to have faith in father figures, fellow IMF members, or himself? Ethan has just spent much of the movie trying to distinguish himself from failed father figure Jim, but now *he* is in the position of the father. Who's to say that, when subjected to the same pressures that broke his mentor, Ethan won't fail, too? "Would you like to watch a movie?" the flight attendant asks, but Ethan, knowing what he knows, looks none too sure that he wants to participate in a sequel to this mission. Perhaps, in a way, De Palma is being asked, "Would you like to make a movie?" Having exploded the formulas of the spy thriller, De Palma naturally declined to film a sequel.

Besides this coda, there are several other scenes in *Mission: Impossible* that can be read as having an autobiographical resonance for De Palma. Regarding the scene where Ethan is a helpless witness to the death of his friend and fellow teammate Jack, who is killed in the elevator when father figure Jim pushes a button, we are reminded of the times when young De Palma would see his father "laying into my brother Bart" but "I couldn't intervene and I felt powerless."[13] It is no accident that, when he blows up Jim at the end, Ethan uses the explosive chewing gum that Jack gave him, for in doing so Ethan enacts a rebellious son's fantasy of revenge on "father" Jim for what he did to "brother" Jack, much as De Palma must have sometimes imagined taking revenge on his own father for Bart's suffering. When Ethan uses his "eyeglass-cam" to catch Jim in the act (of collecting the money), to gain visual evidence of Jim's betrayal (of his country), how can we not think of the teenage De Palma's attempt to obtain proof of his own father's betrayal, to film him in the act of committing adultery?

After De Palma confirmed with his own eyes that his father was cheating, Anthony moved out of the house and De Palma had his mother all to himself: "This crisis allowed me to resolve my Oedipus complex. I had removed my father, and my mother was mine and mine alone!"[14] Similarly, Jim's (apparent) death during the Prague mission leaves Claire, Jim's wife, in Ethan's arms. We recall that Ethan revives Claire from near-death at the beginning of the film, much as De Palma brought his mother to the hospital to be revived after she had taken an overdose of pills in response to Anthony's adultery. In a sense, then, De Palma rescued his mother from his father, but did he do it as a pure savior or because he wanted her for himself?

De Palma's reference to his "Oedipus complex" suggests that he was troubled by mixed motives. (Normally, the Oedipus complex is resolved when the son renounces his desire for the mother by yielding her to the father.) During the time that Ethan spends with Claire, he is similarly troubled by a mixture of desire for her and guilt over the feeling that he is betraying Jim by being with her. Ethan also fears that Claire may be fooling him with deceptive maneuvers, much as De Palma came to feel that his mother was distorting the truth and using his love for her to manipulate him. The fact that, in the end, Ethan first denounces Claire for being deceptive and manipulative but then, after she has been shot, holds her in his arms in a desperate attempt to save her would suggest that, at some level, De Palma had not yet resolved his mixed feelings about his mother.

Mission: Impossible was the most expensive film De Palma had made to date, but the $80 million gamble paid off spectacularly, yielding $457 million in worldwide grosses. "I'm feeling quite invigorated as I come to the end of my fiftieth year," De Palma said, "because I've made the most successful movie of my career."[15] However, having experienced so many ups and downs over his long history as a director, De Palma was not going to let success go to his head—or be fooled into thinking that it would necessarily last: "It's always exciting to have a blockbuster," he said, but added that "everybody thinks you're a genius for 30 seconds."[16]

What De Palma did do was use his newly restored status as an A-list director to make a film that might otherwise not have been bankrolled—a tricky film about a killing seen from multiple points of view. He had done something similar in *Mission: Impossible*, and despite reviewer complaints, audiences had not seemed overly daunted by the complexity. But now, in *Snake Eyes*, he would push this multi-perspectivism to even more complicated levels.

CHAPTER 24

Snake Eyes (1998)

Snake Eyes has Atlantic City police detective Rick Santoro (Nicolas Cage) seated ringside at a casino boxing match when the U.S. secretary of defense, sitting behind him, is shot by a sniper. Rick then undertakes an investigation, interrogating witnesses and studying video footage from the casino's many surveillance cameras to determine whether there might have been a conspiracy behind the assassination. Here we have another film rooted in De Palma's obsession with the John F. Kennedy assassination and the far-reaching inquiry to which it gave rise.

However, by tracking De Palma's treatment of this topic over the course of several films, we can see that he has moved from cynical realism to a more idealistic fantasy regarding the hero's success at solving the crime and making it public. In *Greetings*, Lloyd (Gerrit Graham) enlarges frames from the Zapruder film only to be confronted with grainy images, and his investigation is terminated when he either dies of paranoid fright or is himself shot down by a sniper. In *Blow Out*, Jack (John Travolta) is able to match sound to still images and show that a politician's death was no accident, but Jack's attempts to prove that it was a conspiracy fail when the killer destroys the evidence and murders Sally, Jack's girlfriend. By the time of *Mission: Impossible*, Ethan (Tom Cruise) is not only able to obtain ocular evidence of the mole Jim's conspiracy to betray the United States, he is also able to make this proof public, via his "eyeglass-cam," to CIA boss Kittridge. Yet Ethan's similarity to the mole does contribute to his failure to save Claire, who is herself compromised by criminal behavior.

In *Snake Eyes*, the perspective of each witness Rick interviews, and the angle of every segment of video footage that he reviews, add up like jigsaw pieces to complete the puzzle, revealing who all the players were in the conspiracy to assassinate the defense secretary. Furthermore, the main culprit—naval commander and head of security Kevin Dunne (Gary Sinise)—is actually caught on camera trying to kill a witness to his crime, Julia, whom Rick is able to save from death. Compared to Lloyd, Jack, and Ethan, Rick is the most conventional Hollywood hero: he saves the girl; he exposes the villain; and he successfully pieces together and makes public an assassination conspiracy. According to De Palma, "*Snake Eyes,* like a lot of dramatic works, describes an ideal situation. But that's basically an illusion. In real life, the more information you gather, the less you learn. That was the lesson of the inquiry into the Kennedy assassination, where the proliferation of information never solved the mystery. If I make movies about investigations that succeed, with puzzles that have a solution, it's because they work well on film. But that doesn't reflect my own convictions at all."[1]

If Rick is more successfully heroic than previous De Palma protagonists, Julia is a purer heroine. Whereas Sally (Nancy Allen) in *Blow Out* is involved in sexually blackmailing married men, and Claire (Emmanuelle Béart) seduces and betrays Ethan in *Mission: Impossible,* Julia (Carla Gugino) proves to be innocent and good-hearted. At first, Rick suspects her, for when she sits near the defense secretary, her blonde wig, red lipstick, and skimpy outfit suggest seduction and deception, but it turns out that Julia is in disguise because she's a whistleblower trying to pass on information that could save soldiers' lives. The real villainess is Serena, a woman in a red wig and low-cut red dress who *is* there to entice and distract attention during the assassination. At one point, we see Serena and Julia almost cross each other's paths, the one leaving while the other is arriving at the arena. It is as though, in order to preserve Julia's purity as a heroine, the film splits Serena off from her so that the other woman can carry the opprobrium of being the "bad girl." Serena is an alluring and deceptive part of the conspiracy so that Julia doesn't have to be. (The movie even tries to hold on to some virtue within Serena by having her revealed to be a soldier who mistakenly believes that killing the secretary will be good for the country. There is thus some pathos when Serena is shot by Kevin to cover up the conspiracy.)

Yet, despite the film's tendency to simplify and idealize its characters in the Hollywood tradition, there are some darker complexities worth noting. Our hero, Rick, enters the film in a bravura long take which emphasizes his arrogant sense of power over the entire casino world. As he puts it, "I was made for this sewer, baby. I am the king!" He adroitly juggles alternating calls on his cell phone from his wife and his mistress, succeeding at keeping the two separate better than "Master of the Universe" Sherman did in *The Bonfire of the Vanities.* Even though the heavyweight champion Tyler and the secretary of defense are far more important men than he, Rick behaves as though he were the center of attention, glorying in the spotlight like prize-winning and obnoxious journalist Peter Fallow in the opening long take of *Bonfire*. Rick parades in front of the TV cameras, for he is thinking of running for mayor, but once out of their view, he shakes down some guy for money and then places a bet with a bookie. Being a cop seems to give Rick license to misuse his authority, lording it over petty criminals and engaging in his own illicit behavior. "At the start of the film, [Rick] is a handsome young guy on the move," said cinematographer Stephen H. Burum. "He's very attractive to women, he's in control of everything because he's a cop, he grew up in Atlantic City and he's got the whole town wired. So . . . he's made to look brash and open, very much in control."[2]

When Rick discovers from a video replay that Tyler took a dive, going down for the count when his opponent gave him only a phantom punch, it is curious how devastated Rick is, given the extent of his own corruption. Rick had looked up to Tyler, making a point of their having gone to the same high school: "Neptune High, right? . . . Go, Sea Devils! You and me, Tyler!" Rick even pointed to his class ring as a symbol of the connection between them. Upon finding out that Tyler threw the fight, Rick remonstrates, "What kind of a Sea Devil is that?" Referring to Tyler's complicity in the assassination (his taking a dive was part of the plot), Rick says, "I guess they don't call you the Executioner for nothing!"

It is as though Tyler's hypocrisy exposes Rick's own, which is something that he can't bear to see. As long as his boxing idol seemed pure, Rick could hide his own criminal behavior from himself; they could both project an image and take that to be the reality. But once Tyler's villainy is revealed, Rick sees his own shortcomings brought to light. "I saw you and you saw me," Rick says to Tyler, referring to the fact that the cop witnessed the fighter open his eyes when he was supposed to have been knocked out, but the implication is also that Tyler spied Rick's fakery, too. Rick realizes that he was not being a good cop at that moment by protecting the secretary, and is thus similarly complicit in the man's death.

Like Tyler, Kevin is initially someone Rick greatly admires. Faithfully married for twenty years (while Rick has been fooling around on the side), scrupulously honest in serving his country (while Rick has been taking bribes and kickbacks), naval commander Kevin is Rick's ideal hero. "There's the man whose life I want," Rick says, adding, "Look at you: 007. Man, I'm so impressed." When Rick is led to believe that Kevin was distracted from duty by the voluptuous Serena, that's okay with him ("I like you better—golden boy screwed up"), but when Kevin is revealed to have masterminded the assassination conspiracy, Rick is deeply distraught. Rick and Kevin have been best friends since boyhood, and it is almost as if Rick considers Kevin an extension of himself. "Are you my conscience?" he asks at one point. As long as he could have faith in his friend's goodness, Rick could believe that there was a part of himself that was still unspoiled, but when Kevin's corruption is revealed, Rick is forced to confront the extent of his own.

The idea of boyhood innocence seems to be connected in De Palma's mind with his own childhood when he used to visit Atlantic City before its fall into sin: "Having grown up on the New Jersey coast, near Ocean City, I knew Atlantic City very well. Before the arrival of the casinos, this town was truly a paradise on earth. Afterward, it became hell."[3] "I consider that world like hell," De Palma explained, "because it's completely cut off from light and life. All it is is phony lights and sounds going, like everybody's winning all the time, and you're given this false sense of 'isn't this great?' Meanwhile, your soul is being stripped as your pocket is being emptied."[4] Kevin, who gives the appearance of doing good even while he is secretly committing evil (by having the secretary shot behind Rick's back), becomes a symbol for Atlantic City itself and its hypocrisy.

If Rick is to retain any faith in goodness, he's going to have to find it in himself, for Kevin can no longer be relied on to embody it. Much of the film's drama lies in Rick's attempt to distinguish himself as less corrupt than Kevin. For example, after the assassination of the secretary, both Rick and Kevin go in separate pursuit of Julia—Rick because he considers her a suspect in the conspiracy, and Kevin because he knows she's a whistleblower and he wants to silence her. Julia's glasses were crushed in the commotion following the assassination, so she can no longer see clearly. One blurry point-of-view shot from her perspective shows a man (it turns out to be Rick) coming toward her down a casino hotel corridor, while a later shot shows another man (it turns out to be Kevin) pursuing her down a nearly identical corridor. The fact that Rick and Kevin appear almost indistinguishable is a commentary on their similarly dubious characters.

In her attempt to escape, Julia pretends to be a prostitute so that a hotel guest (Ned) will take her to his room. In one split-screen shot, Kevin is standing in an elevator next to Julia and Ned on the right side of the image, while Rick is standing in another elevator on the image's left side, as if Rick and Kevin were close to combining as one man, both of them pursuing and surrounding Julia. We see the wedding ring on Kevin's finger and then a wedding ring on Ned's. Ned is a married man intending to cheat on his wife with Julia, and Kevin—though he seemed faithful to his wife—confessed to ogling Serena and is now predatorily tracking Julia. Before the assassination, when Julia sat in a seat next to married Rick, he, too, had leered at her. In their pursuit of Julia after the assassination, both Rick and Kevin make use of video surveillance cameras, voyeuristically following her as she goes with Ned to his hotel room. Will Rick find a way to differentiate himself from these two hypocrites, Kevin and Ned, who feign gallantry toward Julia but really only want to use her for their own ends?

Rick locates Julia in Ned's hotel room before Kevin does and hides her in a ground-floor storage room after hearing her account of the assassination, including Kevin's key role in it. Earlier, Kevin appealed to their long-standing friendship in order to manipulate Rick. Now, in an effort to get Rick to tell him where Julia is hidden, Kevin tries to bribe him ("How much is it gonna take for you to look the other way like you have all your life?") and then has him beaten up by his former idol, Tyler. With Kevin and Tyler having turned against him, with both men who used to prop up his sense of goodness having fallen away ("You're all alone on this"), Rick is finally forced to reach deep inside himself for a sense of morality. He stands firm, refusing to give away Julia's location. Even when he is tricked by a tracking device into leading Kevin to where Julia is, Rick covers her body with his own, as he is willing to die to save her.

In the original ending planned for the film, Rick's last-minute stand against evil, his finally finding some remnant of good within himself, would not have been enough to bring about a happy conclusion. In this bleak vision, the corrupt Rick's righteous stand in the end is too little, too late; his isolated iota of virtue is weak, relative to the pervasive forces of evil surrounding it. Instead, only divine intervention can save him and Julia, and it comes in the form of a tidal wave that takes out Kevin just as he is about to shoot them. More specifically, the wave would have caused a giant globe—the symbol of the casino—to be knocked from its perch and to roll over Kevin, crushing him. Thus, both the villain and the corrupt casino of which he was the symbol would have been destroyed. "The whole idea at the end of *Snake Eyes* was *deus ex machina*," De Palma said. "We were dealing with such a corrupt world that the only way to solve the problem is to have a hurricane come through and wipe it all away." However, audiences at preview screenings thought the wave was confusing or ridiculous, failing to appreciate its religious import: "They don't believe in God looking down from above and saying, 'The only way to deal with this is a flood. There's so much corruption here, let's wipe it away and get an ark out and start from scratch.' . . . We did shoot this big wave that swept through the casino but we ultimately cut it out."[5]

The "tidal-wave" ending would have been interesting for its negative judgment on the weakness of Rick's last-minute heroism, on humanity's inability to save itself. In a sense, this ending was already foreshadowed when, despite all the human witnesses he interviewed and all the surveillance footage he studied, Rick had to have recourse to a special eye-in-the-sky blimp camera and its transcendent perspective in order to discover the truth about the conspiracy. Without this God's-eye view of events, the merely human Rick would have failed to solve the crime, just as without the divine wave, he would have failed to save Julia or himself.

But the idealistic ending we do have presents Rick, in league with other human forces of justice, as a much more successful hero. Having secured Julia's safety, Rick fixes his gaze on Kevin, while behind Rick the eye of a news camera is also focused on Kevin's villainy. As if that weren't enough, there are also two cops staring at Kevin, with their guns trained on him. The combined pressure of the assorted accusing eyes prompts Kevin to commit suicide. Rick himself is sentenced to serve some time in prison for his petty crimes, but a coda indicates that Julia may well be waiting for him when he gets out, ready to begin a romance. Julia succeeds in exposing the conspiracy, and the casino owner who financed it as part of a plan to make more profit is sent to jail. "Things have really changed," she tells Rick, believing that "it's going to be so different in Atlantic City," while behind them a new casino rises from the wreckage of the old. (In this ending, there was no tidal wave, but there was still a hurricane that destroyed the original, corrupt casino.) The end credits roll over a shot of workers constructing the new casino, and most viewers will leave the theater thinking that this is a conventional Hollywood happy ending.

However, those few who stay to the very end will discover a red ruby embedded in a concrete pillar. The ruby is from a ring that was worn by Serena, the woman whom Kevin killed and whose body is buried under the building's foundations. The new casino is thus literally built on murder, suggesting that nothing has changed and that the corruption will continue. The ruby's red light glints in the sun—a reference to some earlier dialogue about pirates who built phony lighthouses to draw sailors onto the rocks where their ships could be looted. In similar fashion, as De Palma noted, the "phony lights and sounds" of the casinos trick people into believing that "everybody's winning all the time,"[6] when in fact they're being robbed by a house that always wins. Thus, buried within this Hollywood fantasy of heroic triumph, De Palma has hidden a bit of cynical realism for his more vigilant viewers to find.

Snake Eyes was a modest success, returning $103 million worldwide on its $73 million cost, but it did not do as well as had been hoped. De Palma attributed the film's less-than-stellar performance at the box office to the fact that it offered a "very dark view of humanity, which Americans in general don't appreciate. They prefer to see [*The Untouchables'*] Eliot Ness win in the end and don't like to see the hero [of *Snake Eyes*] go to prison."[7] De Palma himself was at a turning point in his career, believing that he had gone deeply enough into the dark side for now. Betrayal by a close friend or father figure had been the theme of *Carlito's Way* (Carlito traduced by Dave), *Mission: Impossible* (Ethan by Jim), and *Snake Eyes* (Rick by Kevin). "In my last three films, I was very cynical and I was beginning to feel it was enough!" De Palma said. "Frankly, do you want to see even more about our corrupt world? In any case, I couldn't make anything more cynical than *Snake Eyes*."[8] As we shall see, De Palma was also beginning to re-evaluate his own past in the light of a changed present, leading to a new sense of understanding and reconciliation. The result would be his most hopeful and idealistic film, *Mission to Mars*.

CHAPTER 25

Mission to Mars (2000)

Married astronauts Jim (Gary Sinise) and Maggie (Kim Delaney) have trained for years to be co-commanders of the first manned spaceflight to Mars, but they drop out of the rotation when she falls ill and he devotes himself to caring for her during her final months. Instead, Luke (Don Cheadle) leads the mission, but a tornado on the planet's surface kills all of his crew and leaves Luke stranded on Mars. A rescue mission is mounted, manned by Woody (Tim Robbins), his wife, Terri (Connie Nielsen), Phil (Jerry O'Connell), and Jim. However, micro-meteorites puncture their ship's hull, and although an attempt to patch the holes seems successful, a leak in a fuel line leads to an explosion, forcing the crew to evacuate the ship. Now, protected only by their pressure suits, they are floating in space, connected by a lifeline. Woody is able to hook their tether to an orbiting satellite but cannot grab on to it himself, overshooting it. Woody commits suicide by removing his pressure helmet so that Terri and the others will not die in a futile attempt to rescue him, since she does not have enough jet-pack fuel left to reach him and get back to the satellite.

Once on Mars, the crew is at first attacked by Luke, who seems to have been driven crazy by his year spent in isolation from all humanity on the red planet, but this proves to be only a temporary derangement. Luke shows them the giant image of a woman's face on the planet's surface, and once the crew has solved an alien puzzle—converting sounds into a DNA double helix and then adding the final chromosomes to make it human DNA—the face opens up, allowing Jim, Terri, and Luke to enter. Inside, the holographic projection of a female alien shows them that life on Earth was started by aliens from Mars, that in fact the two races are one: "They're us; we're them," as Jim puts it. While

Terri and Luke join Phil and take their spaceship back to Earth, Jim decides to go with the female alien to a different "home planet," to journey with her to his ancestral home (the planet where the Martians went when Mars became uninhabitable).

Early in the film, which begins on Earth, we see Jim, Woody, and Luke seated in a treehouse fort, as if they were still boys dreaming of spaceflight. Jim refers to Woody as having "read too much science fiction as a kid" since he's wearing a necklace with a toy rocketship, and Woody says to Jim, "You read every damn science fiction book I did." As Jim reaches for the rocketship, Woody pulls it away from him, saying that he may want it but he's not getting it. Before this, Woody and Luke have been arguing over the proper action to take during a spaceflight, and Luke asks Jim to settle the dispute. The good-natured bickering leads Luke to conclude, "Three commanders, one ship—I don't think that's gonna work. There's not enough rocket fuel in the world to get those egos off the ground."

Jim, Woody, and Luke can be compared to the three De Palma brothers—Brian, Bruce, and Bart. Speaking of science fiction, Brian said, "I was crazy about this genre of books. My brothers were, too."[1] We also know that Brian and his brothers "grew up in a competitive environment: it was about who would be the best, 24/7!" As an example of this rivalry, Brian noted that "Bart, Bruce, and I loved science fiction, but it never occurred to us to share our magazines. We each had our own collection. When a new issue of a science fiction magazine came out, I bought my brand-new one; Bruce and Bart bought theirs; and when we got home, all three of us went to our own little rooms, each with the same collection of magazines on the shelf."[2] Given this kind of competitive atmosphere, it is easy to imagine youngest brother Brian in the uncomfortable position of being asked by Bart, the middle brother, to decide some argument he was having with Bruce, just as it is easy to picture the three boys fighting over possessions (when they didn't have their own) and trying to occupy the dominant position as leader.

Despite Brian's best efforts to compete, Bruce always seemed to be there before him as the first to build technologically advanced machines, to win prizes at science fairs, and to study physics. "Brian was trying real hard to be Bruce," their mother said,[3] but no matter what the youngest brother did, as De Palma himself lamented, "it didn't have any value for my parents. Whatever happened, Bruce remained the family genius, and I was his imitator."[4] Brian felt closer to his other brother, Bart, who may have tried to comfort him for feeling a sense of inferiority and belatedness, much as Luke attempts to make Jim feel better about his not being the one to lead the first manned mission to Mars. "It should have been your mission," Luke tells Jim, "yours and Maggie's. Nobody ever wanted Mars the way you two did, not even Woody."

Later, it is Luke who sends Jim a "happy birthday" message via video to let him know that, even though he is not the one going to Mars, he has not been forgotten. Luke adds that NASA boss Ray (Armin Mueller-Stahl), the crew's father figure, may not approve of such a message but that there is nothing he can do about it. When we recall how hurt Brian was that birthdays were never celebrated in the De Palma home, this rebellious moment of recognition between Luke and Jim almost seems like one between the brothers Bart and Brian in defiance of their father. Certainly, Luke appears to care more than Woody does about Jim's unhappiness, much as Bart exhibited more compassion for Brian than Bruce did.

Although Woody often seems pleasant enough, the film hints that he is actually quite aggressively competitive, as when he brags that he could beat a Russian astronaut in a baseball game: "Half you guys are foreigners; we'd crush you." Woody "jokes around" in similar fashion with his own wife, Terri, even playing the alpha male with her when he says that "technically, I outrank her, so for the first time in our marriage, she's gonna have to do everything I say—right, honey?" Woody is like James, the Bruce character in *Home Movies*, who was not only intensely competitive, he also ordered around his fiancée and insisted that she be deferential to him. Even in a tender moment when Woody is doing a zero-gravity dance with Terri while they are on board the spaceship, he can't help quipping that he wants her to address him as "sir." This dance is watched by Jim, who suffers the keen discrepancy between himself, who should have been dancing on this mission with his own wife, Maggie, and Woody, who is there in Jim's stead and who has Terri to dance with. The moment seems reminiscent of the time when young Brian used to feel jealous of his older brother Bruce: "You look through a door and see . . . your brother with a girl. I spent a lot of my time watching."[5]

The "fraternal" rivalry among Jim, Woody, and Luke—all of them sci-fi aficionados with big dreams—might also recall the friendly competition among De Palma, George Lucas, and Steven Spielberg, who started out together as young directors. Leonard Schrader remembers hearing them "talk for hours" about how "we wanted to make great films, we wanted to be artists, we were going to discover the limits of our talent."[6] Lucas hit it big with *Star Wars*. (De Palma helped with the writing of the famous opening crawl: "A long time ago, in a galaxy far, far away . . .") Spielberg launched *Close Encounters of the Third Kind* and *E.T.* to great success. It's fair to say that, to a certain extent, De Palma felt left behind. As he put it, "I was more than ready for big-time success. All my best friends in the business—[and De Palma included Lucas and Spielberg in this list]—had already made it in a huge way, and there was I . . . still struggling."[7] "Steven has always said, 'Gosh, I wish I could make a movie like *Hi, Mom!*' Well, *I* wish I could make a movie like *E.T.*!" De Palma commented.[8]

Ever since he read *The Demolished Man* as a teenager, De Palma had been trying to direct this novel as *his* big science fiction movie, but he always failed to get this project off the ground. In 1982, De Palma noted that "Lucas and I are planning to make a film together with Spielberg, and that would be good. This collaboration between directors is something I miss.... We all started like this in the early 1970s, but we don't do it any more. It's a shame."[9] That film, whatever it was, never materialized.

But now, with *Mission to Mars*, De Palma has finally succeeded in "catching up" with his two longtime friends, much as Jim within the film finally makes it into space after Luke and Woody. *Mission to Mars* is even, to some degree, a collaborative effort between De Palma and Lucas, given that the latter's company, Industrial Light & Magic, was responsible for a number of the film's visual effects. Furthermore, De Palma's film allows him to tip his hat to his old friend Spielberg via the many allusions to *Close Encounters*, such as the coded sounds used to make contact with the extraterrrestrials, the sleek look of the alien, and the fact that the hero—Jim in *Mission to Mars*, Roy (Richard Dreyfuss) in *Close Encounters*—decides to depart with the alien in the mothership.

Of course, De Palma's, Spielberg's, and Lucas's entries into science fiction were belated in relation to the great father figure of the genre, Stanley Kubrick, whose *2001: A Space Odyssey* first paved the way for all their films to follow. De Palma pays homage to Kubrick throughout *Mission to Mars*: the exterior of the Mars recovery spaceship, the giant centrifuge inside it, and the totally white room within the alien spacecraft all refer to scenes in *2001*. Most importantly, De Palma takes his message from Kubrick, carrying on his predecessor's key idea that we must overcome the distances which separate us and the rivalries, based on a fear of otherness, which divide us and realize that we are all connected at the deepest level. *2001* and *Mission to Mars* both have birthday messages sent via video to astronauts in an attempt to maintain human contact and to relieve the loneliness of space. Both movies show characters whose lifelines are cut off and who drift to their deaths in outer space, far from their fellow human beings.

Both movies imply that the next stage in our evolution will not come through dominating and destroying the other, but through the peaceful realization that, in the same way that primitive life forms on Earth are linked to us, so we are connected to "alien" life forms with which we can merge. *2001* presents warring apes, then paranoid humans threatened by nuclear war, and finally an astronaut who transcends all fear of otherness to evolve into a higher consciousness, merging with the alien mind that first prompted this evolution by planting a monolith on Earth. In *Mission to Mars*, the astronauts begin in alpha-male rivalry over who will be first on Mars. The crew of the first mission is then attacked by a phallic tornado, which suggests that they were not yet ready to overcome their own belligerence and perceive their underlying link with the aliens. The second crew, realizing that the DNA of humans and aliens is shared, is granted a vision of how the evolution of all life on Earth was first started by Martians—a vision which leads Jim to join hands with the female alien at the end and leave with her.

Mission to Mars can thus be seen as De Palma's attempt to imagine a way beyond male rivalry, whether that competition be among the movie's astronauts (Jim, Woody, and Luke), among the De Palma brothers (Brian, Bruce, and Bart), or among fellow filmmakers (De Palma, Lucas, and Spielberg). (It might be noted that De Palma was also in competition with other filmmakers. Much as Luke replaced Jim on the first manned mission to Mars, De Palma replaced *Mission to Mars'* original director, Gore Verbinski. Asked about whether he had any reservations about helming the picture in Verbinski's stead, De Palma said, "The director of *Mouse Hunt*? No."[10] De Palma was also in a race to finish his film and get it into theaters before a competing Mars movie, Antony Hoffman's *Red Planet*, could arrive there first.)

We have seen the astronauts contending with each other for leadership and vying over who will be first on Mars. However, even when he knows that Luke will be going in his stead, Jim presents him with a congratulatory bottle of champagne. De Palma seems to approve, for soon after this gesture of continuing friendship, he has his own credit appear: "Directed by Brian De Palma." Later in the film, after Luke has been hit by the tornado and stranded on Mars, De Palma imagines another moment of fraternal solidarity when Woody pleads with father figure Ray, who has doubts about Jim, to take his brother astronaut with him on the rescue mission: "We can do this, Ray. You give me [Jim] McConnell as copilot and we will bring Luke home."

More often than not, Bruce—the Woody equivalent in real life—sided with their father against Bart (Luke) and Brian (Jim): "There was a brutality that ran rampage over the weaker ones in my family," De Palma explained. "That was true of my father . . . and my older brother Bruce. I was 10, my other brother Bart was 12, he was very sensitive and vulnerable, and I wanted to protect him from such rage. But I was never able to do it because I was a child."[11]

In *Mission to Mars*, however, De Palma rewrites this family history by having Woody (Bruce) join with Jim (Brian) in an effort to save Luke (Bart). De Palma even imagines Woody (Bruce) sacrificing his own life—"I am not retrievable," he says, removing his pressure helmet—so that Jim (Brian) and the other members of the recovery crew can reach Luke (Bart). The goal of rescuing his brother, dreamed of as a child by De Palma, comes true in the film, with Luke (Bart) even shaking Jim's (Brian's) hand in the end and saying, "Thank you for saving my life, buddy." And the recognition that De Palma always wanted from his father but never felt that he got is finally granted to him when father figure Ray says approvingly about Jim (Brian), "Nobody else could have pulled this off—nobody else."

Bruce died in 1997, just a few years before *Mission to Mars*, and it is possible to view this film as an effort by De Palma to understand, accept, and make peace with his brother on the occasion of his passing. There is, as we have seen, a sense that Woody, despite his aggressive one-upmanship, was ultimately devoted to trying to help others, and there is real pathos in his self-sacrificial death. Terri hands Woody's rocketship necklace to Jim in the end, wishing that Woody were still here, and Jim replies, "He is here, Terri. We wouldn't have made it without him."

Could this be De Palma thinking back on the love of science fiction that he and his brother shared as boys—a love which inspired Bruce to become a scientist-inventor and which led Brian to become a director of science fiction films like this one, both of them exploring new worlds in their different ways? Bruce's belief that he had surpassed all known physics, creating an "N-machine" that exhibited antigravity characteristics and that could tap into "space energy" to solve the world's environmental problems, marked him as a far-reaching visionary, not unlike the film's astronauts who journey to Mars where they encounter an alien form of energy that is the key to all life on Earth.

Disbelieved by the scientific establishment and feeling more and more paranoid in his isolation, Bruce "ended up losing his reason and went off to an island in New Zealand where he lived cut off from the world," according to De Palma.[12] This sounds a lot like Luke who, in a fit of paranoia, attacks his rescuer, Jim, and who may have gone insane after being "marooned alone on Mars for a year." At first, the other astronauts are incredulous when Luke claims to have discovered an alien form of space energy in the coded sounds. "You don't believe me," he says. "That's okay. But I'm not crazy—I know that much." By having Luke's discovery proven to be genuine and of real value to humanity, De Palma in a sense rescues his brother from insanity and oblivion, recognizing the value of Bruce's spirit of inquiry, his desire to help humanity, and his conviction in the face of disbelief. Thus, both Luke and Woody, at different moments in the film, seem to represent aspects of De Palma's brother Bruce.

Before the death of his brother-astronaut Woody, Jim experiences the loss of his wife, Maggie, who dies before the two of them are able to fulfill their dream of journeying to Mars together. This dream is figured as an image of Jim holding Maggie in his arms in front of a wall-size photo of a "Greetings from Mars" postcard—an image of a future that now will never come to be. De Palma's brief marriage to Darnell Gregorio ended in divorce in 1996, and it is possible that *Mission to Mars* represents his coming to terms with the loss of their future together. We recall that *Carlito's Way* ended with that film's protagonist unable to join his beloved Gail, who was pictured dancing "inside" the "Escape to Paradise" travel poster he sees on a wall, and that this may have figured De Palma's own sense of having lost his wife, Gale Anne Hurd, to divorce at that time.

Despite the failure of these marriages ("I haven't been too successful with my wives"),[13] De Palma has endeavored to emphasize the fact that they resulted in two wonderful daughters: "I have two little girls that I adore."[14] When Jim reviews the events of his life at the end of the film, he remembers a video image of Maggie as a young girl with her telescope ("The universe is not chaos; it's connection—life reaches out for life") and then he recalls the female alien reaching out to take his hand. It is as though Maggie lives on through the female alien, whose form serves as an intermediary preserving the connection between Jim and his wife. It also seems as if Maggie's girlhood spirit of adventure is reborn in the female alien, who is like a daughter. "That's what we were born for," Maggie had said, "to stand on a new world and look beyond it to the next one. It's who we are."

After taking the female alien's hand, Jim is led to step into a chamber which fills up with water. At first, he fears death by drowning, but this turns out to be a womb from which he is reborn. The chamber carries him to the alien spacecraft, which blasts off, emerging from inside the giant image of an alien female face on the planet's surface. In describing this face, producer Tom Jacobson said, "Brian wanted to design something that looked like a sleeping goddess, something that was serene and beautiful and beckoning, 'cause the idea was that these were our ancestors and that the artifact that they left behind should feel peaceful to us, should feel welcoming."[15]

De Palma's own mother died in 1998, and this film may represent a tribute to her for having given him life, as well as a way for him to imagine that, despite her death, they are still connected. The film is, after all, about the interconnectedness of life through DNA. Just as his mother lives on in him, so De Palma is "reborn" through his daughters. "This is an invitation for us to follow them home," Jim says about the realization of the shared DNA. "I'm going. It's what I was born for." And so, moving beyond male rivalry and fear of otherness, Jim recognizes the value of connectedness, joining hands with the female alien—his mother, his wife, his daughter—and going home.

With a $111 million return on its $100 million budget, *Mission to Mars* was modestly remunerative but far from being a blockbuster hit. Rob Humanick of *Slant* magazine identified the main problem when he wrote that "*Mission to Mars* might be the greatest '50s sci-fi film ever, even if [it] came half a century late." The film's "irony-deprived B-movie euphoria"[16] just seemed too old-fashioned for twenty-first-century audiences, who found it hard to take the movie's unalloyed optimism seriously. Ironically, in being less cynical than usual, De Palma had swung to the opposite extreme and made a movie that was so idealistic it provoked mockery. "I never realized that they would start laughing at *Mission to Mars* so universally," De Palma lamented. "What people don't understand is that you have to watch . . . *Mission to Mars* through a child's eyes," he explained,[17] adding that the film was "full of innocence. You have to go into it abandoning your prejudices. If you start to get sarcastic, it's finished; you won't take any pleasure from it."[18] De Palma had hoped that, in seeing the film, viewers would connect with their own childhood as he had with his: "I tried to bring the sensibility of the kid I was when I went to see *Destination Moon* [a 1950 science fiction film]. It's kind of a magical thing. And my experience working with people from NASA is, they have that kind of magical glow. . . . There are areas where there's a scientific purity and an idealism, and all those kinds of things that we believed in growing up in the 1950s."[19]

To weather the negative critical storm over *Mission to Mars*, De Palma left America for Paris. As he noted, "The debut of a new film in the United States is always a painful moment for me, which is why at present I prefer not to find myself there."[20] Also, *Mission to Mars* had been the most expensive and technically complicated film De Palma had ever made, and he was ready for a change: "There are more than 400 digital [visual effects] shots in this film. So you spend your life in front of a computer. I don't want to do that again, not at my age, not at this point in my career."[21] It was time for De Palma to return to making the kind of smaller-budget suspense thrillers that he so enjoyed. But this time he would bring his newfound sense of optimism with him. His next film, *Femme Fatale*, would be a different kind of film noir—one with a happy ending.

CHAPTER 26

Femme Fatale (2002)

On a television set, we see a scene from Billy Wilder's *Double Indemnity* featuring Barbara Stanwyck as Phyllis. Reflected in the TV screen over Phyllis is our film's lead character, Laure, who is watching the movie in her hotel room. Over Laure, we see the opening credit for the actress playing her—Rebecca Romijn-Stamos—in the movie that *we* are watching. Then, as Phyllis pulls a gun and shoots Neff (Fred MacMurray) in the film-within-a-film, we see the title credit for our film, *Femme Fatale*. This Brechtian opening emphasizes the connection between a person's character and movie characters. We recall that *Scarface* opened with Tony (Al Pacino) saying how he learned from watching movie gangsters like Humphrey Bogart and James Cagney. This new movie's opening causes us to wonder whether Laure will—or will not—behave like Phyllis, a femme fatale in a film noir. The femme fatale is sometimes known as a phallic woman because she appropriates emblems of male power. Phyllis and Laure are both smoking cigarettes—something that women at one time were frowned upon for doing. Will Laure also adopt other masculine tools, like the gun that Phyllis uses to shoot Neff?

At first, it would seem that Laure is the quintessential phallic woman, as she assists her two male accomplices, Black Tie (Eriq Ebouaney) and Racine (Edouard Montoute), in the commission of a diamond robbery, which occurs on opening night of the Cannes Film Festival. The heist that the two men pull off presents them in hypermasculine mode. Racine, for example, dons a scuba wetsuit and enters a circular air duct. He uses a laser gun to bore a hole in a steel-plated box. He scouts terrain using a micro-camera affixed to the head of a flexible stalk that protrudes "like a cobra in search of its prey."[1] Laure joins in on all this eyeing and penetrating of targets. In a shot that makes her look very butch, Laure—with her close-cropped hair—is presented from behind while, posing as a photographer, she uses her camera to snap photos of Veronica (Rie Rasmussen), the model who is wearing a serpentine gold brassiere studded with the diamonds they want to steal. Rather than being the object of the male gaze, Laure is aligned with the camera's eye and doing the looking. As Romijn-Stamos commented, "I never thought I'd be on that side of the camera, the paparazzi camera."[2]

Laure lures Veronica into a ladies room stall and, under the pretense of making love to her, strips her of her diamond-studded bra. This Laure accomplishes by running the point of some scissors across the model's bare flesh before using them to cut the bra's clasp, and then by pushing her own body up behind Veronica's against the translucent wall of the stall while switching the real diamonds for fake ones behind her back. Laure's "ravaging" of the model is reminiscent of *Dressed to Kill*'s scene where a strange man rapes Kate in the shower or of *Body Double*'s scene where Jake uses his vampire fangs to penetrate a female victim in the shower—but this time the attacker is a woman. "Laure uses her beauty and sexuality like powerful weapons to obtain what she wants," Romijn-Stamos said, and De Palma noted—in a comparison that makes her sound very phallic indeed—that "we fall under the spell of her charm and eroticism and willingly offer ourselves to her scorpion sting."[3]

However, Laure only appears to be in league with the male predators. In fact, she is working in conjunction with Veronica, the two women putting on an elaborate charade that allows them to dupe the men and steal the diamonds for themselves. The women are like the cat that uses its paw to play with Racine's snakelike camera: they toy with men's lust and power, turning these to their own advantage. For example, when the control room guards have their eyes glued to the screen, watching camera footage of Veronica in her sexy, serpentine bra, the distraction enables Racine to sneak into the air duct. Racine seems to have put one over on the guards, but it is Veronica who has bested him, for unbeknownst to Racine, he is furthering her and Laure's robbery plan. While another guard is ogling the sight of Veronica on the video monitor, honey is spilled on his key. In his sexual excitement, the guard is seduced and distracted so that his key can be stolen by Pierre, the robbery's "inside man," but it is Laure who will eventually take possession of this key, using it to make good her escape. Laure and Veronica put on a show of lesbianism, as in a hetero porn film, for Black Tie, who is on the other side of the translucent ladies room stall, diverting him from the fact that Laure is handing him fake diamonds so that she and Veronica can steal the real ones. The tail of the snake in Veronica's serpentine bra points down to her crotch, and all the men seem eye-poppingly mesmerized by it, overcome by their lust. The alluring women toy with each man's ogling eye on its stalk, causing them to miss the *female* robbery plot.

The women also use the men's phallic power against them, letting them defeat each other in rivalrous competition so that the females can walk away with the jewels. Pierre gives the key he stole from a control room guard to Black Tie. Black Tie knocks out a security guard by using a stun gun on him while the man is standing at a urinal. Black Tie shoots another guard in the eye, but this man shoots back, hitting the robber in the chest. Black Tie retaliates by pummeling the guard in the face with his fist. The robbers battle the guards over keys, guns, eyes, and diamonds.

While the men are busy fighting to maintain possession—or to deprive each other—of these tokens of power, the women unite and secretly turn the male forces to their own advantage. When Black Tie pulls a gun on Veronica, Laure kicks him to the floor with her stiletto-heeled shoes ("Asshole, you said no fucking guns!") and then holds his own gun to his head, stealing the escape key from his pocket. In this way, she both protests against his use of phallic force and appropriates it to save her girlfriend and herself. She is momentarily halted by a security guard with a gun, but when Racine shorts out the power box with his laser gun, plunging everyone into darkness, Laure is able to make her escape wearing night goggles. It is as though the guard's gun and the robber's gun cancel each other out. Once again, male rivalry enables female triumph. The women unite to outsmart the men, who are left in the dark.

Significantly, one of the men who has his plans diverted by the women is a film director (played by real-life director Régis Wargnier). First, Wargnier is walking down the red carpet at Cannes with the sexy Veronica on his arm, only to have her and her jewel-encrusted bra stolen from him by Laure. When Veronica does not return from the ladies room, the screenplay has Wargnier wondering, "Where the hell is his date? She's going to make him late to his own premiere."[4] Then, as Wargnier is sitting in the theater with Veronica's empty seat beside him, the projection of his film begins, but just as his director's credit appears on the screen, it goes black as everyone is plunged into darkness due to the power cut, which is a diversion allowing the women to escape with the diamonds. Thus, not only is the director deprived of his date, but his film does not go as planned; both are diverted from his control.

De Palma himself attended Cannes in 2000 to present his film *Mission to Mars*: "I got that idea for the whole heist at the Cannes Film Festival, walking down the red carpet with a girlfriend [Elli Medeiros] covered with Chopard jewelry, with guards around us."[5] (De Palma had Medeiros design the serpentine bra worn by Veronica, and he shot the film's opening sequence at the 2001 Cannes Film Festival. *Femme Fatale* later premiered at Cannes in 2002.) In a sense, then, *Femme Fatale* shows De Palma imagining his own date being stolen from him. Perhaps this is a self-critical moment aimed at powerful men, like film directors, who use women as arm candy.

De Palma also imagines his own film being thrown off course by its female characters, for what begins as a typical film noir or heist movie—conventional genres often helmed by male directors—gets diverted into something new by Laure and Veronica. It is as though Claire in *Mission: Impossible*, instead of playing the role assigned to her by Ethan and the other men (including De Palma), had hijacked the heist (and the film) in order to steal the NOC list from CIA headquarters for herself and a girlfriend. In fact, the jewel heist at Cannes, with all its high-tech gadgets and phallic competition, is very much like *Mission: Impossible*'s CIA break-in, but what makes the new film different is the female characters' hijacking of the male plot.

Following the opening sequence's detour from the male-defined heist genre, the remainder of the film considers the question of whether or not Laure will depart from her predetermined role as a femme fatale in a typical film noir. (We recall that *Carlito's Way* asked a similar question about whether its title character [Al Pacino] would be able to leave the gangster life—and the gangster film genre—rather than coming to the same bad end as Tony [also Pacino] in *Scarface*.) Fleeing Black Tie and Racine, who want the diamonds as well as revenge for her double-cross, Laure is almost killed by the latter when he throws her over a hotel balcony. She is rescued by an elderly couple who mistake her for their daughter-in-law, a lookalike named Lily. Lily has just lost her husband and her daughter to an accident and there are sympathy flowers all over her apartment, but rather than feel much sympathy, Laure seems more interested in imagining what it would be like to wear the rich clothes hanging in her lookalike's closet, to live life with this woman's identity.

After falling asleep in the bath, Laure is awakened by the sound of Lily's return and hides in a curtained alcove to watch her. Lily writes a suicide note and puts a gun to her own head. Laure looks worried and seems on the verge of rising to intervene, but instead remains in hiding. Lily and Laure both close their eyes, bracing themselves for the pull of the trigger, but there is no explosion. Lily then spins the chamber and holds the gun to her head again. As Laure watches, her eyes half-covered by her arm, Lily's gun fires, killing her. At the sound of the bang, Laure closes her own eyes and looks down.

Laure's behavior is that of someone torn between empathy and distance. She would not brace herself along with Lily or find Lily's suicide almost unbearable to watch if she did not feel some compassion for her. However, Laure's self-interest wins out over sympathy. Even though the other woman looks like Laure, Laure does not see her *as herself*. Instead, Laure views her as an expendable object, a "dead ringer" that could be "the solution to all [Laure's] problems"[6] if she can steal her identity, according to the screenplay.

We recall that Laure did feel solidarity with another woman, Veronica, when she saved her from being shot by the robbers. But now that the robbers have come after Laure for revenge, she feels that she must look out for herself alone, sacrificing others to save her own skin: "The last time she kept someone from getting killed it almost cost her her neck. So if this suicidal look-a-like, holding Laure's ticket to a new life, wants to blow her head off . . . well, so be it. Now the only question is: Where to hide the body?"⁷ Thus, though she is at first tempted to "see feelingly," Laure moves from watching Lily with some compassion to gazing at her like a predator. Conflicted in her attitude toward Lily, Laure does not act to save her, but instead remains a spectator, then robs the dead woman of her identity.

Yet there is more to Laure's character than what is readily apparent. Later, when Laure looks back on having taken Lily's identity in order to save herself, she thinks, "if [that] meant letting some pathetic asshole shoot herself and burying her body. . . . So be it."⁸ Laure's contempt for Lily's suicidal surrender is not the kind of indifference one feels toward an object. Rather, it suggests that Laure sees and condemns in the other woman a pathetic passivity toward life's challenges that Laure herself is struggling to overcome. In letting Lily—her lookalike—commit suicide, Laure hoped to separate and distance herself from that kind of weakness and vulnerability. However, what Laure comes to realize is that, when she let her lookalike pull the trigger, Laure was in effect killing herself. Being a predatory femme fatale is ultimately self-destructive.

Having stolen Lily's identity, Laure meets a rich politician named Watts (Peter Coyote) on a plane leaving Paris and marries him. However, seven years later, she must return to France, where Watts is posted as the American ambassador. Laure's photo is taken by a photographer, Nicolas (Antonio Banderas), who sells it to a tabloid magazine. Black Tie and Racine track down Veronica, throwing her in front of a truck, and then spot Laure's photo on a kiosk poster advertising the cover of the magazine.

Terrified that her former accomplices will track her down and kill her, Laure decides that she needs some getaway money, so she seduces Nicolas and then embroils him in a fake kidnapping plot so that her husband, Watts, will pay to ransom her. When Nicolas reveals the truth to Watts, Laure shoots her husband and then Nicolas, too. As he lies there bleeding, she presses her gun into his hand and pulls the trigger, firing into his heart, in order to make it look as though Nicolas killed Watts and then committed suicide. Laure's shooting of Nicolas is like Phyllis's shooting of Neff in *Double Indemnity*, even to the point of Laure using the same words—"I'm . . . rotten to the heart"—that Phyllis used to describe herself. And like the femme fatale Phyllis, Laure also ends up dead, because despite all of her scheming, Black Tie and Racine do find her and throw her off a bridge where she drowns in the river.

Or, rather, that *would* be the ending if *Femme Fatale* had a conventional femme fatale and if it came to a dark conclusion like a generic film noir. But De Palma describes his film as a "surrealistic rethinking of the noir form."[9] After being plunged into the river, Laure resurfaces in Lily's bathtub, waking up to the realization that she just had "a film noir dream," as if "it's late at night, you're watching *Double Indemnity* in bed [as Laure did in the Cannes hotel room], you fall asleep, and you dream *Double Indemnity*!"[10] No wonder Laure's words and actions repeat those of Phyllis, since Laure is dreaming what it would be like to be a femme fatale in a film noir—and discovering thereby how her life would end. What Laure realizes is that, by putting the gun in Nicolas's hand and having him fire it into his own heart, she was in fact shooting herself. Killing him didn't save her; it only brought on other men—Black Tie and Racine—to throw her off the bridge. Similarly, when Laure let Lily—her lookalike—shoot herself, Laure might as well have pulled the trigger on her own head, for stealing the dead woman's identity did not save her; it only started her down a predatory path that led to her own ruin.

Before Lily killed herself, Laure had heard an announcer on TV say, "If you could see the future in a crystal ball . . . or in a dream, would you change it?" Now Laure has had this dream, and she is presented with the possibility of deviating from the femme fatale role that was scripted for her. "Most noir ends very badly," De Palma noted.[11] "Live like a Scorpion. Die like a Scorpion" is how he described the moral of Laure's "prophetic nightmare."[12] But he added that "once I had finished off the noir dream I said, 'Well, what would happen if I turned this around 180 degrees?' Things that we learn in our lives, if we know the history, are we doomed to repeat them? Well, I don't feel that. I think you learn from your experiences; that's what wisdom is supposed to be about."[13]

Lily enters the apartment and gets the gun to commit suicide, while Laure hides in the alcove as before. But this time when Laure is torn between distance and compassion, between seeing Lily as an "other" and acting to save Lily as a version of herself, Laure chooses the more empathetic option. Emerging from her hiding place and grabbing the gun, Laure points it at Lily, an action which we see from the latter's perspective, as if the gun were pointed at us. (Since the two women are lookalikes and played by the same actress, Laure's pointing the gun at Lily is just one step removed from Lily's pointing the gun at herself, but that one step is important for Lily to gain a critical perspective that helps keep her from committing suicide.)

Laure tells Lily, "I just dreamt your future—and mine, too. And all I know is, if there's a snowball's chance in hell of any of that shit happening, we're gonna change it right here." "I" and "you" have become "we." What Laure realizes is that, when Lily was pointing a gun at her own head, she was also holding a gun to Laure's. The two women are connected, for if Laure lets Lily pull the trigger on herself, this will also seal Laure's own fate. If she fails to meet her moral responsibility to save Lily, Laure, too, will die, as though she were shooting herself in the head if she allows Lily to commit suicide. Now, by taking the gun and pointing it at Lily, Laure shocks her—and herself—into choosing life. "Do I pull the trigger?" Laure asks, and Lily decides to go on living.

Significantly, the sense of survival and redemption achieved at the end of this film is presented in terms of female connectedness. In saving Lily, Laure tells her that "I'm your fucking fairy godmother." Before Laure emerged from the alcove to help prevent Lily's suicide, we saw wall photos of Lily with her daughter—photos that Laure had looked at very closely. Lily had been pulled toward suicide by the feeling that she couldn't go on living without her daughter, who died in an accident. In becoming Lily's "fairy godmother," Laure establishes a maternal connection with her like the one that Lily had with her daughter. Lily's grief over her dead daughter seems to bring out the mother in Laure, her own desire for a compassionate connection with another woman, and this could be what finally tips the balance in that crucial moment when Laure decides to leave her hiding place and take empathetic action to save Lily.

Because Laure prevents her lookalike's suicide and does not steal her identity, Lily is able to live out her own life, including meeting her future husband on the plane to America. But, while on her way to the airport in a truck, Lily gives the driver a crystal ball pendant that she had originally bought for her daughter so that, by hanging it on his rearview mirror, he will continue to feel connected to *his* daughter: "When you're on the road, your little girl will always be with you." Some time later, Veronica meets Laure outside a Parisian café to give her an aluminum briefcase filled with cash that Veronica got from fencing the diamonds that she and Laure stole together. Laure leaves with the briefcase, but she has only gone halfway down the street before turning back to see that the vengeful Black Tie and Racine have found Veronica and are manhandling her. Will they then proceed to throw Veronica in front of a truck, as Laure foresaw in her nightmare vision of the future?

Not this time. As Laure covers her mouth with her hand in sympathy for her girlfriend's suffering, a ray of sun ricochets off her aluminum briefcase and hits the crystal ball pendant on the truck's rearview mirror. The light reflected off the pendant momentarily blinds the truck driver, causing him to swerve his vehicle in a way that misses Veronica and crushes Black Tie and Racine instead. The two women exchange empathetic smiles that they are both still alive, whereas their vengeful male pursuers are dead.

The film's conclusion is an extended metaphor for the power of female connectedness. Because Laure saved her girlfriend from being shot by Black Tie during the jewel heist, Veronica is there at the end to give Laure the briefcase of money for the fenced diamonds. Because Laure saved Lily from commit-ting suicide, keeping alive the spirit of motherly connection even after Lily had lost her daughter, Lily was able to give the crystal ball pendant to the truck driver in the belief that it would help him feel connected when he had to be apart from his daughter. Because Laure's aluminum briefcase and Lily's daughter's crystal ball pendant are both there to catch the sunlight, Veronica is saved from being thrown by Black Tie and Racine in front of the truck, which swerves to hit them instead.

Male aggression self-destructs, while female alliances save. This is what Laure saw in her prophetic nightmare—that if she became a phallic woman, a predator like the men, she would in effect be shooting herself, dying from her own scorpion sting. By heeding the message of her film noir dream ("If you could see the future in a crystal ball . . ."), Laure is able to come through to the light, to survive by means of the connections she makes with other women. The crystal ball is itself a symbol of the links among all the females: Lily's love for her daughter (the pendant), Laure's love for Lily (the suicide foreseen and prevented), and Laure's love for Veronica (the light bouncing off Laure's brief-case to illuminate the crystal ball pendant and save Veronica's life).

De Palma has certainly made films with strong female characters before, including ones with at least implicit alliances between women (Grace and Danielle in *Sisters*, Sue and Carrie in *Carrie*, Liz and Kate in *Dressed to Kill*), but *Femme Fatale* marks the first time that this director has placed such emphasis on the moral strength and redemptive consequences of female soli-darity. Could there be something new in De Palma's life that accounts for this change? We know that De Palma has always felt guilty about having been a passive witness to his brother Bart's suffering, even though Brian was really too young at the time to intervene. Unlike Brian with Bart, Laure, after remain-ing a mere onlooker the first time, gets a second chance and acts to save Lily. But this is an old De Palma dilemma, a sense of guilt that he has been trying to overcome for some time. What's new is the switch in gender from male to female, which seems to have some connection with the rescue's success.

Perhaps there is an autobiographical clue in what the truck driver says to Lily about wanting to find a birthday present, like the crystal ball pendant, for his daughter's tenth birthday. We recall how upset De Palma was that his parents never celebrated his birthday, which is why, he has said, "I attach such enormous importance to my daughters' birthdays, which I take care to cel-ebrate as they should be."[14] De Palma's daughter, Lolita, turned ten in the year *Femme Fatale* was filmed. When Lily gives her deceased daughter's pendant to the truck driver, it is as though her daughter lives on through his little girl. The gift is a sign of Lily's renewed hope after almost succumbing to a sui-cidal death after the loss of her daughter and her husband. De Palma's first wife, Nancy Allen, has said that she "almost died" as a result of an "[ectopic] pregnancy" and a miscarriage. According to Allen, she and De Palma "never dealt with what I subsequently learned was tremendous grief. A lot of couples split up after there's a loss of a baby. I didn't know that [at the time]. We never talked about it or cried about it."[15] Laure's observation of Lily's suicidal grief over the loss of her daughter and her husband could represent De Palma's belated attempt at understanding his first wife's suffering over the miscarriage and the divorce. And Laure's giving Lily new hope, which leads her to pass her daughter's pendant on to another girl, could be De Palma coming to terms with his own grief and finding solace in the thought of his surviving daughters, Lolita and Piper.

We have spoken of Laure as a "fairy godmother" to Lily, but given that the two are lookalikes of the same age, it might be more accurate to think of them as sisters. (It is also interesting, when we consider De Palma's fascination with doubles, that both *Lily* and *Lolita* have two *l*'s and that Piper has two *p*'s.) Could it be that, by having Laure save Lily, De Palma is imagining a more successful solidarity between the sisters Piper and Lolita than the one that brothers Brian and Bart shared? As we know, all three De Palma brothers were often at odds with one another, engaged in a competition for superiority. Perhaps, in the compassionate collaboration among Veronica, Laure, and Lily, De Palma envisions a different future for his daughters, one where female bonds win out over male rivalry.

As we think about *Femme Fatale*, it is interesting to compare it to another female-centered "dream" version of a film noir, David Lynch's *Mulholland Drive*. In fact, prior to Wargnier, Lynch was the first filmmaker that De Palma asked to be the director who walks the red carpet at Cannes with Veronica on his arm. De Palma has said about Lynch: "We're very close in terms of the territories we occupy. I have the impression of seeing the same thing he does and sharing his thoughts."[16]

Much as Laure in *Femme Fatale* initially models her behavior after that of Barbara Stanwyck in *Double Indemnity*, so *Mulholland Drive*'s Rita takes her name from Rita Hayworth in the film noir *Gilda*. The closeness between Laure and Veronica can be seen when they make love in a translucent bathroom stall. In Lynch's film, Betty (Naomi Watts) first sees Rita (Laura Harring) naked behind a glass shower door, and they later have a lesbian love scene together in bed. Both Laure and Betty dream part of their movies, and both have male characters who try to awaken them: "Hey, pretty girl, time to wake up," the Cowboy tells Betty, while Black Tie says to Laure, "Wake up, bitch, before you die!"

Yet what is dream and what is reality for each woman is significantly different. In real life, Betty, consumed with jealous rage when she finds out that Rita is cheating on her with a male director and has been given a starring movie role, puts a hit on her girlfriend and has her killed. Betty's dream that she has a second chance to show her love for Rita is an escapist fantasy, belied by the fact that Rita is actually already dead. By contrast, Laure has a bad dream of the fatal consequences that will result if she lets Lily shoot herself, one of which is that bad men like Black Tie and Racine will kill Veronica and Laure. In reality, Laure seizes her second chance, preventing Lily's suicide and as a consequence saving Veronica and herself. De Palma allows Laure to learn from her bad dream and change reality, whereas Lynch presents Betty with a second chance that is mere illusion, for, in actuality, her beloved Rita is past saving.

In *Mulholland Drive*, men (Rita's lover, Betty's hit man) come between the women, leading to divisiveness and death, while in *Femme Fatale*, the women remain united, standing and surviving together despite the onslaughts of Black Tie and Racine. De Palma's film is about the redemptive power of female connections. Lynch's film is about realizing that power too late to stop the destructive forces of jealous rivalry and career competitiveness.

Lest it seem as though only the women in *Femme Fatale* can be redeemed, we should note that some of the male characters also appear to change as a result of Laure's prophetic nightmare: either they are seen in a different light after the dream or, like Laure, they actually decide to reform. When Laure meets her future husband, Bruce Watts, in the dream, he says that he started out in computers and then got interested in other things, "like the whole world." It is his desire for "public glory" that leads him to move from Washington, D.C., as the American ambassador to France. When Laure, in fear that she will be recognized and killed by her robbery accomplices, tries to leave her husband rather than return to Paris with him, he beats her up, giving her a black eye—or so she says in the dream.

This nightmare version of Bruce Watts bears some resemblance to De Palma's brother Bruce, who began by building computers and then attempted to gain recognition for solving the world's energy problems. "I will get invited to Washington only after I generate a lot of publicity," Bruce once said.[17] In *Home Movies*, James—the Bruce character—is possessive of and abusive toward his fiancée, Kristina, much as Bruce Watts mistreats Laure. However, in the revised reality that follows the dream, Laure describes Bruce as "a really good guy" and assures Lily that, if she decides not to kill herself, she can have "a wonderful life" with him. Perhaps Laure's more generous view of Bruce reflects a softening in De Palma's own attitude toward his brother, akin to the sympathetic understanding that the director displayed regarding him in *Mission to Mars*.

Another male character in Laure's life, the photographer Nicolas Bardo, is also markedly different in his dream and real-life versions. In the dream,

Nicolas's photos of Laure threaten to expose her in her assumed identity as "Mrs. Watts" to her vengeful robbery accomplices. In one scene, Laure is sitting with Veronica outside a Parisian café. In a split-screen shot, we see Nicolas on the left with his camera pointed at them, while Racine is shown viewing them through binoculars on the right. Will Nicolas sell Laure's photos to the tabloids, using her as a means to make money, much as Black Tie and Racine tried to use her during the robbery and now want to get their diamonds or their money from her? The split-screen shot presenting Nicolas and Racine side by side makes us wonder how different their characters really are. Later, when Laure goes to a hotel, Racine impersonates a passport photographer, his blinding flash in her face going off like gunfire. Will Nicolas's photographic exposure of her also have a killing effect?

Nicolas trails Laure to a red-light district where he snaps pictures of her in the window of a sex shop with another man. It turns out that she is buying a gun, but the scene brings out another dubious side of Nicolas's character, the sense that he is watching her with lustful eyes. Antonio Banderas described Nicolas as a "professional voyeur."[18] In another scene, Nicolas follows Laure to a seedy bar where he and a lecherous sailor named Napoleon both watch her perform a striptease. When the sailor has had enough of being teased and tries to rape Laure on a pool table, Nicolas throws the man off her body, beats him with a pool stick, and then proceeds to make out with her himself, kissing her roughly and taking her from behind while she is bent over the pool table. While he may have saved Laure from being assaulted by the other man, did Nicolas do so in order to protect her or so that he could possess her himself? Much as he was earlier "twinned" in that split-screen shot with the nefarious Racine, so here Nicolas seems to be Napoleon's double—another one of Laure's attackers rather than her savior.

This nightmare version of Nicolas does have violent sex with Laure and he does sell photos of her to a tabloid magazine. Compromised by lust and greed, he is the antihero of a film noir—the lethal counterpart to Laure in her "femme-fatale" mode. Nicolas and Laure end up pointing and firing guns at each other in mutual distrust. However, since she has filled his weapon with blanks, he in effect self-destructs when he fires at her, bringing on her bullet. When Laure goes on to make his death look like a suicide, this only further reveals the fact that, metaphorically, it was exactly that. Moreover, in shooting Nicolas, she might as well have shot herself, for once she has killed the man who could have helped to protect her, Laure is promptly attacked by Black Tie and Racine, who throw her into the river where she drowns.

And yet, just as Laure seems to learn her lesson from the tragic outcome of this bad dream, so Nicolas appears changed when we next see him in reality. Even within the nightmare, Nicolas had sometimes seemed on the verge of an awakening, as when he told Laure that he hated being a paparazzo and wanted to "reinvent myself," referring to a street scene in Paris "with these light reflections" where "I saw something that changed my life." Now, in reality, we see Nicolas in another split-screen shot, but this time he is not "twinned" with the evil Racine and that character's predatory gaze at Laure. Instead, on the left side of the image, Nicolas is on the phone with his agent, *declining* to sell his picture of Laure to the tabloids ("Did you find fuckin' God or something?" his agent asks), while on the right side, some newlyweds wait to have their picture taken in front of a church. That Nicolas refuses to exploit Laure is a sign of the divine goodness within him, a loving care that might make him a perfect match for Laure's own newly reformed character. Nicolas does take photos of Laure, but only because he is looking for the ideal image to complete a photo collage that he is creating on the wall of his apartment. That image comes when sunlight reflects off Laure's aluminum briefcase, ricocheting onto the crystal ball pendant whose blinding light will cause the truck driver to swerve and hit Black Tie and Racine, saving Veronica and Laure.

Whereas the tabloid exploitation of Laure's photo connected Nicolas with greed and lust, his capture of her ideal image for his work of art links him to heavenly grace. Nicolas Bardo is similar to Barton De Palma, the director's beloved brother who for years taught the art of photography to college students. In fact, it was Barton who took the 3,200 photos from which were chosen the ones that make up Nicolas's photo collage. Earlier, we noted that when Laure saves Lily and herself, it is as though Brian imagined being given a second chance to rescue Barton from family abuse and himself from guilt, and this time succeeding. The last thing we see in *Femme Fatale*'s redemptive ending is an image of Laure in the reflected light, having been saved. This image is the final piece needed to perfect Bardo/Barton's photo collage—and to complete Brian's movie. It is an image of redemption for all concerned. "With this picture, Brian got to create a work of art," Barton has said.[19] Brian's images combine with Barton's and Bardo's to envision a happy ending where there was none before.

When Laure gets knocked down in the commotion following the truck accident, Nicolas leaves his camera behind and rushes to her aid, much as Laure had moved from her vantage point in the alcove to take action and save Lily. By transitioning from a mere spectator to an engaged participant, by acting on his compassion, Nicolas proves that he is a worthy match for Laure. (By contrast, when Wanley [Edward G. Robinson] awakes from his film noir dream in *The Woman in the Window*, he decides *not* to get involved with any female who may be a femme fatale.) As Nicolas helps Laure get back on her feet and they take the first tentative steps toward a romantic future together, we see that they are standing in front of a French café called Le Paradis. We recall that Carlito had hoped to join Gail for an "Escape to Paradise," but he was unable to seize his second chance and escape the tragic fate of a film noir gangster. Given the redemptive light that creates a swerve from *Femme Fatale*'s otherwise tragic ending, the future looks brighter for Nicolas and Laure.

Femme Fatale was financed for $35 million, which De Palma scraped together from a variety of sources throughout Europe. Working without Hollywood backing meant that the money was harder to raise, but as a result De Palma did not have to deal with studio interference. He could make the movie exactly the way he wanted, just as he had done in the 1960s and early '70s: "I come from independent cinema, and I can tell you that returning to that way of doing things after so many years made me happy."[20] Thus, he was able to experiment with *Femme Fatale*'s unconventional form, wherein a significant portion of the plot was later revealed to have been a nightmare.

Interestingly, this narrative innovation was at least partly inspired by video games. De Palma, forever interested in the latest technological developments, had found in video games a "way to tell stories in a nonlinear fashion": "Unlike the usual narrative forms where the director takes you from point A to point B, here a range of much more varied trajectories is offered to you. . . . What's going to make a character take this direction and not that one?"[21] As we have seen, De Palma presents this forking path to Laure and explores why she goes down one road and then backs up to take another.

Despite opening to some critical acclaim—Roger Ebert called the film "an exercise in superb style and craftsmanship,"[22] and Armond White praised it as a "flawless breakthrough in form and content"[23]—*Femme Fatale* performed poorly at the box office, returning less than half its cost. Was the film's narrative too tricky for most moviegoers to follow or appreciate? Or perhaps, at least in America, the film's failure was due to its extensive amount of subtitled dialogue. "At first they thought it was a foreign film," De Palma lamented, noting that "the fact that it had subtitles really confused them. The concept that you can't have a film with subtitles without killing it in the marketplace! I was brought up on films with subtitles!"[24] It could be that this latest failure prompted De Palma to turn back to exploring more of the dark side of things in his next film, *The Black Dahlia*—or he may have had more personal reasons for revisiting some of his old obsessions.

CHAPTER 27

The Black Dahlia (2006)

With the possible exception of its somewhat hopeful ending, *The Black Dahlia* shows De Palma plunging back into the nightmarish world of film noir. It could be that the death of his father, which occurred shortly before filming began, brought on a return of troubling family memories in the director's mind. We know that De Palma considered his father to be a commanding, even overbearing figure who was often rather cold and distant—traits which the son traced back to Anthony's traumatic witnessing of horribly injured bodies on the battlefield during World War II. Anthony, who was the son of Italian immigrants, worked as a surgeon until his retirement to Florida, where De Palma would go to visit him. He died in 2005, at the age of 100.

In *The Black Dahlia*, lead character Bucky (Josh Hartnett) has an aged father who is a German immigrant. As Bucky drives up to his father's apartment building and gets out of the car, he sees his father shooting at pigeons from an upstairs window; Bucky is standing right next to the targeted birds. Then, when Bucky enters his father's apartment, the old man points his gun at his son. Later, Bucky is able to relocate his father, who is increasingly suffering from senile dementia, to a retirement home, but his father only glares at him with a strange animosity. As we shall see, this sense of the father as a threat, perhaps rooted in De Palma's past relationship with his father, will be a significant element in *The Black Dahlia*.

In addition to father-son tension, the film also picks up on the kind of fraternal rivalry that formed such a significant part of De Palma's youth. As we recall, Brian and his big brother, Bruce, were forever vying for their parents' affection and contending for the top prize at science fairs. No matter how hard he fought for recognition, Brian always felt that Bruce received all the adulation, partly owing to the fact that as the older brother, Bruce could beat Brian to the punch. Thus, Bruce was lauded for taking third place in the Philadelphia Science Fair, but when a few years later Brian won first prize and even went on to the national finals, the belated younger brother felt that his greater achievement received less recognition.

Brian and Bruce can be compared to Bucky Bleichert and Lee Blanchard (Aaron Eckhart) in *The Black Dahlia*. Bucky and Lee are both ex-boxers who have become detectives. The two work as a team during the Zoot Suit Riots of 1940s Los Angeles that open the film, but it is Lee who gets the lion's share of the publicity for his bravery. (In fact, there are several times during the early part of the film when Lee gets so much attention that Bucky's very presence goes unnoticed.)

Bucky and Lee agree to return to the ring to fight a publicity match as a fundraiser for the police department. When, reflecting on their past lives as boxers, Bucky says that he "never made it up to the big boys' division like [Lee]," it is almost as though young Brian were talking about his own past with Bruce. Of course, most of the money is on Lee to win the publicity match, so Bucky is expected to lose, including throwing the fight if necessary. As Bucky tells Pete, who funnels money to a bookie, "I'm not bettin' on me, Pete. [Lee] Blanchard's the hero here. That's the way the story's supposed to go. I'm just the other guy." (It is interesting that Bucky has this conversation about his own supposed inferiority with Pete, who is played by Gregg Henry, since the talk is very similar to ones that sad-sack Jake had with his false friend Sam, who was also played by Henry, in *Body Double*.) And so, on the night of the match, Bucky and Lee duke it out, with Bucky doing some serious damage to his partner, but in the end Bucky deliberately drops his guard, allowing Lee to deliver some knockout punches.

As we think about the boxing match between Bucky and Lee, we should also consider De Palma's relationship with his directorial "sparring partner," Martin Scorsese. Since 1965, when they worked on their own separate films in adjacent editing bays at New York University, the two directors have been friendly rivals. Before the publicity fight in *The Black Dahlia*, we see the director's credit—"A Brian De Palma Film"—and then Bucky seated in the locker room, preparing to enter the boxing arena. This locker room shot and many of the camera techniques used to film the fight itself, such as the Steadicam moves and the editing of the punches, inevitably recall Scorsese's *Raging Bull*. As if in an attempt to best his rival, De Palma has now made two boxing movies, *Snake Eyes* and *The Black Dahlia*, but the fact is that Scorsese got there first with *Raging Bull*, a film that garnered significantly more media attention and awards. (And if *Snake Eyes* is De Palma's casino movie, Scorsese got there first with *Casino*, made a few years earlier.)

As with the match between Lee and Bucky, De Palma is expected to lose to Scorsese: "That's the way the story's supposed to go"; De Palma is "just the other guy." In casting for *The Black Dahlia*, De Palma even lost his first choice to play the character of Lee, actor Mark Wahlberg, to Scorsese and his film, *The Departed*.

"Every time you think you have an original or great idea, there's always Marty Scorsese!" De Palma has said. "It's like that Western where he's always looking back and these guys are always chasing him."[1] De Palma attempted to beat Scorsese's *Raging Bull* record for a long take with *The Untouchables*, but then Scorsese achieved an even longer sequence-shot in *Goodfellas*, which De Palma sought to outdo in *The Bonfire of the Vanities* and *Snake Eyes*. "Brian never believed he was as successful as Marty," producer George Litto commented. "That made him very uncomfortable."[2] "Scorsese is considered the greatest director of his generation," De Palma said. "He gets a prize every week. They sing his praises all year long; everything he does is applauded. All the critics talk about 'the genius of Martin Scorsese' . . . I don't rank in the same category. When my films come out . . . I get four hundred bad reviews." To his annoyance, De Palma is sometimes mistaken for Scorsese, since both of them have beards. But, De Palma insists, "I believe I was the first to grow a beard."[3] Although he retains a sense of humor about it, De Palma has clearly felt some dismay at having received fewer accolades than Scorsese.

The rivalry between Bucky and Lee for fame and recognition becomes a competition over a young woman named Kay (Scarlett Johansson), Lee's girl-friend. Soon after Lee introduces Kay to Bucky and hears her ask him if *he* has a girlfriend, Lee knocks a man out (a proxy for Bucky?) in the boxing ring. Later, when Lee sees Bucky dancing with Kay and kissing her at a New Year's Eve party, Lee smiles and blows them a kiss, but once their backs are turned, his face is consumed with fury.

Lee moves strangely from promoting the relationship between Bucky and Kay to reacting in a rage against it. It turns out that Lee had a sister who was killed when they were young. Although he was unable to save her, Lee did rescue Kay from a gangster named Bobby DeWitt, who had carved his initials into her back and was pimping her out. As Bucky discovers when he moves in with them, Lee's relationship with Kay has been entirely platonic. Despite her desire for him, Lee seems to regard her as a substitute for his sister, whose purity must be preserved. Yet Lee also throws Bucky together with Kay, as if wanting to watch what happens while simultaneously enraged at the result. Lee is at once voyeuristically excited at the prospect of Kay (or his sister) being taken by a man and deeply disturbed by it. He is torn by an internal conflict over his own desire, which he fears might be predatory, and his compassion for the woman, whom he would like to save from victimization.

This is why Lee becomes obsessed with the lust-murder of Elizabeth Short (dubbed the "Black Dahlia"), the wannabe starlet who ended up in stag films before having her face slashed from ear to ear and her body cut in half. As Lee and Bucky view one of these stag films at police headquarters and see Elizabeth tied up and tortured with a dildo, Lee has a look of strange fascination on his face, conflicted between lust for her and rage at her assailant. When Lee goes to the movies with Bucky and Kay and watches a scene where a woman is menaced by a man whose face has been carved into a perpetual grin (Conrad Veidt as Gwynplaine in *The Man Who Laughs*), Lee is spellbound, haunted by the wounds linking this scene to Elizabeth's mutilated face and to Kay's scarred back. Lee is torn between a need to protect these women and a desire to possess them himself, to mark them sexually as his.

And Bucky, who is watching these films alongside his "big brother," Lee, is catching the same obsession, experiencing the same internal conflict. When Bucky later sees Kay's near-nakedness exposed in an open doorway, revealing her former pimp's initials carved into her back, he is both appalled and excited. Bucky is like a young boy getting a glimpse of something forbidden and wondering if this is what sex means. "Who are these men who feed on others?" he thinks. "What do they feel when they cut their names into somebody else's life?" Sexually inexperienced, Bucky seems to be wondering if he will grow up to be this kind of man, if he, too, has predatory desires. (It is worth noting that the pimp's initials on Kay's back—"B.D.," for Bobby DeWitt—are strangely similar to Bucky's own: "D.B.," for Dwight ["Bucky"] Bleichert. "B.D." are also the initials of Brian De Palma.) Although Kay has expressed her desire for him, Bucky has resisted having sex with her, ostensibly because she is the girlfriend of his partner. But like Lee, Bucky seems to associate sex with lust and degradation, so his avoidance of contact with Kay may be due to a need to keep her pure and protected—from men like himself.

Bucky is similar to Denis, the character De Palma patterned after himself in *Home Movies*, and Lee is like James, the character based on De Palma's brother Bruce, with the Kay equivalent in that film being Kristina (played by Nancy Allen, De Palma's girlfriend at the time and soon to be his wife). Like Lee in competition with Bucky, James is physically dominant and vainglorious, engaged in a macho rivalry with his brother, Denis. However, despite James's much-vaunted masculinity, he won't sleep with his fiancée, Kristina. James rescued her from a life of stripping and prostitution dictated by her pimp, "Bunny." Associating sex with degradation and viewing Kristina as a mother-substitute, James insists that she remain pure. However, James also contrives scenarios whereby Kristina will be subjected to sexual encounters, as when he has her dress like a whore and then be filmed from outside a bedroom window while a biker tries to assault her. This kind of scene suggests that, while outwardly protective, James is actually tempted by the contrary desire to ravage and possess Kristina.

And James's younger brother, Denis, is tempted right along with him. It is James who first introduces Denis to Kristina and who manages to leave his brother alone with her on numerous occasions. Although young Denis idealizes Kristina as a kind of mother figure, he also lusts after her, as when he spies on her half-naked through the keyhole of a door or when he watches her in the window as that biker is trying to strip and attack her. Denis, a budding filmmaker, had earlier trained his camera's eye on a woman undressing in another window. Thus, given the many ways in which Bucky and Lee resemble Denis and James—the Brian and Bruce characters—from De Palma's *Home Movies*, it seems fair to conclude that these scenes from *The Black Dahlia* may well have an autobiographical resonance for De Palma.

In addition to the stag films, Bucky and Lee also watch screen tests of Elizabeth (Mia Kirshner) auditioning for a part in a potentially legitimate film, attempting to please an off-screen director who is voiced by De Palma himself. These tests begin with a naively optimistic Elizabeth telling transparent lies about having impressed David O. Selznick with her reading of Scarlett O'Hara's "I'll never be hungry again" speech from *Gone with the Wind*. She is innocently flirtatious with the director, laughing with him at her own foibles as if she could somehow cajole him into being Selznick to her Scarlett, and at times we may hear hints of compassion for her vulnerability in the director's voice. After all, De Palma himself had once come to Hollywood as a starry-eyed youth hoping that his first film for a major studio would be a success: "Imagine: walking along Sunset [Boulevard] and staying at the Beverly Hills Hotel at age twenty-nine. You think that your dreams have come true! All the magic of Hollywood was still there. The incredible opulence, the luxury cars, the fantastic women."[4]

But then, as we know, the neophyte director felt betrayed by the film's star, whose unhappiness contributed to De Palma's being fired from *Get to Know Your Rabbit*: "I was young and I hadn't yet understood how the studios function. I believed their lies; I let myself be manipulated; and I lost control of the film."[5] Having had some firsthand experience with "the dark side of the Hollywood myth factory,"[6] De Palma considers himself "very conscious of what actors have to endure during auditions, and of how cruel the Hollywood system can be."[7]

It is this cruel side that eventually comes out in the director who auditions Elizabeth, as he induces her to beg for a departed lover's return, mocks her ability to "play" sadness, and then implies that if she wants the part, she must succumb to the casting couch: "You look like you have a helluva lot of fun. . . . I get it [love] about five times a night." As the director's voice grows increasingly lecherous and demeaning, the movie she is trying out for comes to seem less like a Hollywood production and more like a stag film. Much as Bucky and Lee find themselves torn between compassion and predatory lust, so De Palma here plays a director who is similarly conflicted.

Thus, Bucky, Lee, and the director of the screen test all share an obsession with Elizabeth, the Black Dahlia. Bucky even begins to date a Black Dahlia lookalike, Madeleine (Hilary Swank), with whom he has torrid sex at a cheap motel—the kind of sex he abstains from having with Kay, the woman he idealizes.

Bucky's visits to Madeleine's family, the Linscotts, provide De Palma with an opportunity to present a grotesquely caricatured version of his own family. One of the first things that the father, Emmett Linscott, says to Bucky, the ex-boxer, is that Bucky *could* have been a contender, reminding us that De Palma's father was disappointed in him for not pursuing a successful career in medicine or science. Mealtimes at the De Palma home were tense, charged with an atmosphere of competition among the brothers—Brian, Bart, and Bruce—for their father's approbation. Dinner at the Linscott house involves a similar competition between the daughters, Martha and Madeleine. "Maddy's my pretty one," Emmett says, "but Martha's my certified genius," and we recall how De Palma's father, Anthony, often spoke of Bruce's "brilliant mind,"[8] considering him "the family genius,"[9] while minimizing the achievements of the other brothers. Like Bart, who became a painter and photographer, Martha is an artist, and she sketches an obscene drawing of Bucky and Madeleine having sex. Later, Madeleine tells Bucky that "Martha was always jealous of me." We know that De Palma has referred to "sexual things you don't understand as a teenager," such as when "you look through a door and see . . . your brother with a girl,"[10] so the brothers' competitiveness may well have included jealousy.

Madeleine refers to her mother as "a snob," and indeed Ramona Linscott turns down her nose at Bucky's lowly origins, and despite the family's apparent affluence which includes a luxurious mansion with maidservants, she criticizes Emmett for his failure to get a prestigious street named after her, and accuses him of having married her for her father's money. De Palma's mother, Vivienne, was a lawyer's daughter, whereas Anthony was the son of an immigrant hatter. Even in their early years, when the family still lived in what De Palma has called "a New Jersey Catholic ghetto," they already had a live-in maid, and De Palma "suspected that my mother was a social climber"[11] whose class aspirations prompted a move to Philadelphia and a conversion to Protestantism so that the family could fit in with others of higher standing. (Regarding the conversion, De Palma later found out that it was Vivienne's father who first changed religions.)

Ramona puts on a respectable front, but deep down she is terribly depressed, an alcoholic and a prescription pill addict in response to her husband's infidelity, a betrayal which ultimately drives her to commit suicide. Vivienne's discovery of Anthony's adultery resulted in a suicide attempt from an overdose of pills, though fortunately she survived. Besides her addictions, another way that Ramona copes with her husband's cheating is to have an affair with his best friend, George. In the absence of her husband, Vivienne channeled her affections toward her son Bruce. "My father's life was elsewhere; he was rarely home," De Palma recalled. "My mother was absorbed with my oldest brother."[12] Though there is no reason to believe that the relationship between Vivienne and Bruce was sexual, it was intense: "My mother was very much in love with him," De Palma said. "My other older brother, Bart, and myself were basically not paid the attention we thought we deserved because of my mother's infatuation with my older brother, and that never really changed."[13]

Like the mother Ramona, the father Emmett also has a relevance to De Palma's home life. Emmett, a war veteran and a real-estate tycoon, celebrated his success by shooting the family dog, Balto, when the animal fetched him the morning paper with news of his first million. Emmett then had his war buddy, George, disembowel and stuff Balto. When Emmett finds out that Ramona has been sleeping with George and that Madeleine is really George's daughter, Emmett carves up his buddy's face so that it will not remind him of Madeleine's. Emmett wants Madeleine to be his and his alone, a possessiveness which includes kissing her on the mouth. George, deprived of his daughter Madeleine, sees her lookalike Elizabeth as she is making a stag film and feels that same combination of protectiveness and predatory desire that most of the male characters feel toward the Black Dahlia. Ramona, who has been having an affair with George, finds him with Elizabeth and is overcome by jealous rage. She enlists George's aid in slashing Elizabeth's face and then in bisecting and disemboweling her body.

Anthony was a surgeon during and after the war, a man whose success involved cutting into bodies. As we know, the teenage De Palma witnessed a number of these bloody operations: "I've seen my father amputate legs and open people up."[14] Through the destructive character of Emmett, who is himself almost certainly a victim of the war, De Palma imagines the psychological damage done by Anthony to his sons, particularly Bruce and Brian himself, who idolized and emulated their father. If George participates in slashing Elizabeth's face, it is only after his own face has been carved by Emmett and after Emmett had him cut into Balto. Speaking to Emmett about George, Ramona says, "You did him enough damage!" George's relation to Emmett is like that of Bruce to his father, Anthony. In fact, we learn that George's father was a famous surgeon, just as Anthony was. If George "liked to touch dead things," that destructive desire seems traceable back to Emmett, who first involved him in ghoulish deeds and gave him the wound he would then inflict on others. We should note that Anthony wrote a medical thriller called *The Anatomist* about "a killer necrophiliac"[15] and that he once expressed concern that "Brian will steal my ideas and make them into movies."[16] Rather, the stabbings and slashings in such films as *Murder à la Mod*, *Sisters*, *Dressed to Kill*, *Blow Out*, *Body Double*, and *Raising Cain* might more accurately be described as De Palma's attempt to deal with the damage of his father's influence, with *The Black Dahlia* marking another return to this disturbing family history.

It is not only the father's influence but the mother's, too, that can have a traumatic impact. As we saw, Emmett got George to stuff Balto as a monument to his own ego, and Emmett mutilated George out of jealousy over Ramona and Madeleine. But it was Ramona who took George as her lover when Emmett proved unfaithful, thus opening George up to Emmett's jealous attack, and Ramona also enlisted George in the slashing and disembowelment of Elizabeth. Referring to his own childhood, De Palma has said that "I see the family as a structure that brings about the manipulation and destruction of the individual."[17] He added that "certain parents use their kids as buffers in confrontations which could shred them. That's what I experienced in my family. And that's the dark side of one's upbringing."[18] When Lee finds out about the Linscott parents' involvement in Elizabeth's murder (Emmett paid her to meet with George, and Ramona killed her with George's help), it is not the father or the mother who goes after Lee to ensure his silence. Instead, it is the daughter, Madeleine, and the "son," George, who do their parents' dirty work, acting out their destructive family legacy. George strangles Lee with a rope and Madeleine cuts his throat with a knife, both of them carrying on the family tradition of injuring another's face and body.

And since Bucky Bleichert, arriving just a little too late to save his partner, is the traumatized witness to Lee Blanchard's murder, we have another recurrence of Brian's childhood failure to save his brother Bart, which, as we know, caused such lasting damage to his psyche: "There was a brutality that ran rampage over the weaker ones in my family. That was true of my father, my mother and my older brother Bruce. I was 10, my other brother Bart was 12, he was very sensitive and vulnerable, and I wanted to protect him from such rage. But I was never able to do it because I was a child."[19]

Bucky's guilt is intensified by the feeling that one reason he may not have acted in time to save his partner was a jealous desire to get Lee out of the way so that Bucky could have Kay. "I saw him there," Bucky confesses to her after Lee's murder. "I couldn't move. I didn't move. . . . I could've saved him." Ostensibly to console each other in their grief, Bucky and Kay then make love, but he is also fulfilling his urge to possess her, now that his partner and rival is no longer an obstacle. As Madeleine later says to Bucky, revealing his darkest desires, "if it weren't for me [killing Lee], you wouldn't have had the balls to fuck your partner's girl."

If Bucky's faith in his own virtue is undermined, so is his belief in Lee's and Kay's goodness. Bucky finds out that Lee, the "brother officer" he idolized, was far from being an untarnished hero. Lee jailed DeWitt for bank robbery and rescued Kay from him, but it turns out that Lee also stole money from DeWitt and, in a sense, "stole" Kay from him, too. Lee's altruism was severely compromised by self-interest, making him not so very different from the gangster he arrested. And Kay not only knew about Lee's corruption and was living off the money he took, she also came on to Bucky, exhibiting her willingness to sleep with him even while Lee was still alive. Kay's behavior sullies Bucky's idealized view of her, making him fear that she might indeed be the kind of whore that DeWitt used to pimp out.

Losing faith in others and in himself, Bucky is increasingly tainted by the corruption that surrounds him and tempted to give in to his worst impulses. He leaves Kay and goes to Madeleine, the Black Dahlia lookalike with whom he can have degrading sex, making her the object of his predatory desires. As Kay says to him about Madeleine, "She looks like that dead girl! How sick are you?" Even when Bucky finds out that Madeleine murdered his partner, he is still tempted to sleep with her, perhaps feeling that the two of them belong in hell together since she acted out his hidden desire to see Lee—his rival—dead. Bucky teeters on the edge of a total surrender to his darkest desires, his urge to take lustful possession of Madeleine. "I think you'd rather fuck me than kill me," she says, as Bucky points a gun at her. "You'd never shoot me. Don't forget who I look like, because that girl—that sad, dead bitch—she's all you have." Will Bucky let himself be dragged down into degradation, succumbing to his own desire to claim Madeleine as his sex object?

Bucky resists being seduced by Madeleine into further sin. Instead of sinking with her into bed, he shoots her, eliminating the evil femme fatale and getting justice for his partner, Lee, whom she murdered. Leaving the vanquished Madeleine behind, dead in her slinky black dress on the floor of a cheap motel, Bucky returns to "good girl" Kay who, blonde and wearing a white top, welcomes him back into the warm light of her home.

But the film's ending is more equivocal than this account makes it seem. Madeleine's supine corpse is disturbingly similar to the dead body of the Black Dahlia, especially since the two women are lookalikes. In killing Madeleine, Bucky does not so much distance himself from the Black Dahlia murder as repeat it. In his violent attempt to separate himself from sin, he becomes a murderer, leaving behind yet another female corpse.

And is he of such sterling character as to be justified in condemning Madeleine to death for her sins? One begins to wonder whether Bucky's shooting of Madeleine is a form of scapegoating, a way of seeing all the evil as hers so that he can remain blind to his own. This suspicion is given further credence when, just before he shoots Madeleine, Bucky twice silences her on the subject of Lee and Kay. "You don't talk about them," he insists, as if he wanted to block out any negative truths about those he idealized, even though he has since learned a great deal about their compromised characters. In killing Madeleine, Bucky also represses the dark truths she is telling about him, including his jealous—and potentially murderous—rivalry with Lee over possession of Kay.

Even more doubt about Bucky is cast at the end. Right before joining Kay inside her warm home, he has a nightmarish hallucination of the Black Dahlia's corpse on the lawn, with a crow flying down to her body. The crow is a symbol of his own predatory desires, the kind that led him to lust after Madeleine, but Bucky *closes his eyes to this vision*, repressing all recognition of the dark impulses within him. When Bucky opens his eyes again, the crow and the body are gone, the truth having been erased. As Bucky enters the house to be with Kay, he closes the door behind him, shutting out the Black Dahlia's body as definitively as he left behind Madeleine's corpse. What kind of life can Bucky expect to have with Kay if it is built on a foundation of lies about their true characters? Bucky *needs* to be haunted by his past misdeeds if he is going to know himself well enough not to repeat them with Kay.

And yet there is the equal and opposite danger of being dragged down by terrible truths, of being overwhelmed by surrounding corruption, of being haunted to death by evils committed in the past by others or by oneself. Perhaps remembering the past so as not to repeat it needs to be balanced with a certain forgetting of history's horrors in order to survive them and have some hope for a future. "I think that if you want to continue living, you must try to forget," De Palma has said. "It's a little like how I see our childhood. It can have a bad influence on our adult conduct. Your parents have communicated neuroses to you, which lead you in turn to be destructive. But at a certain moment you have to be able to wipe the slate clean and say, 'Okay, I get it: they did a very bad job taking care of me, but am I going to spend the rest of my life punishing and destroying myself, or am I going to move on?'"[20]

As we have seen, the negative history pressing in on Bucky is similar in many respects to De Palma's own family history, and by ending *The Black Dahlia* in the way that he does, De Palma would seem to be speaking about his own need to forget certain past traumas—damage inflicted by family members on him, and guilt over his own damaging weaknesses and failures—in order to survive and have faith in a future. It could be that to some extent

Bucky must remain willfully ignorant of Kay's flaws, idealizing her as a perfectly loving light so that he can continue to believe in himself as lovable and not be overcome by guilt over his dark desires. As he approaches Kay's home, Bucky thinks of her and Lee as "ones I'd loved and ones who'd loved me, people I'd betrayed and people I needed to protect. And for the first time in my life, I had people that knew that, for the briefest of times, in the darkest of places, I had been so, so good at some things." Bucky knows that the three of them are all deeply compromised, but he chooses to believe in them as a way of having faith in himself. He chooses to imagine himself as loved, despite the betrayals he's committed. He regains a sense of his own goodness by believing that others recognize it in him.

With worldwide grosses coming in at just under what the film had cost ($50 million), *The Black Dahlia* was not profitable. It seems likely that the film's redemptive ending was not enough "light at the end of the tunnel" for most mainstream viewers, given the two hours of dark crime that preceded it, including bloody murder and the perverse horrors of the Linscotts' family history. Yet, even if it limited his audience, De Palma insisted on confronting viewers with the bisected body of the Black Dahlia and making them think about the predatory desires that led to this true crime. Recall that De Palma had wanted to end his first Hollywood film, *Get to Know Your Rabbit*, by having that film's hero (pretend to) saw a rabbit in half on live television as a way of forcing viewers to face the bloody devastation caused by the Vietnam War. Now, twenty-five years later, *The Black Dahlia* presented the image of Elizabeth's severed corpse as a way to call attention to the sexploitation and victimization of women. Undeterred by public reluctance to consider this difficult subject, De Palma would take it up again in his next film, *Redacted*, which deals with the lust-murder of a woman during the Iraq War.

CHAPTER 28

Redacted (2007)

Based on an actual 2006 incident, *Redacted* tells the story of a squad of American soldiers during the Iraq War who rape and murder an Iraqi girl named Farah (Zahra Zubaidi). The correspondences between this film and *Casualties of War* are remarkable. In each case, the troops do not know why they are fighting their war and they have trouble distinguishing friend from foe. An African-American officer—Brownie in *Casualties*, Sweet (Ty Jones) in *Redacted*—warns an inexperienced soldier not to accept fruit from the local children. Brownie is later shot down by a sniper, and Sweet is blown up by an IED. Feeling that the locals aided and abetted the attack, the squad determines to take revenge by raping a civilian girl. In *Casualties*, the conscience-stricken Eriksson tries to convince the other men not to commit the rape, but they do so anyway. Meserve and Clark are the leaders, with Hatcher a willing participant and Diaz browbeaten into joining them. In *Redacted*, it is McCoy (Rob Devaney) who tries and fails to stop the rape, which is committed by Flake (Patrick Carroll) and Rush (Daniel Stewart Sherman). Another soldier, Salazar (Izzy Diaz), participates for a time by holding the girl down but then flees the scene. In both movies, the troops eventually murder the girl in an attempt to cover up their crime.

If *Redacted* seems like a rerun of the previous film, it is no accident: the repetition is the point. "Once again a senseless war has produced a senseless tragedy," De Palma has said. "I told this story years ago in my film *Casualties of War*. But the lessons from the Vietnam War have gone unheeded."[1] De Palma first read about the Vietnam rape and murder in a 1969 *New Yorker* article, but it was not until 1989 that he made a movie about it—many years after the war's official end in 1975. Although De Palma had filmed some black comedies—*Greetings* (1968) and *Hi, Mom!* (1970)—that opposed the draft and that showed one soldier's predatory lust for a Vietcong woman, these were only indirectly "war films." (*Redacted* alludes to two other such films that were sometimes considered to be indirectly about Vietnam. By showing some ants attacking a scorpion in *Redacted*, De Palma refers to Sam Peckinpah's *The Wild Bunch* [1969], which was ostensibly a Western but which showed how escalating violence, including the use of a machine gun, ultimately proves fatal to both sides. *Redacted* also features the music of Handel's "Sarabande" from Stanley Kubrick's *Barry Lyndon* [1975], a film about the mutual destruction caused by war that was set in the eighteenth century.)

Having been in a sense too late with *Casualties* to make a difference in the Vietnam War, De Palma gets a second chance with *Redacted*, which he makes as a blatant attempt to intervene in the Iraq War. This time there will be no indirection or belatedness. De Palma will confront viewers with the casualties of war while that war is still being fought, even if the U.S. government attempts to keep such images out of the public eye. "The true story of our Iraq War has been redacted from the Main Stream Corporate Media," De Palma argued. "If we are going to cause such disorder then we must face the horrendous images that are the consequences of these actions. Once we saw them in Vietnam our citizens protested and brought that misguided conflict to an end. Let's hope the images from this film have the same effect."[2]

It is interesting that *Redacted*'s voice of conscience, McCoy, the character who tries without success to save Farah from being raped, is named Barton in the original script. As we know, De Palma has been haunted for years by his childhood failure to save his brother Barton from the abuse he suffered. If *Redacted* represents De Palma's attempt to save the civilians (from pain and death) and the soldiers (from guilt) that he could not save in the Vietnam War, perhaps it is also an attempt to save his brother and himself, to imagine a rewriting of *their* past.

There may be another family connection in the fact that, by this time in his life, De Palma now has a teenage daughter (Lolita, born in 1991). The director has mentioned that he was influenced by his daughter's Web surfing when he created the multimedia form of *Redacted*, and he has also noted that several of the film's webcam scenes were shot in the New York apartment he keeps for when she visits, but the significance of his daughter could well be more profound than that. Is it mere coincidence that two of his most recent films both end with the violated bodies of fifteen-year-old girls—Elizabeth in *The Black Dahlia* and Farah in *Redacted*? De Palma's empathy for female suffering and his drive to prevent it seem to have taken on a new urgency, as it must be all too easy for him to imagine his own daughter, who is about the same age, as the victim of such assaults. The elegiac tone of *Casualties of War* is replaced in *Redacted* by a sense of present danger, a warning that these attacks need to be stopped now.

De Palma's connection to his daughter may also account for another difference between the two films: the prominent role played by the girl's father in *Redacted*. In *Casualties*, when Oahn is abducted by the soldiers, her mother runs out to give her her scarf. In *Redacted*, Farah attempts to give her father his jacket when he is dragged from their home; now, it is the link between father and daughter that is emphasized. The rape and murder occur in the father's forced absence, and De Palma highlights the man's pain and remorse over his inability to be there to protect his family. (Farah also has a little sister who is killed in the attack; De Palma has two daughters, Lolita and the younger Piper.) "When you're a father, your children being taken is your greatest fear," De Palma has said. "It's as though there was an attack on you. For the first time, you really have something to lose."[3]

The most significant difference between *Casualties* and *Redacted* lies in their endings. Eriksson has the courage to defy his superiors, who want the crime covered up because it reflects badly on the military. He brings charges against his fellow squad members, facing them in open court. He also makes a public confession of his failure to stop the rape or the murder. Although he does so belatedly—he is too late to save Oahn—Eriksson finally acts to do the right thing in bringing the perpetrators to justice and in acknowledging his own partial responsibility for the crime. The film grants him a measure of forgiveness and redemption in having a young Vietnamese woman, who looks like Oahn, convey an implicit understanding of his anguish and offer him a sense of hope in the end—the possibility that both Americans and Vietnamese will some day be able to overcome the past and live in peace. This redemptive ending was in keeping with De Palma's belief that "what one hopes one learns with age is wisdom, and not to repeat the mistakes that were in the past."

But, according to De Palma, "that doesn't seem to be the lesson we've learned from Vietnam,"[4] for with the Iraq War, "it's as if history were repeating itself."[5] *Redacted* shows that De Palma's faith in our ability to learn from the past has been shaken. Unlike Eriksson, McCoy is at first too afraid to openly defy the military establishment. Instead, he recounts his squad's misdeeds in an anonymous YouTube video, with his face disguised. Then, when he is questioned during the ensuing investigation, McCoy seems to crumble in front of his interrogators, who cast doubt on his account of events. De Palma had deleted an extended scene from *Casualties of War* where Eriksson is interrogated. The fact that this kind of scene is included in *Redacted* seems a sign that De Palma has grown more pessimistic about the ability of the individual to stand up against Establishment forces.

Rather than the compassionate Vietnamese woman who gives Eriksson a moment of grace at the end, the people who surround McCoy offer him no respite from his pain. At a homecoming party being filmed by a friend, McCoy's wife kisses him as if to provide a romantic scene for the camera. She seems to want him to be the way he was before he went to Iraq, but he cannot. The friend requests that McCoy tell "a war story" and another asks, "Did you kill anybody?" They seem bloodthirsty and oblivious to his pain. McCoy, needing to unburden himself of guilt and desperate for some understanding, then launches into an account of the rape-murder and of his own inaction, but he is met only with uncomprehending sadness on the part of his wife and with repressive cheer from his friends.

The friend behind the camera—unseen but voiced by De Palma himself—insists that "this is the celebration of a war hero" and has McCoy and his wife pose together for a snapshot of their "happy" reunion. The film freeze-frames on their forced smiles, an emblem of the false images and the lies that have been spread about this war by the media. Perhaps De Palma, by playing the man behind the camera that takes this image, is critiquing himself for his earlier optimism at the end of *Casualties of War*—an optimism that now seems naïve in light of the Iraq War.

The film concludes with a section entitled "Collateral Damage," which shows photos of the bodies of actual Iraqi civilians, including many children, who were maimed or killed—photos that have gone largely unseen in news coverage of this war. For legal reasons, the faces of the victims have been partially obscured by black bars over their eyes, but this only serves to emphasize the extent to which such images of civilian suffering have been barred from public view. The penultimate photo shows a father holding his young daughter against his shoulder. With his back to us, he is looking out at the black smoke rising from an explosion in the distance. His daughter's face, looking at us, is torn and bloody, and her eyes are covered with a black bar which seems connected with the black smoke, as if to stress the fact that her father could not save her from the horrible impact of the explosion.

The last image is of Farah's dead body after her rape and murder. Because no photo of the actual victim of this crime has been released to the public, this image is a staged reconstruction, a way of bringing to light what has heretofore been hidden. De Palma slowly zooms in on Farah's violated body; her eyes are open, confronting the viewer. McCoy had said that "I have these snapshots in my brain that are burned in there forever, and I don't know what the fuck I'm gonna do about them."

In place of the young Vietnamese woman whose forgiveness brings healing and closure to *Casualties of War*'s redemptive ending, *Redacted* confronts us with traumatic images of continued suffering caused by an ongoing war, including the horrific sight of a young Iraqi woman's corpse. These are the snapshots that De Palma wants to have burned into our brains. It could be that such an ending is entirely pessimistic, an angry indictment of those who didn't—and never will—learn the lessons of Vietnam. But surely buried somewhere in the anger and despair is the hope that, when people *see* the truth, they will take action—if only for the sake of their own daughters.

Despite some significant critical praise (De Palma received his first-ever invitation to the New York Film Festival and won the Best Director prize at the Venice Film Festival), *Redacted* was not seen by many viewers. When the major studios passed on distributing it, the film received only a limited theatrical release in the U.S., grossing a mere $65,000. Worldwide, the film recouped only $780,000 of its $5 million cost. "What I didn't think was that nobody would want to see *Redacted*," De Palma commented, adding that "even the good reviews said, 'Well, this is very difficult to watch.'"[6] Back in 2006, De Palma had told an interviewer, "I'm amazed ... there are not people out there making these incredibly angry anti-war movies. How come? ... You'd have to make it for no money and you'd probably have to make it in Europe and get it independently financed."[7] When independent HDNet Films approached De Palma about filming a high-def movie on a subject of his choice, he took immediate action and made *Redacted*, doing "everything very fast: not in two years, but conceived, cast, shot, edited, released in nine months."[8] At least De Palma could take solace from the fact that he had used his directorial skills in support of a cause he believed in, whether or not his film succeeded in raising consciousness about the war.

Five years would pass before the appearance of another De Palma film. "I did not want to work for a few years," he said. "With two school-age daughters it's been good to stay home with them and not have to travel."[9] The new film, *Passion*, would be made with his daughters' future in mind, but also De Palma's own past, his roots as a revolutionary filmmaker: "When I started as a director in New York in the 1960s, I had an ideal: I belonged to an anti-capitalist movement. Things haven't really changed: capitalism is still well and truly with us. I film its excesses and perversions in *Passion*."[10] With his next film, De Palma would take aim at the selfishness of those driven by the profit motive, remembering the rivalry that had marred his own relationship with his brothers, and hoping that his daughters would not succumb to the same competitiveness.

CHAPTER 29

Passion (2012)

Passion can serve as a *summa* of De Palma's work, incorporating so many elements from his prior films that it constitutes a kind of career retrospective in itself. In the Berlin office of a global advertising agency, Christine (Rachel McAdams) is an executive and Isabelle (Noomi Rapace) is her assistant. Christine says that she once had a twin sister who died under strange circumstances when they were young and for whose death Christine felt that she was blamed. (The theme of female twins or doubles was explored in *Sisters, Femme Fatale,* and *The Black Dahlia.*) Isabelle creates an ad involving a smart phone placed in the back pocket of the jeans worn by her assistant Dani (Karoline Herfurth); the phone-cam catches people staring at Dani's shapely bottom. (This idea of the voyeur caught peeping has been seen before in such films as *Sisters, Home Movies,* and *Body Double.*) Christine takes credit for Isabelle's ad in order to secure a promotion, but when Isabelle uploads the ad directly to YouTube, she is given the promotion instead.

An infuriated Christine has Isabelle's boyfriend, Dirk (Paul Anderson), arrange a date with her and then stand her up. Via Skype, Isabelle sees that Dirk is at Christine's apartment where the two of them are watching a video, which Dirk took with a hidden camera, of him and Isabelle having sex. Choking back tears of humiliation and rage, Isabelle makes the long, lonely walk from her office to the elevator, which she rides down to the parking garage, while the camera films her in one oppressively long take as if she cannot escape its mortifying scrutiny. (Prolonged Steadicam shots were also featured in *The Bonfire of the Vanities* and *Snake Eyes,* but those were focused on protagonists—Peter [Bruce Willis] and Rick [Nicolas Cage]—who wanted to be the center of attention in their moment of triumph.) As further revenge,

Christine then holds a company party where, to all the assembled co-workers, she shows surveillance video footage of Isabelle crashing her car in the parking garage and then having a mental breakdown. (The scene is reminiscent of Carrie's public humiliation in front of her schoolmates at the senior prom. Video surveillance is a prominent feature of *Phantom of the Paradise*, *The Fury*, *Scarface*, *Snake Eyes*, and *Redacted*.)

A deeply disturbed Isabelle returns to her apartment, takes some pills, and falls asleep. It is at this point that the film, which has been mostly realistic in presentation, takes a marked stylistic turn toward film noir, including blue tinting, skewed angles, and shadows of Venetian blinds. (Similar noir tropes, along with an uncertainty over whether what we are seeing is real or a nightmare, can be found in *Dressed to Kill*, *Raising Cain*, *Femme Fatale*, and *The Black Dahlia*.) Christine takes a sensuous shower and then has her throat slashed by an unknown killer (reminding us of the showering women who are attacked in *Murder à la Mod*, *Dressed to Kill*, *Blow Out*, and *Body Double*). A split-screen (like the ones in *Dionysus in '69*, *Sisters*, *Carrie*, and *Dressed to Kill*) seems to show that Isabelle was at the ballet during the time of the murder, but she is locked up after part of a scarf that looks like hers is found stained with Christine's blood. However, when Dani is able to produce an identical but clean scarf from Isabelle's apartment and when the other part of the bloodstained scarf is found in Dirk's car, Isabelle is exonerated and released from prison.

Yet it turns out that Isabelle did kill Christine, framing Dirk for the murder, and that Dani captured video evidence of it with her phone-cam. Dani uses the video as blackmail to get Isabelle to sleep with her. (Compare the use of video as incriminating evidence in *Home Movies*, *Blow Out*, and *Mission: Impossible*.) After sex, Isabelle is awakened by Dani's ringing smart phone, but before Isabelle can delete the incriminating video, Dani grabs for the phone and the two women struggle over it. Isabelle strangles Dani, but as the latter is dying, her toe presses the phone's send button, emailing the video to the police. The doorbell rings, but when Isabelle goes to answer it, no one seems to be there. However, as Isabelle bends down, we see someone who looks exactly like Christine standing behind her. (*Raising Cain* and *Femme Fatale* also have sudden reveals of a threatening character looming behind another.) Christine then proceeds to wrap the bloody scarf around Isabelle's neck and to strangle her with it (much like the stranglings in *Blow Out*, *Body Double*, and *The Black Dahlia*).

Isabelle wakes up in bed, gasping for air but otherwise unharmed. Could it all have been a terrible dream? Yet, as the camera cranes upward, Dani's dead body is revealed lying on the floor beside Isabelle's bed. Did Isabelle really commit the murders after all, or is she still in a nightmare? (Many De Palma films end with the corpses of murdered women who should not be forgotten, from *Murder à la Mod* through *Carrie* and *Blow Out*, right on up to *Snake Eyes*, *The Black Dahlia*, and *Redacted*.)

Passion begins with the director's credit—"A Brian De Palma Film"—appearing over the open lid of a laptop computer. Christine and Isabelle are both seated behind it, watching video ads for smart phones. "Our smart phone has to be the smartest," Christine comments, and they both say "yeah" at almost the same time, then both laugh. The competition between smart phones—like the competition that will occur between these two women—is ridiculous because they are basically the same. Neither is *really* that much smarter or better than the other. Yet, as De Palma notes, the film is about "two women who are fighting for power within this large advertising company."[1] Which one will play the superior role?

Interestingly, Rachel McAdams has said that "when I got the script and read it I thought I was playing the other character"[2] (Isabelle, the lead role in the film), but it turned out that McAdams was being contacted about playing Christine instead. It was Noomi Rapace (Isabelle) who, after working with McAdams on *Sherlock Holmes: A Game of Shadows*, had suggested her for Christine. Rapace had had only a small part in the *Sherlock Holmes* movie, whereas McAdams had a large one. Now the roles would be reversed, with Rapace grabbing the lead—both of the film (the part of Isabelle) and within the film (when Isabelle gets Christine's promotion at the ad agency and then murders her).

Christine and Isabelle use computer technology in their competition with one another. In a Skype conversation with company head J. J. (Dominic Raacke), Christine claims credit for Isabelle's smart phone ad, but then Isabelle uploads it directly to YouTube and receives Christine's promotion. Christine retaliates with the sex video of Isabelle and Dirk and then with the surveillance footage of Isabelle's breakdown.

These two young women with their laptops and smart phones must remind De Palma of his teenage daughters, Lolita and Piper. As he has noted, "Both my daughters are very computer-savvy, so I just sort of watch what they do and see what they're up to";[3] "They sit on their beds with their computers on their stomachs"[4]—as we often see Isabelle and Christine do.

As he observes his daughters growing up and about to enter the working world, De Palma seems to be imagining what it might be like for them to have to compete for dominance in the information age. In the scene where J. J. still thinks that Christine created the winning ad, he speaks from a video monitor above the two women, asking Christine if she has "any interest in coming home to New York." The promotion that Christine and Isabelle are vying for involves the opportunity to move there and to work with father figure J. J. De

Palma himself has for years made New York his home, and he has said that he often uses Skype to talk with his daughters. In reply to J. J.'s question about the move, Christine looks over at Isabelle and says, "And desert the natives? I've grown rather attached to them." Christine seems to view Isabelle as being like her twin sister, from whom she does not want to forgo an emotional attachment—like that which connected the Siamese twins in *Sisters*? But, working against these sororal bonds, there is a sense of business rivalry, a desire to receive greater recognition from the father figure, to be the boss's favorite.

Perhaps De Palma is hoping that his daughters will not succumb to the same competitive environment that had so damaged him and his brothers. In the original French film on which *Passion* is based, there is only a rivalrous duo, but De Palma changed a third character's gender from male to female so that in his film the competition is among three women—Christine, Isabelle, and Dani—all vying for the boss's favor. How could these "sisters" not make us think of the three De Palma brothers—Bruce, Brian, and Bart—in their contest to earn their father's approval? If the "sisters" are associated with computer technology, so, too, are these brothers. (Even today, De Palma's Skype user ID combines the names of Bruce and Bart.) When they were growing up, Bruce and Brian bonded and fought over advances in electronics, much as Christine and Isabelle do. "My brother and I were always completely computer crazy," De Palma has said. "We used pretty much every computer at home, every one that hit the market. We'd have it tested and tried, how powerful it is."[5] The brothers also built computers and entered them in competitions. We recall that even though Brian took top prize in the Philadelphia Science Fair, he felt that Bruce's third-place win was unfairly lauded above his, much as Isabelle feels that Christine hogs all the recognition for the smart phone ad when she herself has the greater talent.

Having been praised and elevated to a prominent position by J. J., Christine lords it over minions like Isabelle and Dani, bending them to her cruel will. Christine is shown garbed in a gold nightgown and seated on a Louis XV sofa. Like Swan in *Phantom of the Paradise*, Tony in *Scarface*, and Al Capone in *The Untouchables*, Christine is one of "those megalomaniacal and malefic types who take themselves for gods and who end up committing evil"—types that De Palma has said were "inspired by my brother Bruce."[6] As we know, De Palma believed that, because Bruce was "considered to be a genius" and "treated . . . like a god,"[7] the adulation went to his head and he became an overbearing narcissist, like those insane monarchs who "live surrounded by a court which venerates them and which reflects back to them the deformed image of the world in which they imagine they are living."[8]

Early in the film, when Christine gives Isabelle an expensive scarf, it is ostensibly to keep her warm and to reward her for her hard work, but beneath this show of care and tutelage, there is manipulation and control. Christine's interest in her protégée is really a concern for her own success, for what Isabelle's work can do to advance Christine's career. When she wraps the scarf around Isabelle's neck, it is already an implicit act of strangulation, for Christine doesn't hesitate to squeeze the life out of her protégée's idea, taking credit for Isabelle's smart phone ad. The luxurious scarf is merely the pretense of love and the lure of material wealth, offered to Isabelle in order to get her to do what Christine wants. Similarly, when she buys Isabelle a fancy pair of red platform shoes and then has her walk up to a prospective client, Christine is not unhappy when her protégée fails to attract the man's attention, in a sense falling on her face (the same way a runway model falls at a fashion show that they attend). Ultimately, Christine's rise up the company ladder will be built on Isabelle's downfall.

In the story that Christine tells about her twin sister Clarissa (whose double-*C* names remind us of the double-*B* names of Brian and Bruce), Christine was determined to show that she could ride a bike as well as her sister. Christine pedaled faster and faster, with Clarissa running behind and trying to catch up. Then, at Christine's moment of triumph, "I let go of the handlebars and I felt like I was flying, and it felt so good. I just wanted to see myself, so I looked into the window and I caught my reflection. . . . I swerved into the street, and this truck was coming right at me. And then I suddenly felt my sister push me from behind out of the way and I flew over the handlebars, and the last thing I remember was this horrible thunk." The "thunk" could have been Christine's fall from her bike, but in fact, as she found out when she woke up in the hospital, it was Clarissa being hit by the truck—a death for which Christine felt she was to blame: "No one ever said anything but I knew what they were thinking: that I killed her. And they never told me that they loved me ever again."

In her sibling rivalry, Christine may have unconsciously wanted her sister dead. She wanted to see *herself* admired and loved rather than having others' approving gaze directed at her lookalike, her twin sister. But when Christine's hidden wish seems to come terribly true, when the sister who was her competition is indeed eliminated (and dies saving her), Christine is traumatized. Despite the guilt she feels over this incident (the confusion over the "thunk" suggests that a part of her died with her sister), Christine now seems doomed to repeat this same scenario over and over again, her insecurity leading to a competitive desire for attention, which is never enough to counteract her inherent feeling of worthlessness. Christine succumbs to a self-defeating narcissism. "I used to want to be admired," she tells Isabelle, and "now I want to be loved"—but no love will ever be enough. Because Christine can only see others as a reflection of herself, she cannot be loved; she doesn't have the recognition of others as separate beings that is necessary in order to receive love from them.

"You know what I like about you?" Christine says to Isabelle. "You are conscientious; you are incredibly bright; and you're driven—like me." The two women sit side by side on the Louis XV sofa, toasting each other with glasses, like twin sisters or like one woman doubled in a mirror. Christine "loves" Isabelle insofar as the other woman's success will redouble her own, adding to her power and allure. Later, Christine has Dirk wear a life-mask of her own face as he is having sex with her so that, as De Palma puts it, she is "making love to herself."⁹ Christine's insatiable narcissism means that she doesn't *see* her lover except insofar as he serves as a mirror to magnify her own desirability. (Christine is like Madeleine in *The Black Dahlia*, who makes love with her lookalike, Elizabeth, in order "to see what it would be like to do it with someone who looked like me.") While Christine is coupling with Dirk (that is, with herself), Isabelle is also in bed, dreaming up the idea for the smart-phone ad, which is also narcissistic: it is about seeing people admire and desire you, as they are caught looking at you (that is, into the eye of the phone-cam in the jeans back pocket of a woman with a shapely bottom).

Christine's competitive egotism would thus seem to be contagious, spreading to Isabelle who now starts to model her behavior after that of her boss. Indeed, even before Christine steals Isabelle's idea for the smart-phone ad, Isabelle sleeps with Christine's lover, Dirk, in a sense stealing him from her. In thinking of herself as *more* desired by the man who desires Christine, Isabelle can imagine that she is supremely lovable, superior to her boss. "What's it like with her?" Isabelle asks him, and when she finds Christine's life-mask in a bathroom drawer, she picks it up and looks at it as both Isabelle and the mask are reflected in the bathroom mirror. In this hall of mirrors, Isabelle finds her own narcissism reflected in Christine's. Just as Christine sought self-aggrandizement by looking at Isabelle, her subordinate and inferior, so now Isabelle imagines herself as the kind of person her boss would love and admire. Isabelle sees herself as someone her boss would look up to, that is, as her boss's boss, possessing everything—the sofa, the scarf, the shoes, the man—that her former superior once had.

Dirk, the third person in this "love" triangle, seems equally narcissistic. He secretly activates his phone-cam to film his sex with Isabelle, showing less interest in pleasing his partner than in gazing at the camera in anticipation of watching his own performance afterward. He even gives a self-satisfied wink to the camera after his climax. Here, De Palma is critiquing the downside of new technology like smart phones. "Think of how everybody these days is carrying a video camera with them at all times," he has said. "The trouble with that is that people are recording themselves and playing back the footage instead of living life. You see a man having dinner at a restaurant with a gorgeous girl, and he's doing this [De Palma mimics looking down, typing on a smart phone]. 'What's going on? Don't you want to see what's right in front of you?'"[10]

This is an interesting comment coming from someone who, as a younger man, used to film himself constantly, including when he would go on double dates with Steven Spielberg in the mid-'70s. As Julie Salamon reports, the women they went out with "weren't always amused to find their evenings recorded on videotape; De Palma used to carry his camera with him all the time."[11] Although technology can help bridge communication gaps, it can also be used as a buffer between people, even as a means of power over the other if the self is afraid of making a connection, as young men often are. De Palma recalled a time when, on a double date with Spielberg, the two of them got hold of one of the first portable phones and "used it to play a joke on a girl. We parked in front of her house; we called her to tell her that we were coming over; and one second later, we knocked on her door! You should have seen her face."[12] This moment of surprise was perhaps a bit more about the males' empowerment than it was about the woman's enjoyment. Salamon notes that De Palma and Spielberg "generally found they had more in common with each other than with their female companions."[13] Something similar could also be said about Isabelle and Christine, whose love/hate bond is stronger than anything they feel for Dirk.

In fact, the ambivalent relationship between co-workers Isabelle and Christine may owe something to the years of friendly rivalry between filmmakers De Palma and Spielberg. At their first meeting in 1971, Spielberg answered a knock on the door of his New York hotel room and, "before he could say hello," De Palma "brushed right past him and walked in the room and checked out his furniture. Spielberg felt that his surroundings were being inspected," reports Salamon.[14] An early shot of Isabelle shows her seated on Christine's Louis XV sofa, appreciating its finery along with the other luxurious trappings of the well-appointed room. Over the next several years spent in Hollywood, Spielberg "attached himself" to De Palma, admiring him for the success he had already had as an independent filmmaker and as "a ladykiller," reports Peter Biskind. Spielberg even began to dress like his mentor, "wearing a safari jacket" like De Palma's and absorbing his directorial advice with "rapt attention."[15] He also adopted De Palma's practice of looking through modeling agency photobooks for women to go out with; he double-dated with De Palma; and he eventually married an actress, Amy Irving, who first had a crush on De Palma. Isabelle takes to wearing Christine's scarf and the shoes she bought for her. Isabelle attends closely to and tries to follow her mentor's career advice: "I watched you; I listened; I learned. I did exactly what you would do." And she adopts Dirk as her lover, after he has been with Christine.

Beginning with the breakout success of *Jaws*, and continuing with such films as *Close Encounters, E.T., Schindler's List*, and *Saving Private Ryan*, Spielberg surpassed De Palma, becoming one of Hollywood's most admired and beloved directors. Like Isabelle after she receives the promotion instead of Christine, Spielberg the protégé became the master, De Palma's superior in terms of corporate power. When Lynn Hirschberg interviewed De Palma in 1984, she found him in an office "borrowed" from Spielberg and furnished entirely with *Jaws* memorabilia, a "shrine" to his friend's "Hollywood success": "There is no sign of De Palma—except for a photo taken with Spielberg—anywhere." Looking back on their early days together, De Palma noted that one thing they had in common as budding filmmakers was that they were both "having our movies recut by the studio and badly distributed."[16] In *Passion*, the corporation that runs the advertising agency wants to reshoot Isabelle and Christine's smart-phone ad. De Palma maintains that, despite Spielberg's greater subsequent success as a big Hollywood director, they have "managed, somehow, to . . . stay friends."[17]

Yet, mixed in with De Palma's undoubted admiration for his junior colleague's achievements (Spielberg is six years younger than he), there is also a certain degree of jealousy. When *Jaws* made a killing at the box office, De Palma hoped to do the same with *Carrie* ("I was more than ready for big-time success. All my best friends in the business . . . had already made it in a huge way"),[18] but even though *Carrie* did well, it was not the blockbuster hit that Spielberg had had. In a 1998 interview with Anne Thompson, De Palma notes that Spielberg no longer shows him rough cuts of his movies to get his advice on them: "Steven has gotten, you know, *Steven*." But lest this sound too critical of Spielberg in his supreme isolation, De Palma hastens to add that the emotional distance between them "has a lot more to do with proximity"[19] (the fact that they live on opposite coasts) than with any sense of superiority on Spielberg's part. And yet when De Palma says laughingly that "I never had one of those runaway successful hits and thought I was God," that "I never had the terrible ego problem" of those who were "more successful,"[20] he implies that achieving such power in Hollywood *can* lead one to become egotistical and that part of him wishes *he* had to face such a terrible temptation.

Speaking to another interviewer, De Palma remarks that "you might think that I'm a celebrity, but in fact I am rarely recognized." Unlike Spielberg whom "everybody recognizes," De Palma says that he is able to "move about freely under my own name,"[21] without becoming the object of public attention. Still, it is hard not to hear in De Palma's words a desire for a little bit more of that kind of acclaim. When De Palma emphasizes that, out of all the filmmakers he started out with (he mentions Spielberg, Scorsese, Lucas, and Coppola), he himself is "the least recognized,"[22] is there not a certain amount of envy?

In *Passion*, Isabelle's envy of Christine culminates in murder. The scene where Isabelle slits her boss's throat—a literalization of "cutthroat competition"—highlights the jealous admiration that characterizes their relationship. The scene begins with Isabelle attending a performance of the ballet *Afternoon of a Faun*, in which a faun dreams of unrequited desire for a nymph. A close shot of Isabelle's eyes makes us think that she remains a spectator at the ballet, but we find out later that at a certain point she leaves the theater and goes to spy on Christine in her apartment. Much of what follows is presented as a split-screen, with the ballet being danced on the left, and with the stalking and murder of Christine being enacted on the right. At first glance, many viewers will see these side-by-side images as a stark contrast, a "juxtaposition of something so romantic and something so violent," as De Palma puts it.[23] However, upon further reflection, it is the *hidden similarity* between the two images that proves to be most interesting.

On the right, Christine finds a note pinned to her door, left by some mysterious suitor, directing her to undress, shower, and await the arrival of her lover; she looks intrigued. In the image on the left, the ballerina playing the nymph is similarly intrigued when she catches sight of the male dancer who plays the faun. He approaches her and lifts her up as part of his courtship dance, but as he puts her down, the camera moves to focus solely on her as she admires herself in a mirror. Her self-interest proves greater than her interest in him. The stage setting is a ballet studio, and we as viewers are placed in the position of her mirror so that, as she gazes at herself in it, she is looking directly at us but seeing only herself. The narcissistic ballerina sees other people only as reflections of her own self-love. She does not really see us or the male dancer, except insofar as these feed her need for admiration. When he tries to kiss her, she turns again toward the mirror, her hands stroking her hair and breasts, her face ecstatic. Meanwhile, Christine is similarly engaged in autoeroticism. Though she takes her shower apparently in anticipation of her lover, she seems to be enjoying herself during it, smiling and pleasuring herself (below frame). Afterward, she looks at her own reflection in the bathroom mirror while sensuously rubbing lotion onto her shoulders and breasts.

Like the faun gazing at the narcissistic ballerina, Isabelle is watching Christine's supreme self-satisfaction, desiring to possess that image of wholeness, that sense of complete perfection for herself. A split-screen showing Isabelle's eyes on the left and Christine showering on the right creates an impression of covetous admiration and voyeuristic desire. It is as though Isabelle herself were split, needing Christine's love in order to feel whole, but feeling that that love is forever out of reach due to the other woman's self-infatuation. Christine is already doubled in the mirror of her own self-regard, so she cannot give Isabelle the look of approval that she so craves.

The left side of the screen then returns to the ballet where the faun, looking at and desiring the ballerina, finally kisses her, but her gaze remains fixed on the mirror, in love with her own image. On the screen's right side, Isabelle approaches Christine, gazing at her with the desire to be admired, to be loved. But Christine does not satisfy Isabelle's need for recognition. When Christine looks at her, she sees only herself, as symbolized by the fact that Isabelle is wearing a life-mask of Christine's own face. The rejected Isabelle slits Christine's throat with a knife.

As De Palma describes this ballet/murder scene, "you can see the [dancers'] *pas de deux* with the kiss [on the left], and on the other half of the split screen you can see Christine at her home, expecting a lover and getting murdered. At the moment of the kiss, the knife cuts her throat."[24] What is the connection between the kiss and the killing? In De Palma's explanation, "the dancer suddenly kisses the ballerina on the cheek and in a way violates her, just as Isabelle is violating Christine [with the knife]."[25] The ballerina would not experience the faun's kiss as a violation if she were not so entirely self-involved. The kiss seems to kill because it breaks in from outside, bursting her narcissistic bubble. Likewise, Christine would have nothing to fear from a lover if she were able to recognize otherness as something besides a threat to herself. Christine's narcissism is thus self-defeating because it views all others as competitors and so prevents her from receiving love from anyone outside herself. It is worth noting that Christine is killed by a woman wearing a life-mask of Christine's own face. In a sense, then, Christine kills herself; she dies from her own narcissism.

After Isabelle slits Christine's throat, she wakes up in bed, sitting bolt upright and gasping for air. Is she a killer or did she just have a bad dream? Is Christine even dead? The doorbell rings and two police detectives arrive to inform her that her boss was indeed found murdered and that a piece of Isabelle's scarf, stained with Christine's blood, was discovered near the body. Having both motive (Christine publicly humiliated her by showing the surveillance video of her breakdown) and opportunity (Isabelle cannot recall anyone who saw her at the ballet on the night of the killing), Isabelle is convicted of the murder and sentenced to prison, even though she herself is not convinced that she committed the crime. However, after falling asleep in her jail cell, Isabelle wakes up again in her own bed. It would seem that she has just had a nightmare of innocence wronged, of being unfairly accused and convicted, and now she has awakened to freedom.

But no—when Isabelle wakes up *again*, she is indeed in prison. However, this time she is not only sure that she is innocent, she is able to prove it, for a theater usher is found who saw her at the ballet, and a clean, un-torn scarf is discovered in her apartment, while the other part of the bloody scarf is located in Dirk's car. Isabelle is exonerated and freed, in what appears to be a dream of innocence triumphant.

But not so fast—it turns out that Dani, Isabelle's assistant, followed her from the ballet to Christine's apartment and shot phone-cam footage of Isabelle slitting her boss's throat and then placing a piece of the bloodstained scarf in Dirk's car. There is even video of Isabelle having bought an identical but clean scarf to "disprove" her own guilt. Isabelle has thus gone from a dream of confirmed innocence to a wicked fantasy of getting away with murder (killing her boss and then cleverly planting evidence on Dirk so that her own conviction will be overturned), and finally on to a guilty nightmare of being caught in her wickedness by Dani.

If Isabelle killed Christine, it was out of rage and envy. The boss who had once seemed her loving mentor had rejected and humiliated her, dominating her as competition. Isabelle cut Christine's throat in revenge but also to *become her*, to be the boss who can exact love and admiration from all her subordinates. (When she murdered Christine, Isabelle was wearing the "Christine" mask: she both eliminated her rival and took her place.)

Isabelle and Dani now sit behind an open laptop computer in the same way that Christine and Isabelle did at the beginning of the film, with the latter occupying her former boss's position. But now that Isabelle has become the boss, she is subject to the same envious rivalry from *her* assistant that she had felt toward Christine. Indeed, when Isabelle tries to lord it over Dani, acting as if she is somehow superior to the other woman (her "twin," her "sister"), Dani responds with the same jealous admiration that Isabelle once felt for her boss. Dani desires to be loved and admired in the way that she now imagines that Isabelle is. So Dani uses the phone-cam footage she shot of Isabelle's crime to blackmail her into having sex.

We recall that, in *Femme Fatale*, Laure (Rebecca Romijn-Stamos) falls asleep in the bath and then has a "film noir" dream in which she allows her lookalike Lily to commit suicide and then takes her place, living a life of paranoid ruthlessness, of rivalry with almost everyone around her, until she herself is drowned by the competition. However, after this "long dream sequence" in which she "steals the identity of the woman . . . who looks like her," Laure "reflects on what she dreamt and changes her life," according to De Palma.[26] Laure wakes up in the bath, prevents Lily's suicide, and in the process saves herself, for Laure's good deed has a knock-on effect that results in the preservation of her own life at a certain point in the future. One sign of when Laure was dreaming was the presence of water in many scenes and the fact that all the clocks showed the same time. In the second half of *Passion*, the clocks also seem to be frozen at a particular hour and Isabelle is constantly dropping sleeping tablets into glasses of water. Could these be signs that, even when she seems to wake up, she is actually still in a dream sleep?

Although the film noir style (canted angles, slatted shadows, ominous music) begins when Isabelle starts taking sleeping pills just before the murder, which suggests that everything from the murder on may be a nightmare, dreams have already figured as a significant element in the first part of the film. An early shot shows a smart phone being placed in a glass of water, and Isabelle's idea for the smart-phone ad comes to her in a dream. (It is almost as though the smart phone were dreaming about itself.) De Palma has said that "I myself get a lot of ideas from my dreams. I wake up many times during the night thinking about certain aesthetic problems, which sort of figure themselves out in my dream. For this movie, I got the idea of the phone commercial in a dream."[27] In Isabelle's ad, viewers are caught looking at the phone-cam—at Isabelle herself, since she is the dreamer—with admiration and desire. When Christine fails to look at her in this way, Isabelle kills her, but this murder is filmed by Dani on her phone-cam and she threatens to send the video to the police. Isabelle's dream of being loved and admired turns into a nightmare of guilt and punishment. The phone-cam that facilitated her rise to the top of the corporate ladder now threatens to precipitate her downfall.

After going to bed with Dani, Isabelle wakes up again, but there are numerous elements to indicate that she may still be having some uncertain combination of a wish-fulfillment dream and a nightmare. On the one hand, police inspector Bach is on his way up the stairs of her apartment building with flowers for her, which are his way of apologizing for having falsely suspected her of Christine's murder. Perhaps Isabelle is innocent after all and thus deserving of these flowers. Maybe that clean, un-torn scarf that was eventually found in her apartment did disprove her guilt, testifying to her pristine character, to the fact that she is not the kind of person who would kill another for revenge or out of envy. On the other hand, Isabelle hears Dani's smart phone ringing and finds it behind the back of a drawer where Isabelle had earlier looked but failed to find that exonerating scarf. Maybe the scarf that proves her innocence never existed and what does exist is the video on the smart phone of Isabelle killing Christine because she did in fact do it. Or it could be that Isabelle is neither innocent nor guilty because *nothing has actually happened yet*. She could be exploring the various possibilities in a dream, trying to maintain her spotless character but also imagining what it might be like to kill Christine and live with the consequences.

One such result could be that she makes herself vulnerable to being blackmailed by her own assistant. When Dani grabs for the smart phone before Isabelle can delete the incriminating video on it, Isabelle puts her hands around the other woman's neck and chokes her to death. Thus, in order to cover up one killing (her slitting of Christine's throat), Isabelle commits another (the strangulation of Dani), in a sense repeating the crime in a kind of downward spiral. Indeed, as Isabelle is strangling Dani inside the apartment, Inspector Bach gives up on his attempt to get Isabelle to come to the door so that he can give her the flowers; instead, he leaves them behind and begins his way back down the building's spiral staircase. As a murderer, Isabelle no longer deserves these flowers or his apology for having unjustly accused her.

If we assume that Isabelle's dreaming mind is still imagining the potential fallout from murder, then what happens next shows that she fears she will never get away with it. At the very height of Isabelle's dominance over Dani, just as her blackmailing assistant is breathing her last gasp and dying of strangulation, Dani's toe presses the send button on the smart phone, emailing the video showing Isabelle's murder of Christine to Inspector Bach. He views it on his smart phone and will now begin to climb the spiral staircase again, this time to arrest her. Perhaps the dreaming Isabelle has a conscience and believes she should be arrested, that this is the only way for her to stop her downward spiral of crime and reverse it in the direction of heavenly goodness.

Isabelle's conscience also seems to intervene when, after she goes to the door and bends down to pick up the flowers she doesn't deserve, a Christine lookalike suddenly appears behind her and strangles Isabelle with a bloody scarf when she stands up. The bloodstained scarf points to Isabelle's guilt over having cut her boss's throat, a sense of guilt which brings on a fitting punishment when Isabelle pays for her crime by suffering an attack on her own neck. Whether the Christine lookalike is her twin sister come to avenge her or Christine herself risen from the grave in order to exact her own vengeance, she is a figure for Isabelle's conscience, which won't let her live in peace if she has committed murder.

Isabelle wakes up again, with her hands struggling to loosen the top of her nightshirt as she gasps for air. Did she learn from her premonitory dream that, if she were to cut Christine and choke Dani, she would in effect be strangling herself? De Palma has said that he too has had "dreams where I've dreamt about friends or people in dire or tragic situations and have actively done something to prevent my prophetic dream from actually happening."[28] Is Isabelle like Laure in *Femme Fatale*, who wakes up in the bath and decides to prevent the death of her lookalike Lily and thus save herself from a similarly tragic fate? Will Isabelle live the life that De Palma must hope for his daughters, one in which she avoids the cutthroat competition of the corporate world and instead sees Christine and Dani as her "sisters"?

When the camera then cranes up from Isabelle lying in bed, we see the dead body of Dani laid out on the floor next to her. "I wake up three or four times in the night, and as soon as I wake up I'm not sure whether I'm in a dream or not," De Palma has said. "It takes me, you know, thirty seconds or a minute to realize 'Oh! I just woke up.' And that's very much what happens at the end of *Passion*, where you aren't quite sure . . . is [Dani] really dead? Did [Isabelle] really kill her?"[29]

The film preserves its ambiguity all the way to the end. If Isabelle did actually wake up at some point and really kill Dani, then she would have failed to heed the nightmarish lesson that her mind had been trying to send: Dani's dead body will soon be her own, for in killing her "sister," Isabelle has condemned herself to terrible remorse, if not to a prison death cell. But there is still the possibility that she remains within a dream. Her conscience might yet awaken in time to recognize the other as just like herself, neither smarter than nor superior to her, wanting as much as she does to be admired and loved. Let us hope that the "film noir" nightmare is still screening in Isabelle's mind where she can choose to bring it to an end before it spills out to become a terrible reality, like the dead female bodies at the end of *The Black Dahlia* and *Redacted*.

Afterword

De Palma's films continue to alternate between dreams and nightmares. However, after an earlier emphasis on male rivalry (*Scarface, Raising Cain, Mission: Impossible*) and heroic failure (*Blow Out, Casualties of War, Carlito's Way*), some of his most recent films have imagined ways of overcoming past trauma. In *The Black Dahlia*, De Palma comes to an understanding of the flaws of his brother Bruce by viewing them as the result of their father's negative influence—the same father who was himself traumatized by his wartime experiences. *Mission to Mars* represents De Palma's attempt to reconcile with Bruce and to recognize the positive aspects of his character. *Passion* reveals De Palma's hope that his daughters, Lolita and Piper, will not fall into the same destructive competition that plagued him and his brothers. *Femme Fatale* envisions the possibility of a solidarity between his daughters that will replace male rivalry with compassion—the kind of empathy which would allow heroines to succeed in saving others where deeply compromised heroes have failed.

"When you're making a movie," De Palma has said, "you think about it all the time—you're dreaming about it, you wake up with ideas in the middle of the night—until you actually go there and shoot it. You have these ideas that are banging around in your head, but once you objectify them and lock them into a photograph or cinema sequence, then . . . they no longer haunt you."[1] De Palma's hope seems to be that, if he can put his nightmares on screen, the haunting will end because the films will wake us up in time to avert catastrophe. If this occurred too late for himself, his brothers, and his parents when they were a family, there may still be time for future generations.

De Palma has not received anything like the recognition that has been bestowed upon the filmmakers and friends who began their careers along with him. Coppola, Scorsese, and Spielberg have all won Academy Awards as

Best Director, in addition to being nominated numerous times. De Palma has neither won nor been nominated—not even once. (Strangely, Hitchcock never received a Best Director Oscar either, so De Palma is following in the master's footsteps yet again. At least Hitchcock was nominated five times, though, and received a lifetime achievement award from the Academy.) "I'm telling you, these award things where people stand up and tell you how great you are, I avoid them," De Palma has said, though it's hard not to hear some bitterness in his added comment that "fortunately, I've never had to deal with it."[2] Asked why he is not considered to be a "Great Director," De Palma replied, "Because I've always been against the establishment from day one. I've never been accepted as that conventional artist. Whatever you say about David Lynch or Martin Scorsese, they are considered major film artists and nobody can argue with that. I've never had that. I've had people say it about me. And I've had people say that I'm a complete hack and you know, derivative and all those catchphrases that people use for me. So I've always been controversial. People hate me or love me."[3]

De Palma has taken his own path, delving into the nightmares beneath the Hollywood dreams, and the resulting films have rarely been big hits with the kinds of general audiences that the studios are trying to please: "My movies have always been dark and strange, and that's why I've had to exile myself [from Hollywood] so that I can continue making the films I want to make."[4] In this director's films, there is no shortcut to success. Only by facing the worst is there the possibility—not the guarantee or even the likelihood—of moving beyond trauma.

"What I don't want is to stop making movies," De Palma has said. "Or to be crushed by the system, which can indeed crush you. It can be very tough, and you can take a lot of terrible, negative criticism, and it's always difficult to get up the next day. But you just have to sort of follow your own light, and evolve as you think you're evolving, and hopefully some people will see that."[5] The references to "light" and "evolving" recall the end of *Mission to Mars* where, only after overcoming deadly rivalry and terrible loss, the hero achieves an enlightened awareness of the interconnectedness of all beings, even as De Palma comes to a new understanding of the brother (Bruce) he had competed with and had recently lost. Woody, the character representing Bruce in that film, cannot be pulled to safety in time, but others—such as Luke, who represents De Palma's other brother, Bart—can. It is not too late for him to be reached with a "lifeline."

In some of his more recent films (Laure saving Lily and Veronica in *Femme Fatale*, Kay saving Bucky in *The Black Dahlia*), De Palma seems able to imagine the kind of compassionate reaching out that eluded Peter when he tried to save his son from falling in *The Fury*, and Liz when she extended her hand to her dying "sister" Kate in *Dressed to Kill.* It is as though, having faced so many failed attempts at rescue, De Palma is finally able to envision overcoming the fear and achieving the empathy that would have been needed for Sue to have accepted Carrie's hand when she reached out to her from beyond the grave at the end of *Carrie.*

In recent interviews, De Palma has been fond of saying, "Every day above ground is a good day."[6] This is advice that Tony was given in *Scarface* by a character who was trying to encourage him to "smile more" and "enjoy" himself rather than being so caught up in competition and revenge over past wrongs. Unlike Tony, whose macho rivalry brought on a spectacular demise, De Palma seems ready to take this advice. "I've done a lot of really nice movies and movies that people are still talking about that are 30 or 40 years old. I'm very happy with my career, and if I make a few other good ones, great," he has said. "I'm basically just working because I enjoy it and it's what I do. I don't feel I have to prove anything to anybody."[7]

De Palma doesn't have to fear that he is inferior to Bruce or Hitchcock or Scorsese. De Palma's directorial achievement is distinctive, impressive, and humane. He is a Great Director.

Acknowledgments

This relatively short book has nevertheless been a long time in the making, and I owe a huge debt of gratitude to the many individuals who have helped me along the way. Without them, this work would not have been possible. (Needless to say, its faults are mine and mine alone.)

I wish to thank Leila Salisbury, at the University Press of Mississippi, for her faith in this project from the beginning, and for her unfailingly helpful and encouraging advice at several stages during its composition. Valerie Jones at UPM should also be credited for providing such able assistance during final revisions of the manuscript. In addition, I would like to thank the two anonymous readers who devoted their time and energy to a careful review of my manuscript with an eye toward offering helpful suggestions for its improvement, and copyeditor Peter Tonguette, who provided corrections to my blunders along with felicitous rephrasings for some of my more awkward sentences. This is a better book because of their generous input.

At Cal Poly, Department Chair Kathryn Rummell and Dean of the College of Liberal Arts Douglas Epperson were instrumental in helping me to obtain a professional leave to enable the completion of this project. I am also grateful to former Department Chair David Kann and former Dean Linda Halisky for the vital support they gave to me during the book's earlier stages. Susan Bratcher, Connie Davis, Dee Lopez, Sue Otto, Kathy Severn, Cassandra Sherburne, and Katie Tool have, day in and day out, offered the most expert and enthusiastic assistance anyone could ever hope for, and I thank them most sincerely for all their help. I am truly fortunate to have such wonderful staff support.

The librarians at Robert E. Kennedy Library were always willing to go above and beyond for me, and their expert assistance over the years is very much appreciated. I would like to thank Sharon Andresen (reserves), Brett Bodemer (College of Liberal Arts librarian), Judy Drake (circulation), Jan

Kline and Karen Beaton (acquisitions), Karen Lauritsen (communications), Heather Lucio (current periodicals), and Michael Price (information technology). A special thank-you goes out to Linda Hauck, Christopher Lee, Holly Richmond, and Janice Stone (interlibrary loan). I would also like to recognize Associate Dean Debra Valencia-Laver, Administrative Analyst Margie Valine, and the CLA Tech Team—Tom Dresel, Jennifer Hodges, and Velanche Stewart—for keeping my computer equipment and software up to date and for answering my sometimes-desperate calls for technical aid. Carroll Baker, Eric Boege, and Pete Woodworth in Media Distribution Services also provided me with help when it was most needed.

For their savvy and prompt research assistance when it comes to finding photos pertaining to De Palma, I am grateful to Dollie R. Banner at Jerry Ohlinger's Movie Material Store; Donna Daley, Melissa Ramhold, and Miranda Sarjeant at Corbis; Derek Davidson and Todd Ifft at Photofest; Kristine Krueger at the Margaret Herrick Library of the Academy of Motion Picture Arts and Sciences; and Jamie Vuignier at Kobal. They were a pleasure to work with, and I am only sorry that I could not use more of the wonderful images they helped to find for me.

Any scholar working on De Palma owes a tremendous debt to those who wrote the pioneering studies of this director (see the Bibliography for full citations of the critical works mentioned in this and the following paragraph). Michael Bliss's 1983 book was an inspiration in being among the first to treat De Palma seriously as an accomplished artist. Laurent Bouzereau also approached this director as a serious auteur in *The De Palma Cut* (1988), supplementing a study of recurrent themes and trademark techniques with important interviews. Robin Wood (1985) and Kenneth MacKinnon (1990) mounted a sophisticated defense of De Palma on ideological grounds, providing a model for understanding him as something more than just a misogynist. Then, when Anglo-American interest in him waned during the '90s, French critics took up the baton and made significant strides in De Palma scholarship. Dominique Legrand (1995) approached the director's films from a psychoanalytic perspective; Leonardo Gandini (2002) considered De Palma's revisions of various film genres; and, after writing an exceptionally detailed formal analysis (1999) of *Mission: Impossible*, Luc Lagier (2003, rpt. and rev. 2008) went on to provide an insightful reading of De Palma's films that viewed them as allegories of his relationship to the Hollywood studios. Perhaps most crucial of all, Samuel Blumenfeld and Laurent Vachaud (2001) published a book-length series of interviews with the director—a work that may well prove as important to De Palma scholarship as François Truffaut's book of Hitchcock interviews has for the study of that director.

I am not the only one to have thought of taking a biographical approach to De Palma's films, and I wish to acknowledge that my study has some significant precursors. In addition to groundbreaking essays by Georgia A. Brown (1983), Norman G. Gordon (1983), and Laurent Vachaud (1998), there are the on-set diaries of Susan Dworkin (1984) and Julie Salamon (1991), books which recount what it was like to be present during filming of *Body Double* and *The Bonfire of the Vanities*, respectively. Add to these the aforementioned Bouzereau book (1998), along with the smart, compact volume by John Ashbrook (2000), written for Paul Duncan's Pocket Essentials series, both of which interweave behind-the-scenes material into their discussions of the films themselves. Most recently, Jason Zinoman (2011) has insightfully explored the biographical roots of De Palma's horror-suspense films, and Chris Dumas (2012) draws a number of links between the life and the oeuvre in his spirited, provocative book on the director.

No accounting of intellectual indebtedness would be complete without recognizing the key role that Geoff Beran and his website, *De Palma à la Mod*, have played in keeping viewers informed about all things directly or even tangentially related to De Palma. Beran's site is an endless treasure trove of facts, interpretations, opinions, and Web links, and it would be impossible for me to count how many times I visited it during the writing of this book. My thanks as well to Bill Fentum, whose website *briandepalma.net* (now sadly defunct) was also an invaluable source of information; Romain Desbiens for his fine French website devoted to De Palma, *Le Virtuose du 7ème Art*; and Ari Kahan, the principal archivist for *The Swan Archives*, a wonderful website about *Phantom of the Paradise*.

Over the past several years, I have benefited greatly from stimulating conversation about film with my colleagues and former students, and I would like to take this opportunity to thank a number of them for their provocative ideas and their rewarding companionship: Phillip Akhzar, Damon Bailey, Preston Brown, Kevin Clark, George Cotkin, Nicholas DePaoli, Kevin Fagan, Michael Flores, William Frederick, David Gillette, John Hampsey, Terry Harrington, Brenda Helmbrecht, Larry Inchausti, David Kann, Bozant Katzakian, Jeanette Keesey, Scott Keesey, Brian Kennelly, Darren Kraker, Josh Machamer, Paul Marchbanks, Steven Marx, Cheryl Ney, Kathryn O'Brien, Tom O'Brien, Todd Pierce, Johanna Rubba, Debora Schwartz, Cem Sunata, Parry Thornton, Patricia Troxel, and Paul Valadao. I am particularly grateful to Carol MacCurdy for sharing with me her approach to, and her advice regarding, biographical research. My special thanks to John Harrington, who continues to mentor me in so many ways that any attempt to enumerate them here would only be inadequate.

I wish to thank the students in my Alfred Hitchcock and my Hitchcock and De Palma courses for their fresh eyes, their challenging questions, and their unwillingness to accept facile answers. It has been a pleasure to discover De Palma along with them and to see new generations excited by his films. I would also like to express my gratitude to Jim Dee of the Palm Theatre for enabling my students to experience these films in their highest-quality form and in the best possible audiovisual environment.

The first De Palma film I ever saw was *Carrie*, and I was dazzled by its slow-motion and split-screen techniques and moved by the varying emotions of its title character. Even back then, I sensed that there was something *personal* behind this film. To me, De Palma did not seem like a mere show-off who was all style and no substance, simply making a standard genre film, but instead like a director intimately invested in his work, someone who expressed feeling *through* technique, commitment *through* style. Even though he had no interest in seeing the film, my father bought himself and me tickets to *Carrie* just so that I, underage but incredibly keen to see it, could gain admission "accompanied by a parent." I present this as one small but significant instance of the innumerable ways in which my parents, Phyllis and Donald Keesey, have been unfailingly supportive of me over the years as a film fan, then student, and then scholar, and I am profoundly grateful to them.

My wife's favorite De Palma film is *Blow Out*, particularly for the tragic pathos of its ending. She admires him for having the courage to conclude the film in the way he felt it had to end, regardless of commercial considerations. I love her for that, and for everything else she is and does. This book is dedicated to her.

Notes

Introduction

1. David Thompson, "Emotion Pictures: Quentin Tarantino Talks to Brian De Palma," in *Projections 5*, ed. John Boorman and Walter Donohue (London: Faber and Faber, 1996), 33.

2. Ibid., 25.

3. Roger Ebert, Ryan Gilbey, and Terrence Rafferty have also written perceptive and appreciative reviews of De Palma's work. See the Bibliography for some examples.

4. Susan Dworkin, *Double De Palma* (New York: Newmarket Press, 1984), 12.

5. Joseph Gelmis, *The Film Director as Superstar* (Garden City, NY: Doubleday, 1970), 29.

6. Michael Pye and Linda Myles, *The Movie Brats* (New York: Holt, Rinehart and Winston, 1979), 169.

7. Dick Adler, "Hi, Mom, Greetings, It's Brian—in Hollywood!" *New York Times*, December 27, 1970.

8. Michael Bliss, *Brian De Palma* (Metuchen, NJ: Scarecrow Press, 1983), 127.

9. Dworkin, *Double De Palma*, 175.

10. Samuel Blumenfeld and Laurent Vachaud, eds., *Brian De Palma: Entretiens* (Paris: Calmann-Lévy, 2001), 15.

11. Lynn Hirschberg, "Brian De Palma's Death Wish," *Esquire*, January 1984: 80.

12. Julie Salamon, *The Devil's Candy* (Boston: Houghton Mifflin, 1991), 397.

13. David Bartholomew, "De Palma of the *Paradise*," *Cinefantastique* 4, no. 2 (March 1974): 14.

14. Luc Lagier, *Les mille yeux de Brian De Palma* (Paris: Cahiers du Cinéma, 2008), 21.

15. Salamon, *Devil's Candy*, 386.

16. Hirschberg, "Brian De Palma's Death Wish," 80.

17. Dworkin, *Double De Palma*, 168.

18. Judy Stone, *Eye on the World* (Los Angeles: Silman-James Press, 1997), 656.

19. Bliss, *Brian De Palma*, 121–22.

20. Marcia Pally, "Double Trouble," *Film Comment* 20, no. 5 (September–October 1984), 14.

21. Richard Rubinstein, "The Making of *Sisters*," *Filmmakers Newsletter*, September 1973: 28.

22. Pye and Myles, *Movie Brats*, 168.

23. Lagier, *mille yeux de Brian De Palma*, 23.

24. Bartholomew, "De Palma of the *Paradise*," 14.

25. Charles Higham, "My Films Come Out of My Nightmares," *New York Times*, October 28, 1973.

26. Mark Cousins, dir., "Brian De Palma," *Scene by Scene*, BBC TV, 1998.

27. Blumenfeld and Vachaud, *Brian De Palma*, 85.

28. Jason Zinoman, *Shock Value* (New York: Penguin Press, 2011), 154.

29. Higham, "My Films Come Out of My Nightmares."

30. Jim Jerome, "20 Questions: Brian De Palma," *Playboy* 32, no. 2 (February 1985), 158.

31. Adler, "Hi, Mom, Greetings, It's Brian."

32. Georgia A. Brown, "*Obsession*," *American Film*, December 1983: 33.

33. Zinoman, *Shock Value*, 155.

34. Jerome, "20 Questions," 158.

35. James Blackford, "*Dressed to Kill* and *Blow Out*," *Sight and Sound* 23, no. 9 (September 2013): 96.

36. Full citations for all the critical studies mentioned in this and the next paragraph can be found in the Bibliography.

37. Blumenfeld and Vachaud, *Brian De Palma*, 86.

38. Canadian Press, "Brian De Palma Knows Erotic Thriller *Passion* Is Divisive," *TheSpec .com*, September 11, 2012, http://www.thespec.com.

Chapter 1: *The Wedding Party*

1. Justin Humphreys, *Interviews Too Shocking to Print!* (Albany, GA: BearManor Media, 2014), 196.

2. Blumenfeld and Vachaud, *Brian De Palma*, 23.

3. Michael Henry, "Entretien avec Brian De Palma," *Positif*, no. 193 (May 1977): 24.

4. Dworkin, *Double De Palma*, 142.

5. Ibid., 143.

Chapter 2: *Murder à la Mod*

1. Jacob R. Brackman, "Horror Comedy," *New Yorker*, July 23, 1966.

2. Zinoman, *Shock Value*, 156–57.

3. Ibid., 158.

4. Brackman, "Horror Comedy."

5. Pally, "*Double* Trouble," 14–15.

6. Vincent Canby, "*Murder à la Mod*," *New York Times*, May 2, 1968.

7. Byro, "*Murder à la Mod*," *Variety*, May 1, 1968.

Chapter 3: *Greetings*

1. Gelmis, *Film Director as Superstar*, 29.
2. Bartholomew, "De Palma of the *Paradise*," 12.
3. Gelmis, *Film Director as Superstar*, 28.
4. Eric Harrison, "Scene 1: A Grassy Knoll," *Los Angeles Times: Calendar*, August 2, 1998.
5. Ibid.
6. Blumenfeld and Vachaud, *Brian De Palma*, 29.
7. Ibid., 15–16.
8. Brian De Palma, "Guilty Pleasures," *Film Comment* 23, no. 3 (May–June 1987): 53.
9. Brian Kellow, *Pauline Kael: A Life in the Dark* (New York: Viking, 2011), 119.
10. Stone, *Eye on the World*, 656.
11. Japa, "Greetings," *Variety*, December 25, 1968.
12. Howard Thompson, "*The Wedding Party*," *New York Times*, April 10, 1969.
13. Joseph Gelmis, "*The Wedding Party*," *Newsday*, March 10, 1969.

Chapter 4: *Dionysus in '69*

1. Jerzy Grotowski, *Towards a Poor Theatre* (New York: Simon and Schuster, 1968), 255–56.
2. Ian Christie, Phil Hardy, and Chris Petit, "Interview with Brian De Palma," *Film Directions* 1, no. 1 (December 1977): 7.
3. Bartholomew, "De Palma of the *Paradise*," 12.
4. Taryn Simon, "Blow-Up: Taryn Simon and Brian De Palma in Conversation," *Artforum* 50, no. 10 (Summer 2012): 252.
5. Richard Schechner, ed., *Dionysus in 69* (New York: Farrar, Straus and Giroux, 1970), 76–79; my pagination, since the text itself is unpaginated.
6. Agnes Varnum, "Richard Schechner at *Dionysus in '69* Q&A," *Persistence of Vision*, December 10, 2009.
7. William Plummer, "Despite His Critics, Director Brian De Palma Says *Body Double* Is Neither Too Violent nor Too Sexy," *People*, December 17, 1984.
8. William Hunter Shephard, *The Dionysus Group* (New York: Peter Lang, 1991), 89.
9. Ibid., 82.
10. Schechner, *Dionysus in 69*, 96.
11. Geoff Beran, "Interview with Brian De Palma," *De Palma à la Mod*, February 26, 2002, http://www.angelfire.com/de/palma/interviewparis.html.
12. Schechner, *Dionysus in 69*, 152.

Chapter 5: *Hi, Mom!*

1. De Palma, "Guilty Pleasures," 52.
2. Gelmis, *Film Director as Superstar*, 32.

3. Antonin Artaud, *The Theatre and Its Double*, trans. Mary Caroline Richards (New York: Grove Press, 1958), 96.

4. Ibid., 99, 86.

5. Gelmis, *Film Director as Superstar*, 27.

6. Christie, Hardy, and Petit, "Interview," 9.

Chapter 6: *Get to Know Your Rabbit*

1. Pye and Myles, *Movie Brats*, 151.

2. Christie, Hardy, and Petit, "Interview," 9.

3. Bartholomew, "De Palma of the *Paradise*," 13.

4. Kevin Thomas, "Film-maker at the Gut Level," *Los Angeles Times*, July 7, 1970.

5. Higham, "My Films Come Out of My Nightmares."

6. Jean Vallely, "Brian De Palma: The New Hitchcock or Just Another Rip-Off?" *Rolling Stone*, October 16, 1980: 39.

7. Bartholomew, "De Palma of the *Paradise*," 13.

8. Christie, Hardy, and Petit, "Interview," 9.

9. Pye and Myles, *Movie Brats*, 152.

10. Lagier, *mille yeux de Brian De Palma*, 32.

11. Chris Nashawaty, "The Lives of Brian," *Entertainment Weekly*, September 22, 2006.

12. Lagier, *mille yeux de Brian De Palma*, 32.

13. Brian De Palma, "A Day in the Life," *Esquire*, October 1980: 118.

Chapter 7: *Sisters*

1. Gelmis, *Film Director as Superstar*, 29.

2. Blumenfeld and Vachaud, *Brian De Palma*, 14.

3. Henry, "Entretien," 28.

4. Christie, Hardy, and Petit, "Interview," 10.

5. Blumenfeld and Vachaud, *Brian De Palma*, 117.

6. Higham, "My Films Come Out of My Nightmares."

7. Blumenfeld and Vachaud, *Brian De Palma*, 44.

8. Salamon, *Devil's Candy*, 40.

9. Blumenfeld and Vachaud, *Brian De Palma*, 14.

10. "Masha and Dasha: Rare Study of Russia's Siamese Twins," *Life*, April 8, 1966: 67.

11. Blumenfeld and Vachaud, *Brian De Palma*, 37.

12. Henry, "Entretien," 28.

13. Credit for having spotted the repeated appearances of the Raggedy Ann doll in De Palma's films goes to Geoff Beran, "Daughters and Dolls," *De Palma à la Mod*, July 4, 2011, http://www.angelfire.com/de/palma/blog/index.blog?topic_id=1069286.

14. Henry, "Entretien," 28.

15. Higham, "My Films Come Out of My Nightmares."

16. John McCarty, "*Sisters*," *Cinefantastique* 3, no. 1 (Fall 1973): 28.

17. Paul Schrader, "*Sisters*," *LA*, no. 19, November 11, 1972.

Chapter 8: *Phantom of the Paradise*

1. Bartholomew, "De Palma of the *Paradise*," 8.

2. Dworkin, *Double De Palma*, 148.

3. De Palma, "Day in the Life," 118.

4. Blumenfeld and Vachaud, *Brian De Palma*, 48.

5. Peter Biskind, *Easy Riders, Raging Bulls* (New York: Simon and Schuster, 1998), 152.

6. Blumenfeld and Vachaud, *Brian De Palma*, 37.

7. T. Simon, "Blow-Up," 253.

8. Robert Cashill, "Outside the Green Zone: An Interview with Brian De Palma," *Cineaste* 33, no. 1 (Winter 2007): 11.

9. De Palma, "Guilty Pleasures," 53.

10. Deborah Znaty, dir., "Paradise Regained," *Phantom of the Paradise* DVD (Opening Distribution, 2009).

11. Hirschberg, "Brian De Palma's Death Wish," 82.

12. Alexander Stuart, "Phantoms and Fantasies," *Films and Filming* 23, no. 3 (December 1976): 12.

13. Stone, *Eye on the World*, 656.

14. Dworkin, *Double De Palma*, 141.

15. Znaty, "Paradise Regained."

16. Pye and Myles, *Movie Brats*, 153.

17. "Scene by Scene: Monitor 2," *Swan Archives*, http://www.swanarchives.org.

18. Bartholomew, "De Palma of the *Paradise*," 10.

19. Hirschberg, "Brian De Palma's Death Wish," 82–83.

20. Blumenfeld and Vachaud, *Brian De Palma*, 50.

21. Ibid.

22. Znaty, "Paradise Regained."

23. Bartholomew, "De Palma of the *Paradise*," 10.

24. Bliss, *Brian De Palma*, 121.

25. Bartholomew, "De Palma of the *Paradise*," 14.

26. Mike Childs and Alan Jones, "De Palma Has the Power!" *Cinefantastique* 6, no. 1 (Summer 1977): 9, 10.

Chapter 9: *Obsession*

1. Harry North and Larry Siegel, "*Sobsession*," *Mad*, no. 191 (June 1977): 46.

2. Paul Schrader, *Déjà Vu*, text supplement to *Obsession* DVD (Arrow Films, 2011), 3; typos silently corrected.

3. Laurent Bouzereau, dir., "*Obsession* Revisited," *Obsession* DVD (Arrow Films, 2011).

4. Schrader, *Déjà Vu*, 44.

5. Ibid., 65.

6. Ibid., 63.

7. Stuart, "Phantoms and Fantasies," 12.

8. John Lithgow, *Drama: An Actor's Education* (New York: HarperCollins, 2011), 254.

9. Ibid., 256.

10. Blumenfeld and Vachaud, *Brian De Palma*, 57.

11. Ibid., 15–16.

12. Ibid.

13. Steven C. Smith, *A Heart at Fire's Center* (Berkeley: University of California Press, 1991), 343.

14. D. Thompson, "Emotion Pictures," 26.

15. Josh Rottenberg, "There's Something about *Carrie*," *Premiere*, August 2001: 62.

16. Hirschberg, "Brian De Palma's Death Wish," 81.

17. Laurent Bouzereau, dir., "Visualizing *Carrie*," *Carrie* DVD (MGM Home Entertainment, 2001).

Chapter 10: *Carrie*

1. Rottenberg, "There's Something about *Carrie*," 63.

2. Blumenfeld and Vachaud, *Brian De Palma*, 65.

3. Ibid., 65.

4. Joseph Aisenberg, *Studies in the Horror Film: Brian De Palma's Carrie* (Lakewood, CO: Centipede Press, 2011), 281.

5. Blumenfeld and Vachaud, *Brian De Palma*, 65.

6. Childs and Jones, "De Palma Has the Power!" 9.

7. Aisenberg, *Studies in the Horror Film*, 281.

8. Laurent Bouzereau, dir., "Acting *Carrie*," *Carrie* DVD (MGM Home Entertainment, 2001).

9. Blumenfeld and Vachaud, *Brian De Palma*, 65.

10. Bouzereau, "Acting *Carrie*."

11. Zinoman, *Shock Value*, 164.

12. Sissy Spacek and Maryanne Vollers, *My Extraordinary Ordinary Life* (New York: Hyperion, 2012), 174.

13. Bouzereau, "Acting *Carrie*."

14. Aisenberg, *Studies in the Horror Film*, 150.

15. Justin Bozung, "She Was . . . An American Girl: An Interview with Actress Nancy Allen," *Shock Cinema*, no. 41 (December 2011): 9.

16. Bouzereau, "Acting *Carrie*."

17. Ibid.

18. Bouzereau, "Visualizing *Carrie*."

19. Bouzereau, "Acting *Carrie*."

20. For more on the other versions of *Carrie*, see Douglas Keesey, "Patriarchal Mediations of *Carrie*: The Book, the Movie, and the Musical," in *Imagining the Worst: Stephen King and the Representation of Women*, ed. Kathleen Margaret Lant and Theresa Thompson (Westport, CT:

Greenwood Press, 1998), 31–45. *Carrie* has also been remade as a TV movie (dir. David Carson, 2002) and as a feature film (dir. Kimberly Peirce, 2013).

21. Aisenberg, *Studies in the Horror Film*, 315.

22. Blumenfeld and Vachaud, *Brian De Palma*, 65.

23. Rottenberg, "There's Something about *Carrie*," 63.

24. Ibid., 104.

25. Judy Klemesrud, "At the Movies: Nancy Allen, Making Good by Being Bad," *New York Times*, September 5, 1980.

26. Aisenberg, *Studies in the Horror Film*, 285.

27. Royal S. Brown, "Considering De Palma," *American Film* 2, no. 9 (July–August 1977): 59.

28. Tony Crawley, "The Sound and the Fury," *Films Illustrated* 8, no. 8 (December 1978): 135.

29. R. S. Brown, "Considering De Palma," 59.

30. Childs and Jones, "De Palma Has the Power!" 6.

31. Mark Emerson and Eugene E. Platt, Jr., *Country Girl: The Life of Sissy Spacek* (New York: St. Martin's Press, 1988), 52.

32. Rottenberg, "There's Something about *Carrie*," 62.

33. Spacek and Vollers, *My Extraordinary Ordinary Life*, 170.

34. Bouzereau, "Acting *Carrie*."

35. Childs and Jones, "De Palma Has the Power!" 9.

36. Aisenberg, *Studies in the Horror Film*, 297.

37. Bouzereau, "Visualizing *Carrie*."

38. Pye and Myles, *Movie Brats*, 167.

39. Aisenberg, *Studies in the Horror Film*, 287.

40. Blumenfeld and Vachaud, *Brian De Palma*, 14.

41. Salamon, *Devil's Candy*, 40.

42. Blumenfeld and Vachaud, *Brian De Palma*, 16.

43. Ibid.

44. De Palma, "Guilty Pleasures," 53.

45. Aisenberg, *Studies in the Horror Film*, 294.

46. Rottenberg, "There's Something about *Carrie*," 106.

47. R. S. Brown, "Considering De Palma," 58.

48. Pye and Myles, *Movie Brats*, 167.

Chapter 11: *The Fury*

1. For a more philosophical approach to traumatic witnessing as a theme in *Carrie*, *The Fury*, *Blow Out*, and *Femme Fatale*, see Eyal Peretz, *Becoming Visionary: Brian De Palma's Cinematic Education of the Senses* (Stanford: Stanford University Press, 2008).

2. Blumenfeld and Vachaud, *Brian De Palma*, 14.

3. Ibid., 15.

4. "Bruce De Palma: Inventor of the N-Machine," http://www.brucedepalma.com.

5. Bruce E. De Palma, *Space Energy Newsletter* 3, no. 3 (October–November 1992), http://www.brucedepalma.com.

6. De Palma, "Guilty Pleasures," 53.

7. Blumenfeld and Vachaud, *Brian De Palma*, 15.

8. Paul Mandell, "Brian De Palma Discusses *The Fury*," *Filmmakers Newsletter* 11, no. 7 (May 1978): 29.

9. Steve Swires, "Things That Go Bump in the Night: An Interview with Brian De Palma," *Films in Review* 29, no. 7 (August–September 1978): 403.

10. Crawley, "Sound and the Fury," 133.

11. John Coates, "The Making of *Phantom of the Paradise*," *Filmmakers Newsletter* 8, no. 4 (February 1975): 27.

12. Alfred Bester, *The Demolished Man* (New York: Vintage Books, 1996), 242.

13. Ibid., 243.

Chapter 12: *Home Movies*

1. Gerald Peary, "Working His Way through College: Brian De Palma at Sarah Lawrence," *Take One*, January 1979: 18.

2. Bill Fentum, "Interview with Keith Gordon (Part I)," *Directed by Brian De Palma*, 1999, http://www.briandepalma.net.

3. Peary, "Working His Way through College," 14.

4. Blumenfeld and Vachaud, *Brian De Palma*, 196.

5. Dworkin, *Double De Palma*, 141.

6. De Palma, "Day in the Life," 117.

7. G. A. Brown, "*Obsession*," 33.

8. J. Hoberman, "Dazzling," *Village Voice*, July 23–29, 1980.

9. Bozung, "She Was . . . An American Girl," 10.

10. Zinoman, *Shock Value*, 173.

11. "Noah Baumbach and Brian De Palma," *HBO on Cinema* (1/4), October 12, 2012, http://www.youtube.com.

12. Blumenfeld and Vachaud, *Brian De Palma*, 85–86.

13. G. A. Brown, "*Obsession*," 32.

14. Ibid.

15. Blumenfeld and Vachaud, *Brian De Palma*, 44.

16. Ibid., 50.

17. Dworkin, *Double De Palma*, 26.

18. Ibid., 141.

19. Blumenfeld and Vachaud, *Brian De Palma*, 196.

20. Fentum, "Interview with Keith Gordon (Part I)."

21. Lee Gambin and Camilla Jackson, "Murder Most Mod," *Fangoria*, no. 332 (May 2014): 15.

22. Paula Span, "Brian De Palma, Through the Lens," *Washington Post*, August 18, 1989.

23. Dworkin, *Double De Palma*, 141–42.

24. Salamon, *Devil's Candy*, 43.

25. Ibid.

26. Ibid., 44.

27. Peary, "Working His Way through College," 16.

28. Fentum, "Interview with Keith Gordon (Part I)."

29. Norman G. Gordon, "Family Structure and Dynamics in De Palma's Horror Films," *Psychoanalytic Review* 70, no. 3 (Fall 1983): 442.

30. Peary, "Working His Way through College," 18.

31. Ibid., 16.

32. Stone, *Eye on the World*, 658.

33. Vallely, "Brian De Palma: The New Hitchcock," 39.

34. Ibid.

35. Ralph Appelbaum, "Techniques of the Horror Film," *Filmmakers Monthly* 13, no. 11 (September 1980).

36. Vallely, "Brian De Palma: The New Hitchcock," 39.

Chapter 13: *Dressed to Kill*

1. Brian De Palma, *Dressed to Kill* screenplay (1979), 3.

2. Chuck Kleinhans, "*Dressed to Kill* Protested," *Jump Cut*, no. 23 (October 1980): 32.

3. Lee Grant, "Women vs. *Dressed to Kill*: Is Film Admirable or Deplorable?" *Los Angeles Times*, September 12, 1980.

4. Bozung, "She Was . . . An American Girl," 11.

5. Nancy Friday, *Men in Love* (New York: Random House Digital, 2010), 451.

6. Laurent Bouzereau, dir., "The Making of *Dressed to Kill*," *Dressed to Kill* Special Edition DVD (MGM Home Entertainment, 2001).

7. Mort Drucker and Arnie Kogen, "Undressed to Kill," *Mad*, no. 222 (April 1981): 5.

8. De Palma, *Dressed to Kill* screenplay, 16.

9. Ibid., 15.

10. Peter Lester, "Redress or Undress?: Feminists Fume While Angie Dickinson Scores in Sexy Chiller," *Dressed to Kill*," *People*, September 15, 1980.

11. G. A. Brown, "*Obsession*," 34.

12. Blumenfeld and Vachaud, *Brian De Palma*, 91.

13. De Palma, *Dressed to Kill* screenplay, 18–19.

14. Bouzereau, "Making of *Dressed*."

15. Blumenfeld and Vachaud, *Brian De Palma*, 95.

16. Pally, "*Double* Trouble," 14.

17. Appelbaum, "Techniques of the Horror Film."

18. G. A. Brown, "*Obsession*," 33.

19. Ibid.

20. De Palma, *Dressed to Kill* screenplay, 106.

21. Bozung, "She Was . . . An American Girl," 11.

22. Ibid.

23. Drucker and Kogen, "Undressed to Kill," 8.

24. Ibid., 10.

25. Andrew Sarris, "De Palma: Derivative," *Village Voice*, July 22–29, 1980: 42, 44.

26. George Morris, "*Dressed to Kill* and No Place to Go," *Film Comment* 16, no. 5 (September–October 1980): 54.

27. Richard Combs, "*Dressed to Kill*," *Monthly Film Bulletin* 47 (November 1980): 213.

28. John Simon, *Reverse Angle* (New York: Clarkson N. Potter, 1981), 416.

29. Combs, "*Dressed to Kill*," 213.

30. Morris, "*Dressed to Kill*," 54.

31. De Palma, *Dressed to Kill* screenplay, 27.

32. Ibid., 82.

33. Michael Caine, *What's It All About?: An Autobiography* (New York: Turtle Bay Books, 1992), 416.

34. Vallely, "Brian De Palma: The New Hitchcock," 39.

35. Bouzereau, "Making of *Dressed*."

36. Blumenfeld and Vachaud, *Brian De Palma*, 96.

37. Bill Fentum, "Interview with Keith Gordon (Part II)," *Directed by Brian De Palma*, 1999, http://www.briandepalma.net.

38. Robert Fischer, dir., "Lessons in Filmmaking," *Pulsions* DVD (Carlotta Films/Fiction Factory, 2012).

39. Fentum, "Interview with Keith Gordon (Part II)."

40. Brian De Palma and Campbell Black, *Dressed to Kill* (New York: Bantam, 1980), 170.

41. Laura Schiff, "Nancy Allen—*Carrie*, *Dressed to Kill*, *Robocop*: The Fantasy Cinema's #1 Femme," *Femme Fatales* 6, no. 7 (January 1998): 51.

42. Hirschberg, "Brian De Palma's Death Wish," 82.

43. Schiff, "Nancy Allen," 51.

44. Robert Fischer, dir., "Dressed in Purple," *Pulsions* DVD (Carlotta Films/Fiction Factory, 2012).

45. Appelbaum, "Techniques of the Horror Film."

46. Bliss, *Brian De Palma*, 132; italics added, except for "*audiences*."

47. De Palma, *Dressed to Kill* screenplay, 103.

48. De Palma and Black, *Dressed to Kill*, 180.

49. De Palma, *Dressed to Kill* screenplay, 100.

50. Salamon, *Devil's Candy*, 44.

51. Norman G. Gordon and Anaruth Gordon, "De Palma's Dreams: Terror and Trauma," *Dreamworks* 3, no. 2 (1983): 148.

52. Ibid.

Chapter 14: *Blow Out*

1. Gary Arnold, "De Palma's Spectacular Sleeper," *Washington Post*, November 21, 1976.

2. *Blow Out* DVD (Criterion Collection, 2011).

3. Bliss, *Brian De Palma*, 135.

4. Blumenfeld and Vachaud, *Brian De Palma*, 99.

5. Ibid., 101.

6. Bozung, "She Was . . . An American Girl," 11.

7. Serge Daney and Jonathan Rosenbaum, eds., *The Hollywood Interviews* (Oxford: Berg, 2006), 96.

8. Stephanie Mansfield, "No Wonder Nancy Allen Has Nightmares," *Sarasota Herald-Tribune*, July 16, 1981.

9. *Blow Out* DVD.

10. Nashawaty, "Lives of Brian."

11. *Blow Out* DVD.

12. Robert Fischer, dir., "Return to Philadelphia," *Blow Out* DVD (Carlotta Films/Fiction Factory, 2012).

13. Blumenfeld and Vachaud, *Brian De Palma*, 99.

14. Neal Williams, *Blow Out* (New York: Bantam, 1981).

15. "The *Take One* Write-a-Script-for-De Palma Contest," *Take One*, January 1979: 19–22.

16. See Brian De Palma, "The Making of *The Conversation*: An Interview with Francis Ford Coppola," *Filmmakers Newsletter* 7, no. 7 (May 1974): 30–34.

17. Dworkin, *Double De Palma*, 68.

18. Kristin McMurran, "Why No Blowups on *Blow Out*?" *People*, August 17, 1981.

19. Carmie Amata, "Travolta and De Palma Discuss *Blow Out*," *Films and Filming*, no. 327 (December 1981): 11.

20. Schiff, "Nancy Allen," 51.

21. *Blow Out* DVD.

22. Ibid.

23. Rob Hill, "Mr. Untouchable," *Uncut*, January 2007: 136.

24. Romain B. and Richard B., "Interview Nancy Allen," *Scifi-Universe*, http://www.scifi-universe.com.

25. Robert Fischer, dir., "Rag Doll Memories," *Blow Out* DVD (Carlotta Films/Fiction Factory, 2012).

26. *Blow Out* DVD.

27. Pauline Kael, *Taking It All In* (New York: Holt, Rinehart and Winston, 1984), 227.

28. Daney and Rosenbaum, *Hollywood Interviews*, 95–96.

29. Dworkin, *Double De Palma*, 173.

Chapter 15: *Scarface*

1. Laurent Bouzereau, dir., "The *Scarface* Phenomenon," *Scarface* Limited Edition Blu-ray (Universal Studios Home Entertainment, 2011).

2. Wade Major, "Brian De Palma," *MrShowbiz*, August 1998, http://www.mrshowbiz.com.

3. David Taylor, *The Making of Scarface* (London: Unanimous Ltd., 2005), 148–49.

4. Laurent Bouzereau, dir., "*Scarface*: The Creating," *Scarface* Anniversary Edition DVD (Universal Studios Home Entertainment, 2003).

5. William Schoell, *The Films of Al Pacino* (New York: Citadel Press, 1996), 128.

6. Bernard Weinraub, "A Foul Mouth with a Following," *New York Times*, September 23, 2003.

7. Stephen Rebello, "The Resurrection of Tony Montana," *Playboy* 58, no. 12 (December 2011): 162.

8. Michael Mills, "Brian De Palma," *Moviegoer* 2, no. 12 (December 1983): 9.

9. Lawrence Grobel, *Al Pacino: In Conversation with Lawrence Grobel* (New York: Simon Spotlight Entertainment, 2006), 132.

10. Karina Longworth, *Al Pacino: Anatomy of an Actor* (Paris: Phaidon Press, 2013), 98.

11. Walter Goodman, "Is There a Moral Limit to the Violence in Films?" *New York Times*, December 18, 1983.

12. Dworkin, *Double De Palma*, 168.

13. Philippe Rouyer and Laurent Vachaud, "Entretien avec Brian De Palma: Violence et passion," *Positif*, no. 397 (March 1994): 19.

14. Douglas Thompson, *Pfeiffer: Beyond the Age of Innocence* (London: Smith Gryphon, 1993), 54–55.

15. Jerome, "20 Questions," 158.

16. Mandell, "Brian De Palma Discusses *The Fury*."

17. D. Thompson, *Pfeiffer*, 165–66.

18. Ibid., 52.

19. Rebello, "Resurrection of Tony Montana," 162.

20. "*Scarface*'s Steven Bauer—Career Interview Time," *Starpulse*, September 6, 2011, http://www.starpulse.com.

21. Ken Tucker, *Scarface Nation* (New York: St. Martin's Griffin, 2008), 66.

22. Gerri Hirshey, "The Bat's Meow," *Rolling Stone*, September 3, 1992.

23. Graham Fuller, "Michelle Pfeiffer: Woman Who Runs with the Wolves," *Interview*, July 1994.

24. Liz Smith, "Nancy Allen Replies," *Sarasota Herald-Tribune*, May 14, 1983.

25. Blumenfeld and Vachaud, *Brian De Palma*, 101.

26. Hirschberg, "Brian De Palma's Death Wish," 82–83.

27. Blumenfeld and Vachaud, *Brian De Palma*, 50.

28. Ibid., 74.

29. Zinoman, *Shock Value*, 233.

30. De Palma, "Day in the Life," 117.

31. Ibid., 118.

32. Bouzereau, "*Scarface* Phenomenon."

33. Mills, "Brian De Palma," 11.

34. Rebello, "Resurrection of Tony Montana," 66.

35. Tucker, *Scarface Nation*, 70.

36. D. Taylor, *Making of Scarface*, 188.

37. "Brian De Palma," *Take One*, The Movie Channel, 1983.

38. D. Thompson, "Emotion Pictures," 31.

39. Dale Pollock, "De Palma Takes a Shot at Defending *Scarface*," *Los Angeles Times*, December 5, 1983.

40. Stone, *Eye on the World*, 658.

41. D. Thompson, *Pfeiffer*, 55.

42. François Truffaut, *Hitchcock/Truffaut*, revised ed. (New York: Simon & Schuster, 1985), 73.

43. Ibid., 109.

44. Service Cinéma, "Un entretien avec Brian De Palma, cinéaste voyeur," *Les Inrockuptibles*, May 12, 2000.

45. Anne Thompson, "The Filmmaker Series: Brian De Palma," *Premiere*, September 1998: 52.

46. D. Taylor, *Making of Scarface*, 185.

47. Pauline Kael, *State of the Art* (New York: E. P. Dutton, 1985), 104, 105–106.

48. Tucker, *Scarface Nation*, 4.

49. Ibid., 81.

Chapter 16: *Body Double*

1. Dworkin, *Double De Palma*, 138.

2. Laurent Bouzereau, dir., "*Body Double*: The Seduction," *Body Double* Special Edition DVD (Sony Pictures Home Entertainment, 2006).

3. Robert J. Avrech and Brian De Palma, *Body Double* screenplay, 1982.

4. Laurent Bouzereau, dir., "*Body Double*: The Setup," *Body Double* Special Edition DVD (Sony Pictures Home Entertainment, 2006).

5. Avrech and De Palma, *Body Double* screenplay.

6. Ibid.

7. Hirschberg, "Brian De Palma's Death Wish," 83.

8. Mills, "Brian De Palma," 11.

9. Martin Amis, *The Moronic Inferno and Other Visits to America* (New York: Viking, 1987), 86.

10. Dworkin, *Double De Palma*, 34.

11. Bouzereau, "*Body Double*: The Seduction."

12. Hirschberg, "Brian De Palma's Death Wish," 83.

13. Bouzereau, "*Body Double*: The Seduction."

14. Laurent Bouzereau, *The De Palma Cut* (New York: Dembner Books, 1988), 70.

15. Dworkin, *Double De Palma*, 34.

16. Bouzereau, *De Palma Cut*, 70.

17. Bouzereau, "*Body Double*: The Seduction."

18. Jerome, "20 Questions," 160.

19. Ibid., 119.

20. Laurent Bouzereau, dir., "*Body Double*: The Mystery," *Body Double* Special Edition DVD (Sony Pictures Home Entertainment, 2006).

21. Avrech and De Palma, *Body Double* screenplay.

22. Bouzereau, "*Body Double*: The Seduction."

23. Avrech and De Palma, *Body Double* screenplay.

24. Stephen Prince, *A New Pot of Gold* (Berkeley: University of California Press, 2000), 353.

25. Ibid., 354.

26. Charles Derry, *The Suspense Thriller* (Jefferson, NC: McFarland, 1988), 215.

27. David Denby, et al., "Pornography—Love or Death?" *Film Comment* 20, no. 6 (November–December 1984): 45.

28. Ibid., 49.

29. Plummer, "Despite His Critics."

30. Jimmy Summers, "*Body Double*," *Box Office*, December 1984.

31. Peter Rainer, "Brian De Palma's Never-Say-Die Brio," *Los Angeles Times*, September 24, 2006.

32. Richard Corliss, "Dark Nights for the Libido," *Time*, October 29, 1984.

33. Kael, *State of the Art*, 264.

34. Scott Ashlin, "*Body Double*," *1000 Misspent Hours and Counting*, http://www.1000misspenthours.com.

35. Bouzereau, "*Body Double*: The Seduction."

36. Blumenfeld and Vachaud, *Brian De Palma*, 126.

37. Bouzereau, *De Palma Cut*, 72.

Chapter 17: *Wise Guys*

1. Blumenfeld and Vachaud, *Brian De Palma*, 14.

2. Salamon, *Devil's Candy*, 41.

3. Blumenfeld and Vachaud, *Brian De Palma*, 75.

4. Ibid., 14.

5. Ibid.

6. Pauline Kael, *Hooked* (New York: E. P. Dutton, 1989), 155.

7. Ibid., 153.

8. Leonardo Gandini, *Brian De Palma* (Rome: Gremese, 2002), 65.

Chapter 18: *The Untouchables*

1. Tom Mathews, "The Mob at the Movies," *Newsweek*, June 22, 1987.

2. Salamon, *Devil's Candy*, 413.

3. Angelo Torres and Arnie Kogen, "The Unwatchables," *Mad*, no. 276 (January 1988): 30.

4. Capone, "Capone Comes Face to Face with One of the Untouchables, Andy Garcia," *Ain't It Cool News*, March 30, 2010, http://www.aintitcool.com.

5. Daniel Dickholtz, *The Untouchables: The Official Movie Magazine* (New York: O'Quinn Studios, 1987), 26.

6. George De Stefano, "Italian Americans: Family Lies," *Film Comment* 23, no. 4 (July–August 1987): 22.

7. Ian Nathan, "The Chicago Way: *The Untouchables* at 25," *Empire*, August 2012: 86.

8. D. Thompson, "Emotion Pictures," 26.

9. Mathews, "Mob at the Movies."

10. Jean-Paul Chaillet, "Une légende fracassante," *Première*, no. 127 (October 1987).

11. Jesse Kornbluth, "*The Untouchables* Shot-by-Shot," *Premiere* 1, no. 1 (July–August 1987): 39.

12. Ibid., 40.

13. Ibid.

14. Ibid.

15. Ibid.

16. Art Linson, *A Pound of Flesh* (New York: Grove Press, 1993), 127.

17. Peter Biskind, "Kevin Costner—*The Untouchables*'s New Ness," *American Film* 12, no. 8 (June 1987): 22.

18. Dickholtz, *The Untouchables*, 20.

19. Laurent Bouzereau, dir., "Production Stories," *The Untouchables* Special Collector's Edition DVD (Paramount Pictures Home Entertainment, 2004).

20. Laurent Bouzereau, dir., "The Script, the Cast," *The Untouchables* Special Collector's Edition DVD (Paramount Pictures Home Entertainment, 2004).

21. Linson, *Pound of Flesh*, 123.

22. Ibid., 106.

23. Ibid., 136.

24. Nathan, "Chicago Way," 84.

25. Linson, *Pound of Flesh*, 137.

Chapter 19: *Casualties of War*

1. Dworkin, *Double De Palma*, 138.

2. Steve Pond, "*Casualties of War*, Shot-by-Shot," *Premiere* 3, no. 1 (September 1989): 98.

3. Ibid.

4. Ibid.

5. Blumenfeld and Vachaud, *Brian De Palma*, 140.

6. Ibid., 14.

7. Salamon, *Devil's Candy*, 40.

8. Blumenfeld and Vachaud, *Brian De Palma*, 139.

9. Bruce Weber, "Cool Head, Hot Images," *New York Times Magazine*, May 21, 1989.

10. John Leguizamo, *Pimps, Hos, Playa Hatas, and All the Rest of My Hollywood Friends* (New York: HarperCollins, 2006), 61.

11. Laurent Bouzereau, dir., "The Making of *Casualties of War*," *Casualties of War* Extended Cut DVD (Sony Pictures Home Entertainment, 2006).

12. Richard T. Kelly, *Sean Penn: His Life and Times* (New York: Canongate U.S., 2004), 214.

13. Ibid.

14. Leguizamo, *Pimps, Hos*, 61.

15. Ibid., 62.

16. Bozung, "She Was . . . An American Girl," 9.

17. Kelly, *Sean Penn*, 212–13.

18. Ibid., 235.

19. Michael Norman, "Brian De Palma Explores Vietnam and Its Victims," *New York Times*, August 13, 1989.

20. Laurent Bouzereau, dir., "Eriksson's War: A Talk with Actor Michael J. Fox," *Casualties of War* Extended Cut DVD (Sony Pictures Home Entertainment, 2006).

21. Bouzereau, "Making of *Casualties*."

22. A split-diopter shot uses a special lens so that the very close foreground on one side of the screen, along with the very far background on the other side, can both appear to be in focus at the same time.

23. Daniel Lang, *Casualties of War* (New York: McGraw-Hill, 1969), 120.

24. Bouzereau, "Making of *Casualties*."

25. Blumenfeld and Vachaud, *Brian De Palma*, 137.

26. Bouzereau, "Making of *Casualties*."

27. David Rabe, *Casualties of War* screenplay, 1989.

28. Blumenfeld and Vachaud, *Brian De Palma*, 133.

29. Bouzereau, "Making of *Casualties*."

30. Cynthia Fuchs, "*Casualties of War*," *Cineaste* 17, no. 3 (February 1990): 40.

31. Elliott Gruner, "Rape and Captivity," *Jump Cut*, no. 39 (June 1994): 54.

32. Kelly, *Sean Penn*, 235.

33. Bouzereau, "Making of *Casualties*."

34. Ibid.

35. David Halberstam, "Law of the Jungle," *Elle*, September 1983: 140.

36. Blumenfeld and Vachaud, *Brian De Palma*, 141.

37. Ibid.

38. David Greven, *Manhood in Hollywood from Bush to Bush* (Austin: University of Texas Press, 2009), 253n28.

39. Stuart Klawans, "*Casualties of War*," *Nation*, September 4, 1989.

40. Paul Rosenfield, "How *Casualties of War* Survived," *Los Angeles Times*, August 13, 1989.

41. Pauline Kael, *Movie Love* (New York: Plume, 1991), 175.

42. Nashawaty, "Lives of Brian."

43. Blumenfeld and Vachaud, *Brian De Palma*, 141.

44. Ibid., 144.

Chapter 20: *The Bonfire of the Vanities*

1. Weber, "Cool Head."

2. Blumenfeld and Vachaud, *Brian De Palma*, 50.

3. Nancy Griffin, "Sherman's March," *Premiere* 4 (December 1990): 75.

4. Ibid.

5. Salamon, *Devil's Candy*, 302.

6. Blumenfeld and Vachaud, *Brian De Palma*, 16.

7. Dworkin, *Double De Palma*, 141–42.

8. Salamon, *Devil's Candy*, 272.

9. Griffin, "Sherman's March," 78.

10. Blumenfeld and Vachaud, *Brian De Palma*, 74.

11. Ibid., 50.

12. Hirschberg, "Brian De Palma's Death Wish," 82–83.

13. Julie Salamon, "Afterword: Ten Years Later," in *The Devil's Candy: The Anatomy of a Hollywood Fiasco* (New York: Da Capo, 2002), 431.

14. Daney and Rosenbaum, *Hollywood Interviews*, 86.

15. Salamon, *Devil's Candy*, 406.

16. Ibid., 168.

17. Ibid., 389.

18. Ibid., 404.

19. Those interested in reading more about why the film failed so disastrously are advised to read Julie Salamon, who has written an entire book devoted to this subject: *The Devil's Candy*.

20. Salamon, "Afterword," 425.

21. Nashawaty, "Lives of Brian."

22. Salamon, *Devil's Candy*, 418.

Chapter 21: *Raising Cain*

1. Amy Taubin, "The Master of Jeopardy," *Village Voice*, August 11, 1992.

2. Blumenfeld and Vachaud, *Brian De Palma*, 152.

3. Ibid., 151.

4. Ibid., 76.

5. Michael Angeli, "They're More Than Just a Pair of Characters: John Lithgow Takes on Five Roles in One Movie," *New York Times*, August 2, 1992.

6. Robert Plunket, "Brian De Palma," *Interview* 22, no. 8 (August 1992): 46.

7. Zinoman, *Shock Value*, 155.

8. Jeremy Smith, "Brian De Palma" (*The Black Dahlia*)," *CHUD*, September 8, 2006, http://www.chud.com.

9. Angeli, "They're More Than Just a Pair."

10. Taubin, "Master of Jeopardy."

11. Peter Keough, "Out of the Ashes," *Sight and Sound*, December 1992: 15.

Chapter 22: *Carlito's Way*

1. Hill, "Mr. Untouchable," 137.

2. Laurent Bouzereau, dir., "The Making of *Carlito's Way*," *Carlito's Way* Ultimate Edition DVD (Universal Studios Home Entertainment, 2005).

3. Laurent Bouzereau, dir., "Brian De Palma on *Carlito's Way*," *Carlito's Way* Ultimate Edition DVD (Universal Studios Home Entertainment, 2005).

4. Blumenfeld and Vachaud, *Brian De Palma*, 160.

5. Ibid.

6. Ibid., 101.

7. Ibid., 160.

8. Frances FitzGerald, "Casualties of Cinema: De Palma Runs Amok," *Village Voice*, August 22, 1989.

9. Gavin Smith, "Body Count: Rabe and De Palma's Wargasm," *Film Comment* 25, no. 4 (July–August 1989): 52.

10. Salamon, *Devil's Candy*, 404.

11. Ibid., 183.

12. Isabelle Huppert, Thierry Jousse, and Camille Nevers, "Brian De Palma," *Cahiers du Cinéma*, no. 477 (March 1994): 82.

13. De Palma, "Day in the Life," 118.

14. Blumenfeld and Vachaud, *Brian De Palma*, 177.

15. Tom Friend, "Man with a *Mission*," *Premiere*, June 1996: 72.

16. Blumenfeld and Vachaud, *Brian De Palma*, 168.

Chapter 23: *Mission: Impossible*

1. Jean-Luc Vandiste, "Peter Graves," *Ecran fantastique*, no. 154 (October 1996).

2. Tom Green, "Handling an Impossible Task: A *Mission* Complete with Intrigue," *USA Today*, May 22, 1996.

3. Blumenfeld and Vachaud, *Brian De Palma*, 168.

4. Roger Ebert, "*Mission: Impossible*," *Chicago Sun-Times*, May 31, 1996.

5. Dick DeBartolo and Mort Drucker, "Wishin' for the Impossible," *Mad*, no. 347 (July 1996): 43, 44.

6. Ibid., 47.

7. A. Thompson, "Filmmaker Series," 50.

8. José Arroyo, "Mission: Sublime," *Sight and Sound* 6, no. 7 (July 1996): 20.

9. David Koepp and Robert Towne, *Mission: Impossible* shooting script, August 16, 1995.

10. Tom Green, "Handling an Impossible Task."

11. "Mission: Remarkable—40 Years of Creating the Impossible," *Mission: Impossible* Special Collector's Edition DVD (Paramount Pictures Home Entertainment, 2006).

12. Koepp and Towne, *Mission: Impossible* shooting script.

13. Blumenfeld and Vachaud, *Brian De Palma*, 75.

14. Ibid., 15.

15. Major, "Brian De Palma."

16. Joshua Sperling, "Brian De Palma Revisits 5 of His Most Unforgettable Films," *Bullett*, August 8, 2013, http://www.bullettmedia.com.

Chapter 24: *Snake Eyes*

1. Laurent Vachaud, "Le casino, c'est l'enfer sur terre," *Positif*, no. 455 (January 1999): 8.

2. Chris Pizzello, "Ringside Riddle," *American Cinematographer* 79, no. 8 (August 1998): 58.

3. Vachaud, "casino, c'est l'enfer," 6.

4. Cousins, "Brian De Palma."

5. Drew Taylor, "Interview: Brian De Palma," *Playlist*, July 30, 2013, http://blogs.indiewire.com/theplaylist.

6. Cousins, "Brian De Palma."

7. Blumenfeld and Vachaud, *Brian De Palma*, 187.

8. Ibid., 194.

Chapter 25: *Mission to Mars*

1. Blumenfeld and Vachaud, *Brian De Palma*, 190.

2. Ibid., 14–15.

3. Salamon, *Devil's Candy*, 42.

4. Blumenfeld and Vachaud, *Brian De Palma*, 15.

5. Stone, *Eye on the World*, 656.

6. Biskind, *Easy Riders*, 282.

7. De Palma, "Day in the Life," 117.

8. Mills, "Brian De Palma," 11.

9. Daney and Rosenbaum, *Hollywood Interviews*, 98.

10. Brian De Palma, *Mission to Mars* press conference, *ABC News*, May 12, 2000, http://www.angelfire.com/de/palma/mars2.html.

11. Brian De Palma, *Passion* press kit, SBS Productions, 2012.

12. Blumenfeld and Vachaud, *Brian De Palma*, 15.

13. A. Thompson, "Filmmaker Series," 53.

14. Blumenfeld and Vachaud, *Brian De Palma*, 182.

15. "Visions of Mars," *Mission to Mars* DVD (Touchstone Home Video, 2002).

16. Rob Humanick, "80. *Mission to Mars*" in "The 100 Best Films of the Aughts," *Slant*, February 7, 2010, http://www.slantmagazine.com.

17. Bill Fentum, "De Palma on *Mission to Mars*," *Directed by Brian De Palma*, March 10, 2000, http://www.briandepalma.net.

18. Blumenfeld and Vachaud, *Brian De Palma*, 193.

19. Geoff Beran, "Interview."

20. Blumenfeld and Vachaud, *Brian De Palma*, 87.

21. Samuel Blumenfeld, "La passion selon Brian," *Le Monde*, February 12, 2013.

Chapter 26: *Femme Fatale*

1. Brian De Palma, *Femme Fatale: Scénario bilingue* (Paris: Cahiers du cinéma, 2002), 26.

2. Laurent Bouzereau, dir., "*Femme Fatale*: Dream within a Dream," *Femme Fatale* DVD (Warner Home Video, 2003).

3. *Femme Fatale* press kit, Warner Brothers, 2002.

4. De Palma, *Femme Fatale: Scénario*, 30.

5. Gavin Smith, "Dream Project: The Name of the Game Is Déjà Vu in *Femme Fatale*," *Film Comment* 38, no. 6 (November–December 2002): 30.

6. De Palma, *Femme Fatale: Scénario*, 62, 64.

7. Ibid., 72.

8. Ibid., 124.

9. Chad Taylor, "Meaningful Stairs," *Chad Taylor/Marginalia*, March 2, 2010, http://chadtaylormarginalia.blogspot.com.

10. Linda Ruth Williams, *The Erotic Thriller in Contemporary Cinema* (Bloomington: Indiana University Press, 2005), 142.

11. Ibid., 143.

12. De Palma, *Femme Fatale: Scénario*, 156.

13. L. R. Williams, *Erotic Thriller*, 143.

14. Blumenfeld and Vachaud, *Brian De Palma*, 14.

15. Bozung, "She Was . . . An American Girl," 12.

16. Yves Alion, "Entretien avec Brian De Palma: *Femme Fatale*," *Avant-Scène Cinéma*, no. 512 (May 2002): 98.

17. Eric Sauter, "Bruce De Palma & Ed Delvers Discover Rotation Force Field," *Sunday Times Advertiser (Trenton, NJ)*, January 11, 1976.

18. *Femme Fatale* press kit.

19. Bouzereau, "*Femme Fatale*."

20. Olivier Joyard and Jean-Marc Lalanne, "Les vacances de monsieur De Palma," *Cahiers du Cinéma*, no. 568 (May 2002): 103.

21. Blumenfeld and Vachaud, *Brian De Palma*, 178.

22. Roger Ebert, "*Femme Fatale*," *Chicago Sun-Times*, November 6, 2002.

23. Armond White, "*The Black Dahlia*," *Cineaste* 32, no. 1 (Winter 2006): 60.

24. L. R. Williams, *Erotic Thriller*, 145.

Chapter 27: *The Black Dahlia*

1. D. Thompson, "Emotion Pictures," 37.

2. Biskind, *Easy Riders*, 243.

3. Blumenfeld and Vachaud, *Brian De Palma*, 86.

4. Lagier, *mille yeux de Brian De Palma*, 31.

5. Ibid., 32.

6. Nashawaty, "Lives of Brian."

7. Olivier Père, "Brian De Palma—La fleur du mal," *Les Inrockuptibles*, November 7, 2006.

8. Salamon, *Devil's Candy*, 42.

9. Blumenfeld and Vachaud, *Brian De Palma*, 15.

10. Stone, *Eye on the World*, 656.

11. Arnold, "De Palma's Spectacular."

12. G. A. Brown, "*Obsession*," 32.

13. Cousins, "Brian De Palma."

14. Bartholomew, "De Palma of the *Paradise*," 14.

15. Blumenfeld and Vachaud, *Brian De Palma*, 14.

16. Gayle Ronan Sims, "Anthony De Palma," *Philadelphia Inquirer*, April 8, 2005.

17. Blumenfeld and Vachaud, *Brian De Palma*, 14.

18. Ibid., 76.

19. De Palma, *Passion* press kit.

20. Blumenfeld and Vachaud, *Brian De Palma*, 141.

Chapter 28: *Redacted*

1. Brian De Palma, "Director's Statement," *Redacted* press kit, Magnolia Pictures, 2007.

2. Ibid.

3. Blumenfeld and Vachaud, *Brian De Palma*, 76.

4. Cashill, "Outside the Green Zone," 10.

5. Emmanuel Burdeau, "En ligne avec Brian De Palma," *Cahiers du Cinéma*, no. 631 (February 2008): 12.

6. Simon Hattenstone, "No One Wants to Know," *Guardian*, March 7, 2008.

7. Steve Rose, "'Crazy, Huh?'" *Guardian*, September 7, 2006.

8. Burdeau, "En ligne avec Brian," 16.

9. Varga Ferenc, "De Palma Talks *Passion*, *Happy Valley*," *Origo*, May 1, 2013, http://www.angelfire.com/de/palma/blog/index.blog?start=1368073967.

10. Laurent Rigoulet and Jacques Morice, "Brian De Palma: 'Ce qui me plaît dans *Passion*, c'est que l'histoire est 100% féminine,'" *Télérama*, February 9, 2013.

Chapter 29: *Passion*

1. Dagmar Wagner, dir., "Talking about *Passion*," *Passion* DVD (Universal Pictures Video, 2013).

2. Mark Olsen, "Brian De Palma Applies His *Passion* to Remaking *Love Crime*," *Los Angeles Times*, September 7, 2012.

3. Cashill, "Outside the Green Zone," 11.

4. Tom Toro, "Brian De Palma on *Redacted*," *Rotten Tomatoes*, November 15, 2007, http://www.rottentomatoes.com.

5. Kerstin Lindemann, *Passion* interview with Brian De Palma, *Weser Kurier*, April 2013, http://www.angelfire.com/de/palma/blog/index.blog?start=1367276794.

6. Blumenfeld and Vachaud, *Brian De Palma*, 44.

7. Ibid., 15.

8. Ibid., 50.

9. De Palma, *Passion* press kit.

10. Fernando F. Croce, "Interview: Brian De Palma," *Slant*, August 26, 2013, http://www.slantmagazine.com.

11. Salamon, *Devil's Candy*, 255.

12. Blumenfeld and Vachaud, *Brian De Palma*, 121.

13. Salamon, *Devil's Candy*, 255.

14. Ibid.

15. Biskind, *Easy Riders*, 259.

16. Hirschberg, "Brian De Palma's Death Wish," 80.

17. Ibid.

18. Ibid., 81.

19. A. Thompson, "Filmmaker Series," 53.

20. Ibid., 52.

21. Blumenfeld and Vachaud, *Brian De Palma*, 180.

22. Ibid.

23. De Palma, *Passion* press kit.

24. Andreas Kilb, *Passion* Interview with Brian De Palma, *Frankfurter Allgemeine*, May 3, 2013, http://www.angelfire.com/de/palma/blog/index.blog?start=1368073967.

25. De Palma, *Passion* press kit.

26. L. R. Williams, *Erotic Thriller*, 142.

27. Jack Giroux, "Brian De Palma: The Strawberry Ice Cream of Filmmakers," *Film School Rejects*, September 26, 2012, http://www.filmschoolrejects.com.

28. G. Smith, "Dream Project," 30.

29. Daniel Kasman, "A Property of Movies: A Conversation with Brian De Palma," *Notebook*, October 1, 2002, http://mubi.com/notebook/posts/a-property-of-movies-a-conversation-with -brian-de-palma; ellipses in the original source.

Afterword

1. T. Simon, "Blow-Up," 248.

2. Amy Nicholson, "Brian De Palma Explains How His Erotic Remake *Passion* Is Better than the Original," *LA Weekly*, August 29, 2013.

3. Rose, "'Crazy, Huh?'"

4. Père, "Brian De Palma—La fleur."

5. Juan Morales, "No Longer a Bad Boy, But Still His Own Man," *New York Times*, November 3, 2002.

6. Anne Thompson, "Brian De Palma Q&A: *Passion*," *Thompson on Hollywood*, August 30, 2013, http://www.blogs.indiewire.com/thompsononhollywood.

7. Olsen, "Brian De Palma Applies His *Passion*."

Bibliography

Adler, Dick. "Hi, Mom, Greetings, It's Brian—in Hollywood!" *New York Times*, December 27, 1970.

Aisenberg, Joseph. *Studies in the Horror Film: Brian De Palma's Carrie*. Lakewood, CO: Centipede Press, 2011.

Alion, Yves. "Entretien avec Brian De Palma: *Femme Fatale*." *Avant-Scène Cinéma*, no. 512 (May 2002): 93–98.

Alvarez López, Cristina, and Adrian Martin. "[De Palma's] Vision." *Notebook*, June 3, 2014. https://mubi.com/notebook/posts/de-palmas-vision.

Amata, Carmie. "Travolta and De Palma Discuss *Blow Out*." *Films and Filming*, no. 327 (December 1981): 8–11.

Amis, Martin. *The Moronic Inferno and Other Visits to America*. New York: Viking, 1987.

Angeli, Michael. "They're More Than Just a Pair of Characters: John Lithgow Takes on Five Roles in One Movie." *New York Times*, August 2, 1992.

Appelbaum, Ralph. "Techniques of the Horror Film." *Filmmakers Monthly* 13, no. 11 (September 1980).

Arnold, Gary. "De Palma's Spectacular Sleeper." *Washington Post*, November 21, 1976.

Arroyo, José. "Mission: Sublime." *Sight and Sound* 6, no. 7 (July 1996): 18–21.

Artaud, Antonin. *The Theatre and Its Double*. Translated by Mary Caroline Richards. New York: Grove Press, 1958.

Ashbrook, John. *Brian De Palma*. Harpenden, Herts: Pocket Essentials, 2000.

Ashlin, Scott. "*Body Double*." *1000 Misspent Hours and Counting*. http://www.1000misspenthours.com.

Avrech, Robert J., and Brian De Palma. *Body Double* screenplay, 1982.

B., Romain, and Richard B. "Interview Nancy Allen." *Scifi-Universe*. http://www.scifi-universe.com.

Bartholomew, David. "De Palma of the *Paradise*." *Cinefantastique* 4, no. 2 (March 1974): 8–14.

Beran, Geoff. "Daughters and Dolls." *De Palma à la Mod*, July 4, 2011. http://www.angelfire.com/de/palma/blog/index.blog?topic_id=1069286.

———. "Interview with Brian De Palma." *De Palma à la Mod*, February 26, 2002. http://www.angelfire.com/de/palma/interviewparis.html.

Bester, Alfred. *The Demolished Man*. New York: Vintage Books, 1996.

Biskind, Peter. *Easy Riders, Raging Bulls: How the Sex-Drugs-and-Rock 'n' Roll Generation Saved Hollywood*. New York: Simon and Schuster, 1998.

———. "Kevin Costner—*The Untouchables*'s New Ness." *American Film* 12, no. 8 (June 1987): 22-23.

Blackford, James. "*Dressed to Kill* and *Blow Out*." *Sight and Sound* 23, no. 9 (September 2013): 96.

Bliss, Michael. *Brian De Palma*. Metuchen, NJ: Scarecrow Press, 1983.

Blow Out DVD. Criterion Collection, 2011.

Blumenfeld, Samuel. "La passion selon Brian." *Le Monde*, February 12, 2013.

Blumenfeld, Samuel, and Laurent Vachaud, eds. *Brian De Palma: Entretiens*. Paris: Calmann-Lévy, 2001.

Bouzereau, Laurent. *The De Palma Cut*. New York: Dembner Books, 1988.

Bouzereau, Laurent, dir. "Acting *Carrie*." *Carrie* DVD. MGM Home Entertainment, 2001.

———. "*Body Double*: The Mystery." *Body Double* Special Edition DVD. Sony Pictures Home Entertainment, 2006.

———. "*Body Double*: The Seduction." *Body Double* Special Edition DVD. Sony Pictures Home Entertainment, 2006.

———. "*Body Double*: The Setup." *Body Double* Special Edition DVD. Sony Pictures Home Entertainment, 2006.

———. "Brian De Palma on *Carlito's Way*." *Carlito's Way* Ultimate Edition DVD. Universal Studios Home Entertainment, 2005.

———. "Eriksson's War: A Talk with Actor Michael J. Fox." *Casualties of War* Extended Cut DVD. Sony Pictures Home Entertainment, 2006.

———. "*Femme Fatale*: Dream within a Dream." *Femme Fatale* DVD. Warner Home Video, 2003.

———. "The Making of *Carlito's Way*." *Carlito's Way* Ultimate Edition DVD. Universal Studios Home Entertainment, 2005.

———. "The Making of *Casualties of War*." *Casualties of War* Extended Cut DVD. Sony Pictures Home Entertainment, 2006.

———. "The Making of *Dressed to Kill*." *Dressed to Kill* Special Edition DVD. MGM Home Entertainment, 2001.

———. "*Obsession* Revisited." *Obsession* DVD, Arrow Films, 2011.

———. "Production Stories." *The Untouchables* Special Collector's Edition DVD. Paramount Pictures Home Entertainment, 2004.

———. "*Scarface*: The Creating." *Scarface* Anniversary Edition DVD. Universal Studios Home Entertainment, 2003.

———. "The *Scarface* Phenomenon." *Scarface* Limited Edition Blu-ray. Universal Studios Home Entertainment, 2011.

———. "The Script, the Cast." *The Untouchables* Special Collector's Edition DVD. Paramount Pictures Home Entertainment, 2004.

———. "Visualizing *Carrie*." *Carrie* DVD. MGM Home Entertainment, 2001.

Bozung, Justin. "She Was . . . An American Girl: An Interview with Actress Nancy Allen." *Shock Cinema*, no. 41 (December 2011): 8–13, 48.

Brackman, Jacob R. "Horror Comedy." *New Yorker*, July 23, 1966.

"Brian De Palma." *Take One.* The Movie Channel, 1983.

Brown, Georgia A. "*Obsession.*" *American Film,* December 1983: 29–35.

Brown, Royal S. "Considering De Palma." *American Film* 2, no. 9 (July–August 1977): 54–61.

"Bruce De Palma: Inventor of the N-Machine." http://www.brucedepalma.com.

Burdeau, Emmanuel. "En ligne avec Brian De Palma." *Cahiers du Cinéma,* no. 631 (February 2008): 12–16.

Byro. "*Murder à la Mod.*" *Variety,* May 1, 1968.

Caine, Michael. *What's It All About?: An Autobiography.* New York: Turtle Bay Books, 1992.

Canadian Press. "Brian De Palma Knows Erotic Thriller *Passion* Is Divisive." *TheSpec.com,* September 11, 2012. http://www.thespec.com.

Canby, Vincent. "*Murder à la Mod.*" *New York Times,* May 2, 1968.

Capone. "Capone Comes Face to Face with One of the Untouchables, Andy Garcia." *Ain't It Cool News,* March 30, 2010. http://www.aintitcool.com.

Cashill, Robert. "Outside the Green Zone: An Interview with Brian De Palma." *Cineaste* 33, no. 1 (Winter 2007): 6–12.

Chaillet, Jean-Paul. "Une légende fracassante." *Première,* no. 127 (October 1987).

Childs, Mike, and Alan Jones. "De Palma Has the Power!" *Cinefantastique* 6, no. 1 (Summer 1977): 4–10.

Christie, Ian, Phil Hardy, and Chris Petit. "Interview with Brian De Palma." *Film Directions* 1, no. 1 (December 1977): 7–11.

Coates, John. "The Making of *Phantom of the Paradise.*" *Filmmakers Newsletter* 8, no. 4 (February 1975): 24–27.

Combs, Richard. "*Dressed to Kill.*" *Monthly Film Bulletin* 47 (November 1980): 213.

Corliss, Richard. "Dark Nights for the Libido." *Time,* October 29, 1984.

Cousins, Mark, dir. "Brian De Palma." *Scene by Scene.* BBC TV, 1998.

Crawley, Tony. "The Sound and the Fury." *Films Illustrated* 8, no. 8 (December 1978): 132–38.

Croce, Fernando F. "Interview: Brian De Palma." *Slant,* August 26, 2013. http://www.slantmagazine.com.

Daney, Serge, and Jonathan Rosenbaum, eds. *The Hollywood Interviews.* Oxford: Berg, 2006.

De Palma, Brian. "A Day in the Life." *Esquire,* October 1980: 117–18.

———. "Director's Statement." *Redacted* press kit. Magnolia Pictures, 2007.

———. *Dressed to Kill* screenplay, 1979.

———. *Femme Fatale: Scénario bilingue.* Paris: Cahiers du Cinéma, 2002.

———. "Guilty Pleasures." *Film Comment* 23, no. 3 (May–June 1987): 52–53.

———. "The Making of *The Conversation*: An Interview with Francis Ford Coppola." *Filmmakers Newsletter* 7, no. 7 (May 1974): 30–34.

———. *Mission to Mars* press conference. *ABC News,* May 12, 2000. http://www.angelfire.com/de/palma/mars2.html.

———. *Passion* press kit. SBS Productions, 2012.

De Palma, Brian, and Campbell Black. *Dressed to Kill.* New York: Bantam, 1980.

De Palma, Bruce E. *Space Energy Newsletter* 3, no. 3 (October–November 1992). http://www.brucedepalma.com.

De Stefano, George. "Italian Americans: Family Lies." *Film Comment* 23, no. 4 (July–August 1987): 22–26.

DeBartolo, Dick, and Mort Drucker. "Wishin' for the Impossible." *Mad*, no. 347 (July 1996): 43-47.

Denby, David, et al. "Pornography—Love or Death?" *Film Comment* 20, no. 6 (November–December 1984): 29–49.

Derry, Charles. *The Suspense Thriller*. Jefferson, NC: McFarland, 1988.

Dickholtz, Daniel. *The Untouchables: The Official Movie Magazine*. New York: O'Quinn Studios, 1987.

Drucker, Mort, and Arnie Kogen. "Undressed to Kill." *Mad*, no. 222 (April 1981): 4–10.

Dumas, Chris. *Un-American Psycho: Brian De Palma and the Political Invisible*. Chicago: Intellect, 2012.

Dworkin, Susan. *Double De Palma*. New York: Newmarket Press, 1984.

Ebert, Roger. "*Femme Fatale*." *Chicago Sun-Times*, November 6, 2002.

———. "*Mission: Impossible*." *Chicago Sun-Times*, May 31, 1996.

Emerson, Mark, and Eugene E. Platt, Jr. *Country Girl: The Life of Sissy Spacek*. New York: St. Martin's Press, 1988.

Femme Fatale press kit. Warner Brothers, 2002.

Fentum, Bill. "De Palma on *Mission to Mars*." *Directed by Brian De Palma*, March 10, 2000. http://www.briandepalma.net.

———. "Interview with Keith Gordon (Part I)." *Directed by Brian De Palma*, 1999. http://www.briandepalma.net.

———. "Interview with Keith Gordon (Part II)." *Directed by Brian De Palma*, 1999. http://www.briandepalma.net.

Ferenc, Varga. "Brian De Palma Talks *Passion, Happy Valley*." *Origo*, May 1, 2013. http://www.angelfire.com/de/palma/blog/index.blog?start=1368073967.

Fischer, Robert, dir. "Dressed in Purple." *Pulsions* DVD. Carlotta Films/Fiction Factory, 2012.

———. "Lessons in Filmmaking." *Pulsions* DVD. Carlotta Films/Fiction Factory, 2012.

———. "Rag Doll Memories." *Blow Out* DVD. Carlotta Films/Fiction Factory, 2012.

———. "Return to Philadelphia." *Blow Out* DVD. Carlotta Films/Fiction Factory, 2012.

FitzGerald, Frances. "Casualties of Cinema: De Palma Runs Amok." *Village Voice*, August 22, 1989.

Friday, Nancy. *Men in Love*. New York: Random House Digital, 2010.

Friend, Tom. "Man with a *Mission*." *Premiere*, June 1996: 68–74, 103.

Fuchs, Cynthia. "*Casualties of War*." *Cineaste* 17, no. 3 (February 1990): 40–42.

Fuller, Graham. "Michelle Pfeiffer: Woman Who Runs with the Wolves." *Interview*, July 1994.

Gambin, Lee, and Camilla Jackson. "Murder Most Mod." *Fangoria*, no. 332 (May 2014): 15.

Gandini, Leonardo. *Brian De Palma*. Rome: Gremese, 2002.

Gelmis, Joseph. *The Film Director as Superstar*. Garden City, NY: Doubleday, 1970.

———. "*The Wedding Party*." *Newsday*, March 10, 1969.

Gilbey, Ryan. "Brian De Palma." In *It Don't Worry Me: The Revolutionary American Films of the Seventies*, 103–19. New York: Faber and Faber, 2003.

Giroux, Jack. "Brian De Palma: The Strawberry Ice Cream of Filmmakers." *Film School Rejects*, September 26, 2012. http://www.filmschoolrejects.com.

Goodman, Walter. "Is There a Moral Limit to the Violence in Films?" *New York Times*, December 18, 1983.

Gordon, Norman G. "Family Structure and Dynamics in De Palma's Horror Films." *Psychoana-lytic Review* 70, no. 3 (Fall 1983): 435–42.

Gordon, Norman G., and Anaruth Gordon. "De Palma's Dreams: Terror and Trauma." *Dream-works* 3, no. 2 (1983): 139–49.

Grant, Lee. "Women vs. *Dressed to Kill*: Is Film Admirable or Deplorable?" *Los Angeles Times*, September 12, 1980.

Green, Tom. "Handling an Impossible Task: A *Mission* Complete with Intrigue." *USA Today*, May 22, 1996.

Greven, David. *Manhood in Hollywood from Bush to Bush*. Austin: University of Texas Press, 2009.

———. *Psycho-Sexual: Male Desire in Hitchcock, De Palma, Scorsese, and Friedkin*. Austin: University of Texas Press, 2013.

———. *Representations of Femininity in American Genre Cinema: The Woman's Film, Film Noir, and Modern Horror*. New York: Palgrave Macmillan, 2011.

Griffin, Nancy. "Sherman's March." *Premiere* 4, no. 4 (December 1990): 70–78.

Grobel, Lawrence. *Al Pacino: In Conversation with Lawrence Grobel*. New York: Simon Spotlight Entertainment, 2006.

Grotowski, Jerzy. *Towards a Poor Theatre*. New York: Simon and Schuster, 1968.

Gruner, Elliott. "Rape and Captivity." *Jump Cut*, no. 39 (June 1994): 51–56.

Halberstam, David. "Law of the Jungle." *Elle*, September 1983: 140–42.

Harrison, Eric. "Scene 1: A Grassy Knoll." *Los Angeles Times: Calendar*, August 2, 1998.

Hattenstone, Simon. "No One Wants to Know." *Guardian*, March 7, 2008.

Henry, Michael. "Entretien avec Brian De Palma." *Positif*, no. 193 (May 1977): 23–31.

Higham, Charles. "My Films Come Out of My Nightmares." *New York Times*, October 28, 1973.

Hill, Rob. "Mr. Untouchable." *Uncut*, January 2007: 134–37.

Hirschberg, Lynn. "Brian De Palma's Death Wish." *Esquire*, January 1984: 79–83.

Hirshey, Gerri. "The Bat's Meow." *Rolling Stone*, September 3, 1992.

Hoberman, J. "Dazzling." *Village Voice*, July 23–29, 1980.

Humanick, Rob. "80. *Mission to Mars*." In "The 100 Best Films of the Aughts." *Slant*, February 7, 2010. http://www.slantmagazine.com.

Humphreys, Justin. *Interviews Too Shocking to Print!* Albany, GA: BearManor Media, 2014.

Huppert, Isabelle, Thierry Jousse, and Camille Nevers. "Brian De Palma." *Cahiers du Cinéma*, no. 477 (March 1994): 79–83.

Japa. "*Greetings*." *Variety*, December 25, 1968.

Jerome, Jim. "20 Questions: Brian De Palma." *Playboy* 32, no. 2 (February 1985): 118–19, 158–60.

Joyard, Olivier, and Jean-Marc Lalanne. "Les vacances de monsieur De Palma." *Cahiers du Cinéma*, no. 568 (May 2002): 102–103.

Kael, Pauline. *Hooked*. New York: E. P. Dutton, 1989.

———. *Movie Love*. New York: Plume, 1991.

———. *State of the Art*. New York: E. P. Dutton, 1985.

———. *Taking It All In*. New York: Holt, Rinehart and Winston, 1984.

Kapsis, Robert E. "Coping with the Hitchcock Legacy: The Case of Brian De Palma." In *Hitch-cock: The Making of a Reputation*, 188–215. Chicago: University of Chicago Press, 1992.

Kasman, Daniel. "A Property of Movies: A Conversation with Brian De Palma." *Notebook*, October 1, 2002. http://mubi.com/notebook/posts/a-property-of-movies-a-conversation -with-brian-de-palma.

Keesey, Douglas. "Patriarchal Mediations of *Carrie*: The Book, the Movie, and the Musical." In *Imagining the Worst: Stephen King and the Representation of Women*, edited by Kathleen Margaret Lant and Theresa Thompson, 31–45. Westport, CT: Greenwood Press, 1998.

Kellow, Brian. *Pauline Kael: A Life in the Dark*. New York: Viking, 2011.

Kelly, Richard T. *Sean Penn: His Life and Times*. New York: Canongate U.S., 2004.

Keough, Peter. "Out of the Ashes." *Sight and Sound*, December 1992: 14–15.

Kilb, Andreas. *Passion* interview with Brian De Palma. *Frankfurter Allgemeine*, May 3, 2013. http://www.angelfire.com/de/palma/blog/index.blog?start=1368073967.

Klawans, Stuart. "*Casualties of War*." *Nation*, September 4, 1989.

Kleinhans, Chuck. "*Dressed to Kill* Protested." *Jump Cut*, no. 23 (October 1980): 32.

Klemesrud, Judy. "At the Movies: Nancy Allen, Making Good by Being Bad." *New York Times*, September 5, 1980.

Knapp, Laurence F., ed. *Brian De Palma: Interviews*. Jackson: University Press of Mississippi, 2003.

Koepp, David, and Robert Towne. *Mission: Impossible* shooting script, August 16, 1995.

Kornbluth, Jesse. "*The Untouchables* Shot-by-Shot." *Premiere* 1, no. 1 (July–August 1987): 36–40.

Lagier, Luc. *Les mille yeux de Brian De Palma*. Paris: Cahiers du Cinéma, 2008.

———. *Visions fantastiques: Mission: Impossible de Brian De Palma*. Paris: Dreamland, 1999.

Lang, Daniel. *Casualties of War*. New York: McGraw-Hill, 1969.

Legrand, Dominique. *Brian De Palma: Le rebelle manipulateur*. Paris: Cerf, 1995.

Leguizamo, John. *Pimps, Hos, Playa Hatas, and All the Rest of My Hollywood Friends*. New York: HarperCollins, 2006.

Lester, Peter. "Redress or Undress?: Feminists Fume While Angie Dickinson Scores in Sexy Chiller, *Dressed to Kill*." *People*, September 15, 1980.

Lindemann, Kerstin. *Passion* interview with Brian De Palma. *Weser Kurier*, April 2013. http:// www.angelfire.com/de/palma/blog/index.blog?start=1367276794.

Linson, Art. *A Pound of Flesh*. New York: Grove Press, 1993.

Lithgow, John. *Drama: An Actor's Education*. New York: HarperCollins, 2011.

Longworth, Karina. *Al Pacino: Anatomy of an Actor*. Paris: Phaidon Press, 2013.

MacKinnon, Kenneth. *Misogyny in the Movies: The De Palma Question*. Newark: University of Delaware Press, 1990.

Major, Wade. "Brian De Palma." *MrShowbiz*, August 1998. http://www.mrshowbiz.com.

Mandell, Paul. "Brian De Palma Discusses *The Fury*." *Filmmakers Newsletter* 11, no. 7 (May 1978): 26–31.

Mansfield, Stephanie. "No Wonder Nancy Allen Has Nightmares." *Sarasota Herald-Tribune*, July 16, 1981.

"Masha and Dasha: Rare Study of Russia's Siamese Twins." *Life*, April 8, 1966: 67–70.

Mathews, Tom. "The Mob at the Movies." *Newsweek*, June 22, 1987.

McCarty, John. "*Sisters*." *Cinefantastique* 3, no. 1 (Fall 1973): 28.

McMurran, Kristin. "Why No Blowups on *Blow Out*?" *People*, August 17, 1981.

Mills, Michael. "Brian De Palma." *Moviegoer* 2, no. 12 (December 1983): 8–11.

"Mission: Remarkable—40 Years of Creating the Impossible." *Mission: Impossible* Special Collector's Edition DVD. Paramount Pictures Home Entertainment, 2006.

Mitchell, Neil. *Carrie.* Leighton Buzzard: Auteur, 2013.

Morales, Juan. "No Longer a Bad Boy, But Still His Own Man." *New York Times,* November 3, 2002.

Morris, George. "*Dressed to Kill* and No Place to Go." *Film Comment* 16, no. 5 (September–October 1980): 54–55.

Nashawaty, Chris. "The Lives of Brian." *Entertainment Weekly,* September 22, 2006.

Nathan, Ian. "The Chicago Way: *The Untouchables* at 25." *Empire,* August 2012: 82–89.

Nicholson, Amy. "Brian De Palma Explains How His Erotic Remake *Passion* Is Better than the Original." *LA Weekly,* August 29, 2013.

"Noah Baumbach and Brian De Palma." *HBO on Cinema* (1/4), October 12, 2012. http://www .youtube.com.

Norman, Michael. "Brian De Palma Explores Vietnam and Its Victims." *New York Times,* August 13, 1989.

North, Harry, and Larry Siegel. "*Sobsession.*" *Mad,* no. 191 (June 1977): 43–48.

Olsen, Mark. "Brian De Palma Applies His *Passion* to Remaking *Love Crime.*" *Los Angeles Times,* September 7, 2012.

Pally, Marcia. "*Double* Trouble." *Film Comment* 20, no. 5 (September–October 1984): 12–17.

Peary, Gerald. "Working His Way through College: Brian De Palma at Sarah Lawrence." *Take One,* January 1979: 14–18.

Père, Olivier. "Brian De Palma—La fleur du mal." *Les Inrockuptibles,* November 7, 2006.

Peretz, Eyal. *Becoming Visionary: Brian De Palma's Cinematic Education of the Senses.* Stanford: Stanford University Press, 2008.

Pizzello, Chris. "Ringside Riddle." *American Cinematographer* 79, no. 8 (August 1998): 52–59.

Plummer, William. "Despite His Critics, Director Brian De Palma Says *Body Double* Is Neither Too Violent nor Too Sexy." *People,* December 17, 1984.

Plunket, Robert. "Brian De Palma." *Interview* 22, no. 8 (August 1992): 44–46.

Pollock, Dale. "De Palma Takes a Shot at Defending *Scarface.*" *Los Angeles Times,* December 5, 1983.

Pond, Steve. "*Casualties of War,* Shot-by-Shot." *Premiere* 3, no. 1 (September 1989): 94–98.

Prince, Stephen. *A New Pot of Gold.* Berkeley: University of California Press, 2000.

Pye, Michael, and Lynda Myles. *The Movie Brats: How the Film Generation Took Over Hollywood.* New York: Holt, Rinehart and Winston, 1979.

Rabe, David. *Casualties of War* screenplay, 1989.

Rafferty, Terrence. "Brian De Palma." In *The Thing Happens: Ten Years of Writing about the Movies,* 52–62. New York: Grove Press, 1993.

Rainer, Peter. "Brian De Palma's Never-Say-Die Brio." *Los Angeles Times,* September 24, 2006.

Rebello, Stephen. "The Resurrection of Tony Montana." *Playboy* 58, no. 12 (December 2011): 64–68, 160–65.

Rigoulet, Laurent, and Jacques Morice. "Brian De Palma: 'Ce qui me plaît dans *Passion*, c'est que l'histoire est 100% féminine.'" *Télérama,* February 9, 2013.

Rose, Steve. "'Crazy, Huh?'" *Guardian,* September 7, 2006.

Rosenfield, Paul. "How *Casualties of War* Survived." *Los Angeles Times,* August 13, 1989.

Rottenberg, Josh. "There's Something about *Carrie*." *Premiere*, August 2001: 60–63, 104–106.

Rouyer, Philippe, and Laurent Vachaud. "Entretien avec Brian De Palma: Violence et passion." *Positif*, no. 397 (March 1994): 16–21.

Rubinstein, Richard. "The Making of *Sisters*: An Interview with Director Brian De Palma." *Filmmakers Newsletter*, September 1973: 25–30.

Salamon, Julie. "Afterword: Ten Years Later." In *The Devil's Candy: The Anatomy of a Hollywood Fiasco*, 421–32. New York: Da Capo, 2002.

———. *The Devil's Candy: The Bonfire of the Vanities Goes to Hollywood*. Boston: Houghton Mifflin, 1991.

Sarris, Andrew. "De Palma: Derivative." *Village Voice*, July 22–29, 1980.

Sauter, Eric. "Bruce De Palma & Ed Delvers Discover Rotation Force Field." *Sunday Times Advertiser (Trenton, NJ)*, January 11, 1976.

"*Scarface*'s Steven Bauer—Career Interview Time." *Starpulse*, September 6, 2011. http://www.starpulse.com.

"Scene by Scene: Monitor 2." *Swan Archives*. http://www.swanarchives.org.

Schechner, Richard, ed. *Dionysus in 69*. New York: Farrar, Straus and Giroux, 1970.

Schiff, Laura. "Nancy Allen—*Carrie, Dressed to Kill, Robocop*: The Fantasy Cinema's #1 Femme." *Femme Fatales* 6, no. 7 (January 1998): 48–55.

Schoell, William. *The Films of Al Pacino*. New York: Citadel Press, 1996.

Schrader, Paul. *Déjà Vu*. Text supplement to *Obsession* DVD. Arrow Films, 2011.

———. "Sisters." *LA*, no. 19 (November 11, 1972).

Service Cinéma. "Un entretien avec Brian De Palma, cinéaste voyeur." *Les Inrockuptibles*, May 12, 2000.

Shephard, William Hunter. *The Dionysus Group*. New York: Peter Lang, 1991.

Simon, John. *Reverse Angle: A Decade of American Films*. New York: Clarkson N. Potter, 1981.

Simon, Taryn. "Blow-Up: Taryn Simon and Brian De Palma in Conversation." *Artforum* 50, no. 10 (Summer 2012): 247–53.

Sims, Gayle Ronan. "Anthony De Palma." *Philadelphia Inquirer*, April 8, 2005.

Smith, Gavin. "Body Count: Rabe and De Palma's Wargasm." *Film Comment* 25, no. 4 (July–August 1989): 49–52.

———. "Dream Project: The Name of the Game Is Déjà Vu in *Femme Fatale*." *Film Comment* 38, no. 6 (November–December 2002): 28–31.

Smith, Jeremy. "Brian De Palma (*The Black Dahlia*)." *CHUD*, September 8, 2006. http://www.chud.com.

Smith, Liz. "Nancy Allen Replies." *Sarasota Herald-Tribune*, May 14, 1983.

Smith, Steven C. *A Heart at Fire's Center: The Life and Music of Bernard Herrmann*. Berkeley: University of California Press, 1991.

Spacek, Sissy, and Maryanne Vollers. *My Extraordinary Ordinary Life*. New York: Hyperion, 2012.

Span, Paula. "Brian De Palma, Through the Lens." *Washington Post*, August 18, 1989.

Sperling, Joshua. "Brian De Palma Revisits 5 of His Most Unforgettable Films." *Bullett*, August 8, 2013. http://www.bullettmedia.com.

Stone, Judy. *Eye on the World: Conversations with International Filmmakers*. Los Angeles: Silman-James Press, 1997.

Stuart, Alexander. "Phantoms and Fantasies." *Films and Filming* 23, no. 3 (December 1976): 10–13.

Summers, Jimmy. "*Body Double*." *Box Office*, December 1984.

Swires, Steve. "Things That Go Bump in the Night: An Interview with Brian De Palma." *Films in Review* 29, no. 7 (August–September 1978): 403–409.

"The *Take One* Write-a-Script-for-De Palma Contest." *Take One*, January 1979: 19–22.

Taubin, Amy. "The Master of Jeopardy." *Village Voice*, August 11, 1992.

Taylor, Chad. "Meaningful Stairs." *Chad Taylor/Marginalia*, March 2, 2010. http://chadtaylor marginalia.blogspot.com.

Taylor, David. *The Making of Scarface*. London: Unanimous Ltd., 2005.

Taylor, Drew. "Interview: Brian De Palma." *Playlist*, July 30, 2013. http://blogs.indiewire.com/ theplaylist.

Thomas, Kevin. "Film-maker at the Gut Level." *Los Angeles Times*, July 7, 1970.

Thompson, Anne. "Brian De Palma Q&A: *Passion*." *Thompson on Hollywood*, August 30, 2013. http://blogs.indiewire.com/thompsononhollywood.

———. "The Filmmaker Series: Brian De Palma." *Premiere*, September 1998: 49–53.

Thompson, David. "Emotion Pictures: Quentin Tarantino Talks to Brian De Palma." In *Projections 5*, edited by John Boorman and Walter Donohue, 24–38. London: Faber and Faber, 1996.

Thompson, Douglas. *Pfeiffer: Beyond the Age of Innocence*. London: Smith Gryphon, 1993.

Thompson, Howard. "*The Wedding Party*." *New York Times*, April 10, 1969.

Toro, Tom. "Brian De Palma on *Redacted*." *Rotten Tomatoes*, November 15, 2007. http://www .rottentomatoes.com.

Torres, Angelo, and Arnie Kogen. "The Unwatchables." *Mad*, no. 276 (January 1988): 27–31.

Truffaut, François. *Hitchcock/Truffaut*. Revised ed. New York: Simon & Schuster, 1985.

Tucker, Ken. *Scarface Nation*. New York: St. Martin's Griffin, 2008.

Vachaud, Laurent. "Brian De Palma—Le voyeur." *Les Inrockuptibles*, November 11, 1998.

———. "Le casino, c'est l'enfer sur terre." *Positif*, no. 455 (January 1999): 6–9.

Vallely, Jean. "Brian De Palma: The New Hitchcock or Just Another Rip-Off?" *Rolling Stone*, October 16, 1980: 38–39.

Vandiste, Jean-Luc. "Peter Graves." *Ecran fantastique*, no. 154 (October 1996).

Varnum, Agnes. "Richard Schechner at *Dionysus in '69* Q&A." *Persistence of Vision: Journal of the Austin Film Society*, December 10, 2009.

"Visions of Mars." *Mission to Mars* DVD. Touchstone Home Video, 2002.

Wagner, Dagmar, dir. "Talking about *Passion*." *Passion* DVD. Universal Pictures Video, 2013.

Weber, Bruce. "Cool Head, Hot Images." *New York Times Magazine*, May 21, 1989.

Weinraub, Bernard. "A Foul Mouth with a Following." *New York Times*, September 23, 2003.

White, Armond. "*The Black Dahlia*." *Cineaste* 32, no. 1 (Winter 2006): 58–60.

Williams, Linda Ruth. *The Erotic Thriller in Contemporary Cinema*. Bloomington: Indiana University Press, 2005.

Williams, Neal. *Blow Out*. New York: Bantam, 1981.

Wood, Robin. *Hollywood from Vietnam to Reagan*. New York: Columbia University Press, 1985.

Zinoman, Jason. *Shock Value: How a Few Eccentric Outsiders Gave Us Nightmares, Conquered Hollywood, and Invented Modern Horror*. New York: Penguin Press, 2011.

Znaty, Deborah, dir. "Paradise Regained." *Phantom of the Paradise* DVD. Opening Distribution, 2009.

INDEX

Lightning Source UK Ltd.
Milton Keynes UK
UKHW012147100122
396906UK00003B/105

9 781496 809728